ALSO BY CAROL TAVRIS

Anger: The Misunderstood Emotion
The Longest War: Sex Differences in Perspective
  (with Carole Wade)
Psychology (with Carole Wade)

Simon & Schuster

New York   London   Toronto
Sydney   Tokyo
Singapore

The Mismeasure of Woman

Carol Tavris

SIMON & SCHUSTER
Simon & Schuster Building
Rockefeller Center
1230 Avenue of the Americas
New York, New York 10020

Designed by Karolina Harris
Manufactured in the United States of America

10   9   8   7   6   5   4   3   2   1

Library of Congress Cataloging-in-Publication Data
Tavris, Carol.
    The mismeasure of woman/Carol Tavris.
       p.   cm.
    Includes bibliographical references and index.
    1. Women—Psychology.   2. Sex role.   3. Sex differences.   4. Sex differences
(Psychology)   I. Title.
HQ1206.T28   1992
305.3—dc20   91-36338
                                                                                    CIP

ISBN 0-671-66274-0

Excerpts from Hope Landrine, "The politics of personality," Psychology of Women Quarterly, 13 *(1989) © Cambridge University Press, reprinted with permission.*

(continued on page 399)

■

For Ronan O'Casey,

with the full measure of my devotion.

■ *Contents*

5   Misdiagnosing the Mind   170
Why women are "sick" but men have "problems"

6   Bedtime Stories   208
Three fables of female sexuality

7   Love's Experts, Love's Victims   246
How women cornered the love market

8   Speaking of Gender   287
The darkened eye restored

We are being given the illusion that woman can accomplish anything today and that it is her fault if she does not. It all goes hand in hand with this so-called new femininity—with an enhanced status for traditional feminine values, such as woman and her rapport with nature, woman and her maternal instinct, woman and her physical being. . . . This renewed attempt to pin women down to their traditional role, together with a small effort to meet some of the demands made by women, —that's the formula used to try and keep women quiet. And, unfortunately, as one can see from the tragic results, it is a really successful approach. Even women who call themselves feminists don't always see through it. Once again women are being defined in terms of "the other," once again they are being made into the "second sex."[1]

—Simone de Beauvoir, 1984

■ *Introduction*

The Universal Male

Man is the measure of all things.

—Protagoras (c. 485–410 B.C.)

Join me, if you will, in a brief flight of fancy. George Jones, age thirty-four, visits the "psychology and health" section of his local bookstore. There he finds an assortment of books designed to solve his problems with love, sex, work, stress, and children:

- *Women Who Hate Men and the Men Who Love Them* explains why he remains in a self-defeating relationship with Jane.
- *The X Spot and other new findings about male sexuality* tells him exactly how to have the right kind of multiple orgasm that women have.
- *The Male Manager* shows why his typically male habits of competitiveness and individualism prevent him from advancing in the female-dominated, cooperative corporate world.
- *Cooperation Training* offers practical instructions for overcoming his early competitive socialization as a man, showing him how to get along more smoothly with others.
- *The Superman Syndrome* explains that because men are physically less hardy than women throughout their lives, men find it difficult to combine work and family. They would live as long as women do if they would scale down their efforts to seek power and success.

- *The Father Knot* and *The Reproduction of Fathering* explore the reasons that George feels so guilty about the way he is raising his children. Women feel comfortable with motherhood, these books argue, because they bear and nurse their offspring. But men for basic anatomical reasons are doomed to feel insecure and guilty in their role as fathers because unconsciously they never quite believe the child is theirs.

- *Erratic Testosterone Syndrome (ETS)—What it is and how to live with it* provides medical and psychological information to help George cope with his hormonal ups and downs. Because men do not have a visible monthly reminder of hormonal changes, they fail to realize that their moodiness and aggressive outbursts are hormonally based. A special concluding chapter helps the wives of men with ETS learn to live with their husbands' unpredictable mood swings.

Lucky George. He will never feel obliged to read books like these, were anyone ever to write them; but of course women feel obliged to read the comparable volumes directed to them. It's a puzzle that they do, actually, because most of these books imply that women aren't doing anything right. Women are irrational and moody because of their hormones. They cry too much. They love too much. They talk too much. They think differently. They are too dependent on unworthy men, but if they leave the men to fend for themselves, they are too independent, and if they stay with the men they are codependent. They are too emotional, except when the emotion in question is anger, in which case they aren't emotional enough. They don't have correct orgasms, the correct way, with the correct frequency. They pay too much attention to their children, or not enough, or the wrong kind. They are forever subject to syndromes: the Superwoman Syndrome causes the Stress Syndrome, which is exacerbated by Premenstrual Syndrome, which is followed by a Menopausal Deficiency Syndrome.

Why do women buy so many self-help books every year to improve their sex lives, moods, relationships, and mental health? Simone de Beauvoir gave us one answer in 1949: because women are the second sex, the other sex, the sex to be explained. Men and women are not simply considered different from one another, as we speak of people differing in eye color, movie tastes, or preferences for ice cream. In every domain of life, men are considered the normal human being, and women are "ab-normal," deficient because they are different from men. Therefore, women constantly worry about measuring up, doing the right thing, being the right way. It is normal for women to worry about being abnormal, because male behavior, male heroes, male psychology, and even male physiology continue to be the standard of normalcy against which women are measured and found wanting.

Despite women's gains in many fields in the last twenty years, the fundamental belief in the normalcy of men, and the corresponding abnormality of women, has remained virtually untouched. Now even this entrenched way of thinking is being scrutinized and the reverberations are echoing across the land. Everywhere we look, it seems, teachers, courses, theories, and books are being challenged to examine their implicit assumption that man is the measure of all things.

Thus, in politics, we have "important issues" (drugs, economics, war) and then "women's issues" (day care, birth control, peace), as if these matters could or should be divided at the gender line. Congress and the United Nations worry about international violations of "human rights," but these rarely include violations of women's rights such as denial of suffrage, wife-beating, genital mutilation, forced prostitution, or sweatshops that run on underpaid female labor. Somehow, these are "women's issues," not "human rights" issues. We worry, as well we should, about the feminization of poverty, but we do not see its connection to the masculinization of wealth. The phrase "unfit mother" rolls trippingly off judicial tongues, but "unfit father" is nowhere to be heard. We ponder the problem of unwed, "sexually irresponsible" teenage mothers, not the problem of unwed, sexually irresponsible teenage fathers. Boys will be boys, we say, but girls better not be mothers. Indeed, reproductive freedom in general is a "woman's issue," as if men were merely disinterested bystanders on the matter of sexuality and its consequences.

The perception of female otherness occurs in every field, as we are learning from critical observers in science, law, medicine, history, economics, social science, literature, and art.[1] In medicine, students learn anatomy and physiology and, separately, female anatomy and physiology; the male body is anatomy-itself. In art, we have works of general excellence and, separately, works by women artists, generally regarded as different and lesser; male painters represent art-itself. In literature, a college course on "black female writers of the twentieth century" is considered a specialized seminar; yet when an English instructor at Georgetown University called her course "white male writers," it was news—because the works of white male writers are regarded as literature-itself.[2] In psychoanalysis, Freud took the male as the developmental norm for humanity, regarding female development as a pale and puny deviation from it.

In history, the implicit use of men as the norm pervades much of what schoolchildren learn about American and Western civilization. Was Greece the cradle of democracy? It was no democracy for women and slaves. Was the Renaissance a time of intellectual and artistic rebirth? There was no renaissance for women—"at least," wrote historian Joan Kelly, "not during the Renaissance."[3] Did the Enlightenment expand "the rights of man" in education, politics, and work? Yes, but it narrowed the rights of women, who were denied control of their property and earnings and barred from higher education and professional training. Was the American frontier "conquered" by single scouts, brave men "taming" the wilderness and founding a culture based on self-reliance? This mythic vision excludes the women who struggled to establish homes, survive childbirth, care for families, and contribute with men to the community that was essential to survival.

In economics, supposedly the study of pure market forces and the "Rational Man" (in comparison to the irrational—whom?), the field relies on measures of gross national product as the main gauge of a nation's economic performance, overlooking the value of women's unpaid labor in the home and the invisible work they do that lies outside market economies. For example, as political economist Marilyn Waring has shown, the work of women farmers in underdeveloped nations is not computed in economic formulas that are the basis for agricultural assistance programs.[4] The result is that women farmers lose government aid, with devastating results for food production and the nutritional health of their families. "Economics-itself" does not concern itself with such matters. Students of economics are left with the impression that women's unpaid labor and the systematic underpayment of women's labor in the work force do not matter, or that they are aberrations in an otherwise rational system, or that women are to blame for allowing themselves to become trapped in low-paying or nonpaying jobs.

In philosophy, the centrality in thought and language of the universal male affects the ability to reason about humanity. The philosopher Elizabeth Minnich reminds us of the famous syllogism:

> All men are mortal.
> Socrates is a man.
> Therefore, Socrates is mortal.

But, Minnich suggests, try this one:

> All men are mortal.
> Alice is ———

Alice is—what? We can't say "Alice is a man." So we say she is a woman. Therefore—what? Alice is immortal? Alice, being female, is in a category that is neither masculine nor mortal:

> Alice ends up in the peculiar position of being a somewhat mortal, somewhat immortal, creature. Or, we must admit, we cannot thus reason about Alice while thinking of her as a female at all. We can think of Socrates as a man without derailing the syllogism; we cannot think of Alice as a woman. Reason flounders; the center holds, with Man in it, but it is an exclusive, not a universal or neutral, center. Alice disappears through the looking glass.[5]

Many people, Minnich adds, find it odd, uncomfortable, or threatening to suggest that it is appropriate to expand a field's horizons to include all humankind. "What does it mean for democracy," she asks, "that only some few kinds of humans can be imagined as our representatives? What does it mean for all of us on this shrinking globe?"[6]

* * *

My inquiry in this book is motivated by the spirit of Minnich's question: I wish to examine the consequences for us all, male and female, when only some few of us set the standards of normalcy and universality. My goal is to expand our visions of normalcy, not to replace a male-centered view with a female-centered one. But to do so we must first unmask the three most popular disguises of the universal male. Each of these currently popular ways of thinking about men and women has its adherents and detractors, and each leads to different consequences for how we live our lives:

- *Men are normal; women, being "opposite," are deficient.* This us-them, yin-yang, masculine-is-good, feminine-is-bad view of the sexes is the oldest tradition in civilization. It regards men and women as polar opposites, with males as the repository of culture, intellectuality, and strength, and females the repository of nature, intuition, and weakness.

- *Men are normal; women are opposite from men, but superior to them.* Proponents of this view emphasize aspects of female experience or female "nature"—such as menstruation, childbirth, compassion, spirituality, cooperation, pacifism, and harmony with the environment—and celebrate them as being morally superior to men's experiences and qualities. In this view, nevertheless, man is still the standard against which woman's behavior is judged, even if the judgments are kinder.

- *Men are normal, and women are or should be like them.* Proponents of this approach, which would seem to be the antidote to the fundamental-difference schools, actually commit an intrinsic error of their own. By ignoring the differences that *do* exist between men and women—in life experiences, resources, power, and reproductive processes—the basically-alike school assumes that it is safe to generalize from the male standard to all women.

These three errors, in their various incarnations, have done serious harm to women's feelings about themselves, to their relationships, and to their position in society. They are responsible for the guilt-inducing analyses that leave women feeling that once again they lack the right stuff and aren't doing the right thing. They have made sicknesses and syndromes of women's normal bodily processes, and "diseases" of women's normal experiences. They have framed the debate over solutions to social problems, and led reformers down unproductive paths. They have excluded men from the language of love, intimacy, and connection, perpetuating unhappiness and outright warfare in the family, where many men and women remain baffled by the mysterious opposite sex.

The confusion over whether women are the "same" as men, and whether they can be "different but equal," is at the heart of the current debates between (and about) the sexes. In contrast, I take as my basic premise that there is nothing *essential*—that is, universal and unvarying—in the natures of women and men. Personality traits, abilities, values, motivations, roles, dreams, and desires: all vary across culture and history, and depend on time and place, context and situation. Of course, if you photograph the behavior of women and men at a particular time in history, in a particular situation, you will capture differences. But the error lies in inferring that a snapshot is a lasting picture. What women and men *do* at a moment in time tells us nothing about what women and men *are* in some unvarying sense—or about what they can be.

▪ *The mismeasure of woman*

Not long ago the firm of Price Waterhouse was charged with discrimination in not granting partnership status to a woman named Ann Hopkins. Everyone agreed that Hopkins did her job well. She brought in over $40 million in new business to the firm, far more than any of the eighty-seven other nominees, all of whom were male, and forty-seven of whom were invited to become partners. Most of the opposition to Hopkins came from brief comments from law partners who had had limited contact with her and were unaware of her track record. They described her as "macho," harsh, and aggressive, and one speculated that she "may have overcompensated for being a woman." One man, trying to be helpful, advised her to "walk more femininely, talk more femininely, dress more femininely, wear make-up, have her hair styled, and wear jewelry."

Hopkins's supporters described her behavior as outspoken, independent, self-confident, assertive, and courageous. Her detractors interpreted the same behavior as overbearing, arrogant, self-centered, and abrasive. "Why is it," asked Lynn Hecht Schafran, an attorney on Hopkins's case, "that men can be bastards and women must wear pearls and smile?"[7]

At the same time that the Hopkins case was wending its way to the Supreme Court (where she eventually won), an attorney named Brenda Taylor lost her job because she was *too* feminine: she favored short skirts, designer blouses, ornate jewelry, and spike heels. Her boss told her that she looked like a "bimbo," and she was fired after she complained about his remarks to the Equal Employment Opportunity Commission.

Ann Hopkins and Brenda Taylor illustrate the pressures on modern women to be feminine *and* masculine, to be different from men but also the same. How is a woman supposed to behave: like an ideal male, in which case her male colleagues will accuse her of not being feminine enough, or like an ideal female, in which case her male colleagues will accuse her of not being masculine enough?

We will never know the truth about Ann Hopkins—whether she is outspoken or overbearing, confident or arrogant—because both sets of perceptions are true, from the beholder's standpoint. But by framing the problem as one of her personality, her colleagues deflected attention from the systematic practices of their company and from their own behavior. Suppose, instead, we ask: *Under what conditions* is the negative stereotype of women like Hopkins more likely to occur? The answer, according to research summarized in a brief prepared by the American Psychological Association on behalf of Hopkins, is that men are likely to behave like the Price Waterhouse partners under three conditions: when the woman (or other minority) is a token member of the organization; when the criteria used to evaluate the woman are ambiguous; and when observers lack necessary information to evaluate the woman's work.[8] All three conditions were met in Hopkins's situation. She could have read 435 books on how to behave, and they would have failed her. She could have gone to work dressed in a muu-muu or Saran Wrap, and she still would have lost that promotion. In this case, her personality had nothing to do with it.

Ann Hopkins's dilemma—whether a woman is supposed to behave like a man or a woman—is played out a thousand times a day, in the varied domains of women's lives. A woman who leaves her child in day care worries that she is failing as a mother; but if she leaves her job temporarily to stay home with her child, she worries that she will fail in her career. A woman who cries at work worries whether crying is good, since she is a woman, or wrong, since she is a professional. A woman who spends endless hours taking care of her husband and ailing parents feels that she is doing the right thing as a woman, but the wrong thing as an independent person. A woman who cannot penetrate her husband's emotional coolness alternates between trying to turn him into one of her expressive girlfriends and trying to cure her "dependency" on him.

Of the countless self-help books on the market that address these dilemmas, most direct the reader's attention to women's alleged inner flaws and psychological deficiencies. Women's unhappiness, in many of these accounts, is a result of their fear of independence, fear of codependence, fear of success, fear of failure, or fear of fear. Women are told to be more masculine in some ways and more feminine in others. Each of these explanations has a brief moment in the sun. And each eventually fades from sight, to be replaced by similar explanations that flourish briefly and die, because they do not touch the basic reasons for women's dilemmas: Inequities and ambiguities about "woman's place" are built into the structure of our lives and society. These dilemmas are normal for women. They will persist as long as women look exclusively inward to their psyches and biology instead of outward to their circumstances, and as long as women blame themselves for not measuring up.

It may seem, after two decades of the modern women's movement, that issues of difference and equality have been talked into the ground, that equality has been won. Unquestionably, women have made great progress. But our society continues to fight a war over the proper place of women, and the battleground is the female body. Once again we are in the midst of a pronatalist revival that praises motherhood as women's basic need and talent, and that persists in trying to limit and control women's reproductive choices. Once again we are hearing arguments about women's nature, their unreliable physiology, their unmasculine hormones and brains. And once again we are hearing about the problems that face women who wish to combine careers and families, as experts warn of the dangers of day care, the stresses of being superwomen, the empty satisfactions of being corporate executives.

Researchers in the fields of science, medicine, and psychology all celebrate a renewed emphasis on biological explanations of women's behavior and a medical approach to women's problems and their cures. They enthusiastically seek physiological differences in brain structure and function, biochemical reasons that more women than men suffer from depression, and hormonal changes that supposedly account for women's (but not men's) moods and abilities. Their assertions are more likely to make the news than is the evidence that contradicts them. Similarly, women hear much less these days about the psychological benefits of having many roles and sources of esteem, let alone the benefits of having a personal income.

In *The Mismeasure of Man,* the scientist Stephen Jay Gould showed how science has been used and abused in the study of intelligence to serve a larger social and political agenda: to confirm the prejudice that some groups are assigned to their subordinate roles "by the harsh dictates of nature."[9] The mismeasure of woman persists because it, too, reflects and serves society's prejudices. Views of woman's "natural" differences from man justify a status quo that divides work, psychological qualities, and family responsibilities into "his" and "hers." Those who are dominant have an interest in maintaining their difference from others, attributing those differences to "the harsh dictates of nature," and obscuring the unequal arrangements that benefit them.

Throughout this book, I will be examining the stories behind the headlines and popular theories of sex differences, traveling the trail of the universal male, showing how the belief in male normalcy and female deficiency guides scientific inquiry, shapes its results, and determines which findings make the news and which findings we live by. The following chapters will offer some new ways of looking at the old dilemmas that women and men confront daily. My goal is not to analyze, let alone solve, all the problems that women and men face in their complex lives. But by bringing hidden assumptions into the light, I hope to show how our ways of thinking about women and men lead to certain predictable results for all of us: in law and medicine, in social reforms, in standards of mental health, in the intimacies of sex and love, and in our private reveries of what is possible.

Measuring Up

Why women are not inferior to men

Do you sometimes feel inadequate and worthless? Do you dislike your body? Are you nagged by the fear that you don't really deserve to be happy and successful? Do you frequently compare yourself to others and come up short? When things go wrong, do you automatically blame yourself? . . . If you can answer yes to one or several of these questions, you're probably suffering from low self-esteem, a problem that plagues large numbers of women.[1]

If you were to flip through a random selection of research articles, magazines, and popular books about differences between the sexes, you would encounter many problems that apparently plague large numbers of women. For instance:

- Women have lower self-esteem than men do.
- Women do not value their efforts as much as men do, even when they are doing the same work.
- Women are less self-confident than men; when asked to predict how they will do in the future, they are less optimistic than men about their abilities.
- Women are more likely than men to repress their anger and to say they are "hurt" than to admit they are angry.

▪ Women have more difficulty than men in developing a separate identity, a sense of self.

Well, these are all things to worry about, aren't they? Surely it is desirable for women to have high self-esteem, value their work, be self-confident, express anger clearly, and develop autonomy. Surely it is important to explore the problem of why women are so insecure and what can be done about it.[2]

To find the premises underlying these well-meaning efforts to understand women's problems, let's dissect a very good recent study. The researcher asked some young women and men to take tests of creativity, such as inventing new uses for ordinary objects. She was not actually interested in whether men or women are more creative (in this case, they did not differ), but rather in the reasons they give for their success or failure on the tests during a mock job interview afterward.

The investigator reported that women are less self-confident than men: The women attributed their successes less often to their own abilities than to luck, and they reported less overall confidence in their present and future performance. Why, she asked, do women make "less self-serving" explanations than men do? "The feminine social goal of appearing modest," she concluded, "inhibits women in making self-promoting attributions in an achievement situation which involves face-to-face interaction."[3]

Now, ignore the lumpy language of research psychology and notice that the goal of this study was to explain why the women didn't behave like the men. To see this more clearly, simply rephrase the question and its answer. The investigator might have said: "Why do men make *more self-serving* explanations than women do? The masculine social goal of appearing self-confident inhibits them from making modest explanations of their abilities or acknowledging the help of others and the role of chance."

Of course, the habit of seeing women's behavior as something to be explained in relation to the male norm makes sense in a world that takes the male norm for granted. In this case, the researcher showed that the female habit of modesty actually does women a disservice in job interviews, because they appear to be unconcerned with achievement and unwilling to promote themselves. This bit of information would be useful to women *and* men from England,

Japan, and other cultures that value modesty, if they want to do business in America.

Nevertheless, in this study, as in many others, the men's responses are used to define the norm, framing the very questions and solutions that investigators explore. But suppose for a moment that we lived in a world where psychologists used women as the basis of comparison. We might then be reading articles and books that analyze the following problems that plague men:

- Men are more conceited than women.
- Men overvalue the work they do.
- Men are not as realistic and modest as women in assessing their abilities.
- Men are more likely than women to accuse and attack others when they are unhappy, instead of stating that they feel hurt and inviting sympathy.
- Men have more difficulty than women in forming and maintaining attachments.

Now the same "problems" have to do with male overconfidence, unrealistic self-assessment, aggression, and isolation, not with women's inadequacies. But you won't find many popular books trying to help men like George Steinbrenner or Donald Trump, who, as far as I'm concerned, suffer from excessive self-esteem.

In recent years, women have been uncovering many of the implicit biases that resulted from using men as the human standard. But the universal man is deeply embedded in our lives and habits of thought, and women who deviate from his ways are still regarded as, well, deviant. To illustrate the persistence of the normal man and the difficulty he poses for women who hope to measure up, I offer three stories of how he affects the evaluation of women's bodies, psychology, and brains.

■ Body: Beauty and the bust

The cartoonist Nicole Hollander once described what she thought the world would be like without men. "There would be no crime," she said, "and lots of happy, fat women."

It's a wonderful line, funny because it strikes right at the heart of the guilty secret (or outright worry) of most women: the endless obsession with weight and body shape. Every woman I know has a "weight problem." My thin friends worry about gaining weight, my plumper friends struggle to lose it. My friends are governed by diets: they are either on one, about to start one, delighted at having finished one, or miserable that they can't stick with one. I sympathize with them; I'm that way too. This obsession, which is so damaging to women's self-concept, happiness, and self-esteem, perfectly highlights the dilemma for women of being like men or different from them, and the origins of that dilemma in the larger social picture.

Over the years, the ideal figure for a woman has changed, from eras that accentuate the differences from the male body to those that minimize them. In this century alone we have seen rapid shifts from the Lillian Russell/Marilyn Monroe standard, which was voluptuous and curvaceous, to the 1920s Flapper/1960s Twiggy standard, which was unisex slim, to today's odd hybrid: full-breasted but narrow-hipped. Psychologist Brett Silverstein and his associates have cleverly documented this changing female ideal by calculating "bust-to-waist" and "waist-to-hip" ratios of the measurements of women in popular women's magazines.[4] You get larger ratios in eras that celebrate the big-breasted figure, and a smaller ratio in eras that endorse the boyish shape.

In the early 1950s, for instance, *Playboy* centerfolds, beauty contest winners, and fashion models weighed much more and were several inches more ample in bust and hips than they were in the 1970s and 1980s. The 1951 Miss Sweden was 5'7" tall and weighed 151 pounds; the 1983 Miss Sweden was 5'9" tall and weighed 109 pounds.[5] The phrase "pleasantly plump," which was still a compliment in the 1950s, became an oxymoron in the 1960s. Actress Valerie Harper, who truly was pleasantly plump, was not happy with her body until she became alarmingly gaunt.

Why do these ideals change? Curvy, full-breasted women are in fashion during pro-maternal eras, in which motherhood and domesticity are considered women's most important roles: this was the case in the early 1900s, the 1950s, and, increasingly, today. In contrast, thin, muscular, boyish bodies are in fashion whenever women have entered the work force, specifically the traditionally male occupations: this was the case in the 1920s and again in the late 1960s and 1970s. In the 1920s, women used to bind their breasts with tape so their breasts would not be prominent in the dress styles of the day. The 1970s "working girl" that Mary Tyler Moore played for seven years on television didn't have to do this; she was as thin as a reed. Jane Fonda transformed her voluptuous Barbarella shape into an aerobically toned muscular one.

Why should the kind of work that people do affect ideal body image? Men and women, Silverstein discovered, associate the round, big-breasted body with femininity. And they associate femininity with nurturance, dependence, passivity, domesticity—and, unhappily, incompetence. The normal male body, in contrast, conveys intelligence, strength, and ability. Therefore, women who want to be thought intelligent, professional, and competent—i.e., "masculine"—must look more male-ish. (Men, too, have fallen prey to this equation. Fat, once a sign of a man's wealth and success in the early decades of this century, now signifies womanly softness and lack of masculinity.)

Indeed, in every era when educational and occupational opportunities for women have increased, the ideal body for women became thin, athletic, small-busted, and narrow-hipped. A 1935 *Fortune* article described the professional, "intelligently dressed woman," contrasting her with the "blond stenographer with the slick sleazy stockings and the redundant breasts." Redundant breasts? The idea returned in the careerist 1970s and 1980s. A 1984 career guide for women advised its readers: "The sex goddess look is at odds with a professional business look. If you have a large bust don't accentuate it."

In such egalitarian times, the number of articles and books on dieting increases astronomically, and eating disorders and "fat panic" among women and girls become epidemic. Most white teenage girls no longer regard normal and necessary adolescent weight gain as normal signs of maturation, but as signs of (unpleasant) fatness. A representative survey of more than 2,000 girls in Michigan, ages eleven to eighteen, found that nearly 40 percent considered themselves overweight; dieting and dissatisfaction with body image were the typical responses to the onset of puberty.[6] Many other studies of nationally representative samples find that dieting, unrealistic body image, and dissatisfaction with weight are chronic stressors for women.[7]

Women who value achievement, higher education, and professional careers are especially likely to be obsessed with thinness and to suffer from various eating disorders, such as anorexia and bulimia. "Eating disorders and the obsession with weight control," says Silverstein, "are an ironic price of 'women's liberation.' They occur when the level of discrimination against women decreases enough to let women into higher education and the professions—but not enough to break the association between femininity and incompetence."[8]

This link seems to be particularly troubling for women who are insecure about their competence and who feel that their fathers did not think they were intelligent and did not support their ambitions. To resolve this dilemma, they try literally to measure up: to become as thin as a man, since they can't actually become one. According to O. Wayne Wooley and Susan Wooley, who direct a research program and eating-disorders clinic at the University of Cincinnati's College of Medicine, many bulimic young women are seeking their fathers' recognition of their competence, which they don't get because they are female. "To become like their fathers, our patients feel compelled to be thin," they observe, "—not just to minimize their womanliness, but also because thinness, in this culture, is a sign of achievement and mastery."[9]

All women remain affected to some degree by the portrayals of the ideal woman in the media, and those portrayals, in spite of the popularity of Roseanne Barr, are getting worse. "Women receive more messages to be slim and stay in shape than do men," says Silverstein, who analyzed popular television characters and articles and ads in magazines. On television in the late 1980s, 69 percent of the female characters were very thin, compared to only 17.5 percent of the male characters. Only five percent of the female characters were heavy, compared to 25.5 percent of the males. In 48 issues of popular women's magazines that Silverstein surveyed, the total number of ads for diet foods was 63; the comparable number in popular men's magazines was 1. As for articles dealing with body shape or size, the score was women's magazines 96, men's 8.

With the dawn of the 1990s, media images of women began to

celebrate a hybrid form that is all but impossible for most women: big-breasted but narrow-hipped. (Accordingly, Jane Fonda got breast implants.) This hybrid reflects the ambivalence in American society toward women's roles and the expectation that women must be both professionally competent *and* maternal. The majority of women, including mothers of young children, work outside the home, yet we are also in an era of strong pro-maternal sentiment.

As one sign of the times, those "redundant breasts" are back in vogue: After a decade of the popularity of breast-reduction surgeries, breast-enlargement procedures are on the increase. "Be Your Best," blares an ad for the "Breast Enhancement Medical Center" in Los Angeles. These three words are placed across the model's breasts, as if to convey the real message, "Be Your Bust." The message is catching on. More than 70,000 women in the United States had breast augmentation surgery in 1988 alone, and that number jumped to 150,000 in 1990. Eighty percent are for cosmetic purposes; indeed, breast implants have become the most popular form of cosmetic surgery for women in the nation. They are more popular than liposuction, nose jobs, or face lifts, in spite of the considerable expense and a significant degree of risk of ruptured implants, repeat surgery for complications, infections, allergic reactions, tumors, and disruption of the autoimmune system.[10]

The fashion industry, both haute couture and ready-to-wear, now features the breast, offering swimwear with padded bust lines and underwire bras, dresses with plunging necklines, padded corsets, and bustiers, and fabrics that cling to the bosom to emphasize its curves. "Curves are natural to a woman's form," explained a designer for Van Buren, whose dresses nevertheless now include built-in push-up bras for women who need help being natural. "We're definitely moving in the direction of a softer, more feminine curvaceousness," said a representative of Lancôme cosmetics in New York. "It's much sexier to have some flesh to hold on to," said Gale Hayman, who is president of her own cosmetics company. As if to prove her point, for their respective roles in *Green Card* and *Alice,* Andie MacDowell and Mia Farrow gained ten pounds.[11]

So the cycle is making another turn. A reporter writing on this trend explained, "after years of stick-thin cover girls, their fuller figures [of bigger-breasted models] provided a refreshing, ultra-feminine look."[12] Today the big-breasted "refreshing and ultra-feminine" look competes with "a professional business look." But if breasts are ultrafeminine and also redundant, what's a woman to do? If she accepts nature's body—the one with breasts, fat deposits, and curves—and throws away the diet books, she risks being regarded as incompetent and best suited for motherhood. If she wishes to enter the business and political world, she struggles to have a man's body, one without those nurturing, feminine breasts. It is no wonder that contemporary dress styles dramatically reflect this ambivalence: many business outfits consist of a "male" tailored jacket and a "female" miniskirt. It's an effort to be businesslike and sexy.

Many women justify their efforts to be thin on medical grounds, but even here many of the warnings about the dangers of fat have been based on studies of men. Women are biologically programmed to store fat reserves in the thighs, buttocks, and hips, and fat in these areas is not generally a health risk. On the contrary, this reserve of fat is necessary for menstruation, childbearing, nursing, and, after menopause, for production and storage of estrogen. This is one reason that moderate weight gain after menopause is not as risky to women's health as excess weight can be for men; indeed, such weight gain reduces the risk of osteoporosis.[13]

Joel Gurin, co-author with physician William Bennett of *The Dieter's Dilemma,* believes that much of the research on health and weight has been heavily biased by reliance on a male norm. "The risks of dieting have been underestimated," he maintains, "and the risks of fatness have been overestimated." Of course, obesity does increase the risk of diabetes and high blood pressure, and a diet rich in fats has been implicated in numerous diseases (such as breast cancer). But being very thin is also unhealthy: The risks to longevity show up at the extremes of fat and thin. Moreover, the location of fat is more important than the number of pounds: abdominal fat is implicated in a greater risk of diabetes in women and of heart disease in men.[14] "The irony," says Silverstein, "is that it is men who are at greater risk from obesity, but it is women who diet."

And diets themselves carry physical and psychological risks. Up-and-down dieting changes the body's metabolism, making it easier to gain weight and harder to lose it, and possibly also increasing the chances of becoming hypertensive. When rats are put on a regimen of yo-yo dieting, their blood pressures rise significantly and dangerously after the third "crash diet." The link between hypertension and being overweight that doctors warn about may be a result of the person's having been on several crash diets, not a result of the weight per se.[15] Dieting is also psychologically debilitating. "Food fantasies, obsession with talking about food, depression and irritability, and bingeing when the diet is broken are not signs of failed willpower," says Gurin. "They are signs of hunger." Women who are chronically dieting are in a constant state of stress, which affects their emotional and physical health.[16]

O. Wayne Wooley considers women's obsession with dieting and excess weight to be largely a political matter, not a medical one. "It is political," he argues, "because it keeps women attending to their looks instead of the circumstances of their lives, it pits woman against woman, it destroys physical fitness and energy. And, saddest of all, it represents a rejection of the female body"[17]—the real female body, that is; the one with those "redundant" breasts. The same may be said of efforts to change an equally real female body—the one with small breasts. It is small consolation to be able to throw away the diet books and gain a few pounds if the trade-off is being thought mindless and incompetent.

Nicole Hollander's joke—that in a world without men, women would be fat and happy—reminds us exactly why it is that women subject their bodies to surgery, dieting, and deprivation, and how women might feel about their normal bodies if the world were designed and run by women. As it is, women keep trying to look the right way, but the ideal they aspire to is not based on the normal varieties of the female body. The fact that the large majority of women who have breast implants for cosmetic reasons are in their thirties and forties, and married, reveals a more likely motive than vanity. A news reporter interviewed one woman, age forty-four, who "recently went from 'barely a 32-A' to a 34-C. Before her surgery, she said, her father used to say he 'couldn't tell the difference between the front or the back' when he looked at her. Her husband often joined in the jokes."[18]

Many women today feel superior to Victorian women, who wore excruciating corsets to force their bodies into exaggerated hourglass shapes. (In a woman-centered world, the demise of the corset and the girdle would rank right up there with the electric razor as a major contribution to human welfare.) But modern women who are forcing their bodies into exaggeratedly slim shapes, or, increasingly, into exaggeratedly voluptuous shapes, are no less subject to social pressures and the standards of fashion. These alternating standards, which reflect the perception that the woman's body is never right as it is and always needs to be fixed, will continue as long as women model themselves after the impossible male norm: to be opposite from the male body, or to be like the male body, but never satisfied with the woman's body they have.

■ *Psyche: The problem of women*

> It all goes back, of course, to Adam and Eve—a story which shows, among other things, that if you make a woman out of a man, you are bound to get into trouble. In the life cycle, as in the Garden of Eden, the woman has been the deviant.[19]
>
> —Carol Gilligan, *In a Different Voice*

Women not only fail to measure up to having the right body; they also fail to measure up to having the right life. I remember how annoyed I felt, as a college student, when I first read Erik Erikson's theory of the "Eight Stages of Man." Every few years throughout their lives, Erikson said, people have a psychological crisis to resolve and overcome. Children, for example, must resolve the crisis of "competence" versus "inferiority." Teenagers must resolve the famous identity crisis of adolescence, or they will wallow around in "role diffusion" and aimlessness. Once you have your identity, you must learn to share it; if you don't master your "intimacy" crisis, you become lonely and isolated. Middle-aged adults face the problems of "stagnation" versus "generativity," and, in old age, "ego integrity" versus "despair."

It turned out, of course, that Erikson meant the ages of "man" literally, but none of us knew that then. The fact that female readers were grumbling that their stages didn't seem to fit the pattern was just further evidence of how peculiar and irritating women were.

Erikson's theory was assumed to be a brilliant expansion of Freud's stage theory, which stopped at puberty. If women didn't fit, it was their own fault.

It was worrying. I wasn't having any of my crises in the right order. My sense of competence was plummeting, a result of being a lowly student, and I was supposed to have resolved *that* one at around age seven. My identity was shaky, although I was no longer a teenager, and I hadn't married when I was supposed to, which was putting my intimacy and generativity crises on hold.

Uncertain about my career prospects and having missed the college-age marriage boat, I applied to graduate school. Many graduate schools were reluctant to accept women in the late 1960s, and the reason, they said, was that women were so unpredictable, idiosyncratic, and unreliable—so, in a word, unmasculine. Women were forever dropping out to support their husbands, or have children, or take jobs that allowed them to eat. I remember how relieved I felt to read the research of the time, which provided reassuring evidence to administrators that yes, women would finish their training if you gave them the chance, and yes, they would eventually do as well as men.

In those days, theorists writing on adult development assumed that adults were male. Healthy "adults" follow a single line from childhood to old age, a steady path of school, career, marriage, advancement, a child or two, retirement, and wisdom—in that order. Everyone was supposed to grow "up," not sideways, down, or, God forbid, in circles. In the 1970s and 1980s, popular stage theories offered road maps that plotted a way through the thicket of adult adventures. Psychiatrist George Vaillant wrote *Adaptation to Life*, based on a longitudinal study of privileged Harvard (male) students, and concluded that men go through orderly stages even if the circumstances of their lives differ. Psychiatrist Daniel Levinson and his associates followed with *Seasons of a Man's Life*, which argued that the phases of (a man's) life unfold in a natural sequence, like the four seasons of the year. This book had nothing to say about women's seasons, possibly because women were continuing to irritate academics by doing things unseasonably.

Moreover, almost everyone assumed that healthy adult development meant progress toward autonomy, independence, and separation. It was bad and unhealthy to remain too attached to your parents. Indeed, to many psychologists, the continuing attachment that many women have with their families is a sign of immaturity and their "weak sense of self." Proponents of the "turmoil theory" of adolescent development explained that teenagers must go through a few years of ranting, railing, disobedience, and craziness or they wouldn't become calm, sane, mature adults—the kind who had separated from their parents.

But once a critical mass of women entered psychology, they began asking different questions. Why, they wondered, is it so desirable for an academic career to be uninterrupted by experience, family life, and outside work? So what if women's life paths were less linear than men's? Wasn't this way of structuring one's life as logical as, and more humanly beneficial than, the straight-up-the-ladder model? Shouldn't administrators be worrying about the deficient education of male students, so woefully unweathered by real life? And why, as psychologist Carol Gilligan argued to great acclaim, do we focus so much on the importance of separation from parents, instead of on the continuing affectionate bond that is the norm almost everywhere in the world, the bond that females promote?[20]

These questions, and the new research they generated, have transformed our understanding of human development. We now know that women and men do not resolve crises of competence, identity, nurturance, stagnation, autonomy, and connection once and for all; these issues bubble up throughout life. There is no right time or only time to go to school, change careers, have a baby, retire, or marry. The continuing connection between parent and child throughout life is healthy, a sign of strength rather than immaturity.

Even turmoil theories of adolescence are on the way out. Large-scale studies of normal adolescent males and females show that turmoil is only one way, and not the most common way at that, for getting through the teenage years. Most teenagers of both sexes remain close to and admiring of their parents, and experience a minimum of conflict and rebellion.[21] (This doesn't mean they aren't driving their parents crazy, and vice versa; just that these conflicts are ultimately trivial, to both sides, in the larger scheme of things.)

"We need a new model of adolescent development, one which

makes sense of the continued love between child and parent," argues psychologist Terri Apter.[22] Apter, who began her research with mothers and daughters on the (male) assumption that the task of adolescence is to separate from the parent, expected that daughters would talk frequently of their needs for separation, to be their "own person," to have more freedom. Instead, the daughters talked much more about their connection to their mothers: Their conversations were dotted with "her view is," "she thinks I'm," "the way she sees things." Mid-adolescence is generally thought to be the time of greatest conflict between parent and child, Apter found, yet most of the teenaged girls she interviewed said "the person they felt closest to, the person they felt most loved by, the person who offered them the greatest support, was their mother."[23]

All of these challenges to traditional theories proved to be good news for men and women, but particularly for the women who for so long had compared themselves to the male life pattern and come away feeling guilty for not matching it. "What's the right way to do it?" women often ask the "experts." "When should I have a baby—before, after, or during a career?" Or "When should I go to school—before, after, or during the baby?" The questioners assume that there is a right answer, and a right answer in turn assumes a single linear standard that will fit everybody—or rather, every man. But, as psychologists Grace Baruch and Rosalind Barnett have found, "there is no one lifeprint that ensures all women a perpetual sense of well-being—nor one that guarantees misery, for that matter. Adult American women today are finding satisfying lives in any number of different role patterns. Most involve tradeoffs at different points in the life cycle."[24] The fact that it is women who tend to be making the tradeoffs and not men is another matter.

In the last decade, new interpretations of many other old theories in psychology have flourished like mushrooms after rainfall. No area of investigation has been immune from scrutiny for male bias. For example, the left side of the list below represents the traditional way of looking at sex differences; the list on the right, another way of interpreting the same findings:

What's wrong with women	What's wrong with men
Low self-esteem	Inflated self-esteem
Undervalues her work	Overvalues his work
Gullible	Rigid
Too modest	Too overconfident
No sense of humor	Offensive sense of humor
Selflessness	Selfishness
Works too hard	Doesn't work hard enough
Career line irregular	Career path too narrow
Adult development too erratic	Adult development too conformist
Dependent	Aloof
Too connected, fused with others; weak ego boundary	Too autonomous, isolated, narcissistic
Penis envy	Penis insecurity
Suggestible	Inflexible
Conformist	Unyielding
Too emotional	Too remote, unfeeling
Weak leadership style	Authoritarian leadership style
Unwilling to dominate	Unwilling to negotiate
Stunted moral reasoning	Narrow moral reasoning
Not competitive enough	Not cooperative enough

Most people will see at once that the negative terms in the right-hand column are biased and derogatory, but that is the point. Why has it been so difficult to notice the same degree of bias and denigration in the lefthand list? The answer is that we are used to seeing women as the problem, to thinking of women as being different *from men,* and to regarding women's differences from men as deficiencies and weaknesses.

So it is understandable that many women have responded to the transformation of the list on the left into the list on the right with considerable mirth and relief. It was enormously liberating to believe that women weren't the problem; men were. By smoking the universal male out of his lair, we saw in daylight that he and his ways were not the center of all things. Most women have greeted each attempt to reevaluate him—finding after finding, popular book after popular book—with "At last! That's us!"

My personal favorite is the reanalysis of the perennial male lament, "Why can't women take a joke?" Studies have consistently shown that men and women don't differ in their capacity for humor, but they often disagree about what's funny. In general, what's funny has to do with the target of the joke. On the average, men think it is funnier when a male disparages someone else than when he disparages himself, but women generally prefer self-deprecating humor. One psychologist asked men and women to think of funny endings to stories that involved themselves or others. Most of the men took longer to think of endings to jokes in which the humor was directed at themselves than when it was directed at someone else, while for women the opposite was true.[25] Studies like these transform the problem from "Why can't women take a joke?" into "Why don't men know what's funny?"

As a woman, I like to play the reversal game too. But replacing the "woman as problem" bias with a "woman as solution" bias doesn't take us very far in solving the problem of the universal male. For one thing, it tends to confuse differences in what women and men do in their lives with differences in their basic psychological capacities. It is a small jump from saying "Women's lives are less linear than men's, and that is fine" to saying "Women think in a less linear way than men do, and that is fine too." As soon as we are in the realm of psychological qualities rather than in the activities of life, replacing "woman as problem" with "man as problem" obscures the reality of their human similarities. When the public hears news that men and women differ psychologically in some way, they immediately imagine two nonoverlapping groups that look like this:

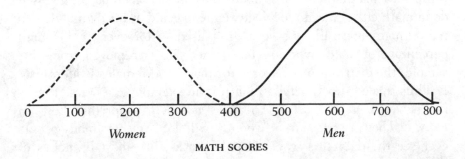

Women   *Men*

MATH SCORES

Sometimes two such nonoverlapping groups occur. As scientist Robert M. Sapolsky has observed, if you take two groups of anthrax victims, only one group of which has been treated with antibiotics, there will be no overlap in survival rates at all: The untreated victims will die within forty-eight hours. Period. This is an example of what Sapolsky calls a "powerful fact": By knowing which group an anthrax victim is in—treated or untreated—you will be able to predict with absolute certainty whether he or she will die of the disease.[26]

But when we get into the realm of abilities and qualities—such as doing well in math, the likelihood of roaring at the children, having a sense of humor, needing friends and family, being able to love, or being able to pack a suitcase—the overlap between men and women is always far greater than the difference, if any. Sapolsky plotted the actual results of a famous study that claimed to find clear evidence of a male superiority in math among junior high school students, and the result looked like this:

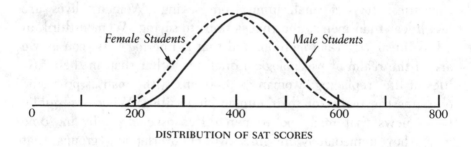

DISTRIBUTION OF SAT SCORES

"Anyone who can look at the graph," Sapolsky says, "and claim that it provides any predictiveness about how an *individual* boy or girl will do in math either has an ideological axe to grind or his own ability to reason mathematically is severely impaired." Moreover, if the small percentage of males who are math prodigies is removed from this sample, the distribution of scores for males and females is identical.

Thus, male "superiority" in math is an example of a "fact" that is not powerful at all, because it does not help us predict how an *individual* boy or girl, man or woman, will do. "Yet how many people ever see the data this way?" Sapolsky asks. "In most branches of science, reporting a difference with this little predictiveness would get you laughed out of the business. . . . Of the teachers, administrators, parents, and guidance counselors who believe that science has shown that boys are better at math than girls, how many know the predictiveness of this fact?"[27]

Suppose, therefore, that we move away from the narrow and limited question of "Do men and women differ, and if so, who's better?" and ask instead: Why is everyone so interested in differences? Why are differences regarded as deficiencies? What functions does the *belief* in differences serve? The answers begin to emerge in the following story from the halls of science, where we can see how even "pure" biological research is besmirched by the dusty fingerprints of those who conduct it.

■ Brain: Dissecting the differences

> It must be stated boldly that conceptual thought is exclusive to the masculine intellect . . . [but] it is no deprecation of a woman to state that she is more sensitive in her emotions and less ruled by her intellect. We are merely stating a difference, a difference which equips her for the special part for which she was cast . . . Her skull is also smaller than man's; and so, of course, is her brain.[28]
>
> —T. Lang, *The Difference Between a Man and a Woman*

In recent years the sexiest body part, far and away, has become the brain. Magazines with cover stories on the brain fly off the newsstands, and countless seminars, tapes, books, and classes teach people how to use "all" of their brains. New technologies, such as PET scans, produce gorgeous photographs of the brain at work and play. Weekly we hear new discoveries about this miraculous organ, and it seems that scientists will soon be able to pinpoint the very neuron, the very neurotransmitter, responsible for joy, sadness, rage, and suffering. At last we will know the reasons for all the differences between women and men that fascinate and infuriate, such as why men won't stop to ask directions and why women won't stop asking men what they are feeling.

In all this excitement, it seems curmudgeonly to sound words of caution, but the history of brain research does not exactly reveal a noble and impartial quest for truth, particularly on sensitive matters such as sex and race differences. Typically, when scientists haven't found the differences they were seeking, they haven't abandoned the goal or their belief that such differences exist; they just moved to another part of the anatomy or a different corner of the brain.

A century ago, for example, scientists tried to prove that women had smaller brains than men did, which accounted for women's alleged intellectual failings and emotional weaknesses. Dozens of studies purported to show that men had larger brains, making them smarter than women. When scientists realized that men's greater height and weight offset their brain-size advantage, however, they dropped this line of research like a shot. The scientists next tried to argue that women had smaller frontal lobes and larger parietal lobes than men did, another brain pattern thought to account for women's intellectual inferiority. Then it was reported that the parietal lobes might be associated with intellect. Panic in the labs—until anatomists suddenly found that women's parietal lobes were *smaller* than they had originally believed. Wherever they looked, scientists conveniently found evidence of female inferiority, as Gustave Le Bon, a Parisian, wrote in 1879:

> In the most intelligent races, as among the Parisians, there are a large number of women whose brains are closer in size to those of gorillas than to the most developed male brains. This inferiority is so obvious that no one can contest it for a moment; only its degree is worth discussion.[29]

We look back with amusement at the obvious biases of research a century ago, research designed to prove the obvious inferiority of women and minorities (and non-Parisians). Today, many researchers are splitting brains instead of weighing them, but they are no less determined to find sex differences. Nevertheless, skeptical neuroscientists are showing that biases and values are just as embedded in current research—old prejudices in new technologies.

The brain, like a walnut, consists of two hemispheres of equal size, connected by a bundle of fibers called the corpus callosum. The left hemisphere has been associated with verbal and reasoning ability, whereas the right hemisphere is associated with spatial reasoning and artistic ability. Yet by the time these findings reached the public, they had been vastly oversimplified and diluted. Even the great neuroscientist Roger Sperry, the grandfather of hemispheric research, felt obliged to warn that the "left-right dichotomy . . . is an idea with which it is very easy to run wild."[30] And many people have run wild with it: Stores are filled with manuals, cassettes, and handbooks that promise to help people become fluent in "whole-brain thinking," to beef up the unused part of their right brain, and to learn to use the intuitive right brain for business, painting, and inventing.

The fact that the brain consists of two hemispheres, each characterized by different specialties, provides a neat analogy to the fact that human beings consist of two genders, each characterized by different specialties. The analogy is so tempting that scientists keep trying to show that it is grounded in physical reality. Modern theories of gender and the brain are based on the idea that the left and right hemispheres develop differently in boys and girls, as does the corpus callosum that links the halves of the brain.

According to one major theory, the male brain is more "lateralized," that is, its hemispheres are specialized in their abilities, whereas females use both hemispheres more symmetrically because their corpus callosum is allegedly larger and contains more fibers. Two eminent scientists, Norman Geschwind and Peter Behan, maintained that this sex difference begins in the womb, when the male fetus begins to secrete testosterone—the hormone that will further its physical development as a male. Geschwind and Behan argued that testosterone in male fetuses washes over the brain, selectively attacking parts of the left hemisphere, briefly slowing its development, and producing right-hemisphere dominance in men. Geschwind speculated that the effects of testosterone on the prenatal brain produce "superior right hemisphere talents, such as artistic, musical, or mathematical talent."[31]

Right-hemisphere dominance is also thought to explain men's excellence in some tests of "visual-spatial ability"—the ability to imagine objects in three-dimensional space (the skill you need for mastering geometry, concocting football formations, and reading maps). This is apparently the reason that some men won't stop and ask directions when they are lost; they prefer to rely on their right brains, whereas women prefer to rely on a local informant. It is also supposed to be the reason that men can't talk about their feelings and would rather watch television or wax the car. Women have interconnected hemispheres, which explains why they excel in talk, feelings, intuition, and quick judgments. Geschwind and Behan's theory had tremendous scientific appeal, and it is cited frequently in research papers and textbooks. *Science* hailed it with the headline "Math Genius May Have Hormonal Basis."[32]

The theory also has had enormous popular appeal. It fits snugly, for example, with the Christian fundamentalist belief that men and women are innately different and thus innately designed for different roles. For his radio show "Focus on the Family," James Dobson interviewed Donald Joy, a professor of "human development in Christian education" at Asbury Theological Seminary, who explained Geschwind and Behan's theory this way:

JOY: . . . this marvelous female brain, is a brain that's not damaged during fetal development as the male brain is, but the damage gives a specialization to the male brain which we don't get in the female.
DOBSON: I want to pick up on that concept of us brain-damaged males. [laughter, chuckling]
JOY: . . . It's giving a chemical bath to the left hemisphere and this connecting link between the two hemispheres that reduced the size and number of transmission passages that exist here . . . So males simply can't talk to themselves across the hemispheres in a way that a woman does.
DOBSON: So some of the sex differences that we see in personality can be tracked back to that moment.
JOY: Oh, absolutely. And when we're talking about this now, we're talking about a glorious phenomenon because these are intrinsic sex differences . . . this is glorious because we are fearfully and wonderfully differentiated from each other.
DOBSON: Let's look at 'em, name 'em.
JOY: We're, we're mutually interdependent. Every household needs both a male brain and a female brain, for example. The woman's brain works much like a computer . . . lateral trans-

mission in her brain allows her to consult all of her past expe-rience and give you an instant response. She can make a judgment more quickly than a male can. . . . [but how she arrives at it is] hidden even from her, because it is like a com-puter, all it gives is the answer, it doesn't give you the process.[33]

The male brain, Joy added, is more like an "adding machine," in which facts are totaled and a logical solution presents itself. So males are good at logical reasoning, and females at intuitive judgments, because of the prenatal "chemical bath" that affects the male brain.

The same explanation and language—down to the same joke that men are "brain-damaged"—turns up in a book by two Christian fundamentalists, *The Language of Love,* published by Dobson's orga-nization. The authors, Gary Smalley and John Trent, write:

Specifically, medical studies have shown that between the eigh-teenth and twenty-sixth week of pregnancy, something happens that forever separates the sexes. . . . researchers have actually observed a chemical bath of testosterone and other sex-related hormones wash over a baby boy's brain. This causes changes that never happen to the brain of a baby girl. . . . The sex-related hormones and chemicals that flood a baby boy's brain cause the right side to recede slightly, destroying some of the connecting fibers [*sic:* the authors have it backward; the theory actually says that the left side is affected]. One result is that, in most cases, a boy starts life more *left*-brain oriented [*sic*]. Because little girls don't experience this chemical bath, they leave the starting blocks much more two-sided in their thinking. . . .

Now wait a minute, you may be thinking. *Does this mean that men are basically brain-damaged?*

Well, not exactly. What occurs in the womb merely sets the stage for men and women to "specialize" in two different ways of thinking. And this is one major reason men and women need each other so much.[34] (Emphases in original.)

Now it may be true that men and women, on the average, differ in the physiology of their brains. It may even be true that this difference explains why James Dobson's wife Shirley can sum up a person's character right away, while he, with his slower, adding-machine brain, takes weeks or months to come to the same impressions. But given the disgraceful history of bias and sloppy research designed more to confirm prejudices than to enlighten humanity, I think we would all do well to be suspicious and to evaluate the evidence for these assertions closely.

This is difficult for those of us who are not expert in physiology, neuroanatomy, or medicine. We are easily dazzled by words like "lateralization" and "corpus callosum." Besides, physiology seems so *solid;* if one study finds a difference between three male brains and three female brains, that must apply to all men and women. How do I know what my corpus callosum looks like? Is it bigger than a man's? Should I care?

For some answers, I turned to researchers in biology and neuroscience who have critically examined the research and the assumptions underlying theories of sex differences in the brain.[35] The first discovery of note was that, just like the nineteenth-century researchers who kept changing their minds about which *lobe* of the brain accounted for male superiority, twentieth-century researchers keep changing their minds about which *hemisphere* of the brain accounts for male superiority. Originally, the left hemisphere was considered the repository of intellect and reason. The right hemisphere was the sick, bad, crazy side, the side of passion, instincts, criminality, and irrationality. Guess which sex was thought to have left-brain intellectual superiority? (Answer: males.) In the 1960s and 1970s, however, the right brain was resuscitated and brought into the limelight. Scientists began to suspect that it was the source of genius and inspiration, creativity and imagination, mysticism and mathematical brilliance. Guess which sex was now thought to have right-brain specialization? (Answer: males.)

It's all very confusing. Today we hear arguments that men have greater left-brain specialization (which explains their intellectual advantage) *and* that they have greater right-brain specialization (which explains their mathematical and artistic advantage). *Newsweek* recently asserted as fact, for instance, that "Women's language and other skills are more evenly divided between left and right hemisphere; in men, such functions are concentrated in the left brain."[36] But fundamentalists Smalley and Trent asserted that most women spend the majority of their days and nights camped out on the right side of the brain [which] harbors the center for feelings, as well as the primary relational, language, and communication skills . . . and makes an afternoon devoted to art and fine music actually enjoyable.[37]

You can hear the chuckling from men who regard art museums and concert halls as something akin to medieval torture chambers, but I'm sure that the many men who enjoy art and fine music, indeed who create art and fine music, would not find that last remark so funny. Geschwind and Behan, of course, had argued that male specialization of the right hemisphere explained why men *excel* in art and fine music. But since Smalley and Trent apparently do not share these prissy female interests, they relegate them to women—to women's brains.

The two hemispheres of the brain do have different specialties, but it is far too simple-minded (so to speak) to assume that human abilities clump up in opposing bunches. Most brain researchers today believe that the two hemispheres complement one another, to the extent that one side can sometimes take over the functions of a side that has been damaged. Moreover, specific skills often involve components from both hemispheres: one side has the ability to tell a joke, and the other has the ability to laugh at one. Math abilities include both visual-spatial skills and reasoning skills. The right hemisphere is involved in creating art, but the left hemisphere is involved in appreciating and analyzing art. As neuropsychologist Jerre Levy once said, "Could the eons of human evolution have left half of the brain witless? Could a bird whose existence is dependent on flying have evolved only a single wing?"[38]

These qualifications about the interdependence of brain hemispheres have not, however, deterred those who believe that there are basic psychological differences between the sexes that can be accounted for in the brain. So let's consider their argument more closely.

The neuroscientist Ruth Bleier, who at her untimely death was Professor of Neurophysiology at the University of Wisconsin, carefully examined Geschwind and Behan's data, going back to many of their original references.[39] In one such study of 507 fetal brains of 10 to 44 weeks gestation, the researchers had actually stated that they found *no significant sex differences* in these brains. If testosterone had an effect on the developing brain, it would surely have been apparent in this large sample. Yet Geschwind and Behan cited this study for other purposes and utterly ignored its findings of no sex differences.

Instead, Geschwind and Behan cited as evidence for their hypothesis a study of *rats'* brains. The authors of the rat study reported that in male rats, two areas of the cortex that are believed to be involved in processing visual information were 3 percent thicker on the right side than on the left. In one of the better examples of academic gobbledygook yet to reach the printed page, the researchers interpreted their findings to mean that "in the male rat it is necessary to have greater spatial orientation to interact with a female rat during estrus and to integrate that input into a meaningful output." Translation: When having sex with a female, the male needs to be able to look around in case a dangerous predator, such as her husband, walks in on them.

Bleier found more holes in this argument than in a screen door. No one knows, she said, what the slightly greater thickness in the male rat's cortex means for the rat, let alone what it means for human beings. There is at present no evidence that spatial orientation is related to asymmetry of the cortex, or that female rats have a lesser or deficient ability in this regard. And although Geschwind and Behan unabashedly used their limited findings to account for male "superiority" in math and art, they did not specifically study the incidence of genius, talent, or even modest giftedness in their sample, nor did they demonstrate a difference between the brains of geniuses and the brains of average people.

Bleier wrote to *Science,* offering a scholarly paper detailing these criticisms. *Science* did not publish it, on the grounds, as one reviewer put it, that Bleier "tends to err in the opposite direction from the researchers whose results and conclusions she criticizes" and because "she argues very strongly for the predominant role of environmental influences."[40] Apparently, said Bleier, one is allowed to err in only one direction if one wants to be published in *Science.* The journal did not even publish her critical Letter to the Editor.

At about the same time, however, *Science* saw fit to publish a study by two researchers who claimed to have found solid evidence of gender differences in the splenium (posterior end) of the corpus callosum.[41] In particular, they said, the splenium was larger and more bulbous in the five female brains than in the nine male brains they examined, which had been obtained at autopsy. The researchers speculated that "the female brain is less well lateralized—that is, manifests less hemispheric specialization—than the male brain for visuospatial functions." Notice the language: The female brain is *less specialized* than, and by implication inferior to, the male brain. They did not say, as they might have, that the female brain was *more integrated* than the male's. The male brain is the norm, and specialization, in the brain as in academia, is considered a good thing. Generalists in any business are out of favor these days.

This article, which also met professional acclaim, had a number of major flaws that, had they been part of any other research paper, would have been fatal to its publication. The study was based on a small sample of only fourteen brains. The researchers did not describe their methods of selecting the brains in that sample, so it is possible that some of the brains were diseased or otherwise abnormal. The article contained numerous unsupported assumptions and leaps of faith. For example, there is at present absolutely no evidence that the number of fibers in the corpus callosum is even related to hemispheric specialization. Indeed, no one knows what role, if any, the callosum plays in determining a person's mental abilities. Most damaging of all, the sex differences that the researchers claimed to have found in the size of the corpus callosum were not statistically significant, according to the scientific conventions for accepting an article for publication.

Bleier again wrote to *Science,* delineating these criticisms and also citing four subsequent studies, by her and by others, that independently failed to find gender differences of any kind in the corpus callosum. *Science* failed to publish this criticism, as it has failed to publish all studies that find no gender differences in the brain.

Ultimately, the most damning blow to all of these brain-hemisphere theories is that the formerly significant sex differences that brain theories are attempting to account for—in verbal, spatial, and math abilities—are fading rapidly. Let's start with the famed female superiority in verbal ability. Janet Hyde, a professor of psychology at the University of Wisconsin, and her colleague Marcia Linn reviewed 165 studies of verbal ability (including skills in vocabulary, writing, anagrams, and reading comprehension), which represented tests of 1,418,899 people. Hyde and Linn reported that at present in America, there simply are no gender differences in these verbal skills. They noted: "Thus our research pulls out one of the two wobbly legs on which the brain lateralization theories have rested."[42]

Hyde recently went on to kick the other leg, the assumption of overall male superiority in mathematics and spatial ability. No one disputes that males do surpass females at the highly gifted end of the math spectrum. But when Hyde and her colleagues analyzed 100 studies of mathematics performance, representing the testing of 3,985,682 students, they found that gender differences were smallest and favored *females* in samples of the general population, and grew larger, favoring males, only in selected samples of precocious individuals.[43]

What about spatial abilities, another area thought to reveal a continuing male superiority? When psychologists put the dozens of existing studies on spatial ability into a giant hopper and looked at the overall results, this was what they reported: Many studies show no sex differences. Of the studies that do report sex differences, the magnitude of the difference is often small. And finally, there is greater variation *within* each sex than *between* them. As one psychologist who reviewed these studies summarized: "The observed differences are very small, the overlap [between men and women] large, and abundant biological theories are supported with very slender or no evidence."[44]

Sometimes scientists and science writers put themselves through contortions in order to reconcile the slim evidence with their belief in sex differences in the brain. The authors of a popular textbook on sexuality, published in 1990, acknowledge that "sex differences in cognitive skills have declined significantly in recent years." Then they add: "Notwithstanding this finding, theories continue to debate why these differences exist." Pardon? Notwithstanding the fact that there are few differences of any magnitude, let's discuss why there are differences? Even more mysteriously, they conclude: "If Geschwind's theory is ultimately supported by further research, we will have hard evidence of a biological basis for alleged sex differences in verbal and spatial skills."[45] "Hard evidence" for *alleged* sex differences—the ones that don't exist!

It is sobering to read, over and over and over again in scholarly papers, the conclusions of eminent scientists who have cautioned their colleagues against generalizing about sex differences from poor data. One leader in brain-hemisphere research, Marcel Kinsbourne, observing that the evidence for sex differences "fails to convince on logical, methodological, and empirical grounds," then asked:

Why then do reputable investigators persist in ignoring [this evidence]? Because the study of sex differences is not like the rest of psychology. Under pressure from the gathering momentum of feminism, and perhaps in backlash to it, many investigators seem determined to discover that men and women "really" are different. It seems that if sex differences (e.g., in lateralization) do not exist, then they have to be invented.[46]

These warnings have, for the most part, gone unheeded. Poor research continues to be published in reputable journals, and from there it is disseminated to the public. Many scientists and science writers continue to rely on weak data to support their speculations, like using pebbles as foundation for a castle. Because these speculations fit the dominant beliefs about gender, however, they receive far more attention and credibility than they warrant. Worse, the far better evidence that fails to conform to the dominant beliefs about gender is overlooked, disparaged, or, as in Bleier's experience, remains unpublished.

As a result, ideas enter the common vocabulary as proven facts when they should be encumbered with "maybes," "sometimes," and "we-don't-know-yets." Scientist Hugh Fairweather, reviewing the history of sex differences research in cognition, concluded: "What had before been a possibility at best slenderly evidenced, was widely taken for a fact; and 'fact' hardened into a 'biological' dogma."[47]

Now, it is possible that reliable sex differences in the brain will eventually be discovered. Will it then be all right for Dobson to go on the air to celebrate how delightfully but innately different men and women are? Should we then all make sure we have a male brain and a female brain in every household? Should we then worry about the abnormality of households like mine, in which the male is better at intuitive judgments and the female has the adding-machine mentality?

The answers are no, for three reasons. First, theories of sex differences in the brain cannot account for the complexities of people's everyday behavior. They cannot explain, for instance, why, if women are better than men in verbal ability, so few women are auctioneers or diplomats, or why, if women have the advantage in making rapid judgments, so few women are air-traffic controllers or umpires. Nor can brain theories explain why abilities and ambitions change when people are given opportunities previously denied to them. Two decades ago, theorists postulated biological limitations that were keeping women out of men's work like medicine and bartending. When the external barriers to these professions fell, the speed with which women entered them was dizzying. Did everybody's brain change? Today we would be amused to think that women have a brain-lateralization deficiency that is keeping them out of law school. But we continue to hear about the biological reasons that keep women out of science, math, and politics. For sex differences in cognitive abilities to wax and wane so rapidly, they must be largely a result of education, motivation, and opportunity, not of innate differences between male and female brains.

Second, the meanings of terms like "verbal ability" and "spatial reasoning" keep changing too, depending on who is using them and for what purpose. For example, when conservatives like Dobson speak of women's verbal abilities, they usually mean women's interest in and willingness to talk about relationships and feelings. But in studies of total talking time in the workplace, men far exceed women in the talk department. In everyday life, men interrupt women more than vice versa, dominate the conversation, and are more successful at introducing new topics and having their comments remembered in group discussions.[48] What does this mean for judgments of which sex has the better "verbal ability"?

Third, the major key problem with biological theories of sex differences is that they deflect attention from the far more substantial evidence for sex similarity. The finding that men and women are more alike in their abilities and brains than different almost never makes the news. Researchers and the public commit the error of focusing on the small differences—usually of the magnitude of a few percentage points—rather than on the fact that the majority of women and men overlap. For example, this is what the author of a scientific paper that has been widely quoted as *supporting* sex differences in brain hemispheres actually concluded:

> Thus, one must not overlook perhaps the most obvious conclusion, which is that basic patterns of male and female brain asymmetry seem to be more similar than they are different.[49]

Everyone, nevertheless, promptly overlooked it.

The habit of seeing women and men as two opposite categories also leads us to avoid the practical question: How much ability does it take to do well in a particular career? When people hear that men are better than women in spatial ability, many are quick to conclude that perhaps women, with their deficient brains, should not try to become architects or engineers. This reaction is not merely unfortunate; it is cruel to the women who *do* excel in architectural or engineering ability. The fields of math and science are losing countless capable women because girls keep hearing that women aren't as good as men in these fields.

None of this means that biology is irrelevant to human behavior. But whenever the news trumpets some version of "biology affects behavior," it obscures the fact that biology and behavior form a two-way street. Hormones affect sexual drive, for instance, but sexual activity affects hormone levels. An active brain seeks a stimulating environment, but living in a stimulating environment literally changes and enriches the brain. Fatigue and boredom cause poor performance on the job, but stultifying job conditions produce fatigue and boredom. Scientists and writers who reduce our personalities, problems, and abilities to biology thereby tell only half the story, and miss half the miracle of how human biology works.

Ruth Bleier, who after all was herself a neuroscientist, put the whole matter in perspective this way:

> Such efforts directed at the callosum (or any other particular structure in the brain, for that matter) are today's equivalent of 19th-century craniology: if you can find a bigger bump here or a smaller one there on a person's skull, if you can find a more bulbous splenium here or a more slender one there . . . you will know something significant about their intelligence, their

personality, their aspirations, their astrological sign, their gender and race, and their status in society. We are still mired in the naive hope that we can find something that we can *see* and *measure* and it will explain everything. It is silly science and it serves us badly.[50]

Once defined as fundamentally different from—and inferior to— men in body, psyche, and brain, women have tried various ways of coping with being "the other." The most common approach, the one that most women today have adopted, has been to try to prove that they are as good as, as competent as, as intelligent as, as valued as, the men who set the norm. Of course, after a while all the efforts to be "as something as" men get tiring. In 1991, after twenty-five years of trying to be accepted by her male colleagues, Dr. Frances K. Conley, a tenured professor in the department of medicine at Stanford and one of the few female neurosurgeons in the country, resigned her post. She had had enough of being called "hon," of having other surgeons fondle her in the operating room, of the relentlessly "hostile" environment, of having her opinions dismissed as evidence of her "PMS." Dr. Conley resigned because, she wrote, "I was tired of being treated as less than an equal person."[51] (She has since returned to her job at Stanford, with renewed conviction in the importance of persistence.)

And so, weary of the seemingly fruitless struggle to be like men and repeatedly having to demonstrate their human competence, many women have set off in a separatist direction to define their own standards of excellence and to redeem qualities and experiences that had long been disparaged. This approach has offered a beguiling, exhilarating, luminous alternative to the impossibility of measuring up. Yet it too has its perils, as we shall see next.

2

Beautiful Souls and Different Voices

Why women are not superior to men

When the War in the Persian Gulf broke out in January 1991, a reporter from a major newspaper called me to discuss what I knew about the much-publicized "gender gap" in attitudes toward war. "What is it about women's nature," he wanted to know, "that makes them more likely to oppose war?" I thought about the thousands of women in the military, many of whom were, for the first time in history, in the thick of the battle; the women interviewed on television and writing to the newspapers, enthusiastically endorsing the war effort; the women who were busily draping yellow ribbons over every tree in their neighborhood; and the men *and* women who were organizing protests against the war. I declined the interview.

A few years ago, Richard Restak wrote an essay to explain why he thought the increased number of women in medicine will reduce health care costs and humanize the profession. "If you combine a woman physician's natural intuitional and emotional assets," he said, "with her willingness to work for less income and her willingness to settle for less autonomy, health care planners are provided with a means to achieve several important goals."[1]

This idea, that women have "natural assets" when it comes to intuitions, emotions, nurturing, professional self-effacement, and opposition to war, crops up across the political and social spectrum. A speaker at a Moral Majority conference put it this way:

> Women's nature is other-oriented. . . . To the traditional woman, self-centeredness remains as ugly and sinful as ever. The less time women spend thinking about themselves, the happier they are. . . . Women are ordained by their nature to spend time meeting the needs of others.[2]

And the feminist writer Lindsy Van Gelder, who would disagree heartily that women "are ordained by their nature" to be compassionate (or to be anything else), nevertheless agrees that:

> [As] the traditional caretakers, women in this culture easily affiliate and identify with others, value people's feelings, and tend to base moral codes on the good of the entire group. . . . [These] traditionally female values are our best shot at changing consciousness—and saving the world.[3]

Many women and men accept the idea that there are profound differences between the sexes in their values, moral codes, and connection to others, and that women's ways are better than men's. The opposite sex is the superior one; the qualities associated with being female are better than the qualities associated with being male. This view is gaining ground in many areas. In psychoanalysis, religion, academic psychology, psychotherapy, politics, philosophy, science, and art, so-called women's ways of thinking, acting, and feeling are being reappraised and revalued, transformed from deficiencies and weaknesses into strengths.

For example, in this society, autonomy—generally meaning self-sufficiency, independence, and the ability to pursue one's own goals —has been considered the sign of maturity and health. In the early years of the women's movement, therefore, many feminists advocated that women should become more independent, more "like men." Now many are arguing that the pursuit of autonomy is a snare and delusion, a male value that serves no one but the Marlboro Man, and that women should value their natural relatedness and nurturance as healthier signs of maturity.

In politics, we are witnessing the rise of movements such as ecofeminism, which rests on the basic premise that patriarchal philosophies are harmful to women, children, and other living things because such philosophies emphasize the need to dominate and control unruly females and the unruly wilderness. Throughout history, men have associated women with nature (it's "Mother Nature," after all) because of the female's mysterious capacity to give birth, whereas they have associated themselves with the higher intellectual functions of "culture" and "civilization." Ecofeminists believe that women should stop trying to break this ancient association (women = nature, men = culture) and capitalize on it. The real problem, they suggest, is men's alienation from nature and their resulting willingness to exploit the planet even at growing risk of destroying it. As Ynestra King, a leading ecofeminist and professor of women's studies, says, "the problem isn't women's proximity to nature, but men's nonproximity."[4]

In the last decade, feminist scholars have divided into those who believe that there are no significant personality differences between the sexes (other than temporary ones caused by differences in power and society) and those who believe that there *are* fundamental differences but that women's ways are better. The latter group, generally known as "cultural feminists," hopes to overcome society's sexism by celebrating women's special qualities, women's ways, women's experiences.[5] As legal scholar Robin West describes the movement:

> Women's art, women's craft, women's narrative capacity, women's critical eye, women's ways of knowing, and women's heart, are all, for the cultural feminist, redefined as things to celebrate. . . . Most vital, however, for cultural feminism is the claim that intimacy is not just something women *do,* it is something human beings *ought* to do. Intimacy is a source of value, not a private hobby. It is morality, not habit.[6]

I thoroughly endorse the effort to retrieve the best qualities and experiences associated with women from the scrap heap of slander in which they have reposed. It was about time for psychologists to realize that capacities such as intimacy, cooperation, nurturance, vulnerability to others, and empathy are healthy and necessary for both sexes, not oddities of the female psyche. It was outrageous for history and other fields to be limited to the study of men, with footnotes on a couple of notable women. Anthropology's validation of Man the Hunter as the exclusive model of human evolution and human nature needed the humbling realization that Woman the Gatherer was and is as critical to evolution and survival.

My concern here is not with these important efforts to dethrone the universal male; they are intellectually and ethically essential and long overdue. My concern is with a growing tendency to turn the tables from us-them thinking (with women as the problem) to them-us thinking (with men as the problem). Framing the question in terms of polarities, regardless of which pole is the valued one, immediately sets up false choices for women and men. It continues to divide the world into *men* and *women* as if these categories were unified opposites. It obscures the fact that the opposing qualities associated with masculinity and femininity are caricatures to begin with. It perpetuates what I will argue is a misguided belief that there is something special and different about woman's nature, an attitude that historically has served to keep women in their place. It continues to use the male norm, although this time to define what is supposedly right with women instead of what is wrong with them.

Moreover, celebrations of "women's natural ways of being" have, I believe, the potential to be as oppressive to women as the denigrating attitudes they replace. I don't mind if women wish to transform normal female experiences, such as menstruation, into a "summer solstice ritual" like this one:

> The women simulated a birth canal and birthed each other into their circle. They raised power by placing their hands on each other's bellies and chanting together. Finally they marked each other's faces with rich, dark menstrual blood saying, "This is the blood that promises renewal. This is the blood that promises substance. This is the blood that promises life." From hidden dirty secret to symbol of the life power of the Goddess, women's blood has come full circle.[7]

It is good for women to feel positive about themselves, particularly when society for so long has regarded women's normal reproductive processes either as sicknesses or as evidence of women's earthy, instinct-driven nature. Certainly it is healthy to reaffirm child-bearing as a unique female experience. It is healthy to regard menstruation as a normal part of a woman's life and to reject views of menstruating women as being unclean, untouchable, or irrational (as we will see further in Chapter 4).

Yet I worry about the compensatory impulse to worship a woman's "menstrual powers" that supposedly link her to Nature and Life. It makes about as much sense to me as would a male celebration of the "scrotal powers" that produce "life-giving sperm" in a constant cycle of depletion and renewal. As the writer Hilary Standing says, "The exhortation to be positive about our bodily cycles is in danger of producing new mystifications based on myths about women's psychic communion with the moon or with nature."[8]

These new mystifications, which sentimentalize women's "magical" reproductive capacities, have the potential to backfire on the very group they are intended to liberate. They restore the familiar pronatal pressures on women who cannot or choose not to have children. They make women who have a difficult time with menstruation or childbirth feel guilty that they have pain or might be helped by "male" medicine; and many women, in spite of Lamaze's promise of *Painless Childbirth,* do experience intense pain during childbirth and then feel like failures.[9] Women do not benefit from doctrinaire regulations of the one right way to be, whether the right way is an outmoded notion of medical correctness or a modern notion of spiritual correctness.

Some proponents of the glorification of Womanhood, having endorsed stereotypes of female qualities to begin with, actively reject the qualities, practices, and experiences associated with males. Are men political? Then women must be spiritual. Are men overly rational? Then women must be intuitive. Is modern medicine patriarchal and overly technological? Then women must choose natural healing and cure themselves, as Hallie Iglehart advocates in *Womanspirit: A guide to women's wisdom,* with fasting and yoga, health food and herbal teas, a laying on of hands and a channeling of energy.[10] Is society hopelessly male-dominated? Then women must find or invent societies in which women once dominated. Forcing choices between such exaggerated extremes, I believe, is fruitless. The endorsement of what is good about women does not require a rejection of what is good about men. A rejection of what is bad about men does not require the manufacture of a natural sweetness in women.

Are women really kinder, gentler, and more interconnected with people and the environment than men are? It is not easy to stand back from our intuitions or from flattering stereotypes and evaluate them critically. The questions are these: Are the qualities of peacefulness and connection to others endemic to female nature, or are they a result of the nurturing, caretaking work that women do because of their social and family roles? For that matter, are these qualities truly more characteristic of women than men, or are they merely human archetypes—stereotypes of female and male—that blur when we look more closely at actual human beings?

The answers are important for our visions of possible futures, because if women are kinder and gentler by nature, then we can predict that they will indeed transform the world when they get the power to do so (Margaret Thatcher, Jeane Kirkpatrick, Indira Gandhi, and Ilse Koch being apparent aberrations). But if women's daily behavior, like men's, is more influenced by the roles they play, the ideologies they believe in, and the work they do than by anything fundamental to their gender, then we need to transform roles, ideologies, and work so that humane qualities can be encouraged in both sexes.

■ *Fighters and pacifists*

A typical woman . . . innately understands the basic principles of conflict resolution.

—Helen Caldicott, 1985

Non-violence is a natural method of action for women.[11]

—Paper presented at a 1983 Peace Conference

One of the constructive impulses behind cultural feminism is the dream of a better world, one that will be egalitarian, peaceful, and environmentally sound. For some ecofeminists and other members of the woman-is-better school, this dream, and visions of how to achieve it, rest on the most basic male-female dichotomy: that men are the warlike, dominating, aggressive, planet-destroying sex and women are the peacemaking, empathic, nonaggressive, planet-saving sex. It then follows that saving the world depends on the ascendancy of women, who will turn the planet into an ecologically sound environment in which all will live in harmony. (Except men, who presumably will have to be enclosed on restricted preserves.)

I admit that I've entertained this fantasy too from time to time. The trouble is that the only sex that might replace men is women, and to date there is no persuasive evidence that women are naturally or even actually more pacifistic, empathic, or earth-loving than men.

New studies find that the behavior that we link to gender depends more on what an individual is doing and needs to do than on his or her biological sex. For example, sociologist Barbara Risman compared the personality traits of single fathers, single mothers, and married parents. If biological predispositions or childhood socialization create stable personality differences between men and women, she reasoned, then fathers should differ from mothers in their baby-care skills and nurturing talents in general, regardless of marital status. Instead, Risman found that having responsibility for child care was as strongly related to "feminine" traits, such as nurturance and sympathy, as being female was. The single men who were caring for children were more like mothers than like married fathers. These men were not an atypical group of especially nurturant men, either. They had custody of their children through circumstances beyond their control—widowhood, the wife's desertion, or the wife's lack of interest in shared custody.[12]

Similarly, a study of 150 men who were spending up to sixty hours a week caring for their ailing parents or spouses found that the men provided just as much emotional support as women traditionally do. The obligation of providing this care usually falls to women, but when men have to do it, they do it just as well and lovingly. Lenard Kaye, who directed the research, reports that these men spent as much time as women doing nurturant things—holding the sick relative's hands, listening, showing concern. The men were not providing this care grudgingly; they derived great satisfaction (as well as stress) from doing it.[13]

What about the female advantage in empathic skills? Isn't it obvious that women are better than men in reading another person's emotional state, being able to take another person's point of view, sharing another person's feelings? The feminist psychoanalyst Nancy Chodorow argues that because girls remain connected to their mothers, whereas boys must learn to separate from their mothers, girls emerge from childhood "with a basis for 'empathy' built into their primary definition of self in a way that boys do not . . . with a stronger basis for experiencing another's needs or feelings as one's own (or of thinking that one is so experiencing another's needs and feelings)." [14]

It turns out that the operative word in this sentence is *thinking*: Many women (and men) *think* that women have the empathic advantage, so when psychologists ask people to rate themselves on their empathic skills, women tend to score higher than men. But when studies measure physiological signs of empathy (actual physical responses to another person's suffering or unhappiness) or behavioral signs of empathy (actually doing something to help another person in distress), gender differences vanish. Men and women may be helpful in different ways, of course, depending on their roles and talents; men will be more likely to help a woman change a flat tire, and women will be more likely to bring over some food for a bereaved friend. But the impetus to help is present in both genders. Two psychologists, summarizing numerous studies of empathy done with children and adults, reported that there is "little basis for the conclusion that the [self-described] sex difference in empathy . . . is due to an innate mechanism or predisposition." [15]

In everyday life, women do appear to have the edge on some kinds of empathy: They are, on the average, better able to "read" men and interpret male behavior than men are at reading women and interpreting female behavior. Men are often charmed and amused by what they regard as the mysterious behavior of women, but they typically feel no need to decipher it. "That's women for you," they say with a shrug or a smile, "who knows what they want?" Songs, plays, novels, and cartoons have long relied on this joke, although I've never understood why the answer never occurs to the songwriter or cartoonist: Just ask them—and then listen.

In contrast, most women learn that for their own safety and security they had better try to understand and predict the behavior of men. But this is not a *female* skill; it is a *self-protective* skill, and the sex gap fades when the men and women in question are equal in power. In a brilliant experiment on women's intuition, psychologist Sara Snodgrass paired men and women in work teams. Sometimes she assigned the man to be the leader, sometimes the woman. She found that the person in the subordinate (follower) position was more sensitive to the leader's nonverbal signals than the leader was to the follower's cues. This difference occurred whether a man or a woman was the leader or follower, leading Snodgrass to conclude that "women's intuition" should properly be called "subordinate's intuition."[16] Men, like women, manage to develop empathic skills when they need to read a boss's temper and intentions for their own security or advantage.

Alfie Kohn, in *The Brighter Side of Human Nature*, examined scores of studies having to do with that brighter side: the human willingness and ability to feel compassion, to behave altruistically, to care for others even at the expense of one's own interests, to help in emergencies. Over and over, he reports that while girls and women have a reputation for being more empathic and altruistic, and while they are more likely than males to express sympathy verbally for another person, few studies find any real behavioral difference of any magnitude. "Where gender differences do emerge," he writes, "they are typically weak, partial, and buried in qualifications."[17]

Much of the stereotype of women's innate advantage in empathy derives from the different jobs that women and men do and their different average levels of power. Women are more likely than men to be the caretakers and monitors of relationships. They do the interaction work in conversations, making sure feelings aren't hurt and keeping the ball rolling. They do the invisible but time-consuming "kin work" of managing extended family relationships, such as organizing celebrations, sending holiday and birthday cards, making phone calls to keep in touch, and arranging dinner parties. Much of the paid work they do falls in the service sector, where they are expected to anticipate and respond to the emotions of customers and clients. And they work fully an extra month of twenty-four-hour-days per year in comparison to husbands, doing what sociologist Arlie Hochschild calls a "second shift" of child care and housekeeping.[18]

Although there is no question that mothers spend far more time, on the average, than fathers in terms of the daily care of their children—noticing when the children need new shoes, taking them to the doctor and to soccer practice, supervising their homework and chores—it does not follow that mothers are necessarily more empathic about understanding their children's feelings or actions. As many mothers as fathers are prepared to yell at their children or spank them to "get" them to obey, instead of talking and explaining rules to them.[19] I have yet to see a new mother know what to do with a baby or know why it is crying unless she has been raised in a large family or already has had considerable experience with infants.

Males and females in all primate societies must learn how to be parents. Human beings have a capacity for empathy, the ability to see things from another person's perspective, but its expression is a learned skill. Anyone who rummages for even ten minutes in the history of motherhood, or who merely watches harried mothers in supermarkets, or who *is* a harried mother in a supermarket, will quickly lose the belief in a "maternal instinct." Throughout the centuries, women have been as likely as men to abuse, reject, or simply fail to understand their own children.[20]

Sexual stereotypes have further polarized men into the warlike, aggressive sex, and women into the peaceful, nonaggressive sex: Man the Life-Destroyer versus Woman the Life-Creator. Certainly it is true that the oldest division of roles in human society put men in charge of war and hunting, and women in charge of raising children. Moreover, this stereotype is based on an undisputed and universal truth that men are more physically violent than women. They are more likely to get into fistfights, more likely to respond combatively to insult, far more likely to commit murder. In our society today, women and men fear the violence of men—the horror of heartless and random murders, assaults, and serial killings—and women cannot walk on city streets without hoping that the footsteps behind them prove to be those of another woman.

Without disputing this real and alarming difference between the sexes, I wish to make another argument here. "Man the Killer" and "Woman the Peacemaker" are symbols of two potentials in human nature. By focusing on the men in power who make war (and the men in armies who fight), we overlook the women who support and endorse war, making it possible. By focusing on male violence, we overlook the men who promote pacifism and negotiation. By regarding aggressiveness as an entrenched and exclusively male quality, and pacifism as an inherent feminine quality, we overlook the ways in which societies in turmoil create dangerous, violent men, and we conveniently forget that most of the greatest pacifists and reformers in history have been men. Archetypes are not blueprints; flesh-and-blood men and women conform to them in only the most general of ways.

As political scientist Jean Bethke Elshtain has showed in *Women and War*, throughout history women have been just as militant in wartime as men. Women have always participated in wars, in whatever ways their societies permitted: as combatants, as defenders, as laborers in the work force to produce war materials, as supporters of their warrior husbands and sons. Women have been all too willing to join in the glorification of nation above family, and to find honor in playing the "Spartan Mother" (the woman, nameless to history, who lost five sons in battle and gave thanks to the gods that Sparta won). A Spartan Mother in World War II, Aletta Sullivan, became a "Gold Star Mother" five times over after all five of her sons were killed when their ship was sunk off Guadalcanal. Was Mrs. Sullivan angry at the Navy, which incredibly stationed all of her sons on one ship? Did she call for an end to war? Now is a good time, she said to a crowd of shipworkers who had turned out to honor her, "to keep your chin up."

The persistence of Spartan Mothers, along with the weight of evidence of history and psychology, gives the lie to the sentimental yet appealing idea that because women give birth they are more inclined to oppose the destruction that accompanies warfare. " 'Mother' got drafted into propaganda service over and over, in all warring nations," observes Elshtain. She cites the "blood-curdling patriotism" of an English woman in World War I, who wrote a letter to the London *Morning Post* and signed it only "A Little Mother":

[We] mothers of the British race . . . play the most important part in the history of the world, for it is we who "mother the men" who have to uphold the honour and traditions not only of our Empire but of the whole civilized world. . . . We women, who demand to be heard, will tolerate no such cry as Peace! Peace! where there is no peace.[21]

Women have revealed their patriotic fervor not only by sending their sons to battle, but also, over the centuries, by being actively involved in warfare themselves as soldiers, resistance fighters, and terrorists. In the first century B.C., Plutarch described barbarians

whose fierce women charged with swords and axes, and fell upon their opponents uttering a hideous outcry. . . . When summoned to surrender, they killed their children, slaughtered one another, or hanged themselves to trees.[22]

In the Second World War, upward of one million Soviet women served in combat as snipers, machinegunners, artillery women, and tank women; they flew in three women's air regiments on bombing missions. Nadya Popova, a bomber pilot, recounted her experiences as matter-of-factly as any male pilot would: "War requires the ability to kill." Marisa Masu, an Italian Resistance fighter in World War II, described feelings that are no different from those of most male soldiers:

At that time it was clear that each Nazi I killed, each bomb I helped to explode, shortened the length of the war and saved the lives of all women and children. . . . I never asked myself if the soldier or SS man I killed had a wife or children. I never thought about it.[23]

We think of war as a male activity and value, but war has always given even noncombatant women an escape from domestic confinement—the exhilaration of a public identity and a chance to play a heroic role, usually denied them in their private lives. In American history, the Civil War was a major springboard for women's advancement into men's spheres, and the World Wars of the twentieth century had an even more liberating effect for many women: wars earned them the vote, got them into the arena of politics, got them better jobs, and vindicated the importance of their labor on the home front. Black women in World War II moved into higher-paying factory jobs.[24]

Without understanding what war accomplishes for women, in emotional excitement, expanded opportunities, and tangible freedoms (and likewise what thrills and terrors war offers men), we perpetuate mythic notions that men love war and women loathe it. This notion infuses most of the current debates about whether women should be allowed in combat. Proponents on both sides tend to base their arguments on women's *nature*—whether women are or are not as able as men to fight, whether combat does or does not destroy their femininity, and so on. This debate deflects attention from the question that really matters, namely, "What do women gain or lose by this decision?" Currently, women in the military lose money by not being allowed directly in combat, although, as we learned in the Persian Gulf War, they are at as great a risk of death by working in support services; they lose status and prestige; and they lose political clout. Military experience, especially in combat, is still an asset for those who run for high office (except for Ronald Reagan, who merely believed he had served in the Army).

Quite apart from what men and women do in wartime, bellicose and genocidal attitudes are by no means a male preserve. The same propaganda and ideology that motivate male members of a society ensnare its female citizens too. Iranian women joined Iranian men in chanting Death to America; British women joined British men to support a war with Argentina over the Falkland Islands; German women joined German men to support Hitler's dreams of world conquest; American women have joined American men in supporting virtually every one of our invasions, "police actions," and wars, most recently in the Persian Gulf. Women, for all their reputed empathic skills, have been as willing and able as men to regard the enemy as beasts or demons to be exterminated rather than as fellow human beings.

Thus, a Milwaukee woman, endorsing use of the atomic bomb at Hiroshima, wrote to her newspaper: "When one sets out to destroy vermin, does one try to leave a few alive in the nest? Certainly not!"[25] Women have supported the Ku Klux Klan and its bloody outrages every bit as much as their men did; women didn't light the fires, perhaps, but they sewed the costumes that the cross-burners wore. In the late 1970s, David Duke (then Grand Wizard of the Knights of the KKK, now posing as a mainstream Republican) allowed women to become actual members, so Klanswomen today can attend den meetings and ritual cross burnings along with men—which they do. Across the country, women are organizing their own "white power" and "Aryan women's" groups, and they constitute upwards of a third of the *active* membership of hate groups such as skinheads, neo-Nazis, and "Christian Identity" sects.[26]

None of this means that at any given moment in society, men and women will be precisely alike in their attitudes and values. Much has been made in recent years of the American gender gap in support for militarism. For instance, after Iraq invaded Kuwait in August 1990, a survey conducted by the Public Agenda Foundation reported that "support for launching a massive counterattack or an all-out war is 25% lower among women (35%) than among men (60%)."[27] Similarly, two thirds of American men but "only" half of American women supported the U.S. invasion of Grenada, and, before the political revolution in Eastern Europe, more men than women said the United States should be "more forceful" with the Russians even if it leads to war.

What is behind this gender gap? Certainly, as historian Ruth Rosen points out, women "do not suffer from the dreaded 'wimp factor.' If they support peace, their womanhood is not endangered." On this point, I entirely agree. But I disagree with the second reason Rosen offers for the gender gap, the one most commonly heard: "As primary care-givers, women learn early to nurture life rather than destroy it." How I wish this assertion were true, but regrettably I see little evidence for it in the case of war. Men and women do not differ in their willingness to go to war, an enterprise that tends to destroy life. They merely differ in the reasons that would make them willing to go to war.

Psychologist Ofer Zur closely examined opinion polls and surveys that have been conducted in the last forty years, and he noticed a curious bias in the phrasing of questions. For example, one Roper Poll asked respondents "Would you be willing to fight . . . in case a foreign power tried to seize land in Central America?" Standing tall lest they be mistaken for wimps, men were far more likely than women to say yes. So, on polls like these, men consistently appear to be more violent and militaristic than women. However, when women are asked whether they would endorse a war for reasons that reflect other motives—such as saving the lives of loved ones or promoting group cohesion—women turn out to be more violent and militaristic than men. In Zur's research, women agreed more often than men did with statements such as "Any country which violates the right of innocent children should be invaded."[28] Oh, good. Not only will that rationale keep the United States busy invading dozens of countries for the next century, it offers the government just the propaganda it wants to close the gender gap.

The point is that gender gaps widen or narrow with changing times, motives, and political circumstances, and they cannot be accounted for by an intrinsic female pacifism. Feminists who hoped the gender gap would lead to the defeat of Ronald Reagan and George Bush have learned that ideology and economics override gender in the voting booth.

The archetypes of Man as Just Warrior and Woman as Beautiful Soul are complimentary to both sexes. But they are ultimately untrue, defied by a more complex reality that includes ample illustrations of female bellicosity and male pacifism and self-sacrifice. It is time to sing of "arms and the woman": to recognize that women are the unindicted co-conspirators in the making of war.

▪ *The search for the feminist Eden*

The evidence of women's role as supporters and combatants in war has not deterred those who cannot envision an egalitarian future without inventing an egalitarian past, a time when women's ways were the dominant ways and everyone lived in peace. One of the principle tenets of ecofeminism is that current male-dominated societies are relatively new, having developed only in the last 5,000 or 6,000 years. Before that, for thousands of years of prehistory, people lived in benign, woman-centered, goddess-worshipping societies in an ecological balance with nature, without hierarchy, male dominance, or war.

The search for such a feminist Eden has itself a long history. Most recently, in the nineteenth century, J. J. Bachofen proposed his theory of "mother right," the view that human society progressed from a matriarchal structure, in which women controlled religion, property, and marriage, to a patriarchal one. (The change to "father right" and male control of things, Bachofen believed, was fortunate.) The anthropologist Lewis Henry Morgan also agreed that matriarchy was humankind's original state, but argued that "civilization" began when patriarchy took over (likewise, in the nick of time). Only Friedrich Engels suggested that the demise of matriarchy might have been a bad thing. Matriarchy's fall, indeed the *"world historical defeat of the female sex,"* Engels said with emphasis, were a result of the creation of a system of private property controlled by men.[29]

The theory that women once ruled in peace and harmony attracted many adherents a century ago, including the suffragist Elizabeth Cady Stanton. A major obstacle to woman's emancipation, Stanton believed, was the assumption that male dominance was universal and inevitable; men could justify the status quo by simply saying, "It's always been this way." So any evidence that women once were the ruling power, and that they used that power for the best interests of humanity, must, she wrote, give women "a new sense of dignity and self-respect."[30]

Possibly for the same motives, we are witnessing today a resurgence of the belief in Original Matriarchy. For example, Merlin Stone's *When God Was a Woman*, Marija Gimbutas's *The Goddesses and Gods of Old Europe*, Riane Eisler's *The Chalice and the Blade*, and Gerda Lerner's *The Creation of Patriarchy* maintain that long before recorded history, religions were peace-loving and woman-worshipping, deities were female, women were priestesses, and neither sex wore the pants, as it were. As Merlin Stone writes:

> In the beginning, people prayed to the Creatress of Life, the Mistress of Heaven. At the very dawn of religion, God was a woman. . . . In every area of the Near and Middle East, the Goddess was known in historic times. . . . the worship of the female deity survived into the classical periods of Greece and Rome. It was not totally suppressed until the time of the Christian emperors of Rome and Byzantium, who closed down the last Goddess temples in about 500 A.D.[31]

Riane Eisler, whose book has become a bible of the ecofeminist movement, argues that life in these prehistoric cultures reflected the metaphor of the Chalice: People valued home and hearth, women's role in gathering food (as opposed to men's role in hunting it), and the "feminine" spirit. She is particularly fond of ancient Crete, where, she maintains, trade, architecture, and art reached their highest female expression. But by the eleventh century B.C., paradise was lost. Barbarians from the periphery of Europe and Asia, driven by the violent impulses of the sword and Blade, descended over Europe, bringing violence, war, and bloodshed and transforming religion and politics into their currently male-dominated forms. Eisler warns that we must return to the principles of the Chalice, our woman-celebrating origins, or we face annihilation by modern barbarians.[32]

It is a pretty argument with much intuitive appeal, and is the source of lively debate. Much of this debate hinges on the archaeological evidence of figurines of women, voluptuous so-called Venuses found in numerous archaeological sites from Spain to Siberia. For example, figurines found at Dolní Věstonice (in Czechoslovakia), dating from 26,400 B.C., include bone and ivory pendants shaped like breasts, vulvas, and penises; clay figures of animals and humans; and a mysterious small clay statue of an abstract woman. She has fat buttocks and pendulous breasts, but no facial features or genitals, no feet or hands. She is typical of many such figurines found in this era. But was she, as Eisler and others believe, a symbol of a goddess or a priestess? Or was she, as some scholars have argued, a symbol of puberty? Or was her plumpness a sign of the community's concern about hunger rather than sexuality?[33] Bonnie Anderson and Judith Zinsser, authors of the monumental two-volume *Women in History,* conclude:

> Many speculations have been advanced about [these figurines], most as facile as the view that allowed these figurines to be called "Venuses." They have been described as pregnant women and called fertility objects, although few are discernibly pregnant and gathering/hunting peoples tend to limit their fertility rather than enhance it. They have been called mother goddesses, although there is no evidence of what the people who made them believed. These objects tell the historian very little about women or their relationship to men in these early societies.[34]

Theories about the status of women in prehistory, before the invention of writing, are based on conjecture and imagination. It is a fascinating and exasperating dilemma, because the first written documents of the Greeks, Romans, and Hebrews show that women were subordinated to men. Until recently, historians, archaeologists, and theologians maintained that this subordination was "natural" and had always existed. New interpretations argue that this subordination was culturally imposed. But both sides are, in essence, reading tea leaves. The archaeological record gives us physical evidence of what people ate, the tools they used, and how they lived, but not evidence of what people thought about women, the beliefs they held, the values they endorsed.

For example, research has corrected the bias in anthropology that had emphasized the role of Man the Hunter, male competitiveness, and aggression. We now know that Woman the Gatherer was responsible for the food for everyday living, and that early human societies depended for their survival on cooperation rather than competition. What no one knows, however, is whether ancient peoples recognized the importance of the daily work women did, or whether they valued more highly the occasional but riskier work that men did, in hunting meat, a source for many tribes of essential protein.

Similarly, there is no doubt that female deities have been worshipped in many religions and been a central part of many creation myths in virtually every culture: Ishtar of Mesopotamia, Maat of Egypt, Cerridwen of the Celts in Ireland, Nidaba of Sumer, Astarte (in her many names and forms) throughout the Near East. The question is: What do these myths tell us about women's actual status in their societies? Stone and others who have written about these goddesses believe that it is possible to interpolate from legends and myths a great deal about how these cultures regarded women and how women lived. According to Stone, for instance, legends describing the Goddess "as a powerful, courageous warrior, a leader in battle," were not merely responsible for the myth of the Amazons; they reflect reality:

> More thoroughly examining the accounts of the esteem the Amazons paid to the female deity, it became evident that women who worshiped a warrior goddess hunted and fought in the lands of Libya, Anatolia, Bulgaria, Greece, Armenia, and Russia and were far from the mythical fantasy so many writers of today would have us believe.[35]

Undoubtedly, as we have seen, women have hunted and fought. The problem occurs in using myth, legend, and artifact as evidence of human behavior in the absence of a written record.

From about 3000 B.C. to 1200 B.C., Crete was indeed a thriving and successful culture that produced writing and art in many forms —seal rings, vases, bronzes, figurines, and frescoes. Many of these art forms portray women, but most historians remain uncertain as to what women's role and status in Crete actually were. In one study of 103 small human figurines found there, 37.3 percent were female, 9.2 percent male, 40.7 percent had no sexual characteristics, and 12.8 percent were so fragmented that their sex was uncertain.[36] Should we be impressed that 37 percent were female and so few distinctively male? Or is it more important that 41 percent were neutral? Did the figures represent deities or just plain folks?

Likewise, it is certainly interesting to know that Cretan artists produced faience statues of elaborately dressed women holding or entwined with snakes, but what or whom did these statues represent? Goddesses? Priestesses? Snake charmers? (Hallie Iglehart sees an unmistakable Snake Goddess in this figure: "Her wide eyes and the snakes wrapped around her imply the power of spiritual trance, while her strong stance and bare breasts reflect women's freedom."[37]) Although most of the seal rings depict animals, a few portray women with uncovered breasts, surrounded by smaller females and males, animals, and trees. What does the large figure represent? A goddess ruling the planet? The artist's wife? The artist? The answer is unknown.

It is not even clear what kind of religion was practiced by the people of Crete. There is no compelling evidence, as there is for cultures of the Middle East and Egypt, that they worshipped numerous goddesses or one great Earth Mother. Yet even if we were to discover a Rosetta Stone to tell us that the female figurines did represent goddesses, we would not know what this meant for the status of actual women in Crete. Powerful goddesses such as Ishtar, Athena, and Isis were found where men were in firm political and religious control; such goddesses most likely reflected men's images of women, not women's actual power.

Historian Sarah B. Pomeroy, whose book *Goddesses, Whores, Wives, and Slaves* was the first social history of Roman and Greek

women in classical antiquity, describes the goddesses of Greek myth—
Athena the wise warrior, Hera the strong queen, Aphrodite the sex
bomb—as "archetypal images of human females, as envisioned by
males":

> The distribution of desirable characteristics among a number of
> females rather than their concentration in one being is appro-
> priate to a patriarchal society. The dictum of Demosthenes in
> the fourth century B.C. expresses this ideal among mortals: "We
> have mistresses for our enjoyment, concubines to serve our per-
> son, and wives for the bearing of legitimate offspring."[38]

Pomeroy carefully reviewed arguments for Mother Goddess Theory and its corollary, that female dominance in religion indicates a
female dominance in many spheres of society. The Great Mother
may have played a major role in communal cults in prehistory, she
concludes, but "to use the mother goddess theory to draw any conclusions regarding the high status of human females of the time
would be foolhardy." On the contrary, she shows, many religions
that worship the mother or female deities, including Christianity
(with its worship of Mary) and Hinduism (with its worship of the
goddess Kali, the powerful figure who personifies creation and destruction), exist in societies "where male dominance and even misog-
yny are rampant."[39]

The historian Elizabeth Fox-Genovese likewise criticizes the
oversimplification of history in romantic accounts that reduce its
complexities to a morality play of good versus evil, female versus
male. All such simplistic stories omit inconsistent details: "Crete did
manifest a disquieting social stratification," noted Fox-Genovese
in a review of Eisler's book, "but since it developed under female
hegemony it does not provoke Ms. Eisler's critical scrutiny."[40]
Why, she asks, did barbarians abandon their female spiritual origins and move outward to conquer others? Were they consumed by
a desire to dominate, or were they starving? Why do we assume that
all barbarians are male? (Remember Plutarch's description of
those female barbarians.) What about the disconcerting fact that
violence has historically been the means for the progress of en-
slaved groups toward freedom? What about all the nonbarbarian
males, in the past and present, who do not share the view of West-

ern industrial nations that nature is there to be conquered, leveled, and plundered?

Eisler, Stone, and others want to prove that male dominance is not natural or inevitable. They want to give women what Elizabeth Cady Stanton hoped theories of matriarchy would give them: a renewed sense of dignity and self-respect. It is as if they believe that there is no hope for future societies if we cannot find ideal past ones. Hallie Iglehart makes this connection explicit: "Learning about women's cultures has given me a new perspective on myself and my society," she writes, "as well as inspiration for making changes in both. My deep belief that the world need not be and has not always been as sexist, racist, classist, and violent as it is now has been confirmed. . . . An emphasis on female energy is needed to restore the balance in the lives and psyches of both women and men."[41]

But there is plenty of cause for hope, and we need look no further than recent history rather than to the dim recesses of prerecorded time. Centuries ago, Sweden used to be one of the most warlike, aggressive nations of the earth; remember the Vikings? Yet today it is one of the most peaceful, and the status of its women ranks highest in the world. It didn't get that way because it decided to value the Chalice rather than the Blade, returned to Goddess-worshipping, or enclosed all its men on game preserves. It evolved because of historic changes in its world status and power, the social and economic programs it followed, and the shared goals of its citizens, male and female.[42]

Nor is it necessary, in the name of hope, to read history through an all-or-none, matriarchy-versus-patriarchy filter. We need not replace the doctrinaire theory of Original Patriarchy as the model for all humanity with a doctrinaire theory of Original Matriarchy as the model for all humanity. It is neither useful nor accurate to approach history and the structure of society in absolute, universal, polarized terms: Men are universally dominant now, but women originally were dominant; men compete, women cooperate; men destroy nature, women live in balance with nature. This is a pointless debate for both sides. "[It] is as foolish to postulate masculine dominance in prehistory as to postulate female dominance," says Pomeroy. "The impartial scholar will be forced to confess that the question is open and may never be answered."[43]

Instead of framing the question in absolutes, we can examine the varying circumstances, then and now, that make female subordination, competitive values, warfare, and ecological disasters more or less likely.[44] Hunting/gathering and nomadic societies are no less diverse in their customs or the quality of their male-female relations than modern industrial societies are, and for many of the same reasons: the environment in which their practices developed, the functions that their customs and rituals serve.

For example, in small, close-knit cultures in which interdependence and "balance with nature" are understood to be essential for survival, both sexes value cooperation and regard violent and renegade loners with fear and disdain. But living in harmony with nature does not guarantee living in harmony with other humans. Plenty of cultures do not plunder the environment as selfishly as most modern Western societies do, but this fact does not make them any less warlike. Plenty of North American Indian men (the charming film *Dances with Wolves* notwithstanding) kept slaves, made war, and raped women; and women, although not warriors, were not neutral observers. "Indian women customarily prepared raw scalps for exhibit," writes Elshtain; "they stripped, robbed, and mutilated corpses of the 'blue-coats,' killing those 'who still twitched.' " War, and women's role in it, was as natural to the Oglala Sioux, the Cheyennes, the Arapahos, the Kiowas, and other tribes as it was to the Europeans who conquered them.[45]

Unromantic explanations—such as the structure of work—are better predictors of how men and women will get along than are explanations based on male and female "nature." In societies in which the sexes are mutually dependent and work cooperatively, as in husband-and-wife teams, sexual antagonism is lower than when work is organized along same-sex lines and men control the major resources. In general, male dominance and violence are more likely in societies that are undergoing environmental stresses, such as an unpredictable food supply, endemic warfare, chronic hunger, rapid industrialization (which tends to sharpen the sexual division of labor), and the recent migration of males because of work or war.

A practical alternative to the Earth Mother approach to world peace was proposed by a women's group in Nottingham, England— Women Oppose the Nuclear Threat (WONT)—in the early 1980s. "We don't think that women have a special role in the peace movement because we are 'naturally' more peaceful, more protective, or more vulnerable than men," they wrote, "nor do we look to women as the 'Earth Mother' who will save the planet from male aggression":

> Rather, we believe that it is this very role division that makes the horrors of war possible. The so-called masculine, manly qualities of toughness, dominance, not showing emotion or admitting dependence can be seen as the driving force behind war; but they depend on women playing the opposite (but not equal) role, in which the caring qualities are associated with inferiority and powerlessness.[46]

Ecofeminists are right to worry about the future consequences to the planet of the philosophy of the Blade. But it is the *philosophy* of domination and exploitation that must be challenged, in whichever sex supports it, as well as the circumstances that make such a philosophy expedient. As Elizabeth Fox-Genovese says, "future projection does not justify reduction of the past to science fiction. The best possible understanding of history remains the best possible hope for our future."[47]

▪ *Moral voices, moral choices*

[In 1950, psychoanalyst] Bernard S. Robbins first advanced the idea that women's psychological characteristics are closer to certain psychological essentials and are, therefore, both sources of strength and the bases of a more advanced form of living.[48]

—Jean Baker Miller

It seems that the pain of suffering has forged in many women a deeper, stronger capacity to appreciate life.[49]

—Mary Lou Randour

In 1982, psychologist Carol Gilligan published a provocative book called *In a Different Voice*. If *The Chalice and the Blade* is the textbook of ecofeminism, *In a Different Voice* quickly became the textbook of cultural feminism, the movement to celebrate women's virtues. It has made its way into science and politics, art and literature, business and industry, therapy and philosophy.

Gilligan's work was, at first, an important correction of bias in the study of psychological development, which had been based almost entirely on men's lives. In particular, she showed that earlier psychologists, finding that women did not seem to reason like men in evaluating moral dilemmas, concluded that women were somehow morally deficient, lacking in moral reasoning skills, and developmentally retarded. "I cannot evade the notion," Freud had written, "that for women the level of what is ethically normal is different from what it is in men."

Gilligan agreed with Freud that women and men differ in what they regard as "ethically normal," but she maintained that women's ways are just as moral. Women, she said, tend to base moral decisions on principles of compassion and care ("who will be hurt least?"), whereas men base theirs on abstract principles of justice ("what is the fairest thing to do?").[50] Women feel "the moral imperative" to *care* for others; men, to protect the *rights* of others. Gilligan did not say that women's moral reasoning is better than men's; only that it is different, and that both styles of moral judgment have their strengths and weaknesses. Recently she tried to clarify the problem of talking about differences without implying a hierarchy of better-or-worse. "One can think of the oboe and the clarinet as different," she told a reporter. "Yet when they play together, there is a sound that's not either one of them, but it doesn't dissolve the identity of either instrument."[51]

This point was lost on many of Gilligan's adherents, who delightedly replaced the male bias in moral-development studies with a female bias. Nevertheless, by speaking of women's ways and men's ways in such dichotomous terms, Gilligan contributed to the polarization of thinking about these two approaches to moral reasoning and to the assumption that the sexes are profoundly different in their need for attachment, intimacy, and connection.

The origin of women's different voice, according to feminist psychoanalysts such as Nancy Chodorow and Jean Baker Miller, lies in the psychodynamic consequences of being raised primarily by mothers. Girls may continue to stay attached to their mothers as they form their identities, but boys, in order to develop a male identity, must separate themselves psychologically at an early age. The result, in this view, is that adult women find comfort and solace in connection and are frightened of separation; adult men find security in independence and are frightened of attachments, which they fear will swallow them up and obliterate their identity as males. "Since masculinity is defined through separation while femininity is defined through attachment," Gilligan summarized, "male gender identity is threatened by intimacy while female gender identity is threatened by separation." [52]

According to cultural feminists, everything in women's lives follows from this fundamental difference in connection versus independence: women's cognitive development, their "voices" (in writing and speaking), their literary and artistic preferences and expressions, their moral reasoning, their values, their deepest psychology, their greatest fears, their private dreams. Although Chodorow maintained that these two personality styles are a result of mothering arrangements, not mothering instincts or biology, her work, like Gilligan's, has tended to enter public conversation as evidence that the two styles are somehow part of male and female *nature*—enduring and unchangeable. As Chodorow put it, "The basic feminine sense of self is connected to the world, the basic masculine sense of self is separate." [53]

In this sense, even feminist psychoanalysts reinforce Freud's original observation that men and women are, inevitably, psychological worlds apart. These modern analysts turn the tables by praising the women's way, while deploring men's way of emotional aloofness. The problem of development lies with men, not women: Men are too independent and aloof, not connected enough, whereas attachment, connection, and dependency are human needs.

The idea that women operate on a different moral wavelength and speak in a different voice has made its way into many fields and into common consciousness. In business, many employers and managers are using Gilligan's theory to account for sex differences they observe in the workplace. Clinical psychologist Harriet Goldhor Lerner, describing her experiences as a consultant to organizations, says, "I frequently hear Gilligan's research interpreted as demonstrating that women on the job care primarily about people's feelings and personal ties, whereas men, in contrast, think in rational, logical, and abstract terms and are primarily oriented toward the task at hand."[54]

Certainly, in generating public reaction, Gilligan clearly struck a nerve: Thousands of women have seen themselves in her book. "Yes," many women say, "we *do* speak in a different voice, when we are allowed to speak at all, and someone finally has articulated it." One reason for this enthusiasm, I believe, is that Gilligan and others finally recognized and validated the long-disparaged, unpaid work that women do: the work of day-to-day caring for children, the work of keeping extended families together with calls, letters and gifts, the work of worrying about everyone's feelings, the work of monitoring relationships to make sure they are going well. Of course, it seems right to argue that women make moral decisions based on the needs of others more than on the rights of others. Women's entire lives are devoted to the needs of others.

Moreover, Gilligan's work rang more than a few bells about modern relationships and the ongoing misunderstandings between the sexes. Women across the country said to themselves, in effect, "Yes, it's absolutely true, Harry is terrified of true intimacy with me, while I am terrified of leaving him to fend for myself." It was encouraging and life-affirming to read that intimacy and an ethic of care are as valuable as, indeed more valuable than, typical male aloofness and men's ethic of justice. It was infinitely reassuring to read that all the effort they were putting into relationships was not a sign of loving too much but of a normal and mature morality; it was all those commitment-phobic men who had the morality problem. Gilligan's work seemed to explain at last why so many relationships were in trouble, if men could be bothered to get into one in the first place. It was no wonder that Robin West (and many other women) could say: "I don't know of any woman who hasn't recognized herself somewhere in this book."[55]

And yet, accepting ideas solely on the basis of their intuitive application to oneself has its risks. Two psychologists, observing the rising popularity of Gilligan's ideas, sounded a note of caution: "It seems almost philistine to challenge the nature of [Gilligan's] evidence," they wrote. "Many women readers find that the comments by women quoted in Gilligan's book resonate so thoroughly with their own experience that they do not need any further demonstration of the truth of what is being said . . . *intuitively* we feel that Gilligan. must be right. . . . [but, a warning]: Women have been trapped for generations by people's willingness to accept their own intuitions about the truth of gender stereotypes" (emphasis in original).[56]

One problem with intuitions, of course, is that what feels right to one person may feel entirely wrong to another. A friend of mine, a professor in a law school, was discussing Gilligan's theory with her class and met vociferous resistance from the students, male and female. Many of the males felt resentful that their very real affections and attachments were being overlooked or disparaged. Many of the females felt resentful that their professional abilities were being compromised or questioned. "These women are planning to be litigators," said my friend, "and they don't consider themselves 'naturally' soft or pliable, or less capable of a justice-based form of moral reasoning."

Nevertheless, the belief that women have a different moral voice, notes psychologist Martha Mednick, "has been widely and enthusiastically accepted by many feminist scholars in numerous disciplines, as well as by many writers, politicians, journalists, and the public. . . . it appears to be a symbol for a cluster of widely held social beliefs that argue for women's difference, for reasons that are quite independent of scientific merit."[57] Mednick believes that "a different voice" is another of the popular bandwagons that roll along every few years—a concept that catches the public fancy for a while and then rattles off the stage.

There is much that I admire about Gilligan's work, particularly its expanded vision of the importance of an ethic of care in moral reasoning. But Mednick is right: The popularity of this theory does not rest on its scientific merit. On the contrary, research in recent years casts considerable doubt on the notion that men and women differ appreciably in their moral reasoning, or that women have a permanently different voice because of their early closeness to their mothers.

One part of Gilligan's original argument, that women make moral decisions based on who will be hurt least rather than on impartial principles of justice, came from a study she did of how women made decisions about abortion. "When a woman considers whether to continue or abort a pregnancy," Gilligan said, "she contemplates a decision that affects both self and others and engages directly the critical moral issue of hurting."[58] But Gilligan did not ask a comparable group of men how they would come to a decision about their partner's abortion, which makes sex comparisons a bit difficult, to say the least.

The primary basis for Gilligan's argument, however, came from her observations of how schoolchildren make moral decisions. Repeatedly, she took excerpts from her interviews to argue that in resolving a conflict between desire and duty, for example, boys think in "hierarchical" terms (what goes first), whereas girls think in "network" terms (who is left out, who is hurt). Readers of Gilligan's book are usually impressed with her analysis of the children's explanations. But when social psychologist Faye Crosby took the children's comments out of Gilligan's narrative, and asked her students to tell her which were said by boys and which by girls, it turned out not to be such an easy task.[59] See for yourself:

When I really want to go to my friends and my mother is cleaning the cellar, I think about my friends, and then I think about my mother, and then I think about the right thing to do.

I have a lot of friends, and I can't always play with all of them, so everybody's going to have to take a turn, because they're all my friends. But like if someone's all alone, I'll play with them.[60]

Which child is connected to a "network" and which is being "hierarchical"? Or how about these responses to the question "What does responsibility mean?":

It means pretty much thinking of others when I do something . . . [not doing something just for yourself], because you have to live with other people and live with your community, and if you do something that hurts them all, a lot of people will end up suffering, and that is sort of the wrong thing to do.

That other people are counting on you to do something, and you can't just decide, "Well, I'd rather do this or that." [There is also responsibility] to yourself. If something looks really fun but you might hurt yourself doing it because you don't really know how to do it and your friends say, "Well, come on, you can do it, don't worry," if you're really scared to do it, it's your responsibility to yourself [not to do it] . . . because you have to take care of yourself. . . ."[61]

Gilligan sees the boy as operating from "a premise of separation but recognizing that 'you have to live with other people,' " whereas the girl is operating "contextually." Of course, I do not have the space to report Gilligan's full interviews here, but the point is that it is just as plausible to say that the boy *and* the girl recognize that they have a responsibility to themselves *and* to others. (In each pair of quotes, by the way, the first is by a boy and the second by a girl.)

In fact, when subsequent research directly compared men's and women's reasoning about moral dilemmas, Gilligan's ideas have rarely been supported. In study after study, men and women use *both* care-based reasoning (such as "which outcome will cause the least hurt for all of the people involved") *and* justice-based reasoning (such as "whether there is a moral code to which all individuals should adhere"). In study after study, researchers report no average differences in the kind of moral reasoning that men and women apply. In a few studies, women are more care-based; in others, men are more care-based; and in one overview that pooled the findings from a large number of studies, women were actually more justice-based than men.[62] These results confirm Gilligan's argument that people make moral decisions not only according to abstract principles of justice, but also according to principles of compassion and care. But they fail to support her notion that women have any special corner on that compassion. As one researcher summarized:

There is now considerable evidence that justice-defined measures of moral reasoning are not biased against females. Further, there is little support for the notion that males are better able to reason about hypothetical dilemmas, or that moral reasoning is in some way a male domain.[63]

Two other psychologists in the field of moral development, Anne Colby and William Damon, likewise found little scientific support for Gilligan's claims. "While her portrayal of general, sex-linked life orientations is intuitively appealing," they concluded, "the research evidence at this point does not support such a generalized distinction."[64]

Similar efforts to pin down differences between males and females in the value they place on "autonomy" versus "attachment" have been unsuccessful. In one study of 130 college students—who were of an age where we might expect the most exaggerated sex differences—psychologists Susan Cochran and Letitia Anne Peplau found no average differences in the students' desire for attachment. The researchers said they "found no evidence of women's allegedly greater concern with having a secure, committed, sexually exclusive relationship. Most men and women in our sample valued equally these features of intimacy."[65] The young women, if anything, valued autonomy more than the young men did!

Most of the other studies that have attempted to illuminate a difference between men and women in "fear of closeness" have also failed. One research team, reviewing a large number of studies, concluded that the whole idea was "a common and perhaps repressive stereotype."[66] In the few studies that have found differences, the results were not of great magnitude. For instance, researchers in one study announced that men were more than twice as likely as women to see danger and threat in pictures of people described as having an intimate bond between them.[67] More than twice as likely! Persuasive evidence that men fear attachment! The numbers in question, however, turn out to be 18 percent of the men to eight percent of the women. That is more than twice as many, all right, but do we really want to generalize to all men on the basis of 18 percent of a few college students?

Gilligan's own numbers weren't much better. "The men in the class, considered as a group, projected more violence into situations of personal affiliation than they did into impersonal situations of achievement," she wrote. *"The* men"? It turns out she is referring to 25 percent of eighty-eight college males—a goodly number, and a higher percentage than the females, but not even close to a majority.[68]

Now, bear in mind that neither I nor any of these researchers is saying that men and women *express* their needs for intimacy and attachment, or even for autonomy and self-development, in the same way. Many women love to analyze and talk about their relationships, even when everything is going swimmingly. "How do I know *he* thinks it's going swimmingly," they will say, "unless we discuss it?" To most men, this is like pulling a plant up by the roots to see how it's doing. They think that talking about a relationship is a sure sign that it is nearly over. If a marriage is in dire, desperate straits—for example, if the woman has just moved out, taking all the furniture and the cat with her—then, maybe, the man will be willing to talk about it.

I regard such differences in styles of emotional intimacy as very real and a major source of misunderstanding between the sexes, and I will have more to say about this in Chapter 7. But the point here is that differences in style and expression must not be confused with differences in male and female nature, or capacity, or personality traits. If most men do not demonstrate their needs for attachment or their dependency on others in the same way most women do, it is not fair to accuse them of fearing attachment or being incapable of love and an ethic of care in their moral reasoning.

Research has also cast doubt on Gilligan's argument that women develop ways of thinking and relating to others that are embedded in their psyches like plums in a pudding. As Colby and Damon concluded, "to the extent that differences of this sort do exist, there is no evidence whatsoever that they are due to early and irreversible emotional experiences between mother and child."[69] The reason is that once again, when we look more closely, many (but not all) of the qualities associated with "women's voices" prove to be qualities associated with women or men who are powerless.

Let's examine the popular use of Gilligan's theory to explain why women seem to be more "people-oriented" than "task-oriented" at work. If women really are more interconnected than men, more interested in other people than in ideas, challenges, or high pay, we can readily understand why more women than men are in low-paying service jobs. They don't want anything better, and they are well suited to what they do. This old chestnut has been kicking around for decades, commonly used by employers to explain why it isn't necessary for them to promote women into higher-paying jobs with greater responsibility.

In the 1970s, the sociologist and business consultant Rosabeth

Moss Kanter, in studies of men and women in corporations, showed conclusively that *conditions of employment, not qualities of the individual*, determine what most people value about their work. That is, women *and* men who are in dead-end, low-paying, unstimulating jobs tend to focus on the aspects of the job that are, by default, the most pleasurable: namely, relationships with others. Kanter found that

> *men with low opportunity look more like the stereotype of women in their orientations toward work,* as research on blue-collar men has shown; they limit their aspirations, seek satisfaction in activities outside work, dream of escape, interrupt their careers, emphasize leisure and consumption, and create sociable peer groups in which interpersonal relationships take precedence over other aspects of work.[70] [Emphasis in original.]

And psychologist Brenda Major examined the idea that women feel less entitled than men do to higher pay and better working conditions because there is something about women—their low self-esteem, their need for people rather than raises—that causes them to hold different values and preferences about work. Quite simply, Major found no support for this belief.[71] When men and women hold the same prestigious jobs, their values and behavior are similar. When women know what the going salary should be for their jobs, they do not cheerfully accept less. When women and men know that promotions are possible, they are equally likely to strive for them.

When I first read Kanter's research, so long ago, I was sure it would drive a stake through the heart of the idea that women are best suited for work with people and men are best suited for work with money. But this belief is hard to kill. In any form—women have a "caring nature" or a "feminine love of gossip" or a "different voice"—it is a view of women that continues to justify keeping things the way they are.

In light of this evidence, I have numerous misgivings about women's recent enthusiasm about their skills in "relatedness" and the corresponding denigration of male "autonomy." According to psychotherapists Rachel Hare-Mustin and Jeanne Marecek, the fact is that, under current conditions, autonomy is not feasible for many women because of their economic insecurity, responsibility for children, and lack of power in society.[72] The proper response to these conditions is not for women to give up the goal of self-determination because they cannot easily achieve it. The goal must be to understand what it will take for women to have it.

Likewise, by relegating to women's nature what ought to be the human qualities of feeling, attachment, connection, and care, we overlook men's capacity for these qualities or absolve them of responsibility for not demonstrating them. We will all do better to specify what it will take for men to become more related or connected (or to admit that they already are!) than to dismiss them as hopelessly lacking this "female" skill. "The more we continue to glorify women's 'special' nurturant and caretaking abilities as a 'separate but equal' line of development," says Harriet Lerner, the less likely it is that men will be able to recognize their own competence in this arena.[73]

Further, by artificially linking autonomy with men and relatedness with women, theories like Gilligan's obscure the fact that both qualities have good and bad aspects. It is one thing to disdain the kind of autonomy that signifies selfishness, inflexibility, and a psychopathic-like detachment from others; it is quite another to reject the kind of autonomy that means having the power and self-confidence to determine one's own best interests. We may wish to preserve the kind of relatedness that reflects the ability to care for others, but not the kind of relatedness that would relegate either sex to a life of self-obliterating martyrdom.

In real life, no individual is strictly autonomous or connected anyway. Even the most traditional macho men depend on other people to keep their households and businesses running, to make sure they get to the doctor, to raise their children, to provide love and moral support. Even the most traditional women are not so selfless or passive in their devotion to others; many derive enormous satisfaction, power, and sense of achievement from managing their families, having close friendships, maintaining their homes, and raising children.

As a team of family therapists writes: "So much of the literature in family therapy is about getting separate and staying separate, and so little is about getting connected and staying connected." In fact, they say, connection and autonomy are to be equally sought, "and each is a necessary condition for the other."[74] In the last analysis, the problem with endorsing quite so heartily the belief that women speak in a different voice is that we are less likely to find our way toward a common language.

▪ *Why opposites repel*

Human beings love to divide the world and its inhabitants into pairs of opposites. So ingrained and pervasive is this habit of perception that many psychologists now believe it is a fundamental aspect of the mind's organization. It is too easy to fall into language and beliefs that split along us-them, good guys-bad guys, saints-sinners, war-peace, and, of course, male-female. We are drawn to the simplicity of opposites, which clarify the world and obscure the annoying fact that truths come in shades of gray. In wartime, which most sharply distinguishes the Valorous Us from the Beastly Them, people's mental health improves and the suicide rate goes down.[75]

We all lapse into oppositional thinking without being aware of it. In one charming study, parents were simply asked to describe their children.[76] Those who had three or more children spoke about each child in individual terms: Jane is intellectual, they might say, Sam is sociable, and Pam is athletic. Parents who had two children, however, described them as opposites: Pam is a leader, Sam is a follower; Sam is the sociable son, Pam is the unsociable daughter.

Unfortunately for our habits of thought, if not for our other customs, human beings do not come in three sexes. As soon as we start thinking of women and men as opposites (autonomous/dependent, independent/connected, care-based/justice-based, war-mongering/peace-loving), we overlook all the other factors that influence them, such as race, class, culture, and age. We forget what philosophers call "the law of the excluded middle," which, as noted in the last chapter, is where most men and women fall in their qualities, beliefs, values, and abilities.

It is easy to make this mistake. Studies of aggression, for instance, were often based on the assumption that men are aggressive and that females, in not behaving like males, are the *opposite*—that is, that they are unaggressive or submissive. Some people consider this lack of aggressiveness a bad thing; others consider it a good thing. But both interpretations are wrong. Most studies do not show that women are submissive or unaggressive; rather that women are, under some conditions, less likely than men to behave aggressively. It's a matter of relativity and degree, not opposition.[77] By labeling the women's behavior as the opposite of the men's, we not only are mistaken; we also lose critical information about women's aggressiveness.

Thinking in opposites may be a comfortable habit, but the results are often hazardous to our relationships, social policies, and private lives. For one thing, it twists our way of talking about the differences that do exist between men and women into stable, permanent qualities. It obscures the fact that women and men change over their life spans: The exaggerated sex games of adolescence are not, thank God, a blueprint for life. People develop, learn, have adventures and new experiences; and as they do, their notions of masculinity and femininity change too.

Thinking in opposites frames the possibilities for change in limited ways. Some women have decided that the only way to break the Men-are-warlike/Women-are-peace-loving polarity, for example, is to proclaim "a right to fight," to become Just Warriors themselves. Others cling to the paradigm of woman as Beautiful Soul to support dreams of an antimilitarist peace movement, based on fantasies of a utopian future of world government or total disarmament. But both solutions, as Jean Elshtain argues, preserve the old stereotypes and are therefore doomed to fail: "the first, because it is a way of doing business as usual; the second, because it covertly sustains business as usual by proclaiming solutions that lie outside the reach of possibility."[78]

I have no illusions that women, if drafted in large numbers into the military, will transform that institution: Without question, the military will transform women. It already has, as women continue to demonstrate their equal competence with men in the technology, skills, and requirements of modern war. But neither will women be able to change the military, or politics, or medicine, or business, or any other institution by abandoning real-world tactics and the difficulty of real-world change, and by turning instead to spiritualism, ritual, chanting, intuition, and herbal teas. The Doctrine of the Beautiful Soul is comforting, but if it simply allows women to feel better about themselves without doing anything that might offend others or require real change, it is not enough.

Finally, thinking of the sexes as opposites implies that women and men invariably act in opposition to one another. It implies an underlying antagonism or conflict, the pitting of one side against the other, one way (which is right and healthy) versus the other's way (which is wrong and unhealthy). Yet nothing in the nature of women and men requires us to emphasize difference and opposition. We can emphasize similarity and reciprocity.[79] We can continue to reclaim the psychological qualities long associated with female deficiency by celebrating them not as glories of female nature but as potentials in human nature.

As long as people think in opposites, they will be prevented from envisioning a future that would combine, for example, "male" access to power and resources with "female" values and skills. They will continue to define problems in a narrow way, instead of expanding the visions of possibility. They will continue to provoke animosities across the gender line, instead of alliances. That is why the woman-is-better school is ultimately as self-defeating as the woman-is-deficient school it hopes to replace.

3

The 70-Kilogram Man and the Pregnant Person

Why women are not the same as men

What do these stories have in common?

- In the spring of 1990, the Board of Directors of the all-women Mills College, in Oakland, California, voted to admit men for the sake of the school's financial survival. The ensuing protest by the female students, photographed weeping and desolate, outraged the public—especially, judging from phone calls to talk shows and letters to the editor of various newspapers, the male public. The reaction was angry and unsympathetic to the women students' unhappiness: Quit sniveling and join the twentieth century. You women can't have it both ways. If you demand access to all-male schools, you don't get to turn around and demand the right to have all-female schools. A priest, writing to the *Los Angeles Times,* said the students' reaction was a dangerous sign of man-hating.

- "Myra" and "Jim" married as law students and planned to have an egalitarian marriage and independent careers.[1] After a few years, they had a baby—an event that changed Myra's life, but not Jim's.

They couldn't find reliable live-in help; the baby was, Myra said, more "absorbing and exhausting" than she had anticipated; Jim's law firm would not permit him to spend less time at work so he could help with the baby, and he was not prepared to give up his high salary for another position. As a result, Myra quit her job to care for the baby. When Myra and Jim divorced, the judge was unsympathetic to Myra's situation. He awarded her no spousal support and minimum child care, because, he said, a professional woman should be able to take care of herself.

Myra now works full-time to support herself and her child, but not at a career that is remotely comparable to her former husband's (or to her own). She had to take a job that would allow her time off when her son was sick, that would never require late hours or trial appearances, and that would finish at 5:00 so she could pick her son up from the day-care center on time. Many people today have no sympathy for women like Myra. "You wanted to be equal with men under the law," runs their attitude, "and the law is treating you equally. You can't cry now for special protection."

■ A few years ago, the results of a massive study of 22,071 volunteer physicians made headlines across the country: taking small doses of aspirin can reduce the chances of having a heart attack. There were no women in the study. A compilation of studies of the effects of drug treatments on the likelihood of having subsequent heart attacks involved 13,385 patients; there were no women in any of these studies. And in still another research project, a study used a sample only of men to examine the effects of diet on . . . breast cancer. An editor of the *New England Journal of Medicine,* Marcia Angell, replying to charges of gender bias in medicine, said, "Gender bias is not serious in a way that distorts research. It doesn't serve women well to see sexism where it doesn't exist."[2]

What all of these stories share, I believe, is a confusion between gender equality and gender sameness: the idea that to be equal in life and law, the sexes must be the same. But to deny that men and women differ in their basic natures, personality traits, and abilities, as I have done in the previous two chapters, is not to deny that men and women differ at all. Of course they do. They differ in the life experiences that befall them. They differ in the work they do, at home and at "work." They differ in reproductive processes. They differ, most of all, in power, income, and other resources. By ignoring these real differences in men's and women's lives and bodies, people who take the normalcy of men for granted have fallen prey to a third error: Generalizing from the experiences and even the physiology of men to all humanity on the grounds that everyone is like men—and usually a narrow band of middle-class white men, at that.

The assumption that "there are no differences that matter" is the guiding principle of egalitarians who believe that *equality of opportunity and result* rests on *treating men and women as if they were the same.* Because the emphasis on sex differences has, for centuries, been a flimsy disguise for the belief in female deficiencies, the modern women's movement at first downplayed or rejected any discussion of differences, demanding that women be treated like men, no better, no worse. I still share these concerns, but I don't cling to them as fervently or apply them as universally as I once did, and I will try to explain why.

The confusion between equality and sameness must be untangled, because it has now become abundantly clear that in many domains the assumption of sameness has led to unfair and unequal results. Here is an illustration that affects everyone, which we might call "The Exasperating Ladies-Room Problem." Most public restrooms in airports, theaters, movie houses, or restaurants are equal in terms of the size and number of stalls they allot to men and women. But everyone who has ever used a busy public restroom knows that they are not equal in result: Women are always waiting in line. A Cornell engineering student, Anh Tran, discovered why this is so. She and a male assistant monitored "toilet time" for each person at high-use rest stops in Washington, D.C. The men took an average of forty-five seconds each, while the women spent an average of seventy-nine seconds each. Because men and women differ in dress, anatomy, and personal needs, the researchers concluded that restroom allocation, to be *fair*, should be *different*: a fairer allocation of toilets would be 60-40, favoring women.[3] (California was the first to pass such legislation in 1987; in 1990 a "potty parity" law went into effect in New York, requiring all public facilities to have as many stalls in women's restrooms as there are stalls and urinals in men's; and in 1989,

Virginia revised its plumbing code to require twice as many stalls in women's restrooms as in men's—except in restaurants and night-clubs.)

Unfortunately, in several arenas the assumption of sameness has produced rather more disastrous consequences for women than having to wait longer than men in restroom lines. Two of those arenas, which together affect so much of our lives, are medicine and the law.

▪ The 70-kilogram man

> . . . though they of different sexes be,
> Yet on the whole they are the same as we,
> For those that have the strictest searchers been,
> Find women are but men turned outside in.[4]

Modern medicine seems to agree with this bit of nineteenth-century doggerel—women, on the whole, are the same as "we" men. In the field of medicine, both in research and clinical practice, the male body can therefore be used as the medical norm.

In anatomy textbooks, for example, the illustrations that show a full body typically show a male body, except for the illustrations of the female reproductive system. A group of psychologists examined eight major anatomy textbooks now in use in medical schools, documenting the sex ratio for all illustrations of bodies and body parts. In general anatomy chapters, males made up 64 percent of the illustrations, females 11 percent (in the remaining illustrations gender was not apparent). Only in the sections on reproductive anatomy were female and male bodies represented in equal numbers. The drastic omission of women from the realm of "human" anatomy, the authors concluded, "creates the impression that female bodies are somehow uncommon or abnormal" except for their sexual and reproductive functions.[5] The message, they suggest, is that women's bodies are most suited to reproduction, whereas men's bodies are capable of all activities.

It was not always this way, nor is this way inevitable; it reflects an underlying attitude about similarities and differences between men and women. In the late seventeenth century the Dutch anatomist Godfried Bidloo created a set of stunning drawings to illustrate parts of the body, using male and female bodies indiscriminately.[6] For example, a female model, drawn from head to waist, was used to illustrate the muscles in the upper back. Until the nineteenth century, anatomical artists explicitly portrayed the sex of the bodies they were illustrating with genitalia, breasts, beards (for men), or long hair falling on the shoulder (for women). They assumed that most of men's and women's body parts were perfectly interchangeable, and that the parts that were not—those interesting reproductive organs—were nevertheless analogous: women's organs were the same as men's, "turned outside in."

In the nineteenth century, however, scientists in all fields began to attack this premise, and to emphasize instead the chasm between masculine and feminine natures, physical and mental. They concluded that differences between male and female bodies were correspondingly vast, because female development had been arrested at a lower stage of evolution. Women, they said, could be placed on the evolutionary ladder along with children, apes, and "primitive" peoples. Even illustrations of female skeletons reflected this belief in female inferiority. Female skeletons were drawn with tiny skulls and ample pelvises, to emphasize the idea that women were intellectually weak and suited mainly for reproductive functions.[7] The male body became the prototype of the *human* body, and this attitude persists today.

Medical students are trained on the male model—literally. The paradigm patient in medical school is "the 70-kilogram man" (or, in older schools not on the metric system, the "154-pound man"). According to Perri Klass, who is a pediatrician and writer, and Lila Wallis, an internist and former president of the American Medical Women's Association, medical students learn what the average man's heart weighs and what his minimum urine output should be; they treat him for allergies, appendicitis, diarrhea, and prostate problems. They compute dosages of medication based on his weight. And the 70-kilogram man is definitely a macho guy; he never gets ovarian cysts, fibroids, or any other female disorder.[8]

Medical research, too, is overwhelmingly based on men and a male standard of normalcy. A 1990 report released by the Government Accounting Office sharply criticized the National Institutes of Health for continuing to exclude women from most studies of drug effects, diseases, and treatments (a violation of NIH's own 1986 policy of including more women) and for devoting only 13 percent of its research funds to research on women. For years, congresswomen and female physicians have been observing that the bulk of money for medical research in America is directed to the problems that male members of Congress have, apparently on the principle that "we fund what we fear." So there has been ample funding for, say, large-scale studies of heart disease in men, but not for comparably large-scale studies of the causes of breast cancer or the effects of high cholesterol on women.

Psychologist Margrit Eichler, at the Ontario Institute for Studies in Education, and two psychiatrists at the Toronto Western Hospital, Anna Lisa Reisman and Elaine Borins, examined all issues of four professional journals in the year 1988: *The New England Journal of Medicine*, *The American Journal of Psychiatry*, *The American Journal of Trauma*, and *The Canadian Journal of Surgery*. They found evidence of gender bias in all stages of the research process: in the very titles of the articles, in research design, methods, data collection and interpretation, and in treatment recommendations. This bias turned up in American and Canadian journals and cut across all medical specialties.[9]

Titles, for example, reveal the common practice of basing a study exclusively on men but implying or stating that the results are applicable to both sexes. Thus, a typical article in *The New England Journal of Medicine*, "Work Activity and Coronary Heart Mortality," was based on a sample only of males, yet the title implies that the findings apply to people-in-general. An article in *Psychosomatic Medicine* was entitled "A Study of the Effects of Gonadotropin-Releasing Hormone on Human Mood and Behavior"; the hormone affects everyone, but the humans in question are twelve males. A 1984 report from the National Institute on Aging, based on a large-scale study of men, was entitled "Normal Human Aging." In contrast, almost no one assumes that a study done only on women would apply to men also. Studies of women get titles like these: "A Prospective Study of Moderate Alcohol Consumption and the Risk of Coronary

Disease and Stroke in Women" or "The Differential Impact of Diabetes Type on Female Sexuality." (The latter article nevertheless represents an important correction of bias in research on the effects of diabetes on sexuality, a matter that was assumed to affect only men.[10])

Eichler and her colleagues also found that most of the authors of studies in professional journals viewed their research problems from a male perspective and overlooked females altogether. One such team examined the effects of cardiac medication and exercise on recovery from heart attack. In the text of the article, the patients involved in the research are described in general terms; only in a footnote to a table does the reader learn that the patients were fifty-four men and five women. In a second phase of the study, the researchers evaluated the results of the exercise treadmill on thirty-eight male patients; all five of the original females vanished. Nevertheless, the researchers concluded that the treatments were effective, without warning that the findings might not apply to women. The researchers proposed a larger study to test the drug further, but they made no call for a sample that would include women and men.

Of course, experimenters often exclude females from research—even female rats in rat studies—because it is simpler and cheaper to use male animals. The female's estrous cycle disrupts responses in certain behavioral and biological tests, and increases variation among animals. The goal in research is to minimize this variation, the better to determine the precise effects of the drug or treatment in question. So researchers often plead that it would be too costly to add women to their studies. But of course males and females *do* vary physiologically, and eliminating this variation means that the results of many experiments cannot be applied to females in any simple or direct way. If you want to know the effects of Drug X and you throw women out of your study because the menstrual cycle affects their responses to medication, you cannot then extrapolate from your study of men to women, precisely *because* the menstrual cycle affects their responses to medication.

Other researchers actually do include significant numbers of women in their studies, and then proceed to overlook the importance of social and physical sex differences in analyzing the results. In one such study described by Eichler and her associates, investigators were hoping to develop procedures for the genetic testing of people who are at risk of Huntington's Disease, and for helping those who prove to have the gene learn to cope with that knowledge. They worked with thirty-four women and thirteen men, reporting that of those who tested positive for having the disease, half had "periods of severe depression" and half "reported a serious re-evaluation of long-term goals in their careers and marriages"; a year after testing, "the intensity of the emotional response had waned." Because men and women are known to differ in their experiences with work and marriage, and because of the greater incidence of depression among women, these findings raise many questions. "Half" of the women and the men became depressed? Or only the women? Or all of the men and some women? Did the intensity of emotional responses wane for everybody? The researchers do not say.

This blindness about the potential importance of gender pervades many studies that are ostensibly of basic medical procedures. In one article on the measurement of hormones in urine, the authors state that 1,086 patients were assayed; nowhere is their sex mentioned. As Eichler and her associates observe, *"If* the patients were all male, this is a crucial aspect of the study and should have been made entirely clear. *If,* on the other hand, urine samples from both male and female patients were assayed and *not* analyzed separately by sex, this would be grossly incompetent. The reader is left to guess."

Does it matter that only male kidneys are used in a study of the effects of oxygen depletion in kidneys—and only male rat kidneys, at that? A kidney is a kidney, isn't it? Does it matter if dosages of medication are based on the weight and metabolism of the average man? Who cares about the gender of urine samples? "Women are different biological entities," physicians Klass and Wallis answer, "with different hormones, different patterns of health and disease, different responses to stress."[11] This is why the assumption that findings about the 70-kilogram man will apply equally to women has proven wrong, over and over again. Consider this small sampling of topics:

▪ *Alcohol.* In general, alcohol behaves more unpredictably in women than in men, possibly because of its interactions with women's hormonal and metabolism changes. Many women who are taking birth control pills, for instance, are more susceptible to adverse reactions to liquor than are women not on the pill.[12]

- *Drugs.* Medications behave differently in different racial and ethnic groups, in people of varying ages, and in women and men. When psychiatrist Keh-Ming Lin moved from Taiwan to Seattle, he learned that the dosage of antipsychotic drugs given to schizophrenic American patients must often be ten times higher than the dose for schizophrenic Taiwanese patients to get the same therapeutic effect. Similarly, Richard Chaisson, director of the AIDS service at the Johns Hopkins Hospital, has warned against generalizing from drug studies done with middle-class gay white men to women, blacks, and other groups at risk, but this is precisely what most researchers who study AIDS medication do.[13]

The tremendous individual and group variability in response to medication means that researchers who conduct clinical trials, testing experimental drugs before permitting them to be given to patients, must be careful about their generalizability. Unfortunately, many are not. Women receive about 70 percent of all prescriptions for antidepressant medications, but many, perhaps most, of the studies of these drugs have been conducted only on men, and very few studies have specifically investigated the ways in which women and men might differ.[14] The index of a leading 1,000-page text in psychopharmacology lists only two citations under "gender," and minimizes the effects of gender in those two instances.[15]

Researchers seem to have a blind spot in assuming that women and men will respond the same way to the same drug, but studies show more adverse effects from medication in women than in men. Age, body weight, and reproductive events all influence the effects of medication differently for men and women.[16] Yet women of reproductive age are specifically excluded in the first phase of testing of new drugs, and studies that have included both sexes have typically failed to look for gender differences. As a result, psychiatrists and physicians know least about the group they prescribe drugs for most: women.

- *Heart disease.* Almost all of the classic studies in the cardiology field have been conducted solely or primarily with men as subjects.

Endocrinologist Estelle Ramey thinks the reason is not just that it would be too costly or too complicated to add women. "Women have been excluded from these studies," she maintains, "because researchers believe, incorrectly, that women don't die of heart disease. It is true that premenopausal women rarely do, but coronary heart disease is the leading cause of death in women after menopause. I think there is a lot of anger in this field at the fact that women live longer than men."[17]

That men-only study on the benefits of aspirin generated considerable uproar, and subsequent research with thousands of women (nurses) suggests that aspirin reduces the risk of first heart attack in postmenopausal women too. This is good news, but it is not time for complacency, because the pattern of excluding women from research on heart disease is widespread. There was no hoopla, for instance, over this characteristic 1988 study: Stating at the outset that their purpose was to determine the cost-effectiveness of a routine drug treatment (beta-adrenergic-antagonist therapy) in patients of different *age* and *risk* groups, the researchers concluded that all survivors of heart attack who are at medium-to-high risk of having another attack should be given the drug. All survivors! The conclusions were based on a compilation of studies involving 13,385 men.[18]

▪ *Cholesterol.* High cholesterol is associated with elevated risk of heart disease for men—actually, for men between the ages of forty and fifty-five—but not for women. Before menopause, estrogen seems to counteract the risk effects of cholesterol for women, but no one has really studied cholesterol and postmenopausal women specifically to know if high cholesterol is a risk for them. In 1989, an editorial in the *Journal of the American Medical Association* acknowledged that there are "no data regarding the treatment" of high blood cholesterol in women. Even that ideal cutoff point of a cholesterol level of 200 or less is specific to men; it is not known what level, if any, increases the risk of heart disease in women.[19] In fact, in one major study of the factors in coronary heart disease, postmenopausal women with cholesterol levels higher than 295 had heart attack rates that were the same as or lower than those of men with cholesterol readings of less than 204.[20]

There is not even direct evidence from controlled studies that postmenopausal women who lower their cholesterol through diet or by taking estrogen achieve a corresponding drop in their risk of heart attacks. (I'll have more to say about estrogen replacement in Chapter 4.) "Much of the enthusiasm over using estrogen as a cholesterol-lowering drug in postmenopausal women," concludes physician Sidney Wolfe, Director of Public Citizen Health Research Group, "comes from the assumption that women basically turn into men after menopause as far as their cardiovascular protection is concerned."[21]

Yet the belief that cholesterol studies apply equally to both sexes is subtle and pervasive. Consider the following front-page newspaper story, headlined: "Cholesterol Level Is Lower for Nibblers, Study Finds." Since I myself am partial to nibbling, I eagerly read on: "Frequent nibbling may be better for a person's cholesterol level than eating three square meals a day." Only at the end of the study does the reader learn that the "persons" in the study were seven men.[22] Such a tiny sample means that the results cannot yet be generalized to all men, let alone to women.

▪ *Rheumatoid arthritis.* Menstrual cycle phase and pregnancy affect the outbreak of symptoms in many women who have rheumatoid arthritis (and other diseases). For years, physicians regarded these symptoms as "spontaneous" fluctuations. Although studies get mixed results, clearly for some women with this disease the menstrual cycle has an unmistakable influence. In one study of fourteen women who were followed through sixty-nine menstrual cycles, symptoms of rheumatoid arthritis dropped significantly in the two weeks after ovulation; symptoms were significantly related to changes in concentrations of estrogen and progesterone. In another study of thirty-one women who had given birth after the onset of this disease, fully 75 percent had a complete remission of symptoms during the pregnancy, and 62 percent developed fairly severe symptoms after delivery.[23]

▪ *Hypoglycemia.* This disease, low blood sugar, was once thought to affect countless millions of women. It turns out that the average woman has a blood sugar level that is normally considerably lower than that of the average male. "If you took a random sample of women on the street and took their blood sugar levels," says Ramey, "you'd be expecting them all to faint dead away at any moment from insufficient blood sugar. Instead, they're out doing just fine." [24]

■ *Hypertension and responses to stress.* Women with high blood pressure are at less risk than men with the same level of hypertension, perhaps because estrogen makes blood vessels more flexible. Although women can suffer complications from hypertension, these complications appear an average of ten years later than they do for men. Further, a large body of research finds gender differences in neuroendocrine reactions to stressors: for example, males excrete higher levels of epinephrine (adrenaline) in response to pressure (such as threats, insults, and achievement tests) than females do. [25] If a heightened physiological response to stress contributes to heart disease, as many researchers believe, this sex difference may help to explain why women are better protected than men, at least before menopause.

The traditional reliance on the male body as a medical norm has two serious consequences for women's health. First, many physicians regard conditions that are normal or at least medically safe for women as if they were abnormal or dangerous, and treat them inappropriately. The most blatant example of this error is the treatment of pregnant women. Perri Klass, who was pregnant while a medical student, writes that medical school conveys the attitude "that pregnancy is a deeply dangerous medical condition, that one walks a fine line, avoiding one serious problem after another, to reach the statistically unlikely outcome of a healthy baby and a healthy mother." [26]

Second, many physicians ignore conditions that *are* problems for women, for example mistakenly believing, as Ramey says, that "women don't die of heart disease." The results of two recent studies of sex bias in the decision to recommend coronary-bypass surgery are cause for alarm. In a group of patients who had taken specialized tests that showed evidence of heart disease, 40 percent of the men but only *4 percent* of the women were referred by their physicians for the next medical test to see if bypass surgery was warranted. The women had the same symptoms, the same abnormal test results, but apparently the doctors did not take their symptoms seriously. Because many cardiologists tend to neglect heart disease symptoms (such as chest pain) in women, by the time women are referred for coronary artery surgery, they are older and sicker than men would be with comparable symptoms. As a result, women are nearly twice as likely as men to die from this surgical procedure.[27]

There are signs of improvement on the horizon, however. Government institutions and many physicians have become aware of gender bias in research and practice, which is the first step toward correcting it. A few large-scale studies have begun, including a ten-year, $500-million women's health study to be conducted (at last) by the National Institutes of Health. Research on women and heart disease is increasing. For example, it was known that men who quit smoking reduce their smoking-related risk of heart attack within two years; but no one knew if the same would be true for women. Now physician Lynn Rosenberg and her colleagues have found that for women, no matter how long they have smoked or how much, the elevated risk of heart attack due to smoking disappears within a few years of quitting.[28] Lung cancer is an equal-opportunity disease for smokers of both sexes, and it is good to know that both sexes benefit by quitting.

Until research programs are more evenly balanced, women would do well to be prudent yet cautious in following medical advice that has been based exclusively on men—for example, struggling feverishly to get their cholesterol levels down to a fictitious ideal number. (Eating sensibly and nutritiously, of course, has its own benefits.) A friend of mine, a healthy sixty-five-year-old woman, discovered at a routine medical exam that her cholesterol level was 260. Her male physician said to her: "If you were a man, I would know how to advise you, and I might even consider recommending medication. But we just don't know what a level of 260 means for a woman of your age, considering that you have no other risk factors, and I don't want to risk subjecting you to the side effects of medication." At least he was candid; many physicians confidently treat their female patients as they would treat males. I am not advising women to completely ignore research that was conducted with men as if it had no applicability to them at all. The lesson, I think, is to take it with a grain of salt—which, by the way, affects men and women differently.

■ *Can women be "different" and "equal"?*

Equality is a platitudinous concept that practically everybody supports because it can be given any meaning we like. . . . Formal agreement on equality as a value masks the fact that we haven't a clue as to what is supposed to be equal to what, and in what way, or to what degree.[29]
　　　　　　　　　　　　　—Phillip E. Johnson, *Stanford Law Review*

During a recent dinner party, a friend of mine got himself into a charming verbal muddle. In his desire to use the encompassing "he or she" instead of the generic male "he," my friend found himself referring to the "pregnant person"—"he or she. . . ." Surely, we all agreed, this was carrying equality too far! But my friend's gaffe goes right to the heart of the legal dilemma of sexual equality. As in medicine, the law regards the male as the legal standard of a human being. Therefore, women may be treated like men, in which case they are equal to them, or not like men, in which case they are deficient or special. But they are never treated specifically *as women*. There is no concept in the law of what is normal for women.

Robin West, Professor of Law at the University of Maryland, argues that modern jurisprudence (like medicine) is masculine rather than human: the values, dangers, fears, and other real-life experiences of women's lives are not, she says, "reflected at any level whatsoever in contracts, torts, constitutional law, or any other field of legal doctrine." The Rule of Law does not value intimacy, for example, but autonomy: "Nurturant, intimate labor is neither valued by liberal legalism nor compensated by the market economy. It is not compensated in the home and it is not compensated in the workplace—wherever intimacy is, there is no compensation. Similarly, separation of the individual from his or her family, community, or children is not understood to be a harm, and we are not protected against it."[30] The law, she argues, simply does not reflect the female experience: "Women are absent from jurisprudence because women *as human beings* are absent from the law's protection" (emphasis in original). [31]

Christine Littleton, Professor of Law at UCLA, argues that women's inequality in society results from devaluing women's real-life biological and cultural differences from men. Efforts to achieve equality through precisely equal treatment, therefore, are doomed to fail, because men and women are not starting from the same place. "As a concept," she says, "equality suffers from a 'mathematical fallacy'—that is, the view that only things that are the same can ever be equal." [32] Equality has been the rallying cry of every subjugated group in American society, she maintains, but the time has come to examine its inherent dangers and fallacies.

The ideology of equality evolved from legitimate attacks on the "separate spheres" theory of blacks and women—i.e., that blacks and women "naturally" inhabit separate arenas of life (for blacks, their own race; for women, the home and family). The separate-spheres ideology historically put both blacks and women at a disadvantage; it kept black people out of white railway cars and white law schools, for example, and kept women at home. It is no wonder, then, that women and minorities are rightly wary of any legislation or legal ruling based on arguments about natural differences or separate spheres, for such regulations have invariably served to exclude them from many areas of social, political, and economic life.

For example, special protection laws—such as those forbidding women to work at night in some jobs or to lift heavy objects—were used to restrict women's opportunities and relegate them to lower status and poorer-paying occupations. There were no special laws, however, protecting women from long and excruciating labor in sweatshops. So the modern women's movement has understandably opposed any laws or policies that would essentially be female-specific, fearing these would be used against women's best interests. Their attitude reflects Mae West's observation: "Men are always trying to protect me," she said. "Can't imagine what from."

For these reasons, the initial response of legal scholars to the traditionally asymmetrical treatment of women and men under the law was to argue in favor of perfect symmetry: because there are no natural differences and no inevitably separate spheres, both sexes must be treated alike. Women cannot be given any special considerations *and* be considered equal. Wendy Williams, an articulate spokesperson for this view, has warned that "we can't have it both ways [and] we need to think carefully about which way we want to have it."[33] And the lawyer and writer Wendy Kaminer has recently published a brilliant defense of sexual symmetry under the law in her book A *Fearful Freedom: Women's flight from equality.*

Christine Littleton calls the model of legal symmetry the "assimilation" ideal, for it is based, she says, on the "notion that women, given the chance, really are or could be just like men."[34] Thus, institutions should be required to treat women as they already treat men, admitting those who are "qualified," and demanding that once admitted, women behave like men. If a law firm requires that its partners put in long hours and sacrifice their family relationships and child-care obligations, then that's what a woman must do if she wants to be a successful attorney. If a gadget manufacturer requires workers to be at least 5'9" tall, because of the height of the conveyor belt on the assembly line, then only women who are at least 5'9" can be hired. It is a "woman's gotta do what a man's gotta do" model of equality.

The symmetrical model has great appeal for the legal system, for liberals, and for many people who see in this vision a way to eradicate rigid sex roles that constrain men as well as women. It seems to be fair and logical, and applying it universally is certainly easier than trying to grapple with slippery exceptions. Nevertheless, notice that at the core of this vision is our now-familiar male standard of normalcy: The goal is to treat women *as men already are treated.* "To the extent that women cannot or will not conform to socially male forms of behavior, they are left out in the cold," observes Littleton. "To the extent they do or can conform, they do not achieve equality *as women,* but as social males" (emphasis in original).[35]

Now many scholars of legal issues are questioning the wisdom and the consequences of the symmetrical vision of legal equality, and focusing on the male bias at its heart. One of their most powerful arguments against symmetry is the accumulating evidence that treating women like men often produces disastrously unequal outcomes. In 1986 a New York State Task Force on Women and the Law found that on virtually all issues of specific concern to women—notably domestic violence, rape, child support, day care, and pregnancy—

being treated equally under the law leads to unequal results. So did a major review in 1990 of gender bias in the courts conducted by the Judicial Council of California.[36] Following are some illustrations of legal arenas in which women's experience has gone unrecognized in the law, and in which being treated equally has produced unequal results.

• *Divorce and custody laws.* Almost everyone by now is familiar with the highly publicized finding of what happened after changes in the divorce and custody laws. The new laws were designed to treat divorcing couples "fairly" (that is, the "same"), without apportioning fault. The laws were based on the assumption that the sexes have equal social and economic standing, and that now that so many women are working, they should be able to support themselves. Judge Robert Satter, of the Connecticut Superior Court, reflected this attitude in his autobiography, commenting that he awards alimony to unemployed women in their forties for only two to five years, "sufficient for [them] to acquire skills and return to the job market."[37]

This assumption has proved to be false. Women's wages and benefits are not the same as men's: Until recently, women earned, on average, only 60 percent of what men with comparable education and skills were earning. The gap today has narrowed to 70 percent, not because women's salaries have risen appreciably but because in the cost-cutting, union-busting 1980s, men's salaries dropped. Moreover, in spite of Judge Satter's optimism, it is not easy for middle-aged, unskilled women to get good jobs that pay well. Leaving the job market for several years to raise children makes it difficult to re-enter the field later at competitive wages; and good day care is costly, if it is even available. For these reasons, divorce typically lowers a woman's standard of living by an average of 73 percent, and raises a man's by an average of 42 percent.

"The impact of the divorce revolution is a clear example of how an equal-rights orientation has failed women," writes Mary Ann Mason, a professor of Law and Social Welfare, in *The Equality Trap*. "Judges have taken the position that women with children can support themselves as well as men can support themselves. It is as if every time the media announces that a woman has been appointed to a judgeship or a high corporate position thousands of women lose spousal support."[38] And as if every time a celebrity wife gets a settlement of $250,000 a month, thousands of working-class women lose their meager $250 a month.

In most divorce cases today women are awarded no alimony at all, or possibly short-term alimony for "rehabilitative" purposes. In California, after no-fault divorce became the law in 1970, only 13 percent of mothers with preschool children got spousal support. The amount of child support awards has dropped as well. When it is collected, which is less than half the time, it pays for much less than half the cost of raising the child. The New York State Task Force reported that many if not most awards in child-support cases are made with the needs of the father rather than the needs of the children in mind; when women protest or demand enforcement of child-support payments, judges typically regard them as being vindictive.

The elimination of long-term support for older women who were divorced after twenty- and thirty-year marriages caused such grievous hardship for so many thousands of women in California that the state legislature eventually passed the "Displaced Homemakers' Relief Act." Judges were instructed not simply to divide all assets "equally," but to consider "the earning capacity of each spouse," the supported spouse's contributions to the family in terms of child care and domestic work, and history of unemployment. But in many other states, such as Idaho, no such relief exists. Mason reports the case of Edith Curtis, whose husband, a college professor, abruptly left her after thirty years of marriage. Curtis argued before the Idaho Supreme Court that she should be allowed to draw unemployment insurance, because she had worked for her husband during their marriage, helping his career and carrying out the duties of a faculty wife. Curtis, whose B.A. degree in English was useless on the current market, was only able to get a job as a part-time cashier at the minimum wage. She was forced to live in a one-room cabin without plumbing, eating charity food. The Idaho Supreme Court dismissed her case as "frivolous."[39]

No-fault divorce was an "egalitarian triumph," Mason argues, whose main effect was to impoverish women, from young single mothers to older displaced homemakers. More than half of all single-parent families now live below the poverty line; of those, more than 90 percent are headed by women. There is, she adds, no Single Parent Relief Act in sight.

• *Violence.* On December 17, 1988, Robin Elson picked up her husband's gun and shot him in the back of the head while he was sleeping. For years, Elson had been severely battered and abused by her husband, and on this occasion he had been railing around the house, waving the gun and threatening to kill her and their children. Elson was arrested and charged with murder. Should she have been acquitted, on the grounds that she believed she was in imminent danger of death, was unable to escape, and had no choice but killing her husband if she were to survive? Or should she have been convicted, on the grounds that she could have walked away from the marriage, taking the children with her?

Elson's jury found her not guilty of murder. But a short distance away, another jury convicted a battered woman who killed her abusive husband, a conviction that was upheld on appeal. The difference in the two cases was the admission of evidence, in Elson's case, of "battered woman's syndrome," a psychological pattern of fear, helplessness, and passivity that results from living with constant abuse and threats of death. As Sheila James Kuehl, an attorney for the Southern California Women's Law Center, has observed, until recently "the real lives of women have not been reflected in the interpretation of California's law of self-defense. The law has generally been interpreted only from the male experience, which gives no basis for understanding how any decent, sane person would stay with an abuser. This interpretation of the law conceives of self-defense as a kind of schoolboy battle in which people of equal strength are matched, gun for gun and fist for fist." [40]

But a battered woman is psychologically and physically no match for a battering husband, nor is she equal to him in opportunities for escape. (I am not talking about garden-variety verbal hostility, abusiveness, and rudeness in the family, in which men and women are all too equal.) Like prisoners of war, abused women come to believe —indeed, for many of them, to know with certainty—that they have no exit. They know that their husbands will track them down and murder them if they leave, as many battering husbands do, if indeed leaving were even economically feasible. By ignoring the reality of the battered woman's life, the law assumes a woman will behave as a "reasonable man *[sic]*" would: defend herself in the heat of passion. But most battered women who kill their abusers do not dare to do so in the heat of passion. They know they would die if they tried to fight back. So they wait until their husbands are asleep or drunk, and kill them with whatever weapon is at hand.

Until recently, most courts have not even considered the evidence of battered woman's syndrome and have applied the self-defense rule to both sexes equally. Efforts are now underway to make additions to the Evidence Code in a number of states that would admit expert testimony about the possible relevance of this psychological syndrome. "In this way, the real, lived-out experiences of women, not generally found in assumptions made by American law, may be taken into account," says Kuehl.[41] Juries may then decide whether to punish or vindicate battered women who kill, but without falsely assuming that men and women are equally matched in physical strength or in the ability to fight back.

▪ *Rape*. Courts still place much blame on victims of rape rather than on rapists. Judges, juries, and defense attorneys continue to put the victims on trial for their dress, demeanor, previous sexual activities, and relationship (if any) to the rapist. Laws about rape, almost entirely a crime against women, conform to the male experience of violence, not to the female's experience of invasion, fear, and humiliation. Robin West writes:

> Sexual invasion through rape is understood to be a harm, and is criminalized as such, only when it involves some other harm: today, when it is accompanied by violence that appears in a form men understand (meaning a plausible threat of annihilation); in earlier times, when it was understood as theft of another man's property. But marital rape, date rape, acquaintance rape, simple rape, aggravated rape . . . are either not criminalized, or if they are, they are not punished.[42]

The reason is that from the male point of view, these rapes, if they do not involve violence, cannot possibly be "harmful"; why are women making a fuss about "nonviolent" sex? The law expects a raped woman, like a battered wife, to behave like a man when threatened: to try to defend herself even at the risk of death. The law demands that a woman behave like a reasonable man and fight back. It does not demand that a man behave like a reasonable woman and understand the difference between consent and coercion, between the words "yes" and "no."

The male bias in rape laws is further apparent in the fact that several states still define rape as "nonconsensual sexual intercourse by a man with a woman not his wife." Tell that to the San Francisco wife who told an interviewer that her husband "would put a pillow over my head when he wanted to have sex and I didn't. He didn't want others to hear me scream."[43] To consider this episode as an example of marital sex and not rape reflects only the husband's perspective. The experiences of wives who are raped by their husbands thereby become invisible in the law.

For Robin West, such stories are evidence that the law must recognize experiences that happen mostly or exclusively to women if it is going to become a fully human jurisprudence. "We need to show that the harm of invasive intercourse is real even when it does not look like the kind of violence protected by the Rule of Law," she argues. "We need to show that invasive intercourse is a danger *even when it cannot be analogized in any way whatsoever to male experience*" (my emphasis).[44]

Here too there are harbingers of change. The U.S. 9th Circuit Court of Appeals, in an opinion written by Judge Robert R. Beezer, recently adopted a "reasonable woman" standard in finding for a woman in a sexual harassment case—"primarily because," wrote Judge Beezer, "we believe that a sex-blind reasonable-person standard tends to be male-biased and tends to systematically ignore the experiences of women."[45]

■ *Sentencing and stereotypes.* Sometimes a story turns up in the news suggesting that because of the lingering chivalry or sexism of male judges, women get off easy when they commit a crime. U.S. District Court Judge A. Andrew Hauk, declaring that women are "soft touches" for clever men "particularly if sex is involved," gave a reduced sentence of only two years to a woman convicted of five bank robberies.[46] (We all know that men are never vulnerable to clever women when sex is involved.)

These stories always get media attention, whereas the real news is that women get more severe sentences than men for most crimes, and once imprisoned they are treated more harshly. "Judges are simply being harder on women," said Tracy Huling, director of public policy for the Correctional Association of New York. "The rate of incarceration is much higher [for women] than for men." Even the few women who are on Death Row get fewer privileges than condemned men. In the late 1970s, a federal court ordered San Quentin prison to improve living conditions for the condemned inmates on Death Row. But the privileges apply only to condemned *men*, so the single woman on Death Row, Maureen McDermott, lives in isolation, has no access to typewriters, games, or sports, and may see visitors only if separated from them by a glass wall.[47]

While women often get many years in prison for killing their abusers, many men get reduced sentences for killing their wives or girlfriends. In 1986 alone, 1,500 women were murdered by their husbands or boyfriends, and the average sentence for these killers was two to six years. In Illinois, James Lutgen strangled his wife *in front of their children.* His provocation, he said, was that she refused to do the Christmas shopping for him. (She had just filed for divorce and received a court order for protection from him.) Lutgen served twenty months in jail, and then won custody of his children. A woman in Massachusetts asked a judge for protection from a husband who bragged, even to the police, that he would kill her. The judge said, "This court has a lot more serious matters to contend with." The woman was murdered by her husband not long after. This case is not unusual.[48]

The California Judicial Council report describes widespread stereotyping that affects how the courts treat women. For example, information about a mother's sexual behavior is acceptable evidence in probation reports, and puts her at a disadvantage when the court is considering placement of her child. But, as one witness at the Council hearings said, "[if] a father who has been absent for eighteen months shows up on the scene at last, and has fathered sixteen children by whatever number of women, that never becomes material to the court record."[49]

Women are frequently held to a different standard from men, the Council concluded. Judges expect more from mothers than fathers and thus treat them more harshly if the women fall from grace. If a father is seen as "less than proficient in caretaking," in the words of one testifying attorney, "[the court's attitude is] well, gosh, we need to teach him." But a mother who lacks skills in child-rearing, who is poor and illiterate, is seen as unnatural, unfit. "She's not given, in many cases, the same kind of benefit of the doubt that she wants to take care of the child properly," the attorney added.[50]

In custody battles, which without doubt are terrible for everybody, women often find themselves in no-win situations. They have been denied custody both because they *have* paying jobs (which shows they care more about their careers than their children) and because they *don't* have paying jobs (which shows they don't love their children enough to support them well). They have been denied custody if they *are* living with a man (which shows they are promiscuous) and if they *aren't* living with a man (which shows they can't provide a "stable heterosexual environment"). When a woman provides evidence of the husband's abuse of the child, she is often accused of being crazy, hysterical, or sexually cold—which the husband claims is what drove him to commit incest. When a woman provides evidence that the husband is violent, irresponsible, or disturbed, she often finds the tables turned on her. *She* will be portrayed as the one who is crazy; the father, despite his problems, will be praised for caring enough about his children to sue for custody.[51]

- *Property vs. emotions.* The law values physical security and property more highly than emotional security and relationships. This hierarchy of values seems to be neutral, simply a reflection of societal values; but, writes attorney Martha Chamallas, it has "privileged men, as the traditional owners and managers of property, and has burdened women, to whom the emotional work of maintaining human relationships has commonly been assigned. The law has often failed to compensate women for recurring harms—serious though they may be in the lives of women—*for which there is no precise masculine analogue*" (my emphasis).[52] For example, until recently, if a pregnant woman watched her two-year-old child be killed by a hit-and-run driver, and in her shock and fright subsequently miscarried, she would have been treated like any (male) bystander: no special harm was done to her.

For that matter, consider how the law has typically construed the categories of "physical" and "emotional" harm. A husband enraged by his wife's infidelity was treated as if he had suffered a loss of property, compensable under the law; but a wife's outrage at her husband's infidelity was considered a "subjective" harm, noncompensable "hurt feelings." "By locating the wife's injury within her own mind," observes Chamallas, "the court could dismiss the harm and blame the victim for not mitigating her own injuries." But the husband's hurt feelings are transformed by the court into objective harm: loss of a valued object, his property, his wife.

▪ The pregnant person: Woman as flowerpot

Do you agree with Wendy Kaminer?

> Of course, pregnancy is unique, but should its uniqueness matter in the workplace? Shouldn't disabled male workers have their jobs reserved for them as well? The notion that women are affected by pregnancy . . . in a way that no man is ever affected by a slipped disc or prostate surgery has always been used to justify their marginal status in the workforce.[53]

Or do you agree with Betty Friedan?

> . . . there has to be a concept of equality that takes into account that women are the ones who have the babies. We shouldn't be stuck with always using a male model, trying to twist pregnancy into something that's like a hernia.[54]

Both of these views make sense to me, and both of them are true. How might we get out of this impasse?

The simmering ideas of equality versus sameness come to a boil on the one great indisputable sex difference where law and medicine combine forces: The male body doesn't become pregnant; the female body does. Efforts to combat the illogical belief that the female body is not a deficient male body, however, have led to the equally illogical conclusion that the female body is just like the male body—even the pregnant female body.

Certainly the law itself goes around in circles. Sometimes it has regarded pregnant women as being different from men, and, as Kaminer and others fear, it has used that difference to justify inequality. For example, the law has, in various times and places, required pregnant teenagers to leave school (but not penalized teenage fathers); allowed pregnant women to be fired from their jobs; or required nonpregnant women to be sterilized in order to keep their jobs. Sometimes the law has regarded pregnant women as being the same as men, thereby denying them special considerations. And sometimes the law has granted pregnant women, but not men, those benefits.

In the famous case of the *California Federal Savings and Loan Association* v. *Guerra* (hereafter *Cal Fed*), a woman named Lillian Garland took an *unpaid* pregnancy leave from her job at the Savings and Loan. Under a 1978 law, she was entitled to get her job back after four months, but *Cal Fed* challenged the law on the grounds that it discriminated against men. This case polarized many women's groups. Some supported Garland, but others, including the National Organization for Women and the National Woman's Political Caucus, supported *Cal Fed*'s reasoning. The case made its way to the Supreme Court, which had to resolve the conflict in this situation between equal treatment and preferential treatment. They ruled, six to three, that preferential treatment of pregnant women is not unconstitutional. California and other states may pass laws to permit maternity leaves.

According to equal-rights advocates, pregnancy should be treated like any disability that might cause workers of either sex to lose a few days' or a few months' work. Women's-rights advocates disagree. Sociologist Barbara Rothman puts the matter this way:

> A woman lawyer is exactly the same as a man lawyer. A woman cop is just the same as a man cop. And a pregnant woman is just the same as . . . well, as, uh . . . It's like disability, right? Or like serving in the army?

"Pregnancy is just exactly like pregnancy," she concludes. "There is nothing else quite like it. That statement is not a glorification or a mystification. It is a statement of fact. Having a baby grow in your belly is not like anything else one can do. It is unique. How can uniqueness be made to fit into an equality model?"[55] To Rothman, pregnant women are not in need of protection, and they are certainly not weaker or stupider than men or nonpregnant women; but it is ridiculous, demeaning, and antiwoman to ignore the special condition of pregnancy.

In *The Female Body and the Law,* political scientist Zillah Eisenstein illuminates the male bias in the law by showing what would happen if the model of the basic human being were not the male body, but the pregnant female body. (There's an imaginative idea for you!) The law, she shows, would immediately have to become more complex and sensitive to human diversity than it is, because pregnancies range from being uncomplicated and uneventful to being seriously disabling to the mother-to-be, and because some women, like all men, will not become pregnant.

Thus, the law would recognize that the pregnant worker may have needs that are different from those of the nonpregnant worker: to avoid nausea, she may need to eat several small snacks throughout the day rather than have one break at lunchtime. Further, the needs of individual pregnant women will differ: some will require considerable time off, and others will be able to work right up to the delivery (and return two hours later). Some pregnant workers may not differ at all from their nonpregnant coworkers, female or male, and will neither need nor want special considerations. These are all *equal* ways of being, Eisenstein points out, if we remove the male standard of normalcy.

But if pregnancy occurs with so many variations, why not regard it as something comparable to illness and disability, which affect both sexes and which also occur in degrees of seriousness and incapacity? For many, the answer is that once again, it is the male norm that construes pregnancy as a *dis*ability rather than, say, as an additional ability. "Normal pregnancy may make a woman unable to 'work' for days, weeks, or months, but it also makes her able to reproduce," says Littleton. "From whose viewpoint is the work that she cannot do 'work,' and the work that she is doing *not* work? Certainly not from hers."[56]

In addition, medicine and law, based as they are on the male experience, fail to recognize the female viewpoint of what is distinctive about the experience of reproduction. The male perception of pregnancy, as Rothman points out, consists of two steps: In goes a seed, out comes the result. It is a "mother as flowerpot" view of pregnancy.[57] In contrast, the woman's experience is continuous from conception to baby. By making the male experience the norm, Rothman argues, we deny that continuity, the nine-month relationship a mother has with the fetus—calming it down when it's fussy, trying to sleep when it is too big, feeling it grow and change. By regarding pregnancy from the male perspective, and by celebrating high-tech prenatal technology over the continuous maternal relationship, law and medicine have created the impression that women are merely containers for the fetus, and untrustworthy, inefficient containers at that.

Rothman, who has been studying the social consequences of changes in reproductive technology, fears that pregnant women are fast becoming viewed as "the unskilled workers on a reproductive assembly line." They are blamed for producing "flawed products"—i.e., damaged newborns or fetuses with defects. "America is developing a legal and medical system to monitor pregnant women, control them, keep them in line with 'fetal-abuse' statutes," she argues.[58] In the meantime, people conveniently overlook the more likely causes of "flawed fetuses," such as the appalling lack of prenatal services and care for poor women, the growing evidence of the *male* contribution to birth defects, and the exposure to leads and other toxins in the workplace that are hazardous to men's *and* women's reproductive ability.

Once a technological substitute for a thing exists, argues Rothman, the thing itself loses its mystique. That is what has happened to mothering in this complex age of sperm and egg donors, test-tube babies, in-vitro fertilization, and other modern baby-making possibilities. People are now asking what is so special about the mother's relationship to the fetus, compared to anyone else's. This absurd question, says Rothman, occurs because lawyers, physicians, and technicians have focused on the seed, the embryo, and the fetus, "and reduced all of the nurturance, all of the intimacy, all of the *mothering*, to background environmental factors" (emphasis in original).[59] One has only to think of the vehemence directed toward the few surrogate mothers who, although not the genetic parent, changed their minds about giving up the baby after its birth. How dare a flowerpot speak up? How dare it lay any claim to the flower it nurtured?

Once childbearing becomes a technological rather than a human process, market considerations take over. Because there is a market for (white) babies today, the fetus is increasingly valued, while the relationship with the woman in whom it resides is losing value. This elevation of the fetus over the mother has been abetted by the medical establishment, which remains eager to preserve its control over pregnancy and childbirth. Thus, in recent decades, women have rejected the notion that to be pregnant is to be sick; demanded alternatives to being drugged into an obedient stupor during delivery; and begun flocking to "alternative birthing centers" and midwives. One way that doctors fought back, Rothman maintains, was by turning their attention to the fetus, "a separate patient within." Physicians used to tell women: "You need us to protect you from having an unhealthy baby." Now they say: "Your baby needs us to protect it from you."

Many people, touched and heartened by recent advances in prenatal technology, are sympathetic toward the fetal-rights movement. Shouldn't the fetus be protected from a mother who cannot or will not take care of it properly? Shouldn't doctors get a court order to force a diabetic pregnant woman who seems not to be taking care of herself to stay in the hospital during her pregnancy?

Before the public says yes, Rothman reminds us, it would do well to consider this: Should doctors have gotten a court order, years ago, to force a pregnant woman to take thalidomide to prevent miscarriage, or to lose twenty pounds (when it was mistakenly believed that pregnant women should not gain "too much" weight)? Today obstetricians are likely to recommend that women have cesarean sections —major surgery—if they think there is the slightest risk of damage to the fetus; as a result, the United States has the highest rate of cesarean surgeries in the world. Should physicians be able to override the decision of a pregnant woman if she chooses to have a vaginal delivery? Fetal-rights advocates overlook the huge error rate in obstetrical advice over the years. We are dangerously close to creating a second class of citizen, warns Rothman: the pregnant woman, who does not have the rights of bodily integrity and self-determination that all competent adults in this society are granted.

Many of the more punitive recommendations of the fetal-rights movement, such as locking up drug-abusing women during their pregnancies, actually do little for the ultimate protection of children. They deflect attention from the hazardous conditions in which those mothers and children live. And they certainly deflect attention from fathers. Drug-using fathers also contribute to the smaller size and health problems of the fetuses they conceive, but no one is accusing them of producing flawed infants.

How then might we think about the laws and social policies having to do with reproductive issues? How can society preserve women's rights, promote social equality between the sexes, protect the health of both sexes, and foster a woman-centered standard for the experiences that are uniquely or predominantly female?

Let's start by stipulating what a woman-centered standard of pregnancy does *not* mean. It does not mean a return to concepts of "maternal instinct," the "sanctity of motherhood," and other saccharine ideas that historically have relegated women to their roles as mothers. It does not mean that men should concentrate on business and women on babies, or that women are superior to men in the ability and desire to love and nurture children. It does not mean a return to the protective legislation that treats women differently in the name of protecting their "special" reproductive processes, but has the effect of confining them to lesser-paying, lower-status jobs. It does not mean that employers would be able to fire female employees because of possible risks to their possible fetuses, while ignoring the risks to male fertility of the same hazardous job conditions.

But law and social policy can accommodate the ways in which the female and male experiences of procreation differ. According to Barbara Rothman's guidelines, for the entire duration of pregnancy, women would have full rights of personal privacy, bodily autonomy, and individual decision making. The fetus would not be regarded as a separate person or have rights that supersede those of its mother. The fetus would be part of its mother's body as long as it is in her body. The state may not force her to undergo a pregnancy that she does not want, just as it may not force her to abort a pregnancy that she does want.

The point, says Rothman, is that pregnancy, like abortion, "takes its meaning from the woman in whose body the pregnancy is unfolding."[60] That is why for one woman, pregnancy is a mystical and special experience; for another, an experience no different from having a bad back or swollen ankles. That is why for one woman, an abortion (or a miscarriage) is a minor inconvenience or a major relief; for another, or even for the same woman on another occasion, it is the death of a baby. That is why for one surrogate mother, a fetus is a chick that she is merely incubating; for another, or even for the same woman on another occasion, a fetus is an anticipated baby-to-be.

What woman-centered policies share is the premise that it must be the pregnant woman, not the state, who decides what pregnancy means to her. Without such policies, society will continue down its current path, moving toward a chilling invasion of privacy into women's bodies, a severe restriction of women's freedom, and a relegation of women's rights to third place—after men and fetuses.

▪ *Women's rights versus equal rights*

Perhaps if difference were not so costly, we, as feminists, could think about it more clearly. Perhaps if equality did not require uniformity, we, as women, could demand it less ambivalently.[61]

—Christine Littleton, *California Law Review*

Equality under the law would be an excellent goal for women if it weren't that it always seems to travel a one-way street of making women equal to men. Sometimes, women do not fit the male norm in medicine and law, and the problem with the dream of equality is that it excludes such real-life sex differences. Theories of equality can operate only if those differences can be smoothed over, if women's lives and experiences can be made comparable to experiences that men can have too. Equality theories are inherently prejudiced against women, because they focus on the "differences" that are in women (it is women who do the differing from the norm), and because they mistakenly assume that social institutions, such as banks and schools, are already egalitarian and gender-neutral—it's just a matter of fitting women into them.

This is why many legal scholars, men and women, are now arguing that the right to be treated as an equal doesn't always entail identical treatment. Ronald Dworkin writes, "If I have two children and one is dying of a disease that is making the other uncomfortable, I do not show equal concern if I flip a coin to decide which should have the remaining dose of the drug."[62]

It's a good metaphor, for most parents realize that loving their children equally does not necessarily require treating them identically. One child may need more help with homework. One may have a gift for athletics or music that warrants special favors. One may have a disability that requires attention. But parents can hope to treat their children in ways to assure equal *outcomes* for them: people who know they are loved, who can earn a living at work they enjoy, who are valued for the individuals they are. Most parents intuitively operate on a notion of equality that encompasses the real differences among their children. "I was fortunate enough to have a mother who believed her four very different children should be equals," says Littleton. "I now want the same for all of us."[63]

Many alternative ideas to equality-as-sameness are blooming today, and they are sources of exciting possibilities as well as passionate debates over which policies will enhance the status of women and produce the most equitable results all around. Mary Ann Mason urges a return to "the flexible, pragmatic concept of women's rights," rather than the rigid ideology of equal rights.[64] "Equal rights does not challenge the structure of the economy or the role of the government," says Mason. "Asking to be treated as men are treated is a fundamentally conservative position that asks for no special support from the government or special consideration from employers for working mothers."[65]

Mason would not abandon the goal of equal rights entirely; rather, she argues that it is not the only goal for all women. Equal rights, she maintains, is an appropriate strategy for the many women who, like men, "live to work" and wish access to the careers and circles of the male elite. But it is not helpful to the many more millions of women who "work to live," and who are clustered in low-paying, female-dominated occupations.

For this reason, Mason believes, Title VII of the Civil Rights Act of 1964, which forbids discrimination on the basis of race or sex, should not be the sole model of rights for women. "Sex" was added to the language of Title VII at the last minute, as a joke, by Southern congressmen who were hoping to defeat the Civil Rights Act entirely. But if a Woman's Rights Act had been passed at the time, Mason argues, it would have looked quite different. "A bill written for the needs of working women," Mason says, "would not have stressed equal competition, but would address the issues of government-subsidized child care, paid maternity leaves, a higher minimum wage (since 65 percent of all minimum-wage workers are women), medical care and pension rights for part-time workers, affirmative action, and reentry rights. It would also require some form of pay equity between male-dominated occupations and female-dominated occupations. Instead, women have trapped themselves into a competitive model that leaves no room for the special needs of women who are the primary child-rearers." [66]

As Mason's list of provocative suggestions indicates, once the lid of the equal-rights cauldron is lifted, all sorts of possibilities come bubbling out. Some advocates of a women's rights agenda want a potpourri of policies that will vary depending on a woman's age and position in society—whether she is a wife and homemaker, a career women, a part-time worker, a divorcee. Others, wary of returning to the bad old days of protective legislation, would exempt only the biological processes of pregnancy, breastfeeding, and childbirth from the basic equality model, treating all other sex differences under the rubric of symmetrical equality.

Radical legal scholars, for their part, claim that all the talk about equality and differences obscures the one difference that really matters: that in this society women are economically and politically subordinated to men. In their view, therefore, if women and men must be treated differently under the law in order to end the subordination of women, that is only right. "Why should you have to be the same as a man," asks Catharine MacKinnon, an eminent representative of this view, "to get what a man gets simply because he is one?" She adds:

Clearly there are many differences between women and men. One could not systematically elevate one half of a population and denigrate the other half and produce a population in which everyone is the same. . . . The sameness/difference approach misses the fact that hierarchy of power produces real as well as fantasied differences, differences that are also inequalities.[67]

In general, I share Wendy Kaminer's concern that any legal policy that celebrates or implies that women have a special edge in the maternal, nurturing, Gilligan-connectedness front is bound to be bad for women. Yet, overall, I have been persuaded by a flexible new approach that Christine Littleton calls "equality as acceptance" rather than "equality as sameness."

Equality as acceptance means that instead of regarding cultural and reproductive differences as problems to be eliminated, we would aim to eliminate *the unequal consequences that follow from them.* We would ask how to achieve equality *despite* gender differences, not how to achieve equality by getting rid of (or pretending to ignore) gender differences. We would no longer accept the prevailing male norm as always the legitimate one, while trying to find special circumstances to accommodate women or minorities who are trying to measure up to it. We would stop labeling women's experiences as the deviant ones.

This approach is more complicated than equality as sameness, and it does not generate clear, simple right answers. It is easier to try to squeeze human diversity into one universal, "normal" way of doing things. But equality as acceptance offers new strategies for old problems, even as it unmasks our silent assumptions about whose ways are normal and whose are deviant.

In this view, for example, women and men could achieve equality in athletics without requiring football teams to add a few physically powerful females. Equality as acceptance would require, instead, that equal resources be allocated to male and female sports programs in schools, regardless of whether or not the sports themselves are similar. In this way, sports would *accept* women's athletic skills on their own terms; equality would not depend on the ability of individual women to fit in to the male game or vice versa.

Or consider the gadget maker whose employees must meet a minimum 5'9" height requirement because of the height of the conveyor belt used to assemble the gadgets. Let's assume that this is an inherent requirement of the job, and not a conscious effort to exclude women (or Asians, Hispanics, and other groups whose average height is shorter than that of Caucasians). Some women and minorities will meet that requirement, but many, because of average height differences between groups, will not. A policy of equality as sameness would lead to two unsatisfactory results: either failing to hire many women, or lowering the standards of gadget-assembly in order to assimilate women.

But a policy based on equality as acceptance offers other solutions. Perhaps the height of the conveyor belt could be modified. Perhaps a second, lower belt could be added for assembling other gadgets. Perhaps jobs could be established at the plant that do not have height requirements. The resulting de facto sex segregation would be acceptable, says Littleton, "but *only* if the predominantly male and predominantly female jobs have equal pay, status, and opportunity for promotion into decisionmaking."[68] That "only" is the heart of it: Currently, most practices of de facto segregation are not separate and equal; the segregated group pays for it in lower status and opportunity to advance.

In short, equality as acceptance evaluates policies by directing attention to their results rather than their intentions. What is the result of a law that treats divorcing husbands and wives as if they were economically equal? What are the consequences for women of taking off a few years from the work force in order to care for children or elderly parents? What are the consequences for men, women, and families, if men do not get paternity leave? If the results are disastrous for women, as they now are, more equitable remedies must be sought.

"The question we should be asking," observes law professor Vicki Michel, "is: What are the barriers to women's equality? This question does not presuppose that people are the same, must be treated the same, or have the same opportunities. By asking 'what does this law accomplish for women?' we keep our eye on goal."[69] Defining the goal cuts the Gordian knot that entangles equality and sameness.

Consider again the situation at Mills College. Under an equality-as-sameness umbrella, the students of Mills must accept the admission of men to their college; if women want admission to male schools, they must allow men into theirs. An equality-as-acceptance perspective, however, leads to a different conclusion. Because of existing differences between the sexes in power, opportunities, and resulting self-confidence, on the average young women do better in their intellectual development when they have at least a few years to learn and study with one another than when they are in co-ed environments. In contrast, co-ed education is beneficial for males. However, when males are admitted to female colleges, the traditional patterns of male conversational dominance, in class and out of it, quickly return even when everyone tries to avoid them. In education, what's good for the gander isn't always so good for the goose.

Further, men's and women's single-sex institutions are not equal in the amount of power, prestige, and access to the establishment they provide; thus, the consequences of *not* being admitted to them differ for men and women. Men as a group will not suffer in any way by being excluded from Mills; but females (like minorities) have suffered by being excluded from most male institutions. This is why legal challenges to male-only institutions have had to establish that these institutions are not merely social clubs or private gatherings, but places where business is done, the business of America, the business that for so many years excluded outsiders. If Mills were the only school, say, of veterinary medicine in the United States, or if joining the elite alumnae of Mills represented the only access to the prestige career of, say, banking, then of course men must be admitted.

These considerations convince me that it is neither hypocritical nor necessary to support coeducation at Mills in the name of equality. Of course, I know that these young women will one day be working with men, and some may want to learn how to do that sooner rather than later. That is why they should have the opportunity to do so by going to co-ed schools. But, until males and females are equal in power and status—until, for example, men listen to women as often as women listen to men—there is a legitimate place for all-women schools if they give young women a stronger shot at achieving self-confidence, intellectual security, and professional competence in the workplace.

In 1968, the California Supreme Court decision in *Dillon* v. *Legg* found that a mother who witnesses the negligent injuring of her child may be compensated for her own fright-induced injuries, such as miscarriage. This case was a watershed because it opened up the legal category of emotional harm. The *Dillon* decision allows both mothers *and* fathers to recover for fright, and removes the general association of fright-based harm as a female problem. In this respect, *Dillon* is a fine example of how the integration into law of a "woman's" issue makes for a human and humane jurisprudence.

I believe that a guiding philosophy of equality as acceptance, combined with the specifics of a woman's-rights agenda, would benefit both sexes and reduce many of the largest disparities between them. These ideas are gaining popularity, although they have yet to make a dent in the national political scene. Suzanne Gordon has called for a "National Care Agenda" and Sylvia Ann Hewlett raises "A Call to Action" in their recent books, which argue that the traditional women's issues of caretaking, children's welfare, and education must become national, human priorities if we are to survive as a society.

- *Parental leave and child care.* Seventy-five countries (including India, Egypt, Poland, and Argentina) have national policies that guarantee parental leave when a baby is born; the United States has none, being unwilling even to permit unpaid parental leave. (The *Cal Fed* case allows states to pass laws permitting maternity leave.) Unpaid leave was a compromise idea in Congress and may have been necessary as a foot-in-the-door technique, but it is completely useless for the many millions of mothers whose incomes are necessary for family survival.

Currently, employed women feel it is up to them as individuals to find a way to solve the complexities of combining work and family. The individual solution is the American (male) way. Many women are trying hard to be like men, either sacrificing family time (as many men do) or struggling virtually alone to combine jobs with families. No other Western nation that needs the labor of women leaves it up to individual mothers to try to care for their children and carry out a full-time job.

- *Organizational flexibility.* Vicki Michel tells of a law-school colleague of hers who was expecting a baby and asked the Dean to be relieved of teaching that semester. She offered, in exchange, to teach two classes the next term. The Dean wouldn't hear of it. "When you're the only woman on a male faculty, you have to accommodate to their way of doing things," observes Michel. "The attitude we used to have was gratitude—they're doing us a favor to 'let us' take a week off to have a baby. Now women are realizing that we are half the people. We can start demanding changes that benefit us. And reasonable, flexible work arrangements are among them."[70]

One proposed flexible work arrangement that turned up in the news a few years ago was the "mommy-track" solution to the problem of combining careers and families. The idea was to permit career women to choose one of two paths: a "mommy-track" group who work at a slower pace in exchange for having more time at home, and a "fast-track" group who want to devote their energies exclusively to their careers. (The term itself came from journalists, which may indicate how the work of mothering is so easily trivialized.) Many career women objected to this plan because of its potentially unequal consequences: Women who choose to have families, unlike men who choose to have families, would pay the price, down the line, in career achievement and income.

According to Michel, the mommy-track idea wasn't radical enough. "Mothers aren't taken seriously in the way the system is currently set up," she says, "so any proposal that sets them apart is going to be detrimental to them. But we can start thinking of how to reshape work, including the work that mothers do, so that it will not be detrimental to women to have families."

Michel and others have proposed many ideas to reshape work: increased benefits and security for part-time workers; an arrangement of work for reduced income now, in exchange for the possibility of expanded opportunities and greater income later; the acceptance of part-time partners in law firms, or part-time tenured faculty in universities; and permanent part-time arrangements with health and other benefits. In careers that are incompatible with daily child care, because they require traveling, long hours, or erratic schedules, individuals can press for the right to reenter the occupation later.

All of these solutions and many others can be generated as soon as people rethink their priorities, says Mary Ann Mason, without being afraid to challenge the male definition of what it means to have a successful career. And once they do, men as well as women are likely to take advantage of them.

■ *Revaluing, and compensating, "women's work."* Years ago a jury awarded $56,000 to a man who had to do the housework for two whole months because his wife had been injured in a car crash. *Newsweek*, which reported the story, commented that not even the women's movement had valued a housewife's job at $336,000 a year. If it were, you can bet more men would be doing it. And you can bet that no woman would ever say that she was only a housewife!

No one has (yet) set a value on housework of $336,000 a year, but this story reminds us that the housework and child care that women do, although essential, are invisible and unpaid. The real goal of equality, says Littleton, should be to reduce the emotional and financial *cost* of sex differences. At present, it is expensive to be a woman, especially to be a mother: It costs in terms of income, benefits, time, and unpaid labor. If a woman takes years off from paid work to care for her children, aging parents, other relatives, or husband, she pays in her future wage-earning potential, old-age pensions, and an increased likelihood of eventual poverty. This is a horrible dilemma to impose on anyone.

An alternative, Littleton suggests, is a system in which "anyone may follow a male, female, or androgynous lifestyle according to their natural inclination or choice without being punished for following a female lifestyle or rewarded for following a male one."[71] We don't have to pay housewives or househusbands $336,000 a year, but we would as a society have to value, in concrete benefits, the people who bear children, and those who care for them.

Equality as acceptance does not require us to assume that men's ways are superior, so women should be fitted into them. It does not require us to believe that women's ways are superior, so women shouldn't try to be like men or achieve equal power with them. "It does, however," says Littleton, "affirm the equal validity of men's and women's lives"[72]—and seeks to make them equally valued under the law. A legal system which protects and rewards nurturance and community, as well as self-reliance and autonomy, is one that enriches all of us.

4

Misdiagnosing the Body

Premenstrual syndrome, postmenstrual syndrome, and other normal "diseases"

Conversation overheard in a Hollywood casting office, between a man and a woman angry at being kept waiting by a female casting director:

MAN: "It must be her time of the month."

WOMAN: "And how do we explain the rudeness of male casting directors?"

In 1975, when I was working for *Psychology Today* magazine, we ran a short article called "A Person Who Menstruates Is Unfit to Be a Mother." The author maintained that women are hypertense and anxious for the week before menstruation, moody and incapacitated for the week of menstruation, and utterly exhausted for the week after menstruation. How, then, could the complex care of children, which requires stamina, intelligence, and several advanced degrees, be entrusted to persons who are erratic and unreliable three weeks out of the month?

This essay poked delighted fun at the then-common argument that women's abilities are limited by their physiology. Edgar Berman, Hubert Humphrey's personal physician, had recently declared that women's "raging hormonal influences" made them unfit for political office. The Canadian anthropologist Lionel Tiger had publicly worried that female hormones were ruining women's entire intellectual lives: "An American girl writing her Graduate Record Examinations over a two-day period or a week-long set of finals during the premenstruum," he wrote, apparently with a straight face, "begins with a disadvantage which almost certainly condemns her to no higher than a second-class grade. A whole career in the educational system can be unfairly jeopardized because of this phenomenon."[1]

So all of the second-class female students I knew were heartened by the burst of new research in the 1970s that was rapidly debunking many old myths and preconceptions about women's alleged physical limitations. Raging-hormone theories were on the way out, as research showed again and again that women were just as able as men to work, play, think, sing, pass exams, and otherwise carry on, even when they were menstruating, premenstruating, postmenstruating, and nonmenstruating.

It was too good to last, and it didn't. Today we are witnessing a rebirth of the belief in the unruly female body. A U.S. District Judge, hearing a recent sex discrimination case, commented that women "have a monthly problem which upsets them emotionally, and we all know that."[2] Every week another story appears about how women's hormones affect women's personalities and behaviors, another research finding about sex differences in hormones and anatomy. On a basis of a single small study, "Female Sex Hormone Is Tied to Ability to Perform Tasks" was a front-page news story coast-to-coast, although no headline appeared to announce, as a much larger study found, "Male Sex Hormone Is Tied to Antisocial Behavior and Crime."

Hormone studies are part of an ongoing tidal wave of biological research in general, and much of this research has benefited women. Women should know that the physiological changes of the menstrual cycle vary enormously, that *normal* women range from having no pain or discomfort to having considerable though temporary pain. It is important for women to know that morning sickness during pregnancy is entirely a hormonal matter, and not, as a male physician once said to a friend of mine, "a woman's way of saying she doesn't want to be pregnant." It is important for women to know that hot flashes and vaginal dryness during menopause are likewise due to temporary hormonal changes, not to a neurotic loss of femininity or sexual inhibitions.

In short, it is beneficial and empowering for women to understand the normal changes of their bodies, and not to have their feelings dismissed as psychosomatic whining. A friend of mine told me that she felt depressed when she stopped breastfeeding her daughter, and, being a psychotherapist, she immediately reached for a psychological explanation. "I thought my depression must signal a pathological inability to 'let go' of my daughter," she said, "until I mentioned my feelings to my female pediatrician. She said, 'Oh, sure, that depression is due to the hormonal adjustment. It'll be gone in a few days.' "

But while there are many dangers to the overpsychologizing of normal biological processes, as my friend learned, there are also dangers of reducing all of our feelings, problems, and conflicts to them. Everywhere we look today, we find that the normal changes of menstruation and menopause are increasingly being regarded as diseases, problems, and causes of women's emotional woes and practical difficulties. In particular, biomedical researchers have taken a set of bodily changes that are normal to women over the menstrual cycle, packaged them into a "Premenstrual Syndrome," and sold them back to women as a disorder, a problem that needs treatment and attention. Of course, the only thing worse for women than menstruating is not menstruating. When women cease having the monthly "disease" of PMS, they suffer the "disease" of Menopausal Estrogen Deficiency.

The biological mismeasurement of women's bodies poses many emotional and intellectual conflicts for women, who are caught between defending their reproductive differences from men and asserting their intellectual equality and competence. The story of "premenstrual syndrome" highlights this conflict perfectly. Research on the menstrual cycle was long overdue, as it were, and feminist scholars had to press for research funds and scientific attention to be given to a bodily process that only women experience. Many women themselves have responded positively to the language of PMS, feeling validated at last by the attention being paid to menstrual changes. But the enthusiastic support for PMS masks the more important fact that the menstrual cycle does not affect a healthy woman's ability to do what she needs to do. It also diverts public attention from other matters, such as the effects of hormones on men and the fact that men's and women's moods and physical symptoms are more alike than different.

The public and scientific fascination with PMS and allied "normal disorders" of the female reproductive system is, in turn, part of a larger medical zeitgeist, reflected in the continuing effort to reduce all human problems and emotions to the correct gene, neurotransmitter, hormone, or disease. I'm getting very grumpy about this. I must be premenstrual.

▪ The manufacture of "PMS"

Let's start by trying to identify the problem. A small percentage of women report having particularly difficult emotional symptoms associated with the premenstrual phase. Some describe severe Jekyll-and-Hyde-like personality changes that recur cyclically and predictably. In my lifetime of knowing hundreds of women, I have never met such a Jekyll-and-Hyde-like female. But there is something compelling about the testimony of women themselves and of researchers who have observed their behavior clinically. A woman in one study described herself this way:

> Something seems to snap in my head. I go from a normal state of mind to anger, when I'm really nasty. Usually I'm very even tempered, but in these times it is as if someone else, not me, is doing all this, and it is very frightening.[3]

A larger percentage of women describe premenstrual mood changes, notably depression and irritability, that they swear occur as predictably as ragweed in spring. "Unbeknownst to me, my husband kept track of my irritability days in his office diary," one friend reports, "and he could predict like clockwork when I was within a week of my period."

Which group has the premenstrual syndrome? The Jekyll-and-

Hyde phenomenon reflects an abnormality in degree, kind, and severity of symptoms. But many researchers, the media, and women themselves now confuse mood changes that are abnormal and occur in *few* women with mood changes that are normal for *all* women—and, as it turns out, for all men, too.

This confusion is apparent in virtually all contemporary discussions of PMS in the media. Most of the media today regard PMS as if it were a clearly defined disorder that most, if not all, women "suffer." For example, *Science News* called it "the monthly menace," and the *Orange County Register* called it "an internal earthquake." An article in *Psychology Today* began: "Premenstrual Syndrome (PMS) remains as baffling to researchers as it is troublesome to women." *Troublesome?* To *all* women, as implied? The article turns out to be about a study of 188 nursing students and tea factory workers in China. In the tea factory, "almost 80% suffered from PMS." *Suffered?* "Overall, nearly 74% rated their symptoms as mild, 24% as moderate and 3% said they were severe." In other words, for 97 percent of the women the symptoms of this "syndrome" were no big deal.

Likewise, an article in the *Baltimore Sun,* headlined "Why PMS Triggers Hunger," begins by asking "Why is it so hard to diet when you're suffering from premenstrual syndrome?" (There we are "suffering" again.) The answer turns out to have nothing at all to do with PMS, or, for that matter, with suffering. According to the research, women feel hungrier in the few days before menstruation because their metabolism has increased. This is normal, the article states: "Your body is working as it should, building up the uterine lining . . ." Working as it should? Then why am I suffering from a syndrome?

It's easy to understand the media's confusion, because the list of symptoms thought to characterize "PMS" doesn't leave much out. One popular paperback book offers a "complete checklist" of physical, behavioral, and emotional changes, including weight gain, eye diseases, asthma, nausea, blurred vision, skin disorders and lesions, joint pains, headaches, backaches, general pains, epilepsy, cold sweats and hot flashes, sleeplessness, forgetfulness, confusion, impaired judgment, accidents, difficulty concentrating, lowered school or work performance, lethargy, decreased efficiency, drinking or eating too much, mood swings, crying and depression, anxiety, restlessness, tension, irritability, and loss of sex drive.[4] That's just for starters. Other alleged symptoms include allergies, alcoholism, anemia, low self-esteem, problems with identity, and cravings for chocolate. Some physicians have specified as many as *150* different symptoms.

Mercy! With so many symptoms, accounting for most of the possible range of human experience, who wouldn't have "PMS"? Obviously, the more symptoms that are listed, the more likely that someone will have them, at least sometimes. This likelihood is increased in checklists that include mutually contradictory symptoms (such as "was less interested in sex" *and* "was more sexually active," or "had less energy" *and* "couldn't sit still") and the entire range of negative emotions ("irritable or angry," "sad or lonely," "anxious or nervous").[5] On these lists, there is no way you can't have some symptoms.

Because researchers themselves don't agree on whether they are talking about a problem that a few women experience or that all women experience, estimates of the prevalence of the syndrome range from 5 percent (women who are severely incapacitated) to 95 percent (the number of women who will experience, as one article put it, "one or more PMS symptoms sometime in their lives"). In one typical conference on "PMS—an important and widespread problem," sponsored by England's Royal Society of Medicine Services, participating physicians tried to determine the scope of the "widespread problem." One thought it affected "between 20% and 40% of women at some stage in their lives." Another said that "a very large proportion of women are aware of cyclical physical and mood changes, but probably fewer than 5% of them are sufficiently moved by these symptoms to seek medical help." A third said that "Probably all women at some time in their lives have disturbing premenstrual symptoms . . . [but only] 5–10% of women have clear-cut PMS."[6]

It's heartening to know, I suppose, how many experts are worried about the cost to the economy of all those millions and millions of sick women whose premenstrual symptoms keep them from doing whatever work they do. One newspaper reported that "PMS-related absenteeism is estimated to have cost industry $5 billion in 1979 . . . not counting women who are working but who aren't functioning as well because of PMS." A physician writing in the *Wall Street Journal* estimated that "the illness [of PMS] costs U.S. industry 8% of its total wage bill."[7] This is no wonder, because so many PMS symptoms interfere with a woman's ability to work: she suffers from "confusion," "has trouble concentrating," and is "forgetful," "uncoordinated," and "inefficient." Some PMS guidebooks advise women to turn to routine tasks at that time of the month, and leave the really hard thinking work to later. Most of the women I know couldn't afford this luxury.

In short, everywhere you look, you find agreement that PMS is a real disorder, a disease. There's a widespread sickness among women! Up to half of all women are sick every month! Nearly all of us are sick sometimes! We're slowing down the economy! How fortunate that men are running things!

Luckily, help is at hand, because PMS cures are a thriving business. Across the country, nutritionists, psychologists, nurses, physicians, and writers are promoting books, tapes, and seminars. (One typical tape, "PMS: A positive program to gain control," promises to help all those uncontrollable premenstrual women get hold of themselves.) Physicians are setting up PMS Medical Groups, some funded by drug companies, for the specific treatment of premenstrual syndrome and, according to the promotion letter of one such center, its "disabling psychological symptoms [including] depression, mood swings, irritability, confusion, agoraphobia, panic attacks and alcoholism."[8] Many products have appeared to help women manage all these disabling symptoms. Good old Midol, "the menstrual specialist™," now offers Midol PMS, "the premenstrual specialist™." A product redundantly called "prēmsyn PMS" consists of "premenstrual syndrome caplets" which the sufferer is to "take at the first sign of PMS." These products consist of acetaminophen (an aspirin substitute, used in Tylenol), pamabrom (a diuretic), and pyrilamine maleate (a common ingredient in all pain relievers).

Natural remedies for PMS are equally popular. The health and nutrition magazines have jumped on the PMS bandwagon uncritically, offering medical, psychological, and homeopathic treatments for their confused, depressed premenstrual readers who are phobically stuck at home, drinking too much and shouting at the children. Health magazines have frequent news notes and features on PMS. "It *is* true that few women feel at their best during PMS," one item proclaimed, with no evidence for this assertion whatsoever; it went on to describe a study of sixty "PMS sufferers" who benefited from Vitamin E. Another report, titled "New Study Strengthens Link Between Caffeine and PMS," acknowledged that the "causes of PMS are not completely understood" and that "a cause-and-effect relationship between caffeine and PMS has not been firmly established." Nevertheless the article recommended that women stop drinking coffee and tea when they are premenstrual.[9]

In a nutrition magazine called *Delicious!*, the infelicitously named Jeffrey Bland, described as a "nutritional biochemist," advises women on how to "Break the cycle of monthly discomfort." Bland thinks that Judy Garland, Mary Todd Lincoln, and Queen Victoria were all victims of PMS—a rather cavalier reduction of their complicated and difficult lives to the menstrual cycle. (Retrospective diagnoses of famous people are easy, after all, since the "sufferers" can't object.) Undeterred by the lack of scientific validity regarding the variety and prevalence of symptoms, Bland has divided PMS into four subclasses and somehow calculated the alleged proportions of "PMS sufferers" in each one, offering the appropriate nutritional treatments for each. "PMS C" types, for example (for "craving"), should take Vitamin B-6, zinc, and vitamin C to control their "cravings" for sweets or salty foods.[10] Other *Delicious!* remedies include anemone pulsatilla, which may "relieve symptoms of weepiness and emotional sensitivity." Headlines in nutrition newsletters and magazines tell the story:

- "Premenstrual syndrome: coping with the enigma" (*Mayo Clinic Nutrition Letter*)
- "Pasta and potatoes prescribed for PMS" (*the Edell Health Letter*)
- "Oh! those menstrual blues: how to fight back" (*Teen Magazine*)
- "Nutrient therapy relieves pain of PMS" (*Better Nutrition*)
- "PMS? Let 'em eat carbs" (*Vegetarian Times*)

Perhaps these nutritionists should read *Cooking Light* magazine, which admitted that "No scientific evidence shows that any food, nutritional supplement, vitamin, or mineral effectively combats PMS." It couldn't resist adding, however, that "Many women are able to control their symptoms of premenstrual syndrome with proper diet, stress management, and regular exercise."[11] Jeffrey Bland, for one, agrees. Exercise, diet, and stress-reduction programs "may help many women reach their potential," he writes patronizingly, "—every day." So would a good job.

How did women manage before they knew they had a premenstrual syndrome? The story of how we got from then to now is an illuminating tale, for the idea that menstruation is a debilitating condition that makes women unfit for work has its own cycle: It comes and goes in phase with women's participation in the labor market.

In 1931, a gynecologist named Robert T. Frank created the term "Premenstrual Tension" in an article he published in *The Archives of Neurology and Psychiatry*. "The group of women to whom I refer," wrote Frank, "especially complain of a feeling of indescribable tension from ten to seven days preceding menstruation which, in most instances, continues until the time that the menstrual flow occurs. These patients complain of unrest, irritability, 'like jumping out of their skin' and a desire to find relief by foolish and ill considered actions."[12] Frank was concerned about the consequences of these ill-considered actions in the work force, because "employers of labor," he said, must "make provision for the temporary care of their employees," and some women suffer such severe symptoms that a couple of days of bed rest are necessary.

Before we evaluate what Frank was saying, let us consider when he was saying it. "It strikes me as exceedingly significant," observes anthropologist Emily Martin, "that Frank was writing immediately after the Depression, at a time when the gains women had made in the paid labor market because of World War I were slipping away."[13] It strikes me as significant, too, especially after reading Martin's account of how research findings about menstruation change over time, corresponding to women's role in the work force. At the start of World War II, for example, studies suddenly found that menstruation and "premenstrual tension" were not problems for working women. One researcher, who wrote in 1934 that menstruation was debilitating, changed her mind after the war began: "Any activity that may be performed with impunity at other times," she wrote in

1944, "may be performed with equal impunity during menstruation."[14]

But after World War II, the news changed again. The real mover and shaker on behalf of PMS was Katharina Dalton, a British physician, who throughout the 1950s wrote articles on the dangers of menstruation: "Effect of Menstruation on Schoolgirls' Weekly Work," "Menstruation and Crime," "Menstruation and Accidents," "Menstruation and Acute Psychiatric Illness," "The Influence of Mother's Menstruation on Her Child." Reading these articles is enough to make you agree that a person who menstruates is unfit to be a mother.

In the early 1950s, Dalton and a colleague coined the term "premenstrual syndrome" (to include all those women who had more symptoms than simply premenstrual tension), and in 1964 she published a book, *The Premenstrual Syndrome*.[15] The term stuck like lint. In the ensuing decades, PMS became an increasingly hot research topic, as I learned by doing a computer search:

Number of articles in medical and psychological journals on "PMS," Premenstrual Syndrome, and Premenstrual Tension, 1964 through 1989. (This list omits other menstrual-cycle research that did not use these terms or categories.)

Years	Number of articles in: Medical Journals	Psychological Journals
1964	1	—
1965	16	—
1966–1967	67	8
1968–1969	84	9
1970–1971	74	5
1972–1973	87	9
1974–1975	114	16
1976–1977	146	20
1978–1979	128	16
1980–1981	148	25
1982–1983	187	36
1984–1985	218	77
1986–1987	260	107
1988–1989	305	120

As this table shows, research on PMS erupted in the 1970s, a decade when, as Martin observes, "women had made greater incursions into the paid work force for the first time without the aid of a major war."[16] The growing emphasis on PMS, she argues, fits the pattern of recent history: When women's participation in the labor force is seen as a threat instead of a necessity, menstruation becomes a liability.

The table tells another story as well: the coopting of "PMS" by biomedical researchers. Mary Brown Parlee, a psychologist who has been conducting excellent menstrual-cycle research for many years, observes that psychologists who were studying menstruation tended to focus on normal menstrual cycles. The big money, the big grants, increasingly went to the biomedical researchers, on the assumption that PMS was a disease or a physiological abnormality that was best studied by radioimmunoassays of gonadal hormones and by other new weapons in the medical arsenal.[17]

The move toward the medicalization of PMS was and is actively supported by drug companies, Parlee observes, which stand to make a great deal of money if every menstruating woman would take a few pills every month. Drug companies sponsor research conferences and "medical education" seminars on PMS, events, she says, "for which they actively and effectively seek media coverage."[18] It is to the drug companies' interest, she adds, if physicians and the public confuse the small minority of women who have premenstrual or menstrual problems with the majority who have normal, undrugworthy menstrual cycles.

Because of this confusion, researchers are now reduced to speaking of "clearcut" or "true" PMS to distinguish the small group of women who have severe premenstrual symptoms from those who have normal menstrual changes—and from those who have other disorders. In studies of women who come in or are referred for treatment for PMS and who keep a daily diary of their symptoms over several cycles, three groups emerge: women who have significant premenstrual symptoms but no psychological problems; a group whose major problem is depression, and whose depressive symptoms are aggravated by menstruation; and a group that proves not to have premenstrual problems although they believe they do. Women with a history of emotional disorders are overrepresented in the latter two categories.[19]

By 1987, PMS was enshrined as an official psychiatric disorder in the reference manual of the American Psychiatric Association, *The Diagnostic and Statistical Manual of Mental Disorders,* where it is called Late Luteal Phase Dysphoric Disorder, or LLPDD. LLPDD is supposed to apply to premenstrual symptoms that are severe enough to "seriously interfere with work or with usual social activities or relationships with others."[20] Even for women who have severe symptoms that are unrelated to existing emotional disorders, it is bizarre, and many researchers think detestable, to have such a diagnosis in a manual of *mental disorders.* If LLPDD is a medical condition, why is a psychiatric diagnosis necessary? Thyroid abnormalities cause mood and behavior changes, but we don't consider these physiologically based changes a psychiatric disorder. And if LLPDD reflects a psychological problem, such as depression, why is a medical diagnosis of "late luteal phase disphoric disorder" necessary? We might draw an analogy to a man who suffers from chronic anxiety. Several times a month, he plays racquetball, an exercise that raises his heartbeat and sets off an anxiety attack. The man's problem is anxiety, not racquetball; he does not have Post-Exercising Syndrome.

Because of the evidence of sloppy research and confusion over the prevalence, diversity, and nature of premenstrual changes, LLPDD was relegated to an appendix in the manual, in a section of diagnoses needing "further study." Nevertheless, there it sits, a convenient label for physicians and psychiatrists to use in diagnosing patients and in turn receiving insurance compensation.[21]

In the early 1970s, Parlee published a major review of the research that had been done to date on the effects of the menstrual cycle. She put "PMS" in quotation marks, in order to denote it as an odd or unusual concept that "was purportedly scientific but was not supported by data." In a recent speech she described what happened:

A copy editor took out all the quotation marks, and with them the meaning I wanted to establish. I lost—was silenced—then in my effort to shape in a small way the scientific discourse about PMS. The processes through which "PMS" has come to mean what it does today are too powerful, too internally and mutually self-sustaining, for that meaning to be affected by the results of good science. . . . People—women, researchers, the media, drug company representatives—now use the term PMS as if it had a clearly understood and shared meaning; the only question is how to help women who "have" it. Thus PMS has become real. The quotation marks have been removed.[22]

Many institutions and individuals now benefit from the concept of PMS. Biomedical researchers, medical schools, and drug companies profit financially. Gynecologists, many of whom have closed their obstetrical services because of malpractice insurance costs, have lost a traditional source of income and are turning to new patient groups and new diagnoses for replenishment. Many psychiatrists have shifted from conducting long-term psychotherapy to prescribing short-term (repeatable) drug treatments. Indeed, obstetricians and psychiatrists are already engaged in turf wars over who is best suited to diagnose and treat all those women with premenstrual symptoms.

But the success of PMS is not entirely a conspiracy of big institutions, although, as Parlee says, if PMS didn't exist as a "psychologically disturbing, socially disruptive, biologically caused disease" they would have needed to invent it. (They did.) We must also ask why so many women have responded so favorably to the term and use it so freely. Parlee suggests that "the language of 'PMS' is a means by which many women can have their experiences of psychological distress, or actions they do not understand, validated as 'real' and taken seriously."[23] In that sense the language of PMS is empowering for women, she believes, because it gives a medical and social reality to experiences that were previously ignored, trivialized, or misunderstood.

Like all psychological diagnoses, then, PMS cuts two ways: It validates women, but it also stigmatizes them. Psychiatrist Leslie Hartley Gise directs a PMS program at Mt. Sinai Hospital in New York, yet she too is worried about the stigmatizing effects of making PMS a psychiatric diagnosis. "If even the rumor that Michael Dukakis had undergone treatment for depression could be held against him," Gise told an interviewer, "think of what a PMS diagnosis would mean for a woman seeking public office."[24] We've come full circle. The ghost of Edgar Berman must be smiling.

▪ Of menstruation and men: The story behind the headlines

The research on the physiology and psychology of the menstrual cycle paints a very different picture from the popular impression that PMS is a proven, biomedical syndrome. It is clear that some physical changes normally occur: breast tenderness, water retention, and increased metabolism being the most common. The key word here is *normally*. It is normal for premenstrual women to have some aches and pains, to gain a few pounds (because of temporary water retention), or to crave food (because of increased metabolism). Leslie Gise puts it this way: "Although PMS is used for convenience, *premenstrual changes* is a more accurate term."[25]

You might think, with all the studies trying to document the existence of a "widespread" biological disorder that so many women are "suffering" from, that researchers would have some idea of what causes it. Yet in spite of more than a decade of biomedical research, no biological marker has been found that distinguishes women who have severe premenstrual symptoms from those who do not. There is no support for theories suggesting that premenstrual symptoms are caused by abnormally high (or low) hormones, low magnesium, high sodium, abnormal thyroids, a deficiency of hormonelike substances called prostaglandins, steroid fluctuations, or the like.

Moreover, thus far, no drug or vitamin has been found to be effective. There is no evidence that vitamins help, and megadoses of B-6 supplements, which are commonly recommended, carry significant risks, such as causing nerve damage, for some individuals. In most of the double-blind treatment studies, in which neither the women nor her physician knows whether she is being given an active drug or a placebo, the placebo effect is as strong as the drug. Upward of 60 to 70 percent of the women who are given a placebo report improvement in their symptoms.[26]

For many years, the treatment of choice for PMS was progesterone suppositories, in spite of a lack of clinical evidence demonstrating their effectiveness. Recently, however, Ellen Freeman and her colleagues, who conducted the largest and best-controlled study to date of the effects of progesterone, found that "progesterone suppositories have no clinically significant therapeutic effect greater than that of placebo for premenstrual symptoms."[27] Progesterone did not improve individual symptoms or severity of symptoms in any way. If anything, symptoms remained *higher* in the women given progesterone than in those on the placebo!

So what is going on here? Up to the mid-1970s, researchers kept finding what they called the "classic" menstrual mood pattern: greater happiness and self-esteem during ovulation (mid-cycle), followed by depression, irritability, and low self-esteem premenstrually. But as Mary Brown Parlee noticed back in 1973, the professional journals were not publishing negative results—that is, studies that were finding *no* premenstrual differences or mood variations over the menstrual cycle. In the last fifteen years, more of these disconfirming studies have been published, and many errors have been discovered in the earlier research. The new evidence finds that most of the so-called emotional and behavioral symptoms of Premenstrual Syndrome may not have much to do with menstruation, and in any case are not limited to women.

▪ *The problem of memory.* One major problem with much of the research that supposedly documented Premenstrual Syndrome is that many women recall having had premenstrual mood changes when, in fact, they did not. When you ask women retrospectively to describe their symptoms over the month, many of them will cheerfully tell you that they become depressed, weepy, irritable, and moody just before menstruation. Yet when most of these same women keep a daily diary of their moods, their *actual* moods are often unrelated to what they *recall* their moods as having been. Many women "remember" symptoms that didn't occur, and forget changes that did occur.[28]

Moreover, menstruation itself provides women with the cue they need to decide when they have been "premenstrual." Psychologist Randi Koeske finds that many women *retrospectively* make sense of troublesome moods and actions ("Aha, so that's why I was so grumpy Tuesday; I was about to get my period").[29] Yet a large percentage of women claiming to experience PMS fail to demonstrate a cyclic pattern of negative moods when they actually keep daily records. Nevertheless, many physicians and medical researchers, to this day, diagnose PMS by relying on a woman's memory, asking her to fill out a checklist of what she believes her symptoms have been for the last month or two. Survey questionnaires in popular magazines make the same mistake.

▪ *The "premenstrual elation" syndrome and the "no symptoms at all" syndrome.* The way to correct the error of retrospective memory, it would appear, is to ask women to keep daily mood and symptom diaries for a couple of months. When they do, it turns out that women, like men, vary widely over a thirty-five-day span. Some women, like my friend whose husband kept track of her cycle, do tend to become irritable and grouchy premenstrually. But others have no premenstrual symptoms at all—not a twitch or jiggle. Others are grumpiest during the luteal phase (midcycle). Many women report feeling *better* before menstruation; they describe having a "burst of creativity" and energy. Few studies and checklists ever included this possibility; one questionnaire measure of "Menstrual Distress" contains forty-two negative mood adjectives and only five positive ones. The popular books, likewise, list all manner of negative emotions but no positive ones. Their checklists contain anger, hostility, irritability, depression, nervousness, worry, anxiety, sadness, and loneliness, but not enthusiasm, cheerfulness, happiness, satisfaction, optimism, and increased energy.

Mary Brown Parlee asked seven women to fill out mood and activity questionnaires every day for ninety days, but these women did not know that they were in a study of menstruation. The results showed patterns that were exactly the opposite of what those PMS checklists would predict: Depression, fatigue, sleepiness, and hostility were *lower* premenstrually and menstrually than during ovulation! Parlee concluded, wryly, that she had found evidence for a "premenstrual elation syndrome." Yet when she interviewed the women at the end of the study and told them its purpose, they all believed that they had been more anxious, irritable, and depressed premenstrually, although their own diaries failed to bear them out.[30]

▪ *The power of expectations and circumstances.* The belief in PMS has, itself, a powerful influence on a woman's likelihood of noticing some symptoms and ignoring others at different times of the month.

This is why even the day-by-day method of tracking symptoms has a problem: For some women, the strong belief that their moods change predictably over the menstrual cycle affects their actual experience of symptoms.

In one fascinating study, for example, two groups of women and a comparable group of men filled out daily inventories of their moods and physical symptoms. Half of the women were aware that menstrual-cycle changes were a focus of the study, and half were unaware. During the premenstrual phase of their cycles, the "aware" women reported a significantly higher level of negative moods and uncomfortable physical changes (such as headaches and muscle tension), and fewer positive feelings, than did either the "unaware" women or the men.[31] The belief in PMS and the expectation of negative symptoms, apparently, influence a woman's likelihood of noticing some symptoms and ignoring others at different times. And it's a big likelihood. In this study, the "aware" women, premenstrually, reported a 76 percent increase in negative emotions (anxiety, depression, anger) and a whopping 193 percent increase in physical complaints. The "unaware" women did not.

Being aware of bodily changes or expecting them to occur can make us more sensitive to them; conversely, distracting influences can override them. This fact may explain why moods have less to do with a woman's time of the month than with her time of the week. Women's positive moods (and men's) peak on the weekends![32] If you want to predict when a woman will feel happiest, according to several studies, you do better to know when it's a Saturday or Sunday than when she is ovulating.

As this research suggests, the mood effects of the menstrual cycle often depend on whether a woman is paying more attention to her bodily changes or to her immediate situation. A friend of mine put it this way:

> If, one day, I'm aware of feeling too easily annoyed by telephone interruptions, or if my threshold for bureaucratic stupidity plummets, I may suddenly realize that I'm "premenstrual." This mood can be easily overturned, though, if I do something I enjoy, like taking a hike or going to the movies. It just depends on whether I want to indulge my moods or break them.

▪ *The male comparison.* One of the most misleading consequences of the popular focus on Premenstrual Syndrome is that it omits men as a comparison group. Yet if you give men those same checklists of symptoms (reduced or increased energy, irritability and other negative moods, back pain, sleeplessness, headaches, confusion, etc.), men report having as many "premenstrual symptoms" as women do —when the symptoms aren't called PMS. (You do have to omit the female-specific symptoms, such as breast tenderness.) If the identical checklist is titled "Menstrual Distress Questionnaire," however, men miraculously lose their headaches, food cravings, and insomnia. [33]

When men are included as a comparison group in menstrual-cycle research, it turns out that their moods also change over the course of a month, just as much as women's moods do. Among men, as among women, individuals vary enormously in their moodiness, frequency of mood swings, and general levels of grumpiness. It's just that men can't blame their mood changes on a menstrual cycle, and their mood changes are more unpredictable and idiosyncratic.

Psychologist Jessica McFarlane and her associates, who conducted the "weekend happiness" study, observed mood fluctuations in women and men over a span of seventy days. Their findings reinforce all of the points I have been making here:

> . . . the women in this study did not actually experience the classic menstrual mood pattern but when they were asked to recall their moods, they reported that pattern. . . . [They] were relatively unaffected emotionally by menstrual hormonal fluctuations.
>
> . . . young women's moods fluctuated more over days of the week than across the menstrual cycle, and young men also experienced emotional fluctuations over days of the week. The women were not "moodier" than the men; their moods were not less stable within a day or from day-to-day. Evidence of weekday mood cycles in both sexes suggest that *treating emotional fluctuations as unhealthy symptoms, and assuming that only women usually manifest them, is misleading.* [34] [My emphasis.]

Yet very little research has been done specifically on men's hormones and moods; testosterone, in most men, is as much as 25 percent higher in the mornings than in the afternoons, but no one regards these normal fluctuations as symptoms of anything. If you look up research on testosterone and mood, you will find more studies on women than on men. (Both sexes have both sex hormones, although in different proportion.)

But in one nice study, psychologist Betsy Bosak Houser worked with five young men three times a week for ten weeks. She took blood samples to determine levels of serum testosterone and other hormones; she gave the men mood inventories, behavioral tests (e.g., of reaction time and arm-hand steadiness), and the Menstrual Distress Questionnaire, omitting only its title and one item—"painful breasts." Houser found significant links between hormone levels and moods; for instance, as plasma testosterone increased, the men's hand steadiness and good humor decreased. (Alarm! What does this finding mean for millions of men doing brain surgery or assembly-line detail work?) However, she also found—as is the case for women—huge individual variations in the specific links between hormones and mood.[35]

- *The ultimate question: What do hormones have to do with abilities and behavior?* In the fall of 1988, *The New York Times* and the *Los Angeles Times* were among the many newspapers to herald the results of a study that claimed to link a "female sex hormone" with women's "ability to perform tasks." On closer inspection, the abilities in question proved to be tongue twisters and "precise hand movements." The newspaper editors must have thought that these skills matter a great deal in real life, perhaps because women need to be able to say "It's time, Timothy, to transport the totally titanic ton of terrible trash" five times in a row quickly if they are going to get Timothy to take the garbage out. And perhaps women's skill at precise hand movements explains the predominance of females in needlepointing, although it cannot account for the predominance of males in neurosurgery.

On further inspection of the study in question, it also turned out that the researchers hadn't actually *measured* anyone's hormones; they merely asked women what phase of the menstrual cycle they were in (a notoriously unreliable method, since most women don't accurately know). Nor did the researchers control for the women's use of birth-control pills, which of course affect hormone levels.

Now, how did this poorly done study of trivial talents become "Female Sex Hormone Is Tied to Ability to Perform Tasks" on the front page of *The New York Times* and elsewhere? One reason was a normal news slump that, in this case, followed the 1988 Presidential elections. Another is that virtually any brain/biology/genetics/hormones research makes news these days. A third reason, however, is that people have been trying for roughly eight billion years to find a link between women's hormones and their behavior, without success. When someone gets results, that's news.

The behavior question is important. We should be worried if the premenstrual workers in America are costing the economy millions. We should be worried if premenstrual college students are flubbing their exams in great numbers. And we should be worried if growing numbers of premenstrual (or postpartum) females are crashing their cars or murdering their lovers.

Fortunately, we can all relax. Unsung by the media, study after study has confirmed that women manage to manage their households, thoughts, exams, families, and jobs at any phase of the cycle. Hormonal changes in women have never been reliably linked to problems in behavior or intellectual performance. (Few experts have suggested that women's hormones might *improve* their performance in any sphere, except, perhaps, child care.[36])

For example, psychologist Sharon Golub reviewed all the studies that have tried to find effects of menstruation on women's ability to work. The studies measured everything from the ability to perform simple motor tasks to complex problem-solving. The results, she reports, "confirmed the findings of almost 50 years of research in this area. *The menstrual cycle has no consistent demonstrable effect on cognitive tasks, work, or academic performance* despite beliefs to the contrary that persist"[37] (my emphasis).

What about the notion that hormonal changes make women dangerous, to themselves and others? Katharina Dalton offered statistics suggesting that women in the premenstrual and menstrual phases were overrepresented among women who had had car accidents, been admitted to hospitals, or committed crimes. This sounds like worrying evidence. But, like all correlations, this evidence does not necessarily show that menstruation makes women dangerous or sick. For one thing, it refers only to women who have had accidents or been caught committing a crime, a number that is a very small proportion of all women to begin with; women who express their feelings in positive ways at that "time of the month" do not turn up in statistics or urban pathology. Moreover, as Dalton's critics have observed, accidents and crimes are stressful events, and stress is known to bring on menstruation early. The weak link between menstruation and behavioral problems may occur not because the former causes the latter, but because the latter causes the former.[38]

In contrast, male hormones *are* related to behavior. In a major study of 4,462 male veterans, psychologists James Dabbs, Jr., and Robin Morris, of Georgia State University, found that unusually high testosterone was associated with delinquency, drug use, having many sex partners, conduct disorders, abusiveness, and violence. Of course, these are correlational data and it is also true that some behaviors raise testosterone levels. But Dabbs and Morris noted that testosterone is directly associated only with negative actions: "While high testosterone theoretically might lead to prosocial behavior, the present data provide no indication of such redeeming social value."[39] Testosterone can be restrained, it appears, by money and success. Men of higher socio-economic status had lower testosterone levels and were less likely to commit antisocial acts.

When *The New York Times* eventually published a report on these findings (not, by the way, on the front page, but in the science section), the bad news of the link between testosterone and antisocial behavior was buried late in the story. The headline was "Aggression in Men: Hormone Levels Are a Key," with the subtitle "Testosterone is linked to dominance and competitiveness."[40] Aggression, competitiveness, and dominance are considered desirable for men, of course; the implication of the title was that these qualities are hormonally determined. It is only halfway through the article that the writer cites Dabbs's study and quotes him as saying: "The overall picture among the high-testosterone men is one of delinquency, substance abuse and a tendency toward excess." This point, which is the real news, is not featured in the headline.

I do not wish to replace the biological reductionism of women's behavior with a biological reductionism of men's behavior, but rather to highlight the different diagnoses that society favors and to raise some questions. Of course women are influenced by their bodies—

by aches, pains, puffiness, water retention, and headaches—but so are men. Why, then, are women's mood changes a "syndrome," but men's mood changes just "normal ups and downs"? Why are women, but not men, considered "moody," and why are mood changes, which are normal, considered undesirable? Why are variations in testosterone not considered a medical and social problem, whereas variations in female hormones are a focus of national concern? Why is the *Wall Street Journal* unruffled about the cost to the economy of men's hormonal changes? Why is there no psychiatric diagnosis of "Excessive Testosterone Syndrome" or "Nonmenstrual Lability Disorder" that reduces male moodiness and antisocial behavior to their hormones?

Compare the following true cases. In Los Angeles in 1988, Sheryl Lynn Massip was accused of murdering her infant son by running over him with her car. Her defense was diminished responsibility resulting from postpartum depression. The jurors found her guilty, but the judge overruled their decision on the grounds that she was, in his legal terminology, "bonkers." Yet in Texas in 1988, Ronnie Shelton pleaded not guilty to twenty-eight counts of rape, on the grounds that he was a victim of "compulsive rape syndrome," due to his high testosterone levels. Shelton failed to convince his jurors, too, but his judge agreed with them.[41]

Regardless of what you believe about the appropriateness of hormone defenses, the issue here is why so many people are more eager to blame women's behavior on their hormones than to blame men's behavior on theirs. Why do experts focus on the possible blip in the female crime rate one week out of the month, when that rate is so much lower than the number of men who have accidents and commit crimes all four weeks of the month? In this respect Harriet Goldhor Lerner puts the matter of women's hormones and behavior into the appropriate perspective:

> Let's face it. Do *you* stay off the streets at night because you fear attack from uncontrolled, irrational women in the throes of their Premenstrual Syndrome? Probably not. We stay home at night because we fear the behavior of men.[42]

▪ Reading the body:
The psychology of symptoms

Many women are highly resistant to the evidence that their beliefs and expectations about PMS might be influencing their symptoms, or that their memories of symptoms might not be entirely accurate. It sounds as if psychologists are refusing to believe them, singing the old refrain that was so patronizing for so long: "It's all in your head." When I've talked to women about this research, many say, "Well, the research is plain wrong; I *know* my body changes and I *know* I become irritable," or "That research may apply to other women, but not to me."

Something is going on, therefore, between the evidence of the research and the private experience of the body. How might women (and men) begin to regard the normal symptoms of the menstrual cycle, without transmogrifying them into a problem or syndrome, yet recognizing their influence in daily life and emotional well-being?

Recall these puzzles of PMS. There is no special biological marker or abnormality that characterizes women who report having PMS from those who do not. The symptoms include contradictory conditions, such as irritability and euphoria, lack of energy and increased energy, and every sort of emotion. Some women feel "impelled" to yell at their husbands when they are premenstrual, but others feel equally impelled to bake bread. Both women and men have hormonal fluctuations and mood changes in the course of a month, but only women's moods are attributed to their hormones. And although women everywhere in the world experience similar physical symptoms along with menstruation (cramps, tender breasts, aches and pains), a World Health Organization survey of hundreds of women in each of ten nations found that "PMS" and its associated mood shifts are a Western phenomenon.[43]

This collection of anomalous facts suggests that the changes associated with the menstrual cycle are "real," are felt physically, and that they provide a fuel for moods and feelings. But the *content* of those moods and wishes often depends on a woman's attitudes, expectations, situation, personal history, and immediate problems and concerns. To try another metaphor, hormone changes provide the clay; the mind and experience shape and mold it into a form. It's real clay, but it's only clay.

Symptoms are therefore not "all in the mind," but they aren't exactly "all in the body," either. No hormone could, by itself, account for yelling *and* bread-baking. But hormonal changes can make a woman feel edgy, bloated, and "not herself." They can create a feeling of fatigue and enervation. A woman then interprets these bodily changes in a particular way: as symptoms to be ignored, as signs of temporary insanity, as a sickness to be medicated, as an opportunity to tell her husband what she is afraid to say otherwise, as a liberating opportunity to write poetry. This is why the same physiological process expresses itself in so many different psychological forms.

In a series of studies, Randi Koeske has found that positive *and* negative emotions are often enhanced premenstrually and that it is the situation a woman is in, more than her hormones, that determines which emotions (if any) she feels. Her reactions also depend on how she explains her feelings. A woman who says to herself "water retention makes my tear ducts feel full" is going to feel different from one who regards the same physical sensation as evidence that "I am about to cry and must be depressed."[44]

Sometimes women are aware of how their attitudes and expectations affect their experience of the menstrual cycle, as in the case of my friend who decides whether she wants to overrule her premenstrual symptoms or indulge them. But usually women are unaware of the combined and invisible impact of their unique package of physical histories, family attitudes, culture's views of menstruation, and individual experiences. They are usually unaware, for example, of the fact that they selectively notice certain physical signs or emotional states and ignore others. (So do men.) As one woman I spoke with said:

> If I feel irritable and then get my period a day or two later, I'll say, "Oh, it was just my period speaking, thank goodness. What a relief; it wasn't important." But if I feel irritable at other times, I don't usually put it down as just being in a bad mood; I try to figure out why.

PMS is one illustration of the mind-body link in the experience of any noticeable physiological change, such as pain. Of course pain isn't "all in the mind," but psychologists have demonstrated that the mind affects how severely the pain is felt and what pain sufferers do about it.[45] Many if not most human beings live with some recurring or chronic discomfort, such as lower back pain, migraines, stomach problems, or arthritis. All of us draw a personal line that determines when we acknowledge, worry about, and seek treatment for our pains, and when we will say, "Oh, the hell with it" and carry on as if it weren't there.

In general, men are expected to fall on the "carry on" side of pain management, whereas women are expected to fall on the "worry about it" side. Each strategy has its strengths. The ability to talk about the experiences of the body often evokes useful support, sympathy, and advice from others; the "carry on" approach has the virtue of distracting the pain sufferer, which itself is often a successful technique of pain control. But each strategy, pursued to extremes, has its pitfalls: on the one hand, ignoring symptoms that are signs of a serious problem; on the other, overemphasizing or overmedicating symptoms that are not serious problems.

For women and men, the long and varied process of learning how to interpret and respond to their bodily sensations results in a deeply held belief that "this is just the way I am; I can't help myself." This belief feels like, and is experienced as, a biological inevitability over which the person has no control. But a woman's reaction to menstruation is no different in kind from the man who says, "I can't help losing my temper; I was born angry." No, he wasn't. He was born with a physiological capacity for anger, with the adrenaline that fuels the fight-or-flight response; but he has learned, over a lifetime, what provocations warrant his anger, what he can get away with when he feels angry, and that the belief that he cannot control his temper will get him the results he wants.

That is why the "Jekyll and Hyde" language of PMS bears such strong similarities to the arguments of men who drink and become abusive. Sociologists Richard Gelles and Murray Straus, who have been studying the causes of violence in the family for many years, observe that men and women learn how to behave when they are "under the influence"—whether the influence is drink, drugs, pain, disease, or hormonal changes. There is no inevitable biological link between alcohol and violence, but some men learn that alcohol will give them an excuse to behave violently.[46]

In fact, there is considerable evidence that abusive behavior (by men or women) results more from using the excuse of biology than from the biology itself. About half of all men arrested for assaulting their wives, for instance, claim to have been drinking at the time. However, when these men are given blood tests, fewer than 20 percent have enough alcohol in their bloodstreams to qualify as legally intoxicated.[47] Similarly, no one has yet discovered a physiological marker to distinguish Jekyll-and-Hyde women from any others, but certainly some women have learned that premenstrual changes will be accepted as a reason to say or do what they believe they could not say or do at other times of the month.

It turns out, however, that people use biology to excuse only certain kinds of actions and emotions—namely, the negative ones. (No one ever says, "It wasn't my fault that I contributed $1,000 to that shelter for the homeless; my hormones make me feel generous once a month.") When Koeske asked a group of men and women to explain possible reasons for a woman's depression, hostility, or anger during her premenstrual phase, they frequently chose biological explanations like PMS. But if Koeske described the woman as behaving cheerfully or positively during this time, people accounted for her behavior in terms of her personality or the situation she was in. They discounted entirely the possibility that premenstrual anger might be valid. They regarded such anger as more unreasonable and unjustifiable, and more indicative of a temperamental, irrational, and immature personality, than identical feelings displayed either by a man or by a woman who is not premenstrual.

All the talk about the biochemical origins of women's moods, therefore, overlooks the content of those moods. In her studies, Katharina Dalton was remarkably blind to the substance of the stories her interviewees told her. Many of these women spoke of feeling bored to tears by repetitive housework, drudgery, and unsupportive husbands—only premenstrually, of course.[48] So maybe the real question is not why some women become irritable before menstruation, but why they aren't angry the rest of the month, and why they (and others) are so quick to dismiss their irritations as being mere symptoms of PMS. This trend deflects attention away from the real problems that a "PMS sufferer" might have: menstrual-cycle irregularities; chronic depression; or month-long grievances, such as family conflicts, low pay, long hours, or the housework blues. It also deflects attention away from the normal feelings of grumpiness, sadness, weariness, and other mood changes that both sexes can have any day of the month.

The story, unfortunately, doesn't end here. The saga of PMS is about to be replayed with another normal stage of women's lives: menopause. As the baby-boom generation ages, we will be hearing more and more about medical treatments for an entire generation of women who are "suffering" from another kind of syndrome.

It's already started. At the end of 1989, the *Los Angeles Times* featured a major article on "Menopause: Baby Boomers' Next Step."[49] The subtitle read: "Thirty million women are on the verge of the change of life. Although some will suffer little, others are facing challenges their mothers never dreamed of." *Some* will suffer little? This implies that most women will suffer (and need treatment). "More immediately troublesome to a woman approaching or passing menopause, however, is concern about emotional symptoms. . . ." Here we go again.

The "emotional tangle could get even more complicated," the article warned, for menopausal baby boomers whose daughters are entering their teens. ". . . you have a 50-year-old mom and a 12-year-old daughter," one physician said. "So the little girl is going through puberty, Mom is going through menopause. There are all these raging hormones within the household." Fortunately, 50-year-old men have no emotional ups and downs, and teenage boys are famous for the stability of *their* hormones, so the males in the family can see to it that some work gets done.

One woman interviewed in the article admitted she didn't know what to expect of menopause. "Is it like chronic PMS?" she asked. "Or are you going to be depressed for 15 years, or what?"

The answer is: or what. Two epidemiologists, Sonja and John McKinlay, conducted an important study of 2,500 randomly chosen menopausal women living in Massachusetts. Apart from reporting some "temporarily bothersome symptoms," such as hot flashes, sweating, and menstrual irregularity, most of these women said that menopause was simply "no big deal." The vast majority either regarded menopause as a relief and a pleasure (they no longer had to worry about pregnancy or periods) or had no particular feelings one way or the other about it. Only 3 percent felt regretful that they had reached menopause.[50] Moreover, depression was not associated with any of the natural changes from pre- to immediately postmenopause. The women who were most likely to report increased depression were those who had a stack of things to be depressed about, such as job pressures, ailing husbands, and aging parents; or who had had a history of chronic depression.

These are the findings that turn up in all studies of normal populations of women (as opposed to studies of women who have had surgically induced menopause, through hysterectomy, or who have had continuing episodes of depression). In fact, comparable to the evidence for "premenstrual elation syndrome," the studies provide support for what psychologist Jacqueline Goodchilds calls PMF— "Post-Menstrual Freedom"—and for what Margaret Mead called her "post-menopausal zest." But I predict that we won't be hearing much about PMF as baby-boom women go through menopause. It's too big a market to remain undiagnosed and untreated.

■ Doctoring the failed female

Ultimately, the belief that menstruation and menopause are problems for women is part of a larger assumption that female physiology itself is abnormal, deficient, and diseased. Because this view is so pervasive, it is easy to forget that it is not the only one possible.

In fact, the idea that menstruation is a problem for women (and their families) is new to this century. For most of human history, from the ancient Greeks until the late eighteenth century, medical writers assumed that male and female bodies were structurally similar, and that there was nothing inherently pathological or debilitating about menstruation. (They held many misconceptions about the magical powers of menstrual blood, but that's another story.) For example, in seventeenth- and eighteenth-century America, when women were believed to be biologically similar to men, menstruation was considered a natural, unproblematic process.[51]

In the nineteenth century, as I noted in the previous chapter, a major transformation took place in the scientific and popular views of the female body. It was no longer seen as analogous to the male body, but as distinctly opposite, different. Menstruation became a symbol of that difference. Walter Heape, a zoologist at Cambridge University, wrote in his 1913 book *Sex Antagonism* that "the reproductive system is not only structurally but functionally fundamentally different in the Male and the Female; and since all other organs and systems of organs are affected by this system, it is certain that the Male and Female are essentially different throughout."[52] Heape's description of menstruation, a "severe, devastating, periodic action," was, dare I say, hysterical. The menstrual flow, he wrote, leaves behind "a ragged wreck of tissue, torn glands, ruptured vessels, jagged edges of stroma, and masses of blood corpuscles, which it would seem hardly possible to heal satisfactorily without the aid of surgical treatment."[53]

Today, Heape's descriptions seem as outdated as the old brain studies do, and it would surely surprise no one to learn that Heape was a militant antisuffragist. Yet the legacy of this attitude survives. It is much toned down, to be sure, but no less influential, and just as much a part of the political and social culture in which it occurs.

The view of menstruation as a monthly wound from which women must recover, along with the view of its sister sickness, menopause, are subtly enshrined in our language as processes that involve weaknesses, losses, and debilities. In a dazzling analysis of the language that describes menstruation and menopause in medical textbooks, Emily Martin showed how physicians, anatomists, and the public have come to regard these processes. Menstruation is *failed* conception; menopause is *failed* reproductive functions.

Thus, textbooks describe the process of menstruation in terms of deprivation, deficiency, loss, shedding, and sloughing. The fall in hormones "deprives" the uterine wall of its "hormonal support," "constriction" of blood vessels leads to a "diminished" supply of oxygen and nutrients, and finally "disintegration starts, the entire lining begins to slough, and the menstrual flow begins." The imagery of menstruation that Martin found in textbook after textbook is one of "catastrophic disintegration: 'ceasing,' 'dying,' 'losing,' 'denuding,' and 'expelling.' "[54]

I certainly learned about menstruation in those terms, and my first reaction to Martin's criticism of physiology textbooks was to say,

"Well, how else would you describe it?" The answer is immediately apparent, she shows, in the way textbooks describe other bodily processes that are analogous to menstruation. For example, the lining of the stomach is shed and replaced regularly, in order to protect itself from self-destruction by the hydrochloric acid produced for digestion. Textbooks do not describe this process as one of degenerating, weakening, or sloughing of the stomach lining. They emphasize the "secretion" and "production" of mucus, Martin reports, and "—in a phrase that gives the story away—the periodic *renewal* of the lining of the stomach" (emphasis in original).[55] Here is Martin's summary:

> One can choose to look at what happens to the lining of stomachs and uteruses negatively as breakdown and decay needing repair or positively as continual production and replenishment. Of these two sides of the same coin, stomachs, which women *and* men have, fall on the positive side; uteruses, which only women have, fall on the negative.[56]

Martin then casts her observant eye on the way textbooks describe sperm production and ejaculation. She finds not a whisper of information that the ejaculate is composed of shedded cells or any discussion of the processes of deterioration and renewal in the male reproductive system. Instead, there is much celebration of the "remarkable" male reproductive physiology. As one textbook author described it, "Perhaps the most amazing characteristic of spermatogenesis is its sheer magnitude: the normal human male may manufacture several hundred million sperm per day." This gee-whiz, ain't-it-remarkable tone is absent from descriptions of female reproduction. "Although this text sees such massive sperm production as unabashedly positive," Martin observes, "in fact, only about one out of every 100 billion sperm ever makes it to fertilize an egg: from the very same point of view that sees menstruation as a waste product, surely here is something really worth crying about!"[57]

Menopause fares no better in textbooks, Martin shows. If menstruation is a monthly deterioration and failure, menopause represents a permanent deterioration and failure: "ovaries cease to respond and fail to produce. Everywhere else there is regression, decline, atrophy, shrinkage, and disturbance."[58] This condition is apparently so dire and potentially dangerous to women that in 1981 the World Health Organization actually defined menopause as an estrogen-deficiency disease.

Now this is curious. Why should a process that is normal for all women be construed as a disease? Why, instead, aren't we asking whether there might be advantages to women of ceasing reproduction? After all, women don't faint or die at the end of menopause; most live another twenty-five or thirty active years. So how deadly could this disease be? Of course menopause does involve losses, such as a reduced production of estrogen by the ovaries and the inability to conceive (if one wanted to at that age). It is true that the risks of osteoporosis and heart disease rise significantly after menopause. Nevertheless, *most* women do *not* die from these conditions. The uniformly negative description of menopause is by no means the only one possible. Martin found one current textbook that describes the changes of menopause positively, if tentatively so:

> . . . although menopausal women do have an estrogen milieu which is lower than that necessary for *reproductive* function, it is not negligible or absent but is perhaps satisfactory for *maintenance* of *support tissues*. The menopause could then be regarded as a physiologic phenomenon which is protective in nature—protective from undesirable reproduction and the associated growth stimuli.[59] [Emphasis in original.]

The negative view of menstruation and menopause is part of a larger perspective that regards female anatomy as designed entirely for reproduction. When it starts to "fail" and "run down," therefore, it can only be seen as a "problem," a "crisis"; the relevant body parts become "superfluous" or in need of a little medical bolstering. Are a woman's reproductive organs troubling her in any way? The best solution is to get rid of them; who needs her uterus and ovaries when her reproducing days are over? Conversely, is the level of estrogen necessary for maintaining the menstrual cycle naturally diminishing? That can't be good—better fill 'er up. The attitude that the female body always needs fixing and tuning to protect it from itself has led, in this context, to two popular practices in American medicine:

hysterectomies to remove the unnecessary uterus, and hormone re-
placements for all that estrogen "deficiency."

In 1946, a prescient gynecologist named Norman F. Miller wrote
an article called "Hysterectomy: Therapeutic necessity or surgical
racket?" Miller reported that in his study of 246 patients on whom a
hysterectomy had been performed, nearly half of the operations were
wholly unnecessary: 30.8 percent showed no pathology of the organs
removed and 17.4 percent had no symptoms at all. He warned that
"remunerative or hip-pocket hysterectomies" were becoming a dangerous practice.[60]

Miller's colleagues didn't pay much attention to him, and hip-
pocket hysterectomies (and other other hip-pocket procedures on
both sexes) are still widespread. Herbert Winston, Professor of Obstetrics and Gynecology at Albert Einstein College of Medicine, is a
second-opinion consultant for Blue Cross/Blue Shield in New York.
He disagrees with 90 percent of the recommendations for hysterectomy that have come to him. "The patients who had had the recommendations for the hysterectomies," he says, "either had no
pathology whatsoever or had pathology that was so minimal that it
was inexplicable to me how anybody could have recommended surgery."[61]

Today, some 650,000 hysterectomies are performed every year,
and 40 percent of all American women are now expected to have
them eventually.[62] Most of these operations are medically unnecessary. But it seems that doctors and patients disagree on what "necessary" means. Doctors tend to believe that a hysterectomy is
necessary if it relieves symptoms, such as heavy bleeding or the pain
from fibroids (benign tumors that develop in more than one third of
all women, and that generally disappear after menopause). Most
women think that a "necessary" hysterectomy means that there is no
alternative and without it they will die.

In fact, only 10 percent of all hysterectomies are performed because of cancer or other life-threatening diseases. Many of the others
are recommended for "precancerous" conditions, despite the fact
that most women will not develop cancer of the uterus or ovaries.
(They hear the word *precancerous,* however, and take it to mean that
without surgery they *will* develop cancer, not that they have a small
chance of doing so.) "A number of gynecologists consider the uterus

and the ovaries to be precancerous no matter how healthy the organs may be," observes Lynn Payer, author of *How to Avoid a Hysterectomy,* "and recommend their prophylactic removal in all women around the age of forty."[63]

The idea of undergoing a surgical procedure for "precancerous" conditions that are statistically rare ought to be ludicrous on the face of it. The appropriate comparison to the uterus is the male prostate, which, in the large majority of older men, actually does contain precancerous cells. These cells are very slow-growing, however, and do not pose a threat to most men who have them. Nevertheless, although prostate cancer is far more common than uterine cancer, no one recommends preventative surgery on the prostate. The very idea would make most men premurderous.

The view that nonreproductive uteruses are unnecessary has led many physicians to infer that you can just remove them with no medical consequence—a female form of appendectomy, as it were. Of course, hysterectomies can be life-saving when they are performed to control cancer, dangerous infections, and hemorrhage. But most hysterectomies in the United States are performed for benign conditions. These conditions may be annoying and even painful, but they rarely become cancerous and life-threatening; and, as mentioned, menopause often cures them. It makes sense for a woman to consider having a surgical procedure if she faces years of painful fibroids and excessive bleeding. Yet most medical textbooks and physicians recommend hysterectomy if a woman is *close* to menopause, since she won't be needing her uterus anymore.

But a woman does need her uterus, all things being equal, even if she is past childbearing. There is growing evidence that removal of the uterus and ovaries increases the risk of breast cancer and heart disease. "Since heart disease kills more women than all cancers combined (heart disease accounts for at least seven times as many deaths as breast cancer) and since breast cancer kills three times as many women as uterine cancer," Payer observes, "the benefits of prophylactic hysterectomy have to be weighed against the increased risks of these two diseases." They must also be weighed against the increased risks of yet-unknown problems: The lining of the uterus produces many substances whose purpose is still uncertain, but which may be beneficial in unforeseen ways.

When doctors recommend hysterectomy, therefore, women should be asking whether it is the only available treatment for their condition and what will happen if they don't do it. Other procedures are becoming available, such as an endometrial ablation, a nonsurgical procedure that destroys the lining of the uterus, or myomectomy, which removes fibroids but not the uterus. (Nevertheless, myomectomy is still major surgery, and there is a considerable chance that the fibroids will return.) "Instead of asking only, 'Is this hysterectomy necessary?',", Payer says, "women might better ask, 'Necessary for what?' "[64]

Payer's question is also appropriate for an even more prevalent procedure: the widespread use of estrogen to treat female menopausal symptoms and prevent future diseases—and again, not only problems that some women do have, but problems that a woman might eventually have. When my mother was going through menopause, thirty-five years ago, her physician prescribed Premarin, still the most popular form of estrogen. "Do you have any hot flashes and similar problems?" her gynecologist asked her. "No," she said, "though I did get a chill in a movie theater, once." "Take these," he said, writing the prescription, "they'll prevent symptoms." The ones she never had.

Estrogen was first synthesized in the laboratory in the 1940s, and ever since physicians have been prescribing it for all the things that ail women: menstruation, pregnancy, menopause. It was supposed to prevent miscarriage and make pregnancies healthier, until the DES scandal broke and we learned that it was causing cancer in the children of the women who took DES when pregnant. It was supposed to keep women "feminine forever" after menopause, until we learned that it was killing too many of those feminine women with a sixfold increase in risk of uterine cancer. In birth-control pills, it was supposed to prevent pregnancy with only a few side effects, but those side effects eventually proved intolerable and hazardous, and the pills were modified into their current safe form.[65]

Today estrogen is usually combined with progestin in the Hormone Replacement Therapy (HRT) commonly recommended for menopausal and postmenopausal women. (Most physicians no longer prescribe estrogen alone for women who still have their uteruses, because it increases the risk of endometrial cancer.) Without question, estrogen treatments do help reduce difficult menopausal symptoms, such as severe or frequent hot flashes and vaginal dryness. Estrogen is important for women who have gone through premature menopause due to hysterectomy, radiation, or chemotherapy. It does dramatically reduce the rate of bone loss in postmenopausal women. And, according to a major large-scale study of thousands of nurses, it apparently cuts the risk of heart disease significantly, and this is the leading cause of death in postmenopausal women.[66] (We must say "apparently" rather than "definitively" because the nurses were not randomly assigned to take estrogen or no drug. It may be that the women who volunteered to take estrogen had other characteristics that lowered their risk of heart disease; perhaps, concerned about the drug, they had more check-ups or modified their diets.)

For these reasons many, if not most, physicians are unabashed champions of HRT. They agree with gynecologist Fred Benjamin, who told a reporter: "The consensus of doctors, the *worldwide* consensus, is that unless there is a contraindication, every menopausal woman should be given estrogen indefinitely to prevent osteoporosis and because of its other beneficial effects" (emphasis in original).[67] And an article in a medical journal, concerned that American women "can now expect to live for 30 years or more past the menopause in a state of *estrogen deprivation*," concluded that *"with the demonstrated efficacy and safety of [estrogen replacement], such therapy should be considered for all postmenopausal women"* (my emphasis).[68]

All postmenopausal women! Indefinitely! A woman can now take pills all her reproductive life for her premenstrual symptoms, and then take more pills for the rest of her life for her postmenstrual symptoms!

I want to emphasize that it is as foolhardy to argue that *no* woman should take estrogen as to argue that all women should. The point is that these hormones are not a panacea or a cure for aging. They are complex, and their effects are complex, depending on dose, how long they are taken, and how they are administered. A woman may decide she wants to take estrogen to reduce her risk of heart disease and bone loss; but estrogen on its own increases the risk of uterine cancer, so she will probably be given estrogen combined with progestin; but progestin seems to negate the beneficial effect of estrogen alone on the heart. Moreover, if a woman has microscopic breast tumors that are as yet undetectable by mammography, estrogen may "feed" certain kinds of tumors and increase the speed at which they develop.

Further, HRT involves other risks and side effects that women are less likely to hear about: an increase in gallbladder disease, liver disease, migraine headaches, and fibroids (recall that for many women a major benefit of menopause is the shrinking of benign uterine fibroids).[69] Progestin may also cause abdominal bloating, headaches, and menstrual bleeding. Because most women don't much fancy the idea of menstruating at the age of 65, many older women don't take the progestin part of their hormone replacement therapy—which leaves them with the risks of taking estrogen only.

Yet women are rarely warned that hormones are powerful drugs and should be taken only after considerable reflection, weighing the pros and cons against their *own individual level of risk and family history* of heart disease, osteoporosis, or simply having uncomfortable symptoms. My personal physician, whom I love and admire, is an HRT enthusiast, but he always takes the full picture into account in assessing any one woman's medical outlook. If this assessment is not done, some women remain on HRT for years longer than they need to; and many healthy women who are at *low* risk of heart disease or osteoporosis take HRT unnecessarily and thereby increase their risks of other problems.

It is a dilemma. Because of the rocky and often alarming history of estrogen therapy, some women are understandably wary of taking hormones even when doing so would benefit them. But many others are embracing the potential advantages of HRT without wanting to hear from the doubters. A friend of mine, age 50, went to a meeting of her women's group that was gathering to discuss their experiences with menopause. She brought along copies of a computer-generated reference list of studies implicating HRT in numerous side effects and long-term risks. "Now, who wants a copy to refer to in our discussion?" she asked cheerfully. She didn't get a taker: Many of the other women were on HRT (or planned to be) and didn't want to hear bad news.

At present, the debate about HRT is framed against the basic assumption that the female body at menopause is deficient, primed for disease, and in need of treatment. As a result, a woman who is the least bit skeptical about the wisdom of HRT for herself is placed in the curious position of defending the decision *not* to take hormones. In truth, the burden of proof should be on her physician to show why she *should* take them. In the case of osteoporosis, does she have diminished bone mass already and a family history of the disease? Is she thin and white and a cigarette smoker? With reference to breast cancer and heart disease, what is her family history and how many other risk factors does she have?

Many women might do better to let their bodies gain a few natural pounds after menopause, because fat cells produce estrogen and protect against loss of calcium. Women can also reduce their risks of heart disease and osteoporosis by a moderate regimen of exercise, a high-calcium, low-fat diet, and by not smoking. New methods are being developed—including technologies such as dual-photon densitometry—to measure bone mass and bone loss. Assessment of overall risks, along with new methods of monitoring a woman's health, can help a menopausal woman assess the likelihood that she will be among the one in four who will suffer from osteoporosis in old age— or among the three in four who will not; or if she will be among the 31 percent of postmenopausal women who will eventually die of heart disease—or the 69 percent who will not. If her risk is high, HRT may indeed be a wise course of action.[70] But she doesn't have to make that decision the month that menopause begins. She can be medically monitored for a few years to see how she is doing. The benefits of estrogen will accrue even if HRT is begun several years after menopause.

With further research, which at last is in the pipeline, we will better understand the potential benefits and risks of estrogen. But the idea that menopause itself is "one of nature's mistakes," as the author of *Feminine Forever* put it, can occur only in a culture that regards the female body as a deficient version of the real one.

If the female reproductive process were regarded as the norm (or at least as being normal) in this society, our ways of thinking about and treating the female body would be entirely different. Consider just a few changes that would occur:

Women and men would regard changes in moods, efficiency, and good humor as expected and normal variations, not as abnormal deviations from the (impossible) male ideal of steadiness and implacability. Why must women defend themselves from the charge of having mood changes, anyway? Mood changes are perfectly normal. Everyone has them. Even men.

We would, by understanding the interplay of mind and body, be better able to distinguish emotions that signify something important (such as a family conflict that should be dealt with) from those that are momentary blips on the screen of life. We would travel a clearer path between reducing important problems to biological imperatives ("I'm not mad at you for stealing my inheritance, dear; it's just my PMS speaking") and inflating mild biological changes into serious problems ("I feel puffy and ugly; I want a divorce").

We would regard the changes of menstruation and menopause as normal, not as failures, losses, deficiencies, and weaknesses. Some bodily states or transitions (for both sexes) may not be comfortable one hundred percent of the time, but, under normal circumstances, the best remedies are patience, a moderate diet, exercise, and good humor. Morning sickness, menstrual cramps, and hot flashes are hormonal; they will pass.

We would not confuse normal physical changes with symptoms of a disorder or a disease. We can protest the mindless application of the term "PMS" and speak instead of the variety of premenstrual changes in women *and* of hormonal changes in men. The same applies to menopause; we can try to nip in the bud the forthcoming onslaught of diagnoses that will try to turn this healthy, beneficial, and to most women liberating change into an estrogen-deficiency disease. We can also learn how to live with the normal hormonal effects of menopause without regarding them as major psychological disorders. As one friend of mine, a teacher who is going through menopause, says:

> Occasionally I'll have a very uncomfortable hot flash when my whole body feels feverish. I no longer try to pretend it isn't happening. I just say to the class: "OK, everybody, this is what a person having a hot flash looks like. Take five while I get a drink of water and mop my brow." Then we all carry on.

We would regard surgical procedures and drugs as treatments of last resort, when medically necessary to save a woman's life or when, on balance, they will significantly improve the quality of a woman's life. We would not resort to them casually, to "cure" normal female processes. Instead, we would regard menstruation and menopause as processes of renewal and change, processes that do not need to be conquered, cured, or altered.

Most of all, we would recognize that if hormones affect one sex, they also affect the other. The current embrace of hormonal diagnoses of women's behavior feeds the belief that women aren't really responsible for their actions—not in the way men are, anyway. Hormones affect behavior, but we must think carefully and critically about whose hormones, and which behaviors, are legitimate legal defenses, let alone personal excuses to use around the house.

I believe that women long to achieve legitimacy for the unique experiences of the normal female body, and that they embrace the biomedical language of PMS and Estrogen Deficiency Disease as a way of getting there. But trusting to a language that proclaims these experiences deficient and diseased is not the solution. The price, for women's psychological well-being and for their status in society, is too great.

5

Misdiagnosing the Mind

Why women are "sick"
but men have "problems"

A woman I'll call Emily, who is thirty-nine years of age, decides to enter psychotherapy for help with a persistent problem: chronically low self-esteem, a vague but persistent unhappiness, and a general uneasiness about her life. She briefly contemplated going back to school to improve her skills, but her husband and mother have persuaded her that this is not a practical idea. Her husband, Mark, believes that there really isn't much point in her returning to the workplace, since any job she did get would barely be enough to cover the costs of day care for their two preschool-age children, ages two and four. Emily agrees. Mark wants to be helpful, but whenever he offers suggestions to her—such as getting involved with a volunteer program, looking for a part-time job, or taking a weekend for herself at a spa—Emily rejects them out of hand.

Mark is becoming irritated with Emily's complaints and bitterness. Her intransigence about not doing anything for herself is becoming annoying to those who love her. She takes no pleasure even from the things she does well. She doesn't seem to want to do anything that's fun anymore, and it annoys Mark that Emily has taken to wearing a mantle of martyrdom. "She'll do anything for everybody," he complains, "whether they want her to or not." Occasionally, after she has refused once again to even listen to any of his offers of help, Mark erupts in an angry outburst, to which she invariably reacts with tears and withdrawal.

What's the matter with Emily?

You can find Emily's symptoms on pages 373 and 374 of the *Diagnostic and Statistical Manual of Mental Disorders*, Third Edition Revised, published by the American Psychiatric Association in 1987. The DSM, as it is familiarly called by practitioners, is the bible of diagnosis, a compendium of "mental disorders" and the criteria for identifying them (and thereby receiving compensation from insurance companies). According to the DSM, Emily is suffering from Self-defeating Personality Disorder, which is characterized by a "pervasive pattern of self-defeating behavior, beginning by early adulthood and present in a variety of contexts."

In order to be diagnosed as a self-defeating person—as opposed to someone who just occasionally shoots herself in the foot—you must meet at least five of the descriptions on the DSM's checklist:

(1) You choose people and situations that lead to disappointment, failure, or mistreatment.
(2) You reject offers of help.
(3) You respond to good news or successes with depression, guilt, or actions that produce pain.
(4) You provoke others to reject or be angry with you, and then feel hurt, defeated, or humiliated.
(5) You turn down opportunities for pleasure.
(6) You are able to do well but you keep sabotaging your own objectives.
(7) You reject people who treat you well; e.g., you are turned off by considerate sexual partners.
(8) You like to play the martyr, sacrificing your own interests for others who do not solicit or need your help.

It's a portrait of Emily, all right. Of course, it is also a portrait of all of us, some of the time.

Now consider the case of a young woman I'll call Audrey, age twenty-four, who never seemed to become attracted to the right man. The men she fell in love with were always unavailable in one way or another: either they turned out to be married or, unwilling to make a commitment, they vanished after a few months. For the last eight months, however, Audrey has been having an affair with Mike, and at first she thought things would be different. He was attentive, loving, and passionately committed to her. It's true he was a heavy drinker, but she was so thrilled about finding an affectionate man that she readily overlooked what she considered a minor flaw. Recently, nevertheless, Audrey has become worried about Mike's behavior when he drinks. He has been belligerent, forgetful, and occasionally abusive. She finds herself making excuses for his drinking, to herself and others: "He's been under pressure at work," she says, or "he's had a rough life."

What's the matter with Audrey?

You can find many Audreys at any meeting of Adult Children of Alcoholics, one of the thousands of self-help groups that are burgeoning across the country. Although neither of her parents was actually an alcoholic, Audrey learns why she has always been attracted to unavailable men, why she puts up with Mike's bad behavior, and why she can't leave him: As the daughter of a workaholic father and a depressive mother (the group explains to her), she was always trying to woo her father's affections by being good, dutiful, and responsible. Audrey learns that Mike is not really to blame for his abusiveness because he is suffering from the disease of alcoholism. And she learns that she herself is suffering from a chronic disease, which, if untreated by perpetual participation in a twelve-step recovery program, will worsen. The disease she has, Audrey learns, is codependency.

In confirmation of this diagnosis, Audrey discovers that a "codependency checklist" in a popular magazine fits her like a glove[1]:

(1) You find yourself "covering" for another person's alcohol or drug use, work habits, sexual escapades, or other bad behavior.

(2) You spend a great deal of time talking and worrying about other people's problems instead of your own.

(3) You take on more responsibility than you should in relationships, even when you resent it.

(4) You ignore your own needs to meet someone else's.

(5) You fear that if you get angry, the other person will not love you.

(6) You worry that if you leave a relationship, the other person will fall apart.

(7) Your self-esteem depends on what others say and think about you, or on your possessions or job.

(8) You grew up in a family where there was little communication, where expressing feelings was not acceptable, and where there were either rigid rules or none at all.

It's a portrait of Audrey, all right. Of course, it is also a portrait of all of us, some of the time.

Does Emily have a mental illness? Does Audrey have a disease? Some leaders of the codependency and "Adult Child" movements, such as Anne Wilson Schaef and John Bradshaw, believe that almost all of us are sick or crazy: they estimate that 96 *percent* of all Americans come from "dysfunctional" families and thus are in need of therapeutic help. Oddly enough, no one considers this pessimistic computation as a sign of a Grandiose Self-inflating Personality Disorder, whose symptoms are the belief that "I'm cured and you're not" and the claim "Give me ten minutes, and I'll tell you what's wrong with you."

Today, the two therapeutic enterprises represented by self-defeating personality disorder and codependency are at war for the souls, pockets, and self-definitions of women who love others too much and themselves too little. The psychiatric establishment vies to treat these women for a mental illness with long-term therapy. The burgeoning self-help movement proposes to treat them for a life-threatening disease with support groups that follow a specified plan for a never-ending recovery.

It is not an innocuous debate. The power to name and diagnose—as Thomas Hobbes said, the power to make definitions—is the ultimate authority. Labels and diagnoses, as we've seen in the case of "PMS," have tremendous capacity both to liberate and to oppress. They reassure the worried that their problems are identifiable and probably treatable; but they create worries in people who didn't think they had a problem, let alone one that needed treatment. Most of all, the definitions that people choose to explain their personalities and their lives lead to different courses of action. A woman who thinks she has a chronic disease may be persuaded to enlist in unending group therapy; a woman who thinks she has a personality disorder may begin a lengthy course of analytic treatment; a woman who thinks she needs a better job may be persuaded to enroll in school. People must be careful about the labels they choose to apply to their problems, because definitions have consequences.

Self-defeating Personality Disorder and codependency are the latest incarnations of an old American game that we might call "Name What's Wrong With Women." Every few years a wave of best-selling books sweeps over the land, purporting to explain to women the origins of their unhappiness. In many of the self-help versions of these books, the author begins by describing how she herself suffered from the disorder in question, and, through persistence, effort, or revelation, found the cure.

Thus, in the 1950s, women's problem was said to be their inherent masochism, an idea that derived from Freud's theory that female psychology includes an unconscious need for, and pleasure in, suffering. Wrong, said Matina Horner in the late 1960s. The problem is women's fear of success; the cure is to understand and then overcome their internal barriers to achievement. Wrong, said Marabel Morgan, Phyllis Schlafly, and other religious conservatives in the 1970s. The problem is that women *want* success, when they should be spending their energies being obedient to God and husband; the cure is to strive to become "The Total Woman," "The Fulfilled Woman," or "The Positive Woman." Wrong, said Colette Dowling in 1981. The problem is that women have a "Cinderella Complex—a hidden fear of independence"; they must struggle against their desires to be rescued by Prince Charming. Wrong, said a spate of writers in the early 1980s. The problem is that women "say yes when they mean no," and "when they say no, they feel guilty"; the cure is assertiveness training. Wrong, said Robin Norwood in 1985. The problem is that women love too much. Wrong, said a flurry of books in rebuttal. It's not that women love too much but that they love the wrong men—men who are immature, angry, abusive, chauvinistic, and cold. Wrong, said Melody Beattie in 1987; the poor guys aren't to blame, because they are sick. Women love too much because they are codependent—addicted to addicts, addicted to bad relationships.

Long ago in *The Feminine Mystique,* Betty Friedan wrote of "the problem that has no name"—the vague emptiness and desolation that plagued many women in the postwar era. But in fact the problem has gone by far too many names. The symptoms that all of these books attempt to treat are invariably the same: low self-esteem, passivity, depression, dependency on others, an exaggerated sense of responsibility to other people, a belief that it is important to be good and to please others, and an apparent inability to break out of bad relationships. I do not doubt that many women are unhappy, and I do not doubt that these descriptions apply to many women—and to a goodly number of men. But it is time to ask why these psychological diagnoses of women's alleged inner flaws, which keep returning like swallows to Capistrano, year after year, fail to deliver on their promises. And it is time to ask why the explanations we make of female problems differ in kind and function from those we make of male problems.

Thus, the problems that are more characteristic of men than women—such as drug abuse, narcissism, rape, and other forms of violence—are rarely related to an inherent male psychology the way women's behavior is. When men have problems, it's because of their upbringing, personality, or environment; when women have problems, it's because of something in their very psyche. When men have problems, society tends to look outward for explanations; when women have problems, society looks inward.

For example, psychologist Silvia Canetto has compared attitudes toward people who attempt suicide (typically women) with those toward people who abuse drugs (typically men). Both of these actions, says Canetto, are "gambles with death"; both actions can be lethal although the individual may not intend them to be. Suicide attempters and drug abusers share feelings of depression and hopelessness. Yet mental-health experts tend to regard suicide attempts as a sign of a woman's psychological inadequacy, reports Canetto, whereas they regard drug abuse as "caused by circumstances beyond the person's control, such as a biological predisposition."[2]

Likewise, people speculate endlessly about the inner motives that keep battered wives from leaving their husbands. Are these women masochistic? Do they believe they deserve abuse? Are they codependent, unwittingly collaborating in the abuse against them? Whatever the answer, the problem is construed as the battered wives, not the battering husbands. But when experts ponder the reasons that some husbands abuse their wives, they rarely ask comparable questions: Are these men sadistic? Do they believe they deserve to abuse others? Rather, their explanations focus on the pressures the men are under, their own abuse as children, or the wife's provocations. Male violence is not considered a problem that is inherent in male psychology; but the female recipients of male violence are responsible because they "provoked" it or "tolerated" it or "enabled it" or are "masochistic"—problems presumed to be inherent in female psychology.[3] A man who gets into a fight with a stranger and hits him may spur an observer to ask: "Why is this guy so aggressive and hostile?" But if the same man goes home and hits his wife, the same observer is likely to wonder: "Why does she stay with him?"

Of course, almost everyone knows people who are, often or on occasion, self-defeating, sadistic, dependent, martyrish, or who otherwise behave in annoying and exasperating ways. And I do not deny that therapy can be helpful for such individuals. But the question is: Do they have *problems,* or are they sick? Further, as the examples of Self-defeating Personality Disorder and codependency illustrate, many of the problems associated with women today can be considered signs of mental illness only in comparison to a male standard of what is healthy and normal.

▪ *How to create a mental illness: Are you a self-defeating personality?*

In the early years of the nineteenth century, a physician named Samuel Cartwright argued that two particular forms of mental illness, caused by nerve disorders, were prevalent among slaves. One was *drapetomania,* which was diagnosable by a single symptom: the uncontrollable urge to escape from slavery. Slaves who "suffered" from the other disorder, *dysathesia aethiopica,* revealed many symptoms of their "sickness"—destroying property on the plantation, being disobedient, talking back, fighting with their masters, or refusing to work. "Sanity for a slave was synonymous with submission," says psychologist Hope Landrine, "and protest and seeking freedom were the equivalent of psychopathology."[4] Thus, doctors were able to assure slaveowners (and themselves) that a mental illness, not the intolerable condition of slavery, made slaves seek freedom. This explanation conveniently turned the desire for liberty into a "sickness" that was the problem of the slave, not the slaveowner.

"Drapetomania" now sounds as dated as Plato's view that female hysteria is caused by a lonely womb that wanders through the body crying for a baby. Surely, most people would say, the bad old days in psychiatric diagnosis are past, thanks to modern technology and the scientific method. Yet when we peer beneath the surface, we find that the old attitude that transforms normal desires and deeds into pathology is alive and well.

There is something solid, permanent, and official about a list of symptoms in a scholarly-looking tome like the *Diagnostic and Statistical Manual of Mental Disorders.* The DSM is the mental equivalent of the *Physicians' Desk Reference,* the medical dictionary all doctors rely on. You can look up any of a long list of psychological symptoms in the DSM index (including excessive worrying, indiscriminate socializing, indecisiveness, insomnia, untidy appearance, delusions, and cross-dressing), and there find all possible disorders that the symptom might reflect. "Irritable mood," for instance, is associated with twenty-four different disorders, including nicotine withdrawal, pathological gambling, insomnia, and Organic Anxiety Syndrome.

The DSM strives to classify varieties of mental disorders and their symptoms with a degree of precision to a hundredth of a decimal point. A depressed person who has Bipolar Disorder (known commonly as manic depression) might get any of this range of diagnostic identification numbers:

296.56 in full remission
296.55 in partial remission
296.51 mild
296.52 moderate
296.53 severe, without psychotic features

296.50 unspecified
296.54 with psychotic features

The purpose of such precise numbers and diagnostic criteria, say the compilers of the DSM, is to enhance agreement in diagnosis among clinicians and investigators.

It is important to understand the claims, intentions, and methods of the DSM because the manual has had an extraordinary impact, both in the United States and worldwide. It has succeeded in standardizing the categories of who is, and who is not, mentally ill. Its categories and terminology have become the common language of most clinicians and researchers. Virtually all major textbooks in psychiatry and psychology base their discussions of mental disorders on the DSM. Insurance companies require clinicians to assign their patients the appropriate code number of the diagnosed disorder. Attorneys and judges often refer to the manual's list of mental disorders, even though the DSM warns that its categories "may not be wholly relevant to legal judgments," such as those of individual responsibility and competency. The current edition of the DSM, in its full or abbreviated version, has been translated into Chinese, Danish, Dutch, Finnish, French, German, Greek, Italian, Japanese, Norwegian, Portuguese, Spanish, and Swedish. The Manual generates a yearly revenue of over one million dollars for its publisher, the American Psychiatric Association.[5]

Now, the DSM is not called the "Diagnostic and Statistical Manual of Mental Disorders and a Whole Bunch of Everyday Problems in Living." A collection of mental disorders, one might assume, would include serious, universally recognized problems such as schizophrenia, depression, and paranoia. But the territory of psychiatry and clinical psychology keeps expanding, and as it has, so has the DSM. The 1952 edition of the manual contained 60 categories of mental illness. By 1968, the DSM-II contained 145 categories. By 1980, the DSM-III had ballooned to 230 disorders. In 1987, the DSM-III-R—a revision that added enough changes to warrant a new volume, but not enough to warrant calling it a fourth edition— crossed the 300 mark. And the fourth edition, which will be published in late 1993, contains yet more disorders in all their minute variations.

Many of these additional categories are "Everyday Problems," including tobacco dependence, marital conflicts, and sexual difficulties. Of course these matters can be troubling to people and many seek help in dealing with them. But their presence in the DSM raises some nagging questions. What are they doing in a compendium of *mental disorders?* How did they get there? Where do old diagnoses go when they die, and where do new ones come from? And how, in particular, did something called Self-defeating Personality Disorder make its way onto the latest list of official mental problems?

The careful examination of these questions is critical, because once a diagnosis lands in print, in a fat psychiatric reference manual, it acquires a life of its own and becomes difficult to eradicate. As psychiatrist Judith Herman observes, after a while a label such as Self-defeating Personality Disorder is accepted unthinkingly simply because it has been listed in the manual for some time.[6] A clinician can look up the symptoms of poor Emily's unhappiness and find a label for what she "has." If a label is there, many users of the manual assume, it must be valid.

Or is it? The story of the creation of Self-defeating Personality Disorder has a curious history. In the early 1980s, the American Psychiatric Association decided to commission an official revision of the DSM-III. Work Groups were assembled to discuss each category of mental disorder and decide what, if anything, should be done with it. Each Work Group was given a set of guidelines in studying a proposal for change, starting with the most important: "Was the proposal supported by data from empirical studies?" There were other matters to consider as well, including whether there was "a consensus among experts" that the change would be clinically useful.[7]

In the spring of 1984, the Work Group on Personality Disorders recommended that a new diagnostic label be included in the next DSM, which they called Masochistic Personality Disorder. Although the criteria for this alleged disorder were carefully phrased in "his or her" terms, no one was fooled. Everyone knew it was a term that was far more likely to be applied to women than to men.

The proposal generated an immediate firestorm of protest from the

Committees on Women of the American Psychiatric Association and the American Psychological Association. The protesters raised numerous objections: that the proposed new category was biased against women, that it perpetuated Freud's discredited belief that women enjoy suffering, that it blamed the victim of abuse rather than attending to the abuser, and—oh, yes, by the way—that it was utterly without scientific merit.

For the next year, the Work Group listened to an outpouring of objections and read countless research papers from many professionals inside and outside the psychiatric establishment. Its members then decided . . . to keep the new category anyway. But in an effort to placate the opposition, they made what they regarded as three concessions:

- They changed the name of the proposed new category from Masochistic Personality Disorder to Self-defeating Personality Disorder. This change, the compilers of the DSM-III-R (Revised) explained, avoids "the historic association of the term *masochistic* with older psychoanalytic views of female sexuality and the implication that a person with the disorder derives unconscious pleasure from suffering."[8]

- They agreed to include a cautionary note that the disorder would *not* be diagnosed when a patient is showing normal responses to sexual or physical abuse. That is, clinicians should realize that a woman might stay with an abusive man not because she is "self-defeating" but because she knows her life would be in danger if she left him.

- To counter the charges that this diagnosis would apply mostly to women, the Work Group added what its members thought would be a parallel problem applying mostly to men: "Sadistic Personality Disorder," characterizing people who gain pleasure from inflicting pain on others.

The Board of Trustees of the APA then made one further compromise. Instead of placing Self-defeating Personality Disorder in the main text of the DSM-III-R, as its advocates wished, they relegated it to an appendix consisting of "diagnostic categories needing further study." Nevertheless, it was given an official code number (301.90) and a set of supposedly characteristic hallmarks, which meant it could be used as a legitimate diagnosis.

You might assume that for Self-defeating Personality Disorder to make its way into the DSM-III-R, leapfrogging over piles of documents protesting its inclusion, it must have been supported by data from empirical studies, as the Work Group was instructed to consider first and foremost. You would be wrong. The editors of the DSM revision admitted:

> In attempting to evaluate proposals for revisions in the classification and criteria, or for adding new categories, the greatest weight was given to the presence of empirical support from well-conducted research studies, *though, for most proposals, data from empirical studies were lacking.*[9] [My emphasis.]

In the case of this particular proposal, for instance, no one had determined the extent to which self-defeating personality traits were prevalent among normal women and men who were not in treatment. Indeed, some of the defining qualities of the "disorder," such as sacrificing one's own interests and putting other people first, are highly esteemed traits for both sexes in many cultures and are virtually a role requirement for women in our own. Moreover, no one knew whether this new disorder was significantly different from other personality or emotional problems. For example, a self-defeating person might actually be suffering from depression (depressed people also feel chronically pessimistic and "reject opportunities for pleasure") or primarily have the problem of low self-esteem (such individuals also reject offers of help and fail to complete tasks they could easily do).

None of these concerns deterred the Work Group. The reason for the decision to keep the new diagnosis is stated in the preface to the DSM-III-R:

> . . . the diagnostic criteria for Self-defeating Personality Disorder were studied by examining the data from an anonymous questionnaire that was distributed to several thousand members

of the American Psychiatric Association who had indicated a special interest in Personality Disorders.[10]

A vote! The decision was made, in essence, because a lot of psychiatrists, replying to a survey, said, "Yes, I've seen these women in my practice. It's the damnedest thing. They actually want to play the martyr." One psychiatrist, reviewing a paper that was highly critical of the lack of research evidence for Self-defeating Personality Disorder, noted that this criticism "hardly does justice to those who felt there was a rich clinical tradition that justified this category in the DSM-III-R."[11]

When all the pretensions to science are blown away, the "rich-clinical-tradition" approach to defining mental illness proves to be the real basis for DSM diagnoses: "We psychiatrists think this disorder belongs here, because we have seen it in our practice." Perhaps they have. Yet psychiatrists have seen many things as a result of their clinical judgment that, over the years, proved to be ephemera of the biases and beliefs of the time—including hysteria, penis envy, masochism, drapetomania and nymphomania. As times change, so do ideas about mental illness. Over the years, some "disorders," such as masturbation and homosexuality, have been voted out. Other problems, such as Inhibited Sexual Desire, have been voted in. In modern America, after all, it can't be healthy not to want sex, and so clinicians now debate degrees of desire. (In the latest DSM, Inhibited Sexual Desire has been split into "hypoactive sexual desire disorder"—meaning you don't want to do it often enough—and "sexual aversion disorder"—meaning you don't want to do it at all). As recently as 1980, the DSM banished Freud's old standby, neurosis, to what psychiatrist Matthew P. Dumont calls "the limbo of disappeared disorders."[12]

The group-vote approach would have something to commend it, however, if enough clinicians actually achieved something like consensus. Unfortunately, all too often clinicians do not agree with each other on what the patient in question is suffering from. The very purpose of the DSM—to improve agreement among clinicians on what, precisely, they are diagnosing—has repeatedly been questioned by research. Two clinicians, independently evaluating a patient's case, should agree that his problem is, say, "agoraphobia with

panic attacks." But if one says that patient has an "obsessive compulsive disorder," the DSM considers those two clinicians in basic
agreement—because they both think the patient suffers in general
from an anxiety disorder. Despite the use of methods that inflate the
chances of agreement (in some studies clinicians' agreement with
one another was boosted by their being allowed to make several
diagnoses instead of just one), the reliability in tests of many of the
DSM's categories, particularly of personality disorders, has consistently been poor. In spite of the DSM's own generous standards of
what constitutes good clinical agreement, not a single major diagnostic category of personality disorders achieved it.[13]

Even with all these problems, a case could be made for the "rich-
clinical-tradition" approach to a compendium of mental disorders—
if the compilers of such a manual acknowledged their professional
biases, the social context of the times, and the subjective enterprise
of labeling people. But the DSM tries to have it both ways. It repeatedly asserts that it is based on science and empirical validation,
while then admitting that little such validation exists.

Some dissenting psychiatrists argue that the whole enterprise is a
foolhardy effort to impose a veneer of science on what is ultimately
an art form. Diagnosis of mental disorder rests on human judgment,
they say, governed by all the wisdom and prejudice that human
judgment involves. "Who can calculate the wasted hours of foolish,
futile discussion about how to compartmentalize patients who never
seem to fit the numbered cubicles in which we are forced by insurers
to place them?" says Matthew Dumont. "[It] is like being forced to
choose from some endless, infernal Chinese menu. . . . Time and
thought are scattered in making differences which make no difference; instead of simple prose to describe our patients, we are forced
to use numbers and an esoteric jargon based on bits of yes-no data
supposedly adding up to a picture of a mental state."[14]

The goal of all the precise numbers and scientific language is to
convey the impression that teams of scientists, rooting around in the
mind, have uncovered the "real" disorders of mental life. The DSM
wants to sound and look like a medical textbook, a purely descriptive
set of problems, as if there were no bias or subjective choice involved. "In fact," says Dumont, "the entire system is an expression
of a theoretical bias so rigid and pervasive that it renders alternative

ways of thinking about mental disorder not just difficult or even impossible, but inconceivable. It has to do with the attention given to the figure rather than the ground, the case rather than the con- text, the individual rather than the social setting."[15]

Well, many people say, so what if a diagnosis is based only on clinical judgment of some people in therapy? What about Emily, who is making such a mess of her life and can't be cheered up? If Self- defeating Personality Disorder describes her pattern of behavior, shouldn't she be treated for it? Dumont's observation, in my view, holds the key to the answers, unlocking precisely what is wrong with Emily's diagnosis. The reason becomes clearer if we shift the focus, as he recommends, from case to context, from individual to setting.

In a series of experiments, psychologist Hope Landrine found that the various personality disorders listed in the DSM neatly fit the roles and stereotypes of several groups in our society.[16] For example, try to imagine the gender, social class, race, and age of a person who meets this description:

> This person is lively and dramatic and is always drawing atten- tion to him/herself. This person is prone to exaggeration and often acts out a role such as the "victim" or the "prince/ss" without being aware of it. This person's behavior is intensely expressed. Minor stimuli give rise to emotional excitability, such as irrational, angry outbursts, or tantrums. This person craves novelty, stimulation, and excitement and quickly be- comes bored with normal routines. At first this person is per- ceived as shallow and lacking genuineness, though superficially charming and appealing. . . . This person is attractive and se- ductive. This individual tries to control the opposite sex or tries to enter into a dependent relationship. Flights into romantic fantasy are common.

This is the DSM's description of a person with Histrionic (formerly Hysterical) Personality Disorder. The chances are that you, like most psychiatrists and nonprofessionals, will envision this person as a single, middle-class young white woman in her early twenties. Who fits this description?

This person passively allows others to assume responsibility for major areas of his/her life because of a lack of self-confidence and an inability to function independently. This person subordinates his/her own needs to those of others on whom he/she is dependent in order to avoid any possibility of having to be self-reliant. This person leaves major decisions to others. For example, this person will typically assume a passive role and allow the spouse to decide where they should live, what kind of job he/she should have, and with which neighbors they should be friendly.

This is not a rendition of Self-defeating Personality Disorder, by the way, but of what the DSM calls Dependent Personality Disorder; if you noticed some overlap, you are not alone. In spite of all those his/her constructions, almost everyone thinks that this passage describes a slightly older, married, middle-class white woman. Everyone agrees that it describes, in a word, a wife.

Now, who fits this description?

This person habitually violates the rights of others. In childhood, this person engaged in frequent lying, stealing, fighting, truancy, and resisting authority. In adolescence, this person showed unusually early or aggressive sexual behavior, excessive drinking, and use of illicit drugs. . . . This person is unable to sustain lasting, close, warm, and responsible relationships with family, friends, or sexual partners.

Most people will say that this description of Antisocial Personality Disorder (formerly known as the Sociopathic or Psychopathic Personality) is typical of young working-class males.

Landrine found, in short, that untrained observers can predict which individuals are most likely to receive a particular personality disorder diagnosis, based only on knowledge of their age, race, class, gender, and marital status. Two categories were divided exclusively by gender: Everyone saw the Self-defeating Personality as a woman and the Sadistic Personality as a man.

But what if personality disorders are simply distributed that way in society? Aren't more married women than married men likely to be dependent, aren't more young single women histrionic, aren't more men sadistic, and aren't more working-class males antisocial? The answer is that if a mental disorder reliably and stereotypically fits a narrow category of people, then we should be looking at what is wrong with the conditions of people in that category, not exclusively at their individual pathologies. For example, instead of asking, "What's wrong with women that makes them excessively dependent in marriage?", we could be asking, "What's wrong with marriage that makes so many women excessively dependent?" (or "Why are we always labeling the caring work that women do as evidence of 'dependency'?").

Landrine offers an example of how easily modern roles can masquerade as mental illness. As the number of divorced, displaced women in society increases—many of whom lack the resources to support themselves and their children adequately—a new disorder might be discovered:

> This hypothetical future category—the Inadequate-Hostile Personality Disorder—will be characterized by disorientation and perplexity, bitterness and hostility; complaints of helplessness; paranoid ideation regarding lawyers, the ex-husband, and men in general, with a subsequent inability to form close and enduring heterosexual attachments; and failure to provide adequate food and shelter for one's children and thus to function as a responsible parent.[17]

Inadequate-Hostile Personality Disorder will (probably!) not be added to the DSM, because everyone knows that most divorces cause tremendous emotional distress and that a life of hardship, let alone of dealing with the courts, can create paranoia and bitterness.

But the DSM's "rich clinical tradition" does not extend the same understanding to its own personality disorders, at least when it comes to women's roles. Three psychologists did a study very similar to Landrine's, and in an early unpublished version of their paper, they had concluded that "it is particularly disturbing that personality disorder behaviors seen as characteristic of women appear to be . . . close enough to society's stereotype of women that *normal women who adopt traditional roles may be receiving personality disorder diagnoses*" (my emphasis). Yet when the paper was later published in *The American Journal of Psychiatry* this statement was gone, replaced only by a bland call for "further research."[18]

Over the years, the American Psychiatric Association has understood that some mental problems are a normal result of particular experiences, not of individual abnormality. The category of Post-traumatic Stress Disorder recognizes that the traumas of war, torture, rape, and other horrific experiences can have long-term psychological consequences, and it places the origins of the sufferer's unhappiness squarely on the traumatic event.

Further, the APA has acknowledged that some "mental disorders" have a social origin and that they properly do not belong in the DSM. When the APA first dropped homosexuality from its list of official Sexual Disorders, it decided to maintain a category called Ego-Dystonic Homosexuality, referring to homosexuals who were unhappy or conflicted about their sexual orientation. In 1987, the DSM-III-R banished even that variation, as well it should have, when its compilers realized that "In the United States almost all people who are homosexual first go though a phase in which their homosexuality is ego-dystonic."[19] In making this change, the DSM-III-R was acknowledging that it is society's discomfort with and outright hatred toward homosexuals that can create their conflicts, not a mental disorder. (Nevertheless, the DSM-III-R couldn't let the matter go completely. Under a category called Sexual Disorder Not Otherwise Specified, one symptom continues to be "persistent and marked distress about one's sexual orientation.") Yet if a black woman came to therapy with persistent and marked distress about being black in a white world, the origin of her conflict would not, should not, be located within her psyche. There is no mental disorder called "ego-dystonic race identity."

A compelling series of wide-ranging studies now suggests that self-defeating behavior and even "choosing to suffer" are often *normal* reactions of people who are reasonably certain (but not positive) that unpleasant things will happen to them in the future and who have had a history of suffering in the past. It's as if they say: "If I shoot myself in the foot now, maybe I won't lose my leg next week." In laboratory experiments, perfectly normal college students will typically choose a masochistic action, giving themselves moderate electric shock, if they think that will offset more severe shock later on or prevent hostility or injury from others.[20] And, granted that plenty of women have been known to treat men miserably, which sex is, in the real world, more likely to experience hostility and injury from the other?

Yet if a woman goes to a psychiatrist complaining of dissatisfaction, conflict, dependency, pessimism, worries about her future, and passivity, she is still likely to be diagnosed as having a personality disorder, and she will probably be given an antidepressant. (And the content of her complaints is likely to be trivialized. One male psychiatrist told a depressed friend of mine that she should "become more active—cleaning the closets would be a good idea.") Women are considered sick if they play their traditional roles too well; correspondingly, men will be considered sick if they won't play their traditional roles at all. Many psychotherapists harshly judge male patients who are unconventional—for example, who deviate from traditional standards of masculinity by staying home with the children while the wife has the paying job.[21]

To illuminate what is fundamentally wrong with the concept of Self-defeating Personality Disorder, let us consider what would happen if female behavior and female role obligations were taken as the norm, the healthy standard for *both* women and men: putting other people first, behaving modestly, appraising the limitations in one's life. Which sex would now suffer the pathology of deviance? As a group of women psychiatrists noted in their protest of Masochistic Personality Disorder, no one has proposed a diagnosis for the "Aggressive, Power-driven, Exploiting Personality" that currently causes so much trouble in the world.[22]

Now someone has. In 1988, psychologist Paula Caplan and sociologist Margrit Eichler invented a new category for the DSM, which they called Delusional Dominating Personality Disorder—DDPD for short. Individuals with this disorder, they suggested, have at least several of the following symptoms:[23]

(1) They are unable to establish and maintain close relationships.

(2) They are unable to identify and express their feelings and to know how other people feel.

(3) They are unable to respond appropriately to the feelings and needs of others.

(4) They use power, silence, withdrawal, or avoidance rather than negotiation in coping with conflict.

(5) They believe that women are responsible for the bad things that happen to them, while the good things are due to their own abilities or efforts.

(6) They need to inflate their importance and achievements (or those of males in general), while needing to deflate the importance of women.

(7) They suffer various delusions, such as:

   A. the delusion of personal entitlement to the services of any woman with whom they are associated.

   B. the delusion that women like to suffer and to be ordered around.

   C. the delusion that physical force is the best method of solving problems.

   D. the delusion that sexual and aggressive impulses are uncontrollable in all males.

(8) They need to affirm their importance by appearing with females who are submissive, conventionally attractive, younger and shorter, and lower on the socioeconomic scale than they.

(9) They have a distorted approach to sexuality, reflected by a pathological need for flattery about their sexual performance and/or the size of their genitals.

(10) They tend to feel inordinately threatened by women who fail to disguise their intelligence.

The standard reaction of most psychiatrists to Caplan and Eichler's proposal was: "Very amusing, dears, but it is a joke, isn't it?" Delusional Dominating Personality Disorder *is* funny, but only in a system which takes masculinity as the norm and regards femininity as abnormal. DDPD is a description of the exaggerated characteristics of the male role; but that is just what Self-defeating Personality Disorder is of the female role.

Caplan and Eichler did not intend to replace a label that is biased against women with one that is biased against men. Rather, they wanted to show that the extreme consequences of rigid male upbringing can cause as many psychological problems as can the consequences of rigid female upbringing. They wanted to emphasize that if you're going to have the latter disorder in the DSM, you had better have the former as well. They wanted to reveal the inherent bias of explaining stereotyped male behavior as a result of social demands on men, while accounting for stereotyped female behavior as a result of an abnormal personality disorder. They wanted to highlight the tendency to blame the woman for what is wrong in a relationship and ignore the man's contribution:

> A woman may find her nonpathological responses to [the behavior of men] pathologized as evidence of her alleged, intra-psychic, individual Self-defeating Personality Disorder; instead, it would be more appropriate to recognize that the problem originates in rigid male socialization and is acted out by the man. Before rushing to give women psychiatric labels, [a clinician should investigate] whether they are living or working with someone who suffers from DDPD.[24]

"Our goal," says Caplan, "is to rethink what is normal and what is healthy." She and Eichler invented Delusional Dominating Personality Disorder as a little consciousness-raising exercise, but soon they began to wonder why it shouldn't be taken seriously. DDPD was invisible, they maintained, "because it characterizes so many of the powerful people in our society."[25] But, after conducting a wide-ranging review of a variety of research studies in many disciplines, they concluded that DDPD affects the mental health and well-being of the many men (and some women) who suffer from it. People afflicted with DDPD—that is, those who adhere to the most extreme standards of the traditional male role—are more likely than others to have health problems, shorter life spans, problems in relationships, and little capacity for intimacy. They often suffer from anxiety, stress, homophobia, self-doubt, insecurity, and competitiveness. They have high rates of drug abuse and violence, including homicide. Surely, said Caplan and Eichler, if any personality pattern is worth labeling a "mental disorder," this one is!

The story is not yet over. On September 19, 1988, psychiatrist Allen Frances, Chair of the Task Force overseeing the *fourth* edition of the DSM, and Harold Alan Pincus, Director of the Office of Research for the American Psychiatric Association, summarized their thoughts about how the revision should proceed. In a memo to the Work Group on Personality Disorders, they began with a positive flurry of admonitions to be scientific:

> Essentially, we are undertaking a scientific assessment project, not unlike the treatment and technology assessment projects undertaken by federal agencies and other medical and scientific societies. It is essential that our efforts proceed in as systematic and scientifically based a manner as possible.[26]

But by the end of the memo, they added that "if the resolution of an issue is not clear . . . then the Work Group will need to resolve the issue based upon the best *available* data, clinical experience and advice from the field."

What were the available data on Self-defeating Personality Disorder? That same year, Frances and a colleague, psychologist Thomas A. Widiger, reviewed the evidence and concluded: "The diagnosis of SDPD [Self-defeating Personality Disorder] lacks conclusive or established empirical support." Of course, they added, this is not a reason to remove it from the DSM:

> It should be recognized though that many of the psychiatric diagnoses lack conclusive empirical support. . . . The inclusion of SDPD was justified with respect to clinical usefulness, education of mental health professionals, suitability for research studies. . . .[27]

By the same logic, Paula Caplan and her colleagues reasoned, the DSM should look favorably on the addition of Delusional Dominating Personality Disorder. Surely it, too, would be useful to clinicians, would educate mental health professionals, and be suitable for stimulating research. So they submitted their proposal, with supporting evidence, to the appropriate Work Group. Psychiatrist John Gunderson, the group's Chair, replied:

I think it's highly unlikely that enough support will be available in time for DSM-IV. . . . [DDPD] has neither a widespread clinical tradition nor a significant clinical literature. These facts mean that it will take even more empirical support to introduce a category such as DDPD. . . .[28]

Caplan responded that there was ample empirical evidence, far more in fact than for Self-defeating Personality Disorder. In a subsequent letter, Gunderson then replied that, in essence, the research wasn't *that* important:

. . . the most formidable obstacle to overcome is the fact that [DDPD] isn't generally recognized—even if the empirical evidence can be completed.[29]

"Even if the empirical evidence can be completed"! When the DSM-IV is published, Self-defeating Personality Disorder is likely to remain in it, and Delusional Dominating Personality Disorder will not have poked its head through the door of the rich clinical tradition in psychiatry.

▪ *How to create a social disease: Are you codependent?*

I used to bitch at my husband to do housework and nothing happened. Now I'm in an intensive treatment program for codependency, and I'm asserting myself very strongly. My husband is more helpful because he knows I'm a codependent and he supports my recovery.

—A Minnesota woman to psychotherapist Harriet Lerner

Over the past five years I have become progressively angrier as I have listened to other women take the rap for what other people, usually their husbands or boyfriends, have done to them. . . . My own circumstances were much like those of other women who have been abused, but I do not consider myself to be sick or diseased. I got out of my situation, but I was lucky. I had a college education and work experience, and I knew that I could get a job and support myself and my daughter. That knowledge helped me call a halt to the destruction within my family.

—A letter from an Oregon woman to the author

Codependency is a national phenomenon. Melody Beattie's 1987 book, *Codependent No More,* and its sequel, *Beyond Codependency,* occupied top spots on *The New York Times* paperback best-seller list for many months. Hundreds of books on codependency have appeared, including Lynne Namka's *The Doormat Syndrome,* Pia Mellody's *Facing Codependence,* and Anne Wilson Schaef's *When Society Becomes an Addict; Escape from Intimacy: The pseudo-relationship addictions; Co-dependence: Misunderstood—mistreated;* and *Escape from Intimacy: Untangling the love addiction.*

Thousands, perhaps millions of people are buying these books and joining recovery groups such as CoDA (Codependents Anonymous) and ACOA (Adult Children of Alcoholics). Codependents are people "addicted to people with addictions." Usually women, they are the "enablers," the partners whose overconcern with their drunken or drug-addicted spouses allows the addiction to continue. They are identifying themselves at social gatherings and support groups as codependents, "in recovery from their addiction." What message do these books convey, and why does it strike such a nerve?

"Codependency" was originally a term that referred to the spouses of alcoholics, who faced specific common problems. The term quickly absorbed the disease language that was being applied to drug addicts, and from there it was only a short leap to cover "love addicts" as well. Today it seems that the codependency bug has bitten virtually everybody: relatives of alcoholics; anyone in a relationship with any sort of "holic" (foodaholic, workaholic, or sexaholic); people living with partners who are mentally disturbed, chronically ill, or, adds Beattie, generally "irresponsible"; parents of rebellious teenagers or children with behavior problems; professionals in helping occupations, and so on.

Oddly enough for a disease that has afflicted so many victims, no one really agrees on what codependency is or defines its symptoms the same way. "There are almost as many definitions of codependency as there are experiences that represent it," says Beattie. Her own definition of a codependent person is "one who has let another person's behavior affect him or her, and who is obsessed with controlling that person's behavior." (This definition excludes only a few saints and hermits.) Codependency is "an addiction to dysfunctional love relationships," says Lynne Namka, "a preoccupation of meeting the needs of other persons to the point of feeling responsible for them at the expense of yourself."

And in a veritable flourish of psychobabble, Anne Wilson Schaef defines codependency as "a disease process whose assumptions, beliefs and lack of spiritual awareness lead to a process of non-living which is progressive."[30] (A disease that holds assumptions? A process of nonliving, which one apparently is mistaken in thinking means "dead," that can progress?) To Schaef, codependency is a "progressive, fatal disease" that covers up other "addictions" to sex and love.

"Some therapists," Beattie acknowledges, "have proclaimed: 'Co-dependency is *anything*, and *everyone* is codependent.'" This is a curious kind of disease; what physician would write a book on diabetes, saying "Diabetes is *anything*, and *everyone* is diabetic"? But codependency writers are not fazed by such matters, which they regard as defensive quibbling. If a woman is skeptical, that's more evidence that she is codependent. "Your judgmentalism," writes Schaef, "is a characteristic of the disease." If this is a disease, it's a very social one: social in manufacture and in treatment.

The vagueness of these definitions makes it easier, of course, for everyone to have at least one of the symptoms of the problem. It is the formula for wildfire fads and best-sellerdom—if everybody has the problem, everybody needs to read about the cure or join the right group. Just as they share the disease view of addiction, codependency books propose a common cure: the Alcoholics Anonymous twelve-step method, based on a "spiritual awakening" in which the sufferer hands over his or her addiction to a "Higher Power" for salvation. Codependency books are full of warm admonitions to forgive yourself, "celebrate your perfection," and give yourself "permission to be precious." Reading these books therefore feels somewhat like listening to friendly sermons that emphasize the healing power of love. They make perfect sense at the time, and the advice is undeniably good; but an hour later the reader is hungry for substance, and she may be forgiven for wondering the next day how to *implement* these wise ideas. Following the Ten Commandments is a good idea too, but history shows the regrettably human gap between knowing what you should do and being able to do it.

I do not wish to disparage any program or belief that helps people take control of their lives, change bad habits, or break a cycle of abuse. And, certainly, codependency programs do alert people to one key cause of their troubles: the network of family relationships that enmeshes them. Individuals in families are part of a pattern of reciprocal influences. When one family member takes on the role of "person with problem" (for example becoming depressed, drinking too much, not working), the spouse—wife *or* husband—will often fall into the corresponding role of rescuer and problem-solver. It is helpful for people to realize that the rescuer role, born out of a natural desire to help the loved relative, can back-fire, making the spouse with the problem feel less competent, more hopeless, more determined to resist help. Moreover, it is essential for people to learn to set limits on the destructive behavior of others.

But family-systems therapy, from which much of codependency language derives, does not regard family conflicts and even destructive patterns of behavior as a result of individual sickness or pathology. It is normal to want to help a family member or friend in trouble; the problem arises only when a spouse becomes *excessively* involved with solving the other person's problems and stops attending to his or her own needs entirely.

The symptoms of codependency, however, do not discriminate between such excessive, self-obliterating behaviors and normal care-taking or healthy selflessness. Take a close look again at the symptoms that the codependency movement wants to "cure"[31]:

(1) You "cover" for another person's bad behavior.
(2) You frequently talk and worry about other people's problems instead of your own.
(3) You take on more responsibility than you should in relationships.
(4) You ignore your own needs to meet someone else's.
(5) You worry that if you leave a relationship, the other person will fall apart.
(6) Your self-esteem depends on what others say and think about you, or on your possessions or job.
(7) You want to be a good person.
(8) You need other people.
(9) You are dependent on your relationships.
(10) You are too unselfish.

The person who has these problems is familiar, all right; she is . . . the stereotypic woman. The qualities of the codependent person are most of the hallmarks of the female role, writ large. They represent a blueprint of the obligations a "good woman" is taught to value and enjoy, the most basic of which is caring for others. They consist of expectations for proper female behavior that form the basis of most women's self-esteem. The many men who "suffer" from needing and caring for their partners have the additional burden of worrying about their "unmanliness."

These symptoms of codependency describe traditional role relations in America. For example, Robin Norwood, in *Women Who Love Too Much,* argues that women who choose abusive or unavailable men, another apparent symptom of codependence, come from "dysfunctional" families in which the father is unavailable and the mother is inadequate. The daughter spends considerable energy trying to win her father's love by being good, helpful, ladylike, and otherwise perfect. As an adult, she pursues men who are unavailable or who treat her abusively, trying to get from them what she didn't get from her father. But if the man does love her, she loses interest. She's self-defeating to boot.

Certainly this description fits the experiences of many women. But is it really for the intrapsychic reason Norwood offers? The pattern of the "absent" father and the "inadequate" (i.e., submissive) mother reflects traditional sex-role patterns characteristic of most middle-class families a generation ago. Countless numbers of parents are now being blamed for "toxic" forms of child-rearing that were simply the expected way of doing things at the time. And as for girls learning to be ladylike, good, and helpful to win the "absent" father's love—well, that's what they learned to win the "present" father's love, and the mother's love, and the love of anyone else who happened to be around. It was the message of the times. Little girls were supposed to be good, period. That was their job.

And what does a codependent have to do to be cured? A Codependents Anonymous leaflet entitled "Ways to Become Less Dependent" reminds group members that "Independence, not dependence, promotes effective living, healthy parenting, and rewarding interpersonal relationships. Similarly, the hallmark of effective marriage is minimal fusion and optimal autonomy."[32] A recovering codependent has learned to:

- Become independent.
- Be selfish without feeling guilty.
- Become self-reliant.
- Live serenely, without being hooked by the unhappiness and problems of others.
- Develop more of a "self."
- Just say no to the demands of others.
- Want to be loved without being needed.

Are these qualities familiar? The codependent-no-more person is . . . the stereotypic male! "For a codependent to be recovered," writer Alison Humes observes, "her heart would not leap at the sound of another's voice or at the prospect of its departure. She would not want or need to be needed. Once she had a sense of herself and others as self-sufficient human beings, and once she was in touch with all of her feelings, she would be able to find and enjoy nonaddictive mature love. That this definition of 'perfection' is so resoundingly male is, of course, suitably ironic."[33]

There, in a nutshell, is the fatal flaw in the codependency movement: It is based on a model of the normalcy of men. "By labeling the traits of caretaking a disease," Humes argues, codependency "leaves no room for a positive view of women's abilities to take care of others." By and large, "caring too much" is regarded as the problem, not the corresponding "illness," caring too little. Some of the men in the codependency movement, such as Earnie Larson, do emphasize the problems for men who are unable to express their feelings, admit their needs, or reveal their affections. In general, however, the movement scolds women for having the very qualities they were raised to cultivate.

I am certainly not saying that the stereotypic role requirements for women and men are just fine—that, for example, because women are traditionally raised to be deferent and self-obliterating, then we should celebrate deference and martyrdom as ideal female qualities. Such extreme adherence to sex roles has harmful consequences for both sexes. But the point is to direct our attention to the straitjacket, not its dutiful wearer.

"The language of codependency," says social psychologist Jacqueline Goodchilds, "is just a modern way of explaining problems that women have had for decades, especially low self-worth and the role requirement to care for, and take care of, others. Women have been raised all their lives to put men first, to take care of everyone else in their lives, to marry the Right Person and happily take on the role of Assistant Person. Then they are surprised to discover that all this subordination of their personalities, abilities, and needs carries a psychological price."[34]

David Schreiber, a psychotherapist who works in a chemical dependency program in Minneapolis, goes even further in assessing the male norm in his industry. "Alcoholics Anonymous, alcoholism theory and subsequently alcoholism treatment were conceived by males for males," Schreiber argues.[35] In treatment, he suggests, the husband enters in a "one-down position" as the "sick" spouse; the wife enters in an effort to help him and help herself. "During treatment," Schreiber says, "the husband heroically fights his 'disease' and graduates from treatment victoriously one-up. Meanwhile the spouse who has joined in treatment is given the 'disease' of co-dependency. Not only has she been given a contrived disease but she is frequently told that she is sicker than her spouse and it will take her longer to get well."

In this respect, Schreiber warns, codependency burdens women rather than liberating them. Women often learn that they are as much to blame for their husbands' problems as their husbands are, because they, the wives, are the enablers. The men themselves, however, are not really held responsible for their abusive, rotten, or violent behavior. After all, as Schaef writes, they have a "progressive disease" and "can't help themselves." This way of looking at relationships reflects a classic aspect of the female role that is entirely too comfortable for many women. The woman takes on the guilt and the responsibility for fixing things; but the man is forgiven, because he can't help himself.

Codependency, like Self-defeating Personality Disorder, is a phenomenon that thrives without any convincing body of evidence to support many of its assumptions. For example, codependency theory began with the assumption that wives of alcoholics fit a specific personality profile. But when researchers conducted controlled studies—comparing the rate of personality disorder among wives of alcoholics with the rate of disturbance among comparably married women whose husbands were not alcoholics—they have generally found that *most* wives of alcoholics are not disturbed, although they certainly have difficulties.[36] Moreover, the wives' ways of coping are highly varied. It is inappropriate, one study concluded, to speak of "the" wife of the alcoholic, and to assume that one form of therapeutic help is suitable to all:

> The research on the wives of alcoholics now seems to indicate that they are women who have essentially normal personalities of different types, rather than of any particular type. . . . In all of this, these women seem much like other women experiencing marital problems.[37]

In a review of recent studies, Edith Gomberg, a psychologist at the Alcohol Research Center of the University of Michigan, puts it more strongly. "There are *no* data at all," she says, to justify diagnosing members of a family in which substance abuse occurs as being "codependent"—that is, having a predictable personality disorder— "solely on the basis of their family membership." If codependency advocates want to claim that most members of such families show dysfunction, they must prove it, not simply assert it. "Where are the data?" Gomberg asks. "There are no surveys, no clinical research, no evaluations; only descriptive, impressionistic statements."[38]

Indeed, the media are full of countless testimonials from people who swear that codependency groups have helped them to leave abusive relationships, raise their self-esteem, make constructive changes, and learn to accept their alcoholic (or otherwise difficult) relatives for what they are:

> I am a recovering Adult Child of Alcoholics (ACOA) who has made tremendous gains by being in an ACOA group. ACOA simply teaches you that you were affected by your past and now it's time to deal with it and get on with your life.
>
> I don't blame my parents for anything. In fact, I have a better relationship with them than I've ever had.
>
> —A letter to *American Health* magazine

I do not doubt these testimonials, and I have read many of them from people all over the country. But there is just as much anecdotal testimony about group pressure to conform, about absurd degrees of parent-blaming, about the failure of the groups to accomplish what they promise, and about the unhappiness of being labeled "sick" and "diseased":

> I am dropping out of recovery. . . . Week after week, I listen to people in our group go over how their parents "abused" them. The abuse ranges from legitimate physical and emotional abuse to the absurd, such as a parent shaking his child's toe to get him to wake up in the morning.
>
> —A letter to *American Health* magazine [39]

> I had a problem with heavy drinking for a while, but now I don't need alcohol the way I did. Whenever I told the group I didn't want to think of myself as "diseased" to the core, but as a basically good person who had had a temporary problem, they would tell me I was "in denial."
>
> —A letter to the author

Nevertheless, it is abundantly clear that the movement satisfies, at least temporarily, the needs of many women and men. It offers community support and solace. It fills a wish to belong. It offers answers that are spiritual as well as psychological. It is anti-establishment. And it holds out the promise of that most optimistic, that most joyful of words: *recovery.* "The disease of codependency is probably millennium fever," writer Wendy Kaminer has observed. "Everybody wants to be reborn, and in recovery, everybody is. No matter how bad you've been in the narcissistic 70's and the acquisitive 80's, no matter how many drugs you've ingested, or sex acts performed, or how much corruption enjoyed, you're still essentially innocent: the divine child inside you is always untouched by the worst of your sins." [40]

So why raise objections to a movement that offers solace, self-help, and salvation? For women in particular, codependency groups offer many of the attractions that consciousness-raising groups did in the 1970s: comfort, support, the chance to share stories, a place to find explanations and strategies for action. "The difference," says psychotherapist Laura Brown, "is that instead of making a political analysis and going out to change the world, women in the twelve-step programs for process addictions only rearrange their internal furniture."[41]

Ultimately, that is both the appeal and the problem of the codependency movement: It does not recognize or confront the social and economic realities in people's lives. It does not distinguish the dependencies that are healthy and desirable (loving and needing others) from those that are economically imposed (such as not having the financial resources to leave a violent marriage). It speaks of self-esteem as if it were air in a balloon, something that can be inflated and deflated by sheer willpower, unrelated to anything that people *do*, to their experiences in the world, to the context of their lives.

Psychologist Stan Katz and writer Aimee Liu, in their book *The Codependency Conspiracy*, offer an excellent example of the consequences in therapy of this failure to recognize the context and origins of a person's unhappiness. An angry black woman, whom they call Miriam, came to Katz for therapy. She had had a troubled, impoverished ghetto life. Her mother, who was a harsh taskmaster to her children, worked thirteen hours a day to stay off welfare, leaving her children with a neighbor who fed them and let them watch TV all day to keep them quiet. Miriam did well in her (segregated) schools and was admitted to a good college, but she flunked out after one semester. Over the next decade, she went from job to job, gaining eighty pounds and becoming increasingly unhappy.

Finally, at a co-worker's suggestion, Miriam went to Overeaters Anonymous, where she learned that her overweight was a result of the low self-esteem her mother had instilled in her. Miriam became angry at last: at her father for abandoning her, at her mother for neglecting and pushing her, at her siblings for their indifference to her, at the lazy babysitting neighbor who overfed her. OA taught Miriam to be angry at her family, Katz points out, but her family was not the real target:

[OA] encouraged her to remember all the small cruelties her mother had inflicted out of desperation for her daughter to make a better life for herself, but not the effect that TV shows about rich white people had had on her. Not the way she'd recoiled when white boys yelled racial epithets at her. Not the moment she realized that being a star pupil at a black school meant nothing on a white campus. Not the countless subtle digs at her intelligence by employers. . . . Miriam was right to be angry, but her family was not the monster.[42]

Miriam's experience in OA is typical of the focus of most codependency groups. Writer Ellen Herman, who attended a number of them, reported: "I rarely heard any speakers in meetings—whether recounting stories of assault, workplace harassment, or matters of the heart—mention directly the realities of physical power, economic inequality, racial bigotry, or sexual coercion, even in instances where these were clearly being described."[43] Instead, many members of these groups are content to reveal their feelings and strive to adjust their feelings to whatever situation is troubling them, as if that were enough.

Codependency's emphasis on inner feelings and Higher Powers underestimates the importance of two outside forces that social scientists have shown to profoundly influence women's self-esteem: children and finances. "A therapist will spend hours and hours with a woman trying to raise her low self-esteem," says Jacqueline Goodchilds, "while both of them totally ignore the importance of kids and money. In many families, the kids are 'hers' and the money is 'his' —that's a virtual recipe for low self-esteem. Money in our society is enabling; it confers power to get your way. Children in our society are disenabling for women—because it's women who often must choose between financial success and family life, and because children are largely their responsibility. There is no evidence that codependent women are suffering from a disease. They are suffering from a lack of resources; they are embedded in a network of family and friends that makes escape very difficult."[44]

The power of that network becomes all too apparent to women who fail (or merely slow down) in their care-taking duties, regardless of whether the responsibilities are major ones, such as caring for aged parents, or smaller ones, such as remembering to get birthday gifts and sending out Christmas cards. The family rarely says, "Oh, well done, Margaret! Now you're showing spunk and independence!" They say, "Where's dinner? Where's my graduation present? Why aren't you visiting your mother more often?"

Codependency's emphasis on fixing feelings obscures the unromantic realities of resources and families. But there is mounting evidence that most of the women who remain stuck in destructive or abusive relationships do so more for these external reasons than for pathological ones. Psychologist Michael Strube reviewed years of research that investigated why women leave abusive relationships—and why they stay (as up to 50 percent do). "Overall," Strube found, "these studies paint a picture of women who lack the economic means to leave an abusive relationship, are willing to tolerate abuse so long as it does not become too severe or involve the children, and who appear to be very committed to making their relationships last."[45] That is, they have been in their relationships a long time, and feel emotionally and economically invested in them; or they are opposed to divorce for religious reasons. Such women also tend to have friends and family who pressure them to stay in the marriage and look disapprovingly on their efforts to leave.

The codependency movement therefore represents a brilliant compromise for some women entrapped in difficult relationships. It gives them permission to think more about their own aspirations and needs, without directly challenging those of others. As Harriet Lerner has noted, our culture dislikes and fears angry women, but it is not threatened by sick women meeting together to get well. "Society is more comfortable with women who feel inadequate, self-doubting, guilty, sick, and 'diseased' than with women who are angry or confronting," she maintains. "Women are too, which is why they eat up these codependency books like popcorn. Women are *so* comfortable saying, 'I am a recovering addict; the problem is in me.' They are so uncomfortable saying that the problem is in society, in their relationships, in their financial standing. Women get much more sympathy and support when they define their problems in medical terms than in political terms."[46]

Certainly that increased sympathy and support is what happened to Anne Wilson Schaef, who is still apologizing for the anger she felt in the first years of feminism. "I went through a phase where I blamed men for my participation in a sexist society," she told a reporter for the *Los Angeles Times.* "I spent a couple of years of my life being a holy terror."[47] The deepest fear of the good girl! She will lose her temper, become a holy terror, and other people will be angry at her! The consummate irony of the codependency movement is that, in the name of curing women's good-little-girl qualities, it rewards women for being the best little girls of all, and not rocking anyone's boat.

Women tend to feel so guilty and anxious about any joyful assertion of themselves as individuals, Lerner argues, that they accompany each small move "out from under" by an unconscious act of apology and penance (as in "I'm so happy he's letting me go to my friend's house for a weekend that I'll never ask him to wash another dish"). "I believe," says Lerner, "that it is an act of deep apology, especially to the dominant group culture, for women to move forward in the name of recovery, addiction and disease."[48] Certainly it has always been safer for women to feel guilty rather than angry. "As long as popular explanations keep saying that the reason for women's unhappiness is in them," Goodchilds concludes, "women won't deal with their real difficulties. Codependency is an effort to solve the problem without changing the situation."[49]

Ironically, but predictably, codependency may not remain a self-help movement for long. A growing number of psychiatrists who treat families of alcoholics argue that paraprofessionals who counsel alcoholics are simply not knowledgeable enough about codependents.[50] These psychiatrists are developing diagnostic criteria for the diagnosis and treatment of the mental disorder of codependency—for a future edition of the DSM.

▪ *Diagnosing the human condition*

> We came to believe that addiction was a metaphor for the ways that stereotypes of maleness and femaleness deprive both men and women of their full humanity. Addiction, eating disorders, phobias, depression, codependency—all began to make some larger sense as metaphors for unworkable gender arrangements.[51]
>
> —Claudia Bepko and Jo-Ann Krestan, *Too Good for Her Own Good*

If the qualities and experiences associated with the female role were regarded as the norm (or at least as being normal) in this society, our interpretations and treatments of "mental disorders" would be different. Consider just a few changes that would occur:

Psychiatrists would be worried about the national epidemic of narcissism.[52] The National Institutes of Health would fund field studies of Sadistic Personality Disorder and Delusional Dominating Personality Disorder, neither of which has currently sparked much interest among the psychiatric establishment.

Thousands and thousands of Independency groups would flourish to help the many men, and some women, who are too independent and too unresponsive to the needs of others. Members would be cured when they recognized the human need to be needed, when they began to put others first, when they valued the importance of doing things for others. Occasional individuals who were *too* self-denying and martyrish would be admitted to the groups, but only to help them tone down their otherwise admirable qualities.

We would not confuse a role obligation with a mental illness; that is, we would not blame women or men for playing their roles too well or for not playing their roles well enough. If enough people within a specific social category begin showing psychological symptoms, we would extend the explanatory courtesy to them that we now extend to most middle-class white men, asking: What is the matter with the category? What can be corrected in the raising of children, in the structure of work, in the conditions of marriage, in the culture of poverty, in the values of society, that causes predictable groups of people to suffer?

We would not segregate "female mental disorders" and "male problems" according to different explanatory languages and treatments. If men and women express loneliness and despair differently, we would recognize and treat the fundamental issue the same way, to the benefit of both sexes.

For example, the failure to see the shared psychological dynamics that underlie drug abuse and suicide attempts, as Silvia Canetto has shown, reflects the reluctance of mental-health professionals to challenge traditional conceptions of female and male psychology. "Recognizing the common denominator linking suicide attempts and substance abuse," she points out, "would mean considering the possibility that some addicted men, like many suicidal women, may feel insecure, helpless, needy, despondent and suicidal; it would mean acknowledging the possibility that women's suicide attempts may be instigated not by a sick personality, but by pathogenic external conditions." [53] And just as we understand that men's drug abuse can be "enabled" by wives, families, and working conditions, she adds, we would have to examine the ways that women's suicide attempts can be enabled by husbands, families, and social environments.

Therapists would therefore encourage clients to look outward to their environments and relationships *as well as* inward to their souls and psyches. Matthew Dumont, the psychiatrist who is so critical of the DSM's pigeonholing system of classifying mental illnesses, describes how this approach works with an extreme case: victims of torture in Chile. Understandably, these men and women are deeply traumatized, anxious, and depressed. The goal of therapy is to relieve their suffering, but at the same time it places that suffering in the context of the forces that have produced it. Instead of classifying patients according to DSM criteria, the therapists classify the objective conditions that define the experience of the victims. "There are some fourteen categories of torture, disappearance, or death that are (unfortunately) meaningful," writes Dumont. "The very identification of the category of repression is an organic part of the treatment process." [54]

People do not need to be victims of torture in order to profit by identifying the circumstances in their lives that maintain their dissatisfactions. This does not mean transforming one set of self-justifying beliefs ("I am hopelessly self-defeating and can't do anything about it") with another ("the system made me what I am and I can't do anything about it"). But it does mean a move away from obsessive self-focus, free-floating blame, and endless wallowing in one's problems, and a move toward taking constructive action where possible. Psychologist Stanton Peele and his associates offer a "Life Process Program for outgrowing destructive habits," an alternative to defining oneself as permanently sick, diseased, or addicted. [55]

Similarly, Stan Katz and Aimee Liu observe that a person may decide that he or she needs to work on improving assertiveness, but, they add, "you may also need to work on changing the situations that are holding you back. This may involve political or legal action. It may mean moving to a more welcoming or safer environment. It may require a career change. It could also mean joining community groups, such as Neighborhood Watch, day-care organizations, or school associations, which have nothing to do with personal recovery —except that they are absolutely vital for *your* personal recovery." [56]

Katz and Liu worry that the codependency movement infantilizes its members by calling them "adult children" and encouraging them, like egotistical toddlers, to see the world largely in terms of "me," "my pains," "my anger." Codependents are advised to "embrace the child within you," say Katz and Liu; they often do not learn how to embrace the adult they must become. Too many Adult Children are at risk of becoming childish adults.

The signature of adulthood, as the codependency movement recognizes in adopting the Serenity Prayer as its motto, is the knowledge of what we can change and what we must live with. It is also the knowledge that self-absorption is its own worst form of self-defeating behavior. Perhaps, in a country that valued the best qualities and skills associated with the roles of women *and* men, the "divine child" inside us that the codependency movement celebrates—that "baby"-boomer—would, at last, grow up.

6

Bedtime Stories

Three fables of female sexuality

Once upon a time, not all that long ago, psychologists, doctors, and advice columnists used to dispense prescriptions for the treatment of sexually "frigid" women. The goal was to warm these women up a little, but not so much that they were in danger of liking sex *too* much. (Women were supposed to travel a narrow pathway between "frigidity" and "nymphomania.") Professional treatises on the problem of female frigidity typically sounded like this:

> Certain women have the capacity to identify completely with their men and are happy in their role as encouraging and contributing companions. . . . They may be the most intelligent and lovely women, but they are unaggressive and not competitive. . . . These women are not frigid, but only after long courting do they allow any intimacies.
>
> In contrast to the woman described, from whom emanates the extraordinary beauty of femin[in]ity, we find the woman with the masculinity complex, characterized by aggressive tendencies and envy of the male. This attitude frequently originates from frustrating experiences in her role as a woman. Even after marriage and the birth of several children, she must find

satisfaction in a job or profession to overcome her unconscious feelings of inferiority towards the male sex. . . . Because of their rebellion towards what they interpret as superiority of the male, [such women] unconsciously and, in some instances, consciously resist a response to the lovemaking of the male. They are either frigid or they respond rarely.[1]

When do you suppose this passage was written—1895? 1925? These comments appear in *Frigidity: Dynamics and treatment,* written in 1969 by a psychiatrist named Fritz Kant. Poor old Dr. Kant's analysis would never be acceptable today to sexologists or to the psychiatrists who compiled the *Diagnostic and Statistical Manual of Mental Disorders.* His language is far too laden with subjectivity and bias, starting right off the bat with the fraught word *frigidity.* It is clearly a pejorative description; the appropriate diagnosis nowadays is Female Sexual Arousal Disorder. (No more pejorative descriptions for men, either. Impotence is out, with its connotations of a power failure, replaced by Male Erectile Disorder.) And of course Kant's clear dislike of women who want jobs *and* families is a dead giveaway of his prejudice that a sexually healthy woman is happiest in her role as wife and mother. Modern readers may also be tickled by his description of proper feminine women, who yield "intimacies" only after long courtship and who then magically and unfrigidly release their sexual passions with the one right man.

Frigidity: Dynamics and treatment almost immediately became an anachronism in the modern era of sex research. William Masters and Virginia Johnson's *Human Sexual Response* had been published three years before, in 1966, and their book on therapy for sexual problems, *Human Sexual Inadequacy,* followed a year later in 1970. These books were widely hailed as a major scientific effort to chart the physiological changes of human sexual response, and to treat sexual problems in a practical and efficient manner. Writing in the cool jargon of science, Masters and Johnson were at pains to strip their language of any semblance of judgmental tone or antifemale bias. Not for them any Kant-like fulminations about rebellious wives or the erotic potential of feminine submissiveness; not for them the nasty name-calling of labels like "frigid" or "nymphomaniac."

Masters and Johnson's work was also widely hailed as an impressive step forward for women, because their research attacked the lingering Victorian view that women are less sexual than men, less responsive, less interested in sex, less capable of feeling desire and enjoying orgasm. The researchers reported that male and female sexual response cycles were virtually identical; that male and female sexual anatomy was analogous in all respects; and that Freud's theory that women must outgrow having childish "clitoral" orgasms in order to achieve mature "vaginal" orgasms was simply untrue.

This was all very good news, and I remember how exhilarating it was to read Masters and Johnson's books in those days. There was something so liberating about them. Just as Alfred Kinsey had done nearly twenty years before, Masters and Johnson conveyed the optimistic message that the scientific method would defeat archaic sexual prejudices; that reason would trounce superstition; and that modern technology was at last revealing the basic sexual similarities between male and female, so that no one could accuse women of being lesser men in this intimate domain.

Masters and Johnson's work on sexuality has had remarkable staying power. Their description of the four-stage human sexual response cycle—it is always spoken of as "the" human sexual response cycle—is taught as fact in medical schools, sexology textbooks, popular sex manuals, and magazines. It constitutes the professional and popular standard of normal sexual response, and deviation from this norm has become the basis on which sexual disorder or dysfunction is determined. And it has, at its heart, the egalitarian assumption that men and women do not differ in their sexual capacity, desires, drive, or responses in any significant way.

It's a persuasive and pervasive view, and it feels intuitively right. Of course, we say, how could we have been so stupid? It's obvious that without Victorian constraints and the pressures of the double standard, women would turn out to be as sexual as men, as responsive, as likely (or unlikely) to enjoy sex, as orgasmic, as bawdy. Remember the Wife of Bath! Mae West! Madonna! Think of all the women who write to Dear Abby complaining of husbands who never want to make love!

Nevertheless, in the last two decades the "sexual similarity" school has been criticized by proponents of a very different perspective. New incarnations of the Victorian view of an almost unbridgeable sexual chasm between women and men have been gathering supporters. The "sexual difference" school currently consists of several groups that are, dare I say, odd bedfellows: sociobiologists, conservative Christians, and cultural feminists. For example, sociobiologist Donald Symons argues that "there is a female human nature and a male human nature and these natures are extraordinarily different, though the differences are to some extent masked . . . by moral injunctions."[2] These two sexual natures, allegedly caused by genetic differences created through forces of evolution, are said to explain, in general, why men "want it" more than women do; why men are fundamentally promiscuous and polygamous, whereas women are faithful and monogamous; and why men are drawn to sexual novelty, kinks, and aggressiveness, whereas women want stability, intimacy, and affection.

Cultural feminists agree that women are worlds apart from men, although not necessarily for genetic and evolutionary reasons. As Alice Echols observes, "Cultural feminists define male and female sexuality as though they were polar opposites. Male sexuality is driven, irresponsible, genitally oriented, and potentially lethal. Female sexuality is muted, diffuse, interpersonally-oriented, and benign. Men crave power and orgasm, while women seek reciprocity and intimacy."[3] According to cultural feminists, female sexuality, left to develop on its own without being restricted by male rules and male dominance, would be loving, tender, romantic, egalitarian, sensual, and committed.

It's a persuasive and pervasive view, and it feels intuitively right. Of course, we say, how could we have been so stupid? It's obvious that women are sexually opposite from men. Most women are turned off by pornography and violence, turned on by their feelings instead of their genitals, faithful and monogamous where men are inherently faithless and promiscuous. Remember Don Juan! Casanova! Errol Flynn! Warren Beatty! And now Wilt Chamberlain claims 20,000 scores! Think of all the women who write to Dear Abby complaining about philandering husbands or mates who are "sex machines"!

Both visions of sexuality—that men and women are fundamentally the same or that they are profoundly, unredeemably different —share the assumption that there is a "real" essence to human sexual behavior, and that culture, society, and learning are mere glosses on that basic nature. They share the idea that we have only to peel away the veneer of culture, the veneer of learning and habit, the veneer of fantasy, and the true sexual being will emerge. Proponents of each side then debate what women's real sexual nature is—chaste or bawdy, emotional or lustful, the same as or different from men's sexual nature—and try to find confirming evidence for their view. This is easy, because there is plenty of evidence for both sides.

It's fun to argue about which sex is "naturally" sexier, but ultimately it is a fruitless debate. The reason, I will argue, is that there is no underlying sexual nature apart from those veneers, and that trying to find one is as impossible as trying to find a "true self" unaffected by the world in which it develops. Our sexuality *is* body, culture, age, learning, habit, fantasies, worries, passions, and the relationships in which all these elements combine. That's why sexuality can change with age, partner, experience, emotions, and sense of perspective.

It's also why theories of sexuality change depending on the perspective of the scientists who construct them. Modern ideas about sexuality are as marked by the biases of their times as the Victorian theories they replaced; it's just that the bias differs. Sociobiologists reduce sexuality to genetic imperatives and universal biological drives. Sexologists tend to reduce sexuality to its component muscles, tissues, arteries, nerve endings, and "magic spots." Fundamentalists and cultural feminists elevate sexuality to a level of spiritual feelings. But theories that explain sexuality almost entirely in terms of the genitals of the participants are just as limited as those that totally ignore the genitals of the participants.

To know whether and how men and women differ in bed, we need to consider the worlds in which they live, not just the parts with which they make love. We need to reconnect the genitals to the person. And we need to consider the eye, and ideology, of the beholder who is observing those parts in action, as the Parable of the Primates reveals.

▪ *The myth of the coy female*

[Thus] we arrived at the important conclusion that polygamy is the natural order among human beings, just as it is in most species of the animal kingdom. . . . monogamy is responsible for the high incidence of divorce and female grievances in modern society, as well as the genetic deevolution and behavioral degeneration of civilization as a whole. . . . Culture is to blame, and fortunately *culture can be changed.* Mating is the key.[4] [Emphasis in original.]

— Sam Kash Kachigan, *The Sexual Matrix*

Sam Kash Kachigan is not a social scientist; he's just a regular fellow who thinks that the theories of sociobiology offer the best hope of improving relations between women and men. "Mating is the key," he argues. The mating he has in mind, it turns out, would (if we were truly to follow our evolutionary heritage) occur between rich old men and beautiful young girls. Among the annoying contemporary practices that Kachigan laments is the habit of beautiful young girls marrying boys their own age. To Kachigan, in any truly civilized society—that is, one in which our practices fit our sociobiological natures—girls would marry men who were old enough to demonstrate their "true potential":

In every respect, then, it makes much more sense for young women to mate with *older* men, who will have *proven* their genetic endowment as well as their financial and emotional capacity for raising children.[5] [Emphasis in original.]

Why do I suspect that Kachigan is such a man?

The basic ideas behind sociobiology date back to Charles Darwin, who in 1871 described what he considered to be a basic dichotomy in the sexual natures of males and females of all species. Males actively pursue females; they are promiscuous; and those who are strongest, most fit in evolutionary terms, succeed in their sexual conquest. Females, said Darwin, are "comparatively passive"[6]; they may choose their preferred suitor, but then remain monogamous and faithful. That this dichotomy conveniently fit Victorian dating and mating patterns was, naturally, pure coincidence.

For a century after Darwin, research on sexual selection and sexual behavior was based on the belief that males are passionate and undiscriminating (any female in a storm will do), whereas females are restrained, cautious, and highly discriminating in their choice of partner (only a male who meets her shopping list of qualifications will do). According to primatologist Sarah Blaffer Hrdy, this stereotype of "the coy female" has persisted in the public mind —and she adds a phrase that by now should be familiar to us— *"despite the accumulation of abundant openly available evidence contradicting it"* (my emphasis).[7]

The stereotype of the coy female got a major boost in an important paper published in 1948 by Angus John Bateman. Bateman was a distinguished plant geneticist who did dozens of experiments with Drosophila, the tiny fruit fly that many people remember from science experiments in junior high school. Bateman found that successful male fruit flies could, with multiple matings, produce nearly three times as many offspring as the most reproductively successful female. As Hrdy explains, "whereas a male could always gain by mating just one more time, and hence benefit from a nature that made him undiscriminatingly eager to mate, a female, already breeding near capacity after just one copulation, could gain little from multiple mating and should be quite uninterested in mating more than once or twice."[8]

What, you may ask, does a human man have in common with a fruit fly? When it comes to sexual strategies, said Bateman, the answer is everything. Generalizing from his sixty-four experiments with Drosophila to all species, Bateman concluded that there is a universally lopsided division in the sexual natures of all creatures, apart from "a few very primitive organisms." Quite simply, males profit, evolutionarily speaking, from frequent mating, and females do not. This is why, said Bateman, "there is nearly always a combination of an undiscriminating eagerness in the males and a discriminating passivity in the females."[9]

The modern field of sociobiology took this idea still further, attempting to account for complex human social arrangements and customs—warfare and corporate raiding, feeding infants and giving children karate lessons—in terms of the individual's basic need to reproduce his or her genes. Women and men, sociobiologists believe, adopt highly different strategies in order to do this. Males compete with other males for access to desirable females, and their goal is to inseminate as many females as possible. Females, in contrast, are motivated to attach themselves to genetically "superior" males because of the female's greater "investment" in terms of time and energy in her offspring; this, according to sociobiologists, is why females are more faithful and nurturant than males.[10] As biologist Ruth Hubbard observes, "Thus, from the seemingly innocent asymmetries between eggs and sperm [say the sociobiologists] flow such major social consequences as female fidelity, male promiscuity, women's disproportional contribution to the care of children, and the unequal distribution of labor by sex."[11]

Sociobiological explanations of competitive, promiscuous men and choosy, inhibited but flirtatious women fit right in with many elements within the popular culture. "And so it was," Hrdy says, "that 'coyness' came to be the single most commonly mentioned attribute of females in the literature on sociobiology."[12]

It all seems a cruel joke of nature. Certainly many people are convinced, as the King of Siam sings in *The King and I*, that the male is like the honeybee, flitting from flower to flower, "gathering all he can," whereas the female has "honey for just one man." But notice that it is the King who sings that song; until relatively recently, no one was asking Queens for their view of things. Nor were male observers asking why, if human females were so naturally chaste, coy, and monogamous, social taboos from ostracism to death had to be placed on females who indulged in forbidden sexual relationships. For that matter, why did nonmarital affairs need to be forbidden anyway, if females have "honey for just one man"?

Sociobiologists attempt to explain human social customs by drawing on research on nonhuman animals, from the fields of primatology, evolutionary biology, anthropology, and related disciplines. In the last two decades, however, there has been an explosion of new research that casts doubt on many sociobiological assumptions, a change that is largely a result of the growing numbers of women who have entered these fields. Most of these women saw animal behavior in a different light from most of the male observers who had preceded them. Male primatologists, for example, had tended to observe and emphasize male-male competition and the number of times the male animals "got lucky"; the female animals, to the human men observing them, seemed mysterious and unpredictable. This is not unlike the ways in which human females have seemed mysterious and unpredictable to the human males who have observed *them*.

At first, women who went into these research fields saw the world as they had been taught to see it, through the academic perspective of their mentors. But after a while, they began to ask different questions and to bring different expectations to their observations. Hrdy recalls her own first glimpse of a female langur

> . . . moving away from her natal group to approach and solicit males in an all-male band. At the time, I had no context for interpreting behavior that merely seemed strange and incomprehensible to my Harvard-trained eyes. Only in time, did I come to realize that such wandering and such seemingly "wanton" behavior were recurring events in the lives of langurs.[13]

Eventually, Hrdy learned that female langurs often leave their troops to join up with bands of males; and she also found that often a female, for reasons unknown, "simply takes a shine to the resident male of a neighboring troop." In fact, female langurs (and many other primate species) are able to shift from being in heat once a month to being continuously receptive for weeks at a time, a state not unlike the first phase of (human) love. In many primates, female receptivity is often *situation specific,* rather than being dependent exclusively on cyclical periods of being in heat.[14]

As a result of the efforts of many pioneers like Hrdy, we now know that the females of many animal species do not behave like the patient, coy fruit fly. On the contrary, the females are sexually ardent and can even be called polyandrous (having many male partners). Further, their sexual behavior does not depend simply on the goal of being fertilized by the male, because in many cases females actively solicit males when they are not ovulating, and even when they are already pregnant. Here are a few illustrations from hundreds of research studies:

- Many species of female birds are promiscuous. In one study, researchers vasectomized the "master" of a blackbird harem . . . but the females nevertheless conceived.
- Many species of female fish are promiscuous. A female shiner perch who is not ovulating will nevertheless mate with many

males, collecting sperm and storing them internally until she is ready to ovulate.

- Many species of female cats, notably leopards, lions, and pumas, are promiscuous. A lioness may mate a hundred times a day with many different partners during the week she is in estrus.
- Many species of female primates are promiscuous. Among savanna baboons and Barbary macaques, females initiate many different brief sexual encounters. Among chimpanzees, Hrdy reports, some females form partnerships with one male, but others engage in communal mating with all males in the vicinity. And among wild tamarin monkeys, a species long thought to be monogamous (at least in captivity), supposedly faithful females will mate with several males. So do female Hanuman langurs, blue monkeys, and redtail monkeys, all primates that were formerly believed to be one-man women. The old notion that primate females typically form "one-male breeding units," as primatologists would say, is now seriously called into question.

In spite of rapidly accumulating evidence that females of many different and varied species do mate "promiscuously" (a word that itself has evaluative overtones), it was not until 1980 or so that researchers realized that this fact threw, well, a monkeywrench into traditional evolutionary theories. Why would females have more copulations than are necessary for conception? Why would they go off with some guy from a neighboring town, whom none of their friends approves of? Why risk losing the genetic father's support by joining the baboon equivalent of Hell's Angels? And the brooding question over all of them, why did female primates develop continuous sexual receptivity?

These questions stimulated a flurry of new theories to explain why female philandering would make as much survival sense as its male counterpart. Most of these new explanations directly resulted from considering the world from the female's point of view. Traditional theories of sexual selection, after all, were based exclusively on the perspective of the male: Males compete for *access* to the female, who apparently is just hanging around waiting to go out and party with the winner. And it's only from a male point of view that multiple female matings can be considered "excessive," or that female sexual interest is even described as her time of "receptivity." Is she passively "receptive" to the active intentions of the male? The word implies that she's just putting up with his annoying lustfulness yet again.

New hypotheses argue that there are genetic benefits for the offspring of sexually adventurous mothers. According to Hrdy's review of these explanations, the "fertility backup" hypothesis assumes that females need sperm from a number of males in order to assure conception by the healthiest sperm. The "inferior cuckold" hypothesis suggests that a female who has a genetically inferior mate will sneak off with a genetically superior male when she is likely to conceive. (I suppose she knows this by the size of his income.) And the "diverse paternity" hypothesis argues that when the environment is unpredictable, females diversify. Over a reproductive lifetime, females who have numerous partners, and thus different fathers for their offspring, improve their offspring's chances for survival.

Other theories look for the social and environmental benefits of female promiscuity to the mother and her infants. The "therapeutic hypothesis" suggests that having lots of partners and multiple orgasms (in some species) makes intercourse and conception more pleasurable, and therefore more likely to occur. The "keep 'em around" hypothesis maintains that females actively solicit lower-status males (with the tacit approval of dominant males), a behavior that prevents weaker males from leaving the group. Hrdy's own favored theory is what she calls the "manipulation hypothesis," the idea that females mate with numerous males precisely because paternity becomes uncertain. The result is that male partners will be more invested in, and tolerant of, the female's infants. This idea, Hrdy explains,

> grew out of a dawning awareness that, first of all, individual females could do a great deal that would affect the survival of their offspring, and second, that males, far from mere dispensers of sperm, were critical features on the landscape where infants died or survived. That is, females were more political, males more nurturing (or at least not neutral), than some earlier versions of sexual selection theory would lead us to suppose.[15]

Both of these points are essential: Not only are females more than passive receptacles of sperm, but also males are more than "mere dispensers of sperm." They don't just mate and run. They have a key role in determining whether infants survive or die. Among primates, there is enormous variation in the extent to which males nurture and protect offspring:

- Among the ruffed lemur, the male tends the nest while the female forages for food.
- Among New World monkeys, males directly care for offspring in half of all species; often, the male is the primary caretaker, carrying the infant on his back, sharing food with it.
- In a rare study of a monogamous species of night monkey, an observer found that during one infant's first week of life, the mother carried it 33 percent of the time, the father 51 percent of the time, and a juvenile member of the troop the remaining time.
- Among baboons, males do not have much direct contact with infants, but they hover nearby protectively and offer what Hrdy calls "quality" time in a very real sense: They increase the infant's chances of survival. They discourage attacks on the infant from males who are unknown, in both the literal and the Biblical sense, to the mother.[16]

Hrdy's "manipulation hypothesis" assumes that primate males respond more benevolently to the offspring of females with whom they have mated, so the females derive obvious benefits from mating with more than one male. In numerous primate species, the mother's multiple sexual partners act like godfathers to the infant, as primatologist Jeanne Altmann calls them.[17] Each of these males will help care for the female's offspring. Baboon males, many of whom could have served as the model for *Three Men and a Baby*, develop special relationships with the infant, carrying it on their backs in times of danger and protecting it from strangers and hazards. These affectionate bonds are possible because of the mother's closeness to the males, says Hrdy, and because the infant comes to trust these males and seek them out.

The manipulation hypothesis may or may not hold up with further research, as Hrdy acknowledges. It certainly does not apply to most human societies, where husbands do not look too kindly on their wives' "special relationships" with other men, let alone their previous lovers, husbands, and wooers. Hrdy's work, nonetheless, shows that theories depend, first and foremost, on what an observer *observes,* and then on how those observations can be blurred by unconscious expectations. Hrdy initially regarded those "wanton" female langurs as aberrations because their behavior did not fit the established theory. Not until researchers began to speculate on the potential benefits of female promiscuity did they come up with different questions and answers about female sexual behavior than had sociobiologists.

In evolutionary biology, if not in the popular press, the myth of the coy female (and, for that matter, the myth of the absent father) is dead. Hrdy is encouraged by the speed with which primatologists, once aware of the male bias that permeated their discipline, have produced "a small stampede by members of both sexes to study female reproductive strategies." This she takes to be a healthy sign, as do I. But Hrdy cautions against "substituting a new set of biases for the old ones":

> That is, among feminist scholars it is now permissible to say that males and females are different, provided one also stipulates that females are more cooperative, more nurturing, more supportive—not to mention equipped with unique moral sensibilities. . . .[18]

Perhaps it is impossible, as biologist Donna Haraway suggests, for any of us to observe the behavior of other species, let alone our own, in a way that does not mirror the assumptions of our own way of life. It is disconcerting, says Hrdy wryly, that primatologists were finding "politically motivated females and nurturing males at roughly the same time that a woman runs for vice president of the United States and [Garry] Trudeau starts to poke fun at 'caring males' in his cartoons."[19] Informally, scientists admit that their prejudices—such as the tendency to identify with the same sex of the species they are studying—affect their research. One woman primatologist told Hrdy, "I sometimes identify with female baboons more than I do with males of my own species."[20]

The recognition of a male-centered bias in primatology and biology proved to be an enormous step forward, allowing scientists of both sexes to revise their theories of animal behavior. Sociobiologists (and their fans like Sam Kash Kachigan) can no longer justify traditional sex roles, particularly male dominance and female nurturance and chastity, by appealing to the universality of such behavior in other species. Other species aren't cooperating.

But that is not the only moral of the Parable of the Primates. The female perspective is invaluable, but, as Hrdy warns, a female-centered bias will provide its own set of distortions. Cultural feminists who look to evolutionary biology to explain women's allegedly sweeter, more cooperative ways are on as shaky ground as the antifeminists they would replace.

If the sociobiological heroine is the coy female who is so different from males, the heroine of modern sexology is the lusty female who is just like them. I like her better, but I'm afraid that she, too, is (as a student of mine once inadvertently said) a fig leaf of the imagination.

▪ *The myth of the lusty female*

> In spite of the widespread and oft-repeated emphasis on the supposed differences between female and male sexuality, we fail to find any anatomic or physiologic basis for such differences. . . . males would be better prepared to understand females, and females to understand males, if they realized that they are alike in their basic anatomy and physiology.[21]
>
> —Kinsey et al., *Sexual Behavior in the Human Female*

Alfred Kinsey, who had built his early reputation as an expert on the gall wasp, regarded sex as an essential, basic drive, and culture as simply an obstacle to the realization of a person's full sexual potential. According to Kinsey, and to most of the sexologists who followed him, that potential is largely a matter of anatomy and physiology:

> . . . this capacity to respond depends upon the existence of end organs of touch in the body surfaces, nerves connecting these

organs with the spinal cord and brain, nerves which extend from the cord to various muscles in the body, and the autonomic nervous system through which still other parts of the body are brought into action.[22]

This idea reverberates throughout Masters and Johnson's books *Human Sexual Response* and *Human Sexual Inadequacy:* Orgasm is just a natural thing, a matter of nerves connected to organs connected to muscles. Orgasm is a normal physiological reflex, at least if it is unimpeded by external trivia like just having argued bitterly with one's lover or lost one's job:

It seems more accurate to consider female orgasmic response as an acceptance of *naturally* occurring stimuli that have been given erotic significance by an individual sexual value system than to depict it as a learned response.[23] [My emphasis.]

Similarly, sex therapist Helen Singer Kaplan observed:

It is the aim of sexual therapy to allow couples to experience the *natural* unfolding of their sexual responses. . . .[24] [My emphasis.]

One of the major reasons for the emphasis in modern sex research on physiology—on the "naturalness" and universality of sexual response—is that the study of human sexuality has never been and still is not a socially acceptable enterprise. Because sexologists are often relegated to low status within academia, they must continually keep an eye on what research projects will achieve respect, and which ones will get funded.

Sexologists found an answer in physiology. It is not easy to get grant money and promotions if you propose to ask adults intimate questions about their preferred methods of intercourse, birth control, subjective kinds of orgasm, homosexuality, childhood sexual experiences and education, coercive sex, age of sexual initiation, and other sensitive topics. But hardly anyone will be personally offended if you want to study lordosis in the female rat or the bulbocavernosus reflex in the male person. (If you don't know what those terms mean, that's the point.) In this century, writes sociologist Janice Irvine, sexologists have invoked "the mystique of science" in the hope that "scientific methodology will render acceptable their research into issues that mainstream society often considers unacceptable."[25]

To be sure, much of the research of modern sexologists has been of unquestioned benefit to women and to men. "In the era in which Kinsey was writing," Irvine observes, "his use of orgasm as a measuring unit for women's sexuality was progressive. Given the aura of shame around female sexuality, and the lack of widespread support for women's pleasure, modifying the basic sexual yardstick for research on women could have underscored the popular impression that women's sexuality was more 'diffuse' and orgasm less important for them. By retaining orgasm as the measure for both groups, he conveyed the legitimacy and importance of the female orgasm."[26] Although *Sexual Behavior in the Human Female* was published in a particularly repressive time for women, she adds, "Kinsey discussed their sexual pleasure, separated the concept of sexual pleasure from reproduction, cited the pleasures of masturbation, and regarded women as sexual agents." Moreover, Kinsey's work forced people to confront the evidence that normal human sexual behavior is enormously diverse and cannot be stereotyped into simple pairs of categories labeled his and hers, good and bad, healthy and sick.

This research had many benefits and fit a growing trend toward egalitarianism and the equal rights of women. In twentieth-century scientific sexology, the vision of sexual sameness was replacing the Victorian notion of different but complementary, yet both served the same goal: to perpetuate and justify existing relations between the sexes.

Thus, in the Victorian era as among conservative Christians today, sex complementarity was considered the foundation of marriage: Naturally lustful men need naturally chaste women to control male sexuality and keep it within family bounds. In the modern era, erotic equality has become the foundation of marriage; men and women, equally lustful by nature, should together enjoy the pleasures of sex to keep the couple committed to each other. Both views of sexuality compete today, reflecting society's deep schism on the proper role and status of women in the family and in society. Each side looks to what is "natural" in human sexuality to justify its vision of ideal family relations.

And yet, many critics have argued that the scientific vision of sexual sameness—as represented most famously by "the" sexual response cycle—is not really a model of equality at all, but a way of making female sexual experience conform to a male model of normalcy. They maintain that the goal of sexology in this century was to show, as psychologist Leonore Tiefer observes, that "women have sexual needs and desires just like men, and that, no surprise and how convenient, women's sexual needs and desires were just like men's, albeit a bit slower." [27]

Researchers in the sexual-sameness school, eager to achieve scientific credibility and promote sexual equality, consistently had difficulty explaining the differences they *did* find between women and men. For example, Kinsey explained women's lesser frequency of having orgasms, of watching pornography, or of having masturbated in terms of women's lesser "sexual capacity." He attributed the difference largely to this biological origin, not, as he acknowledged elsewhere was the case, to the systematic ways in which women are taught to avoid, dislike, or feel ambivalent about sex. The vast cultural difference in what men and women learn about sex and in the expectations placed upon them was not a difference that mattered.

Like Kinsey, Masters and Johnson downplayed the social and emotional context in which "sexual capacity" exists; such context merely "interfered" with "natural" responses. But they disagreed with Kinsey's assertion of the lesser sexual capacity of women, arguing instead that the woman's capacity for sexual response "infinitely surpasses that of man," because she can have multiple orgasms until exhaustion, small children, or a persistent telephone make her stop. Yet they did not highlight this finding as a significant difference between the sexes. To Masters and Johnson, women's greater sexual capacity offset any sexual problems a woman might have in a culture that discourages female sexuality, let alone in a relationship based on an inequality of power and influence. So it all comes out "equal," more or less.

Thus, throughout *Human Sexual Inadequacy,* as Janice Irvine observes, Masters and Johnson assume that the couples they treat are of equal standing in the marriage. If the woman occasionally seems to be at a disadvantage, her lesser power is canceled out by her superior sexual capacity. According to Irvine, Masters and Johnson's sympathies "lie almost exclusively with men, whom they perceive as bearing an unconscionable responsibility for sexual interaction. While they rarely criticize sexual violence or the oppression of women, they constantly rail against the disproportionate sexual burden shouldered by men."[28]

For example, Masters and Johnson warned against two beliefs that interfere with "natural sexual interaction" and are "a constant deterrent to effective sexual expression": the fallacies "that men by divine guidance and infallible instinct are able to discern exactly what a woman wants sexually and when she wants it" and "that sexual expertise is the man's responsibility."[29] Now, I completely agree that many men and their partners do suffer from the expectation that men are instinctively supposed to be good lovers and sex experts. Indeed, this fact is further evidence against the idea that sexuality is "natural." But where is the "constant deterrent to effective sexual expression" of *women*'s frequent feelings of being unattractive, worried, and insecure?

In spite of Masters and Johnson's efforts to expunge all traces of subjectivity, in spite of their façade of pure science, they revealed their own biases in terms of what they chose to emphasize, what they chose to omit, and what they chose to construe as the problems in relationships. Perhaps the most significant bias in Masters and Johnson's work was the fact that they did not conduct their research in order *to find out* what the normal sexual response cycle was for men and women. They accepted only those volunteers who met their *predetermined* notions of normalcy—for instance, who were readily orgasmic. They then described "the" complete sexual response cycle as consisting of four stages, which were theoretically the same for men and women: excitement; plateau; orgasm; and resolution.

This four-stage description seems intuitively obvious and physiologically inevitable, but it has proved to be neither. As Irvine says, "by positing a response cycle with four distinct phases that entail specific physiological correlates, Masters and Johnson were stretching their data to support their construct. Their research does not clearly show physiological changes occurring in discrete stages rather than as progressive phenomena."[30] Historian Paul Robinson has argued that the very notion of four distinct stages is based on "groundless differentiation" that Masters and Johnson were unable to document scientifically.[31]

Moreover, the four stages were not really the same for men and women. Masters and Johnson themselves had noted that men require a recuperation phase after orgasm (lasting somewhere between a few minutes and a few weeks) before they are able to return to the plateau and orgasm phases; whereas many women, with properly continued stimulation, can continue having orgasms. In fact, there is no evidence of a distinct plateau stage for men or that all women can and want to have multiple orgasms. Masters and Johnson invented a phase of male sexual response that was comparable to women's in order to maintain the equality of their theory of the four stages.

Before long other sexologists, such as Helen Singer Kaplan, were discovering that the problem most people were having in their sex lives was not being unable to do it, but not wanting to do it. Accordingly, these clinicians added "desire" to the start of the sequence, on the grounds that people need to want to have sex before they can become excited about it. So the current, revised four-stage version of "the" sexual response cycle consists of desire, excitement, orgasm, and resolution.

These four-stage descriptions represent an attempt to impose order and predictability on varied sexual responses; to describe a basic similarity between the sexes; and to document the biological naturalness of sexual response. But the effort is like trying to find discrete bands on a rainbow; there are many ways to draw the distinctions among colors (should we keep yellow and gold together, or separate them?). As psychologist Carole Wade says, "These 'stages' are not like the stages of a washing machine. You don't hear a 'click click' when it shifts to a new phase of the cycle."[32] What, exactly, is the desire phase, and how long does it last before shading into something else? Four weeks of anticipating a lover's return? A five-minute fantasy during a busy workday? And why must desire be the first phase, anyhow? Many tired adults, desiring nothing so much as a good night's sleep, find that sexual desire can *follow* arousal when their partners start fondling them fondly under the covers.

To see how arbitrary four-stage concepts of sexual response can be, let us try to describe the biological stages involved in eating a meal. We decide to divide this experience into four phases: feeling hungry, preparing food, consuming the food, and relaxing in stuffed aftermath. Does that sequence seem inevitable? What about the more common one: seeing food, *then* feeling hungry, then not eating because one is on a diet? To extend the analogy, would anyone want to argue that the experience of eating is the same for women and men in American society? Not when the great majority of women, far more than men, are worried about weight, the presentation of self while eating ("feminine" women are expected to eat small and dainty portions), and health.

The biology of eating and digestion is certainly of interest. But if we focus only on biology and sweep away all other factors as merely being cultural influences on eating, we lose sight of everything that makes food and eating *human* experiences: rules about who may eat with whom, and when, and how often; the emotional meaning of food; the pleasure and danger of eating; food taboos and rituals; inhibitions and body image. This is why it is not informative enough to say that hunger and eating are "natural." In everyday life, many people who are hungry choose not to eat (if they are following a religious ritual or are confronted with food they consider disgusting) and many people who aren't hungry do eat (if a persuasive friend or tempting sandwich turns up).

Of course, Masters and Johnson understood that men and women bring emotional feelings to their sexual experiences, and that sex with a beloved partner, a prostitute, a one-night stand, or a dildo will subjectively feel very different. But their focus was on the physiological similarity of orgasms, however they occur. As Masters said in an early interview, "We had one girl who became orgasmic by rubbing the small of her back. So you could say we have a small-of-the-back orgasm, a clitoral orgasm, a vaginal orgasm, a fantasy orgasm—but they're all the same kettle of fish. Physiologically, they're identical."[33]

Although Masters went on to add that "There is no such thing as the pure physiology of sexual response, except as a textbook concept," that "textbook concept" soon became the dominant model of understanding sexuality. New techniques for research and treatment were developed, designed on the assumption that the most significant aspects of sexuality are physiological.

For example, the photoplethysmograph, a device that measures female arousal and vaginal lubrication, has been used to measure sexual arousal in women who are watching erotic films. Researchers have reported that some women deny that they are aroused when the photoplethysmograph clearly says they are. Whom to believe—the woman or the machine? "It is a quintessential reduction of sex to the biophysical," says Irvine, "where lubrication equals arousal."[34] Although the two often go together, they aren't inseparable. Many women can be aroused without lubricating; and lubricating is not always a sign of sexual arousal. It can also be a response to nervousness, excitement, or fear. Similarly, a man can have an erection without feeling sexually aroused, as a response to fear, anger, exercise, or waking up. But it is easier to measure physiological changes than emotional states, and so physiology tends to become the major indication of whether "the sexual response cycle" is working or not.

The relegation of experience and subjectivity to background factors affecting sexual response has had major consequences in the diagnosis of sexual dysfunction. Scientific efforts to categorize and label sexual disorders are, by definition, subjective decisions because they depend on criteria for sexual normalcy, which change with the times. A century ago, some Victorian doctors believed that orgasm in women was abnormal and harmful, and that orgasmic women should rush off to doctors to be treated. Today, most sexologists assert that lack of orgasm in women is abnormal and harmful, and that nonorgasmic women should rush off to doctors to be treated. A century ago, most Victorian doctors believed that masturbation was a practice that could cause "masturbatory insanity"; terrible treatments were invented to keep people from masturbating. Now masturbation is advocated as a healthy activity and a treatment in its own right.

The history of the DSM shows the changing notions in contemporary times of what constitutes a sexual disorder. Early editions, published in 1952 and 1968, contained only two kinds of sexual problems: dyspareunia (pain during intercourse) and impotence. But the Third-Revised edition of the DSM (1987) contains fully six pages of sexual "dysfunctions." As the DSM states in its introduction to this group of disorders, "The essential feature of this subclass is inhibition in the appetitive or psychophysiologic changes that characterize the complete sexual response cycle."[35] Disorders are defined as deviations from this cycle.

The language of the DSM's descriptions of disorders is intended to be value-free and scrupulously gender-equal: Men and women each can have equal difficulties with desire (not wanting sex), arousal (not being able to sustain desire), orgasm (not having one), and pain during intercourse. Recently, however, Leonore Tiefer has deftly dissected some of the hidden lessons about sexuality that are conveyed by the DSM's superficially neutral tone and criteria for having a disorder.[36]

The basic message, says Tiefer, is "that sexuality is apparently universal, unlearned and innate." It's just a matter of tinkering with the right button or stimulating the right gizmo. Of course, if the complete sexual response cycle is so natural, it's hard to explain why the DSM estimates that "approximately 20% of the total population have Hypoactive Sexual Desire Disorder [i.e., they have very little interest in having sex at all], 30% of the male population have Premature Ejaculation and that approximately 30% of the female population have Inhibited Female Orgasm."[37] That's a lot of people who aren't doing what comes naturally.

Second, Tiefer observes, the DSM defines sexuality as the reactions of unconnected body parts. Symptoms of dysfunction include "failure to attain or maintain the lubrication-swelling response of sexual excitement . . ."; "Recurrent or persistent involuntary spasm of the musculature of the outer third of the vagina that interferes with coitus"; ". . . an inability to reach orgasm in the vagina"; "Persistent or recurrent ejaculation with minimal sexual stimulation . . ." and so on. "Despite the bodily obsession throughout this terminology," Tiefer explains,

> the body as a whole has no meaning, but instead has become a fragmented collection of disconnected physical parts which pop in and out at different points in the performance sequence. This compartmentalization of sexual experience lends itself easily to mechanical imagery, to framing sexuality as smooth operation and integration of complex machines, and to seeing problems of sexuality as "machines in disrepair," needing to be evaluated by high-technology part-healers. Much of the mystification of sexuality inherent in the DSM conceptualization derives from this segmented physiologizing, and its inference

that you don't understand sexuality if you don't know a lot about tissues and organs.

Thus, she adds, the DSM never speaks of "men and women," but only of "males and females," as if human sexuality were comparable to that of beagles or rabbits. The one mention of "woman" in the 1980 manual was deleted in later editions. "No 'women' appear in 1987," says Tiefer, "but one additional 'vagina' and a new term, 'penetration.' "

The third hidden message about sexuality in the DSM, says Tiefer, is the focus on the performance of the genitals. "Every category except for sexual desire mentions genitals in one way or another," she observes. "This nomenclature implies that when the genitals perform correctly, there is no sexual problem, and it asserts that when the genitals are not performing properly, there *is* a sexual problem." This vision of healthy sexuality is common in our society, but it by no means applies to everyone. People's genitals can "work," producing the requisite orgasm, but is there really no sexual problem if one partner is using intercourse to control, manipulate, or dominate the other? And what about people who, for reasons of disability, sexual variety, fatigue, or personal preference, happily enjoy non-genitally-focused sexual episodes?

The DSM regards intercourse as *the* normal sexual activity; therefore, failures in intercourse automatically become dysfunctions. "Inhibited male orgasm" refers to an inability to reach orgasm in the vagina. Women who achieve orgasm only with "noncoital" manual stimulation are sometimes considered to have a "normal variation of the female sexual response" and sometimes considered to have a "psychological inhibition that justifies the diagnosis" of Inhibited Female Orgasm. Well, which is it? The DSM admits that this is a "difficult judgment" for the clinician to make.[38] Still, its unmistakable attitude is that the ideal way for women to achieve orgasm is during intercourse, with a penis. But as Carole Wade observes, "Sex is not a soccer game. The use of hands is permitted." For many women the use of hands is required. Manual clitoral stimulation, apart from or during coitus, is for them an essential way, and a perfectly fine way, to have orgasm.

Finally, the most significant message about sexuality in the DSM is what the manual doesn't say. "Although the language of the DSM implies that women's sexuality is as important as men's," Tiefer concludes, "women's actual sexual *experiences* are absent. There's nothing in the DSM about emotion or communication, about whole-body experience, about danger and taboo, about commitment, about attraction, for heaven's sake, about sexual knowledge, about safety, about respect, about feelings about bodies, about breast cycles or pregnancy or contraception or getting old. The only tiny references to age are under 'Inhibited *male* orgasm' and 'premature ejaculation,' where the clinician is reminded to take age into account!"

The DSM, following the trail of Kinsey and Masters and Johnson, emphasizes sexual biology and assumes that men and women are "equal." Men and women may be equal in their capacities and future possibilities, but they are not the same. As Tiefer says, "Women, lacking equal opportunity for sexual freedom and social encouragement to experiment, burdened with poorer physical self-image and a weakened bargaining position in their intimate relationships, frequently traumatized by past sexual exploitation, and harassed by insecure reproductive rights and a limited window of sexual attractiveness, come to sexual opportunities disadvantaged compared to men."

A reader of the DSM would never know this. In assessing a woman's repeated failure to reach orgasm, the clinician is directed to consider whether she has had "a normal sexual excitement phase . . . that the clinician judges to be adequate in focus, intensity, and duration"[39]: nothing about whether she has had adequate emotional support, birth control, participation in family decisions, sleep, affection, or freedom from fear. In contrast, the 1971 edition of *Our Bodies, Ourselves* reminded women that " 'Frigidity' in bed is not divorced from the social realities we experience all the time. When we feel powerless and inferior in a relationship, it is not surprising that we feel humiliated and unsatisfied in bed. . . . there is no reason to expect this sense of inferiority and inadequacy to go away between the sheets."[40]

Nor is there anything in the DSM about the insecurities of men, such as the relentless cultural pressure on men to have the right erections at the right time, right on demand, the right way, for the right length of time. There is nothing about the social and sexual consequences for men of living in a society in which masculinity is primarily defined by the behavior of their penises. "Men don't want to have an erection to dry their socks on," says Tiefer, who works with men who have come to a urology clinic for treatment for impotence. "They want it because they feel the *natural* expression of masculinity is to have one for the practice of heterosexual intercourse. Knowing one can have an erection for intercourse, whether one does it or not, is being a man." [41]

Ultimately, the scientific enterprise of reducing sex to its component physiological elements—the goal of much of modern sexology—itself reflects a traditional male vision of genitally focused sexuality. As *Dragnet*'s Joe Friday might have said, "Just the parts, ma'am, just the parts." But in sexuality, the whole is greater than the sum of its parts.

"The DSM's choice to argue that anatomy is destiny once again limits women," says Tiefer. "Just because they've got orgasm in there doesn't mean this is a pro-woman document." The DSM's view of human sexuality, she adds, is easily summarized: "Men and women are the same, and they're all men." [42]

▪ *The parable of the G Spot*

Several years ago, Leonore Tiefer and I became interested in the brouhaha about the G Spot, among professionals and the public, and we conducted an investigation of the story behind its brief rise and fall. It's a good story, one that illuminates the passions and personal interests that research on sexuality evokes, especially female sexuality. And it highlights the problems of trying to determine whether female sexuality is "like" male sexuality or another kettle of fish entirely.

In September of 1982, Holt, Rinehart & Winston published *The G Spot and Other Recent Discoveries About Human Sexuality*. The authors—Alice K. Ladas, Beverly Whipple, and John D. Perry—argued that there is a small area in the anterior wall of the vagina that is sensitive to deep pressure. They named it the G Spot after Ernest Grafenberg, the gynecologist who first described such an erogenous zone in 1950. When properly stimulated, the authors maintained, this area (variously described by proSpot sexologists as the size of a dime, a quarter, or a half-dollar, perhaps depending on a woman's income) swells and triggers orgasm. Some Spotted women apparently ejaculate at the moment of orgasm, too. This ejaculate, the authors claimed, comes from "prostate-like" tissue in the vaginal wall, and the fluid that is expelled is neither vaginal lubrication nor urine. *The G Spot* told readers that every women has the Spot and can have a new kind of orgasm, if she only applies persistence, practice, and, in a pinch, a device available from the authors for several hundred dollars. No one seemed to wonder why, if the G Spot is so elusive that route maps and exercises are required to find it, it could be so important or common.

If today you were to read a sexuality textbook, a popular paperback on sexuality, or a catalog of sex toys, the chances are good that you would find an assumption that the G Spot is a certified, documented aspect of female sexuality. You might read that its existence is "controversial," but even discussing it as a "debate" confers its legitimacy in the realm of serious scientific issues. Thus, almost all college-level sexuality textbooks mention the G Spot in their index and text; a few of the more scholarly books are skeptical and critical, but the majority are neither. One even offers instructions for students who want to find their Spots.

Likewise, many popular sex books take the spot for granted: Lonnie Barbach's *For Each Other* offers a "G spot stimulation exercise" and Alan and Donna Brauer's *Extended Sexual Orgasm* has a section on "locating the inner trigger—the G spot." (The Brauers' intensive two-day seminars promise to teach participants "The art of using the wonderful G-Spot. The basic digital strokes.") Some vibrators can be outfitted with an attachment called the G-Spotter. In 1989, *Mademoiselle* ran a story with the cover line: "Paradise found? Hot flash on the G-Spot." That same year, a survey of 1,289 professional women in the United States and Canada found that the majority believed that the G Spot exists and that they had "experienced the sensations associated with its stimulation"—including having multiple orgasms and a spurt of fluid at moment of orgasm.[43]

The story of the G Spot, book and phenomenon, reflects three vulnerabilities in American society, which the book's three authors represented and exploited:

■ *Alice Ladas, the Reichian "bioenergeticist":* Enter the vaginal-clitoral debate—what is the "right" kind of orgasm and where does it happen? After a decade of clitoral ascendancy, the G Spot came down on behalf of vaginal sensitivity, which the Reichians had been saying all along. Orgasm was back in the vagina, where it belongs, with a penis to help produce it. *Playboy* actually declared that "the G Spot may help free women from the clitoral tyranny that has been imposed by Masters and Johnson, Hite, and others." This conservative news made *The G Spot* safe enough for seven book clubs, including *Cooking & Crafts* and *Better Homes & Gardens.*

■ *Beverly Whipple, the nurse (now psychologist):* Enter the American obsession with sexual normalcy and the search for medical authority to define it. Whipple first drew attention to the G-Spot phenomenon by personally demonstrating female ejaculation to interested researchers at sexology conventions. But of course it would have been unscientific to say, "Hey, I've got a special spot and I bet you do, too!" She assumed that the phenomenon that is normal for some women is normal for all women.

■ *John D. Perry, the psychologist-entrepreneur:* Enter the technological fix for every problem. Having trouble reaching the "right" kind of orgasm? Modern science is at hand to help. Perry, a biofeedback practitioner, had invented a machine for exercising the pubococcygeus (PC) muscles, the group of muscles that women and men use to stop the flow of urine. In 1952, a gynecologist named Arnold H. Kegel had argued that exercising the PC muscles not only cured urinary stress incontinence (an involuntary release of urine when a person laughs, exercises, or makes love) but also enhanced sexual pleasure. Perry was trying to market Kegel's idea in the form of an "Electric Perineometer" that would measure the strength of the PC muscles.

When Whipple's G met Perry's PC, the magic equation was made: $G = PC^2$. Although there is no demonstrated connection between the alleged G Spot and the PC muscles, the authors created their own link: "We assume every woman has a G Spot and every man has a prostate gland. The way they function depends, in part, on the state of the surrounding muscles."[44] This was a pretty bit of pettifoggery, because now the authors could prattle on about the "importance of healthy pelvic muscles" and, most of all, sell equipment to shape up those flabby PCs. (One's finger is an acceptable "substitute," they noted, but asserted without proof that there are "substantial advantages" to having a mechanical device.) Clinicians could buy the expensive office model, the Clinical Perineometer, for $2,500. Individuals could buy a Personal Perineometer for "private PC muscle training" for $750, or a Pocket Perineometer, presumably useful on camping trips or long car rides, for merely $450. These gadgets did all but beep when they hit the Spot.

It was too perfect. The American mania for fitness met the American anxiety about sex, and found an "electromyographic feedback mechanism" to unite them. It was also too good to be true, and it wasn't. To date, research finds that:

- The G Spot is not characteristic of all women.
- Of those who do have a "sensitive area," most do not "ejaculate" —i.e., produce a fluid at orgasm. And for most of the women who do produce fluid upon stimulation of the sensitive area, this response does not always occur with orgasm.
- In those who "ejaculate," the fluid has proved to contain urine in all cases.
- There is no scientific evidence that strong PC muscles have anything whatsoever to do with orgasmic responsiveness.[45]
- There is enormous anatomical and orgasmic variation among women, and enormous debate among scientists about the nature of, and even the name of, many details of sexual anatomy. They don't even agree on what they're talking about, much less on what it does.

How did the G Spot become a "new medical discovery"? Let's start with Ernest Grafenberg and his 1950 article in *The International Journal of Sexology*, "The Role of [the] Urethra in Female Orgasm." What's this? The urethra? Grafenberg thought there was a sensitive spot, all right, an "erotogenic zone," but he said it was "along the urethra in the anterior vaginal wall"; that a "clear transparent fluid" was expelled "not from the vulva, but out of the urethra in gushes";

and that these gushes were not urine, "but only secretions of the intra-urethral glands."

Is a spot on the boundary between California and Oregon a Californian spot or an Oregonian spot? The anterior side of the vagina and the urethra share the same wall; is it a vaginal spot or a urethral spot? Little suspecting that he would one day lend his name to a bit of territory on this border, Grafenberg went on to write: "Innumerable erotogenic spots are distributed all over the body, from where sexual satisfaction can be elicited; . . . There is no part of the female body which does not give sexual response."[46] But by siding, as it were, with the urethra, Grafenberg lost all possible sex appeal for his new erotogenic zone. Who would ever buy *The U Spot?* Who would want *The Sensuous Urethra?* In this business, timing and titles are all.

Grafenberg's article was greeted with resounding silence in the professional literature for twenty-eight years (although both Kinsey and Masters and Johnson paused to acknowledge, and discredit, the popular belief that some females ejaculate). In particular, few picked up Grafenberg's sensational remark that *"There is no part of the female body which does not give sexual response."* This view of female sexuality was, after all, increasingly at odds with the growing ideology among sex researchers that male and female sexuality were basically the same, and basically a matter of how the genitals were working.

Then, in 1978, *The Journal of Sex Research* published a short article called "Concerning Female Ejaculation and the Female Prostate." Its authors, a female law student named J. Lowndes Sevely and a biology professor named J. W. Bennett, reviewed the historically recurring belief, from Aristotle to Victorian pornography, that some women do *something* akin to male ejaculation. Sevely and Bennett concluded that women have a "glandular structure" similar to the male prostate that produces a female version of ejaculation, but they offered no new evidence to support their claim.

In 1981, *The Journal of Sex Research* published three more articles on female ejaculation, each one noteworthy for its lack of scientific rigor. The first paper was a collection of anecdotes. The second paper consisted of a study of *one* woman by *six* researchers (including Belzer, Whipple, and Perry). Four of the researchers watched as the woman's husband manually stimulated her "sensitive spot," which "led to expulsion of liquid, and reportedly and apparently to orgasm, on several occasions." Biochemical analysis showed that this fluid had a higher level of prostatic acid phosphatase (PAP) than urine, which indeed seemed to suggest that the woman had prostate-like tissue somewhere. In addition, blindfolded observers sniffed the liquid and said they thought it wasn't urine.

The third paper, by Perry and Whipple, was based on reports of forty-seven women who knew all about the G Spot and PC muscles from their sexual self-help classes. All we are told about the women is their average age; nothing about their sexual or gynecological histories. But the authors did explain in detail how to do a G-Spot exam: ". . . it is often necessary to press deeply into the tissue to reach the spot." Now, this is interesting—such pressure not only reaches the alleged spot but also stimulates the urethra. "It is sometimes necessary to continue palpation for a minute or more before the spot begins to swell to a discernible size and shape." After such deep, relentless pressure, all of the women revealed G-Spot sensitivity.[47]

After these articles were published, the G Spot went national with a bang. The media, of course, could not resist an idea as sensational as female ejaculation. The risk of publishing a true story too late outweighed the risk of publishing a false story too soon; everyone feared being caught with their pants down on this one. With few exceptions, such as Linda Wolfe's account of "The Next Sexual Hype" in *New York* magazine, no one waited for anything as boring as scientific verification. *The Philadelphia Inquirer* inquired favorably, as did *Omni, Playgirl* ("Look Freud, No Hands"), and the sex magazines. In September of 1981, Whipple appeared on the Donahue show, drawing more than five thousand letters in the months afterward.

All the hoopla, however, was making it difficult for a team of researchers who were trying to conduct a serious investigation of Spot theory. They were having trouble finding volunteers; many women had to be rejected because they were too suggestible. "After hearing mass media accounts of female ejaculation," the researchers noted, "they thought they might be ejaculating. In fact they were merely lubricating."[48]

Nevertheless, by June 1982 that scientific study was ready—and the first failure to verify the G Spot and female ejaculation was reported at a meeting of the Society of Sex Therapy and Research. The paper was written by psychologist Daniel C. Goldberg and six others, including Whipple. Goldberg had asked Whipple herself to train two female gynecologists in Spot detection. The gynecologists then examined eleven volunteers: six women who said they had a G Spot and did ejaculate, and five women who said they didn't. Most important for the scientific method, the examiners did not know which women were which.

The gynecologists found something like a G Spot—a sensitive area on the anterior wall of the vagina—in four of the eleven women: in two women who said they were ejaculators, and in two who were not. The volunteers were then left alone and asked to stimulate themselves to orgasm, expelling into a container any ejaculated fluid. Six of the women produced such a liquid. It was, the lab tests revealed, "chemically indistinguishable from urine." Goldberg and his colleagues concluded that the notion of a G Spot was "partially supported. . . . Yet another view is that the Grafenberg spot may not exist at all, but represents nonspecific soft tissue irregularities which can be expected in some women."[49]

Here was a fix for the G-Spotters, who were about to publish their book. "The Grafenberg spot may not exist at all" contradicted "We assume every woman has a G Spot." Finding that the female ejaculate was "indistinguishable from urine" certainly contradicted the argument that it was *not* urine. What to do? Perry responded that the gynecologists hadn't been trained properly (even though Whipple herself trained them); that they needed days of training, not merely hours (even though readers of the book are told that the method is easy to learn); and that the problem was that the women weren't sexually aroused (although everywhere else he said that stimulating the Spot causes arousal).

And so *The G Spot* was published on schedule in 1982, with a first printing of 150,000. At that time, the sum total of professionally published evidence consisted of a historical review; some anecdotal hearsay; a case study of a single "ejaculator"; Perry and Whipple's sample of proSpot women; and one scientific experiment that disputed the whole business (this study was omitted from the book). The authors do say that they personally had examined 400 women, all of whom revealed their Spots. We are given no particulars or statistics about these mysterious 400 women, and Perry and Whipple never published anything else about them in any scientific publication.

The G Spot soon faded from public attention, having had its allotted minutes in the limelight, but a small coterie of determined investigators has remained convinced of its sexual importance. Sevely went on to write her own book in 1987, *Eve's Secret: A new theory of female sexuality*. You can guess what the secret is, and whether the theory was any newer than Whipple and Perry's, or for that matter Grafenberg's.

Others have turned their attention to the prostate-like glands in women, called Skene's glands, which are fewer and less densely packed than men's. ProSpotters keep referring to these glands as the "female prostate," to underscore their argument that women and men have analogous structures with analogous capacities. Thus, sexologist Theresa Crenshaw and psychiatrist Desmond Heath claimed to have found prostatic acid phosphatase (PAP) in tissue dissections of corpses.[50] (Perry had earlier protected himself against his own expectation that the dissections would fail to find a Spot. Most anatomical studies are done on the cadavers of elderly women, Perry told [Penthouse] *Forum*, "whose Grafenberg spot has long since degenerated." *Degenerated?* Now the Spot has a use-it-or-lose-it quality?) And a team of Czechoslovakian physicians reported that the "female prostate" produces a higher fructose level than is normally present in urine, although they admit that the "female ejaculate" contains nowhere near the levels of fructose that are present in male ejaculate.[51]

Unfortunately for this line of reasoning, the presence of PAP in tissue (alive or dead) does not tell us anything about the erotic or ejaculatory capacity of that tissue. Moreover, the fact that women have Skene's glands does not mean that these glands are comparable to the male's or that all women have the capacity to ejaculate. Heli Alzate, a South American physician and sexologist, argues that there is no advantage in calling Skene's glands the "female prostate." It is, he says, "as semantically confusing as calling the clitoris the 'female penis.'"[52] Needless to say, no one has ever called the penis the "male clitoris," or the prostate "the male Skene's glands."

This effort to find precise anatomical parallels between men and women has required researchers to make some pretty fancy two-steps around their own evidence. Just as Masters and Johnson imposed their assumption of similarity on men's and women's sexual responses, so do some G-Spotters try to impose anatomical uniformity on evidence of remarkable diversity. The diversity does not simply divide men and women; it occurs within each sex.

For instance, Milan Zaviačič and his colleagues examined twenty-seven women who volunteered to be manually stimulated by the physicians. "A specifically sensitive site (the G-Spot) was located in all 27 women," the researchers reported, consisting of "a manually detectable tumescence." Although all of the women had urinated prior to the experimental stimulations, Zaviačič noted that "the urge for micturition occurred frequently at the very beginning of friction and became more intensive with continued stimulation."[53] Recall that this result of G Spot stimulation is common, because the urethra is being pressed firmly.

If all those women showed their Spots, it sure sounds like vindication for Perry and Whipple. But the findings got more interesting. Seventeen of the women (63 percent) *failed* to produce "urethral expulsions," in spite of four lengthy bouts of manual stimulation and the fact that "the G-spot was easily found in every one of these women." Of the ten women who did produce expulsions, three managed to do so only after stimulation of at least fifteen minutes. Five produced expulsions, which they called "almost agreeable sensation[s]," but without sexual arousal or orgasm. Only two of the original twenty-seven women "ejaculated" easily and quickly, after a minute or two of stimulation, along with accompanying orgasms. One of them, nevertheless, "repeatedly stressed that ejaculat[i]on does not represent the climax of her sexual reaction."[54]

What in the world is going on here?

Many sexologists today regard the G Spot as the most extreme and ludicrous reduction of female sexuality to the male norm—complete with its own kind of ejaculation. They think it is an anatomical oddity, an individual quirk of sexual response. Alzate and colleague Maria Londoño, who believe there is "erotic sensitivity" on both walls of the vagina, vigorously reject the notion of "female ejaculation," which they consider "an interesting but unusual" phenomenon that exists in "a few atypical women."[55] Similarly, Zwi Hoch, an Israeli sex researcher, concludes that "The 'G spot' does not exist as such. . . . The entire extent of the anterior wall of the vagina (rather than one specific spot), as well as the more deeply situated tissues, including the urinary bladder and urethral region, are extremely sensitive."[56]

Yet other commentators believe that this attitude reflects an intellectual coverup, a refusal to take seriously an important aspect of female sexuality, or even a biased determination to maintain the hegemony of the clitoral orgasm. Sociologist Mark Winton believes that the evidence for the G Spot is simply too threatening both to modern sexology and to feminism.[57] Feminists don't want to return to the bad old Freudian days of the "vaginal orgasm," he argues, whereas sexologists find the G Spot and female ejaculation inconsistent with their current theories of sexuality, and therefore regard female ejaculation as an abnormality.

Tiefer and I believe that the story of the G Spot nicely highlights the unfortunate consequences of trying to explain sexuality in terms of the right anatomical configuration and a single paradigm of normal response. The urethral, G-Spot orgasm superseded the clitoral orgasm, which replaced the vaginal orgasm. Each of these efforts to determine the precise latitude and longitude of orgasm, and to impose the politically correct version, was successful while it suited the goals of specific interest groups—Freudians, Reichians, sexologists, cultural and radical feminists, physicians. Each theory proved to be helpful to women who felt that their intimate experiences were vindicated at last. But each theory also proved to be misguided.

The reason, as Grafenberg himself acknowledged so long ago, is that sex occurs in many places, beginning in the brain and including, but not limited to, various interesting anatomical parts. A touch on the knee by a creepy stranger will feel unpleasant and disgusting, but the same touch by an exciting new date will feel incredibly erotic. The identical physiological sensation produces entirely different perceptions and hence experiences. Yet would anyone argue that orgasm depends on correct knee stimulation? Or that all women can and should have knee orgasms? Similarly, in the case of the G Spot, one woman may learn to associate the urge to urinate and stimulation of the urethra with sexual arousal and pleasure; for another, the *same sensation* will not feel erotic at all. The variation occurs in the mind, not in genital anatomy.

The G Spot was popular because it pandered to the popular notion that sex is in the cells. Psychology is so complicated. You have to pay attention to your desires, and motives, and fears. Lust and passion are enigmatic and fickle. But oh for a G Spot! Like the clitoris did before it, it promises unlimited bliss. All you have to do is push the right button, once you find it.

■ *Beyond sexual "natures"*

My opinion is that the American public, both male and female, was afraid to read the [Kinsey] report on female sexuality because it was afraid to confront what it knew it would find there—confirmation of the unsettling idea that in their sexual behavior women are just as good, or bad, as men.[58]

—Commentator in the *Herald Tribune*, 1958

The fables of sexuality that keep recurring in our society serve a purpose, for they justify their storytellers' notions of what is right, of what should be. To do this, they must persuade us that their story is the universal one, the natural one. I think that the results of this effort are often misguided, misleading, and harmful.

Instead of trying to pin down the fundamental nature of men and women, we would do well to put the person back into the study of sex—that rich and complex individual, wandering around somewhere between generalities about the nature of all "women" and "men" and subcutaneous specifics about tissues, organs, and nerve endings. What might such a vision of sexuality include? How can we find our way between theories that impose a vision of unrealistic sameness on men and women and those that impose a vision of hopeless disparity?

To begin with, we might stop comparing women to men and start comparing men to women. Doing so would allow us to recognize, for one thing, the variety of male sexual responses. Some men achieve tremendous waves of sexual sensation and pleasure from whole-body stimulation. They have different kinds of orgasms. They don't necessarily zoom from 0 to 60 in seven seconds, charging as fast as they can along the main highway to a destination; some prefer slow meandering along the byways, seeing what they can discover en route.

Some men like fairly rough fondling of the scrotum; others don't want their partners anywhere near it. Some are quick to reach orgasm; others take much more time. Some learned their sexual habits by speed-masturbating through *Lady Chatterley's Lover;* others were trained on the *Kama Sutra*.

An appreciation of male diversity in sexual response would help to dispel the prevalent myth that male sexuality is natural, unlearned, and entirely beyond a man's control. This myth harms both sexes. It is cruel to women, for it justifies sexual coercion and rape, and it requires women to learn to "manage" and control male sexuality instead of putting the responsibility for men's behavior squarely on men. The myth is also cruel to men, many of whom are desperately afraid of hearing that something psychological might be affecting their sexual responsiveness. Many men, when their parts slow down or stop "performing," believe that there is nothing they can do short of surgery or implants to get the machinery working again.[59]

In approaching sexual problems, we would begin with the common concerns that people have with sex: feelings of insecurity, unattractiveness, anger, and fear; fatigue, overwork, and conflicting pressures; inability to relax; uncertainties about birth control; and living with three children under the age of five.[60] Couples who are sexually dissatisfied can learn not only squeeze techniques and new positions; they can also learn how to ask questions about their relationships in and out of bed. Who (usually or always) makes decisions, who sets the pace? Is there mutuality and consent or does one partner feel coerced, however subtly? Does sex make one person feel powerful at the expense of the other? Is one worried about losing attractiveness, or losing the partner?

We would include women's perspectives in our notions of what constitutes sexual dysfunction, incorporating the problems that women repeatedly describe in surveys: lack of tenderness; partner is interested only in orgasm; partner can't kiss; partner is too hasty; partner has no sense of romance.[61]

We would not only regard sexuality in terms of frequencies of orgasms or numbers of acts, interesting though these may be; we would also examine the motives and feelings behind the behaviors. For example, teenage girls are having sexual intercourse nearly as often as boys are. But what does this finding mean from the perspective of the participants? Is it a sign of equality or pressure? Are both sexes enjoying sex as much and as often, or is one sex worried about her reputation, getting pregnant, and whether he will leave her if she doesn't "put out"? Are both sexes having sex for the sheer pleasure of it, or is one sex worried about his masculinity, virility, and whether she will leave him if he doesn't "make a move"?

We would turn our attention to the external forces that make male and female sexuality different *at this time* in this society—not only the more obvious ones, such as the pervasiveness of sexual harassment and physical danger for women, but also the subtle influences. Are women really encouraged to be as sexual as men? "Slut," "whore," "bitch," and countless other terms still thrive in the popular lingo, applying only to women; yet there is not a single specific word of opprobrium for the sexual behavior of males.

In fact, in spite of living in a culture that seems sexually obsessed, many women still do not even accurately name their genitals. At best, little girls are taught that they have a vagina, which becomes the word for everything "down there"; they rarely learn they also have a vulva and clitoris.[62] (Men have many words for their genitals, and none of them are vague.) And as we have seen, the scientific and popular descriptions of menstruation and menopause are almost uniformly told in a language of loss and deterioration. Should we then be surprised that many women are vulnerable to the diagnoses, labels, and theories provided by experts? That they worry about having the "correct" kind of orgasm? That they confuse lubrication with ejaculation—and, who knows, the latter for the former? As writer Lucy Bland observed, "We face a past and a present in which there has never been a *language* allowing us to think about and define women's sexuality."[63]

Conversely, we would look at the influences that make male and female sexuality more similar over the life span. Consider one sex difference long thought to be the hallmark of our species: that men generally want sex for the physical pleasure of it and women generally want sex for the emotional intimacy of it. Studies of adolescents and young adults usually show this pattern, at least on the average. But people change over the years; more women start enjoying sex for physical pleasure and more men start enjoying the emotional closeness. By observing such changes in the meaning and variety of sexual experience, we can see that sexuality is not necessarily a permanent pattern that is inherent in the individual.

Finally, we would move toward a more generous definition of sex, one that does not try to categorize people as being by nature sexy or sensuous, victim or victimizer, chaste or lusty. Instead of trying to find the universal essences of human sexuality, we would do well to frame the issues in more constructive ways. The question is not whether women are more or less sexual than men. (The answer to that is yes, no, both, and sometimes.) The questions are: What are the conditions that allow women and men to enjoy sex in safety, with self-confidence, and in a spirit of delight? And how do we get there?

"The most positive thing we women have retrieved from the nineteenth century is that sex is about enjoying ourselves," said the English writer Wendy Faulkner. "Let us get on with it."[64]

Love's Experts, Love's Victims

How women cornered the love market

A friend of mine, whom I will call Roberta, has been mildly unhappy for years about one flaw in her otherwise excellent husband, Henry. The flaw rises and falls in importance to her, depending on Roberta's state of mind and general stresses, but it has long been a chronic irritant. Henry's problem is that he doesn't like to "chitchat," as he puts it. This means, Roberta explains, that he doesn't like to gossip about friends and family, he doesn't like to analyze his marriage on a weekly or even yearly basis, he doesn't like to talk about his feelings, and the only time he ever said "I love you" was back in 1974, when he proposed marriage. Once, pressed to reveal his passions, Henry said, "I vote with my feet. If I didn't love you, I wouldn't be here."

Instead of killing Henry at that moment, which was her inclination, Roberta did what she usually does: She called a woman friend, and they met for lunch to discuss Henry. Several hours later, Roberta emerged refreshed, invigorated, and prepared to cope with Henry for another few months.

. . .

When I was growing up, the stereotype was that men had all the great and true friendships: Damon and Pythias, Hamlet and Horatio, Butch Cassidy and the Sundance Kid. Male friendships were said to be based on male bonding, true and faithful camaraderie, and sturdy affection, whereas women's friendships were shallow, trivial, competitive, and vain. Anthropologist Lionel Tiger advanced his view, in *Men in Groups,* that "male bonding" originated in prehistoric male hunting groups and lingers today in their modern equivalents: sports, politics, business, and bars. Because females do not "bond" in the same way, their friendships are a shadow of the real (male) thing.

When I was growing up, the stereotype said that men were the great romantics, the great lovers. Devoted Rhett Butler was more admirable than the heartless Scarlett; adoring Cyrano de Bergerac was superior to the superficial Roxanne; self-sacrificing Sydney Carton did the far, far better thing than his Lucie would ever do. Women, being interested mainly in marrying a meal ticket, were said to be pragmatic and fickle. What did they know of true love?

When I was growing up, social scientists maintained that men were "instrumental" and "task-oriented," whereas women were "expressive" and "person-oriented." This was a fancier way of saying that men were best suited for work and women were best suited for motherhood. Experts explained that such a division of emotional and physical labor was an ideal arrangement for family life, although, overall and if the truth be told, being expressive and person-oriented was not as healthy or desirable as being instrumental and task-oriented.

With the rise of cultural feminism in the late 1970s and 1980s, many people began to argue that women's ways of expressing love and having friendships were better and healthier than men's. They no longer regarded women's ease with self-disclosure and talking about feelings as evidence of weakness but of strength. As we saw, Carol Gilligan and Nancy Chodorow argued persuasively that women are better at love because of their skill at connection, whereas men have trouble with attachments because they are reared to overvalue independence and fear connection. Studies were finding that women's style of intimacy brought them moral support, protected their mental and physical health, and made them easier to talk to. Both men and women, it was found, feel better after talking things over with a woman.

As a result, it was not long before we saw the rise of the "deficit approach" to men's ability to love. A typical article of the 1970s lamented "The inexpressive male: A tragedy of American society," and new theories suggested that men have a "trained incapacity to share."[1] Research began emphasizing the competition, rivalry, emotional inhibition, and aggression that men bring to their friendships and love affairs, in contrast to the emotional honesty and mutual support that women bring to theirs.

Today, it is female friendships that are celebrated as being deep, intimate, and true, based as they are on shared feelings and confidences and on women's allegedly greater capacity for connection with others. Today, male friendships are scorned for being superficial and trivial, based as they are on shared interest in, say, the Detroit Tigers, Michelle Pfeiffer, and classic E-type Jaguars. Today, love is the one domain in which women are thought to excel and to represent the healthy model of normalcy, while men are pathologized —the poor souls who can't love, don't express themselves, and won't allow themselves to become intimate. Roberta, with her emotional demands for "talk" and "love," used to be the problem. Now, for many women, she is the solution, and it is Henry who is the problem.

The new stereotype of Woman as Intimacy Expert is part of the women-are-better movement that has transformed activities formerly thought to illustrate female deficiency into female strength. On the surface, the stereotype praises women, and certainly it validates much that is true of women's experience. Yet both sexes sacrifice a great deal to maintain this stereotype, and the reasons that it has prevailed throughout our society have little to do with either gender's native abilities or deficits. To find the reasons, we need to stop asking "Which sex is better at love? Whose emotional style is better?" and ask instead: What are the consequences for women and men of the belief that women are the intimacy experts, the love experts? What are the consequences in a family when one partner demands and pursues intimacy, and the other retreats into silence? Why, if women's ways of loving are so normal and desirable, aren't men rushing out to buy books to fix themselves, books called *Men Who Love Too Little?*

It is not my intention to take away from women the one area in which they have approval to excel: the realm of nurturance, love, and caretaking. Although "women's ways of loving" have much to commend them, they must be put in perspective. The misunderstandings between women and men on matters of love and intimacy are often very funny, but they are no joke. They are part of a system that relegates the sexes to separate spheres of expertise: the intimate world of love for her, the public world of work for him. This schism is unfortunate for all concerned, because the two spheres, which represent equally valuable activities, are not equally valued in our society. Women's alleged superiority in love is a sop given to women in a system that regards love and care as fluffy topics to begin with, suitable for women's magazines, greeting cards, and sermons.

▪ The feminizing of love

> Dear Abby: Another St. Valentine's Day has come and gone without flowers, candy or any kind of a valentine from my husband. I'm 25 and he is 26, and we've been married for three years. I'd have been thrilled if he had brought me a flower—or even handed me a valentine—but he ignored the day completely. . . . He's a super guy, hard-working and decent, so maybe I shouldn't complain. But it sure would have felt great to have been remembered on St. Valentine's Day. Any suggestions?[2]
>
> —Nobody's Valentine

"Nobody's Valentine" is in good company, but I wonder whether she would be consoled to know that 85 percent of all valentine cards are purchased by women.[3] This is a fascinating statistic. Why aren't more men buying valentines? And why do so many women want them so much?

"Nobody's Valentine" is the target audience for countless books and articles that offer to help women learn to understand, manage, or change men and get them to be more "loving," at least as women define loving—by revealing their feelings. The cover line on an issue of *Self* magazine is typical: Right after "Breakthrough! The easiest diet!" and "6 Steps to a GREAT BODY!" is *"Get him to talk— tonight."*

Of course, for all the women who are asking, "Why won't he talk to me? Why won't he say he loves me?" there is a corresponding number of men who are complaining, "Why doesn't she shut up? Why does she keep needing reassurance that I love her?" Many women say that their greatest wish for their marriages is that their husbands be more intimate, better at communication. "If only my husband would tell me what he is thinking," they say, "everything would be perfect." For their part, men say, "If only she were happy, if only she would stop complaining, everything would be fine. She expects me to read her mind and know why she is unhappy; I'm truly baffled by what she says she wants."

Underlying these reciprocal complaints is the real problem: that men and women tend to define intimacy and express love differently. For many men, love is action: doing things for the other person. For many women, love is talking: acknowledging the immediate feeling of the other person's adorableness.

For example, psychotherapist Richard Driscoll, in *The Binds That Tie,* describes the following scene: A wife, Paula, asks her husband, Don, if he "really" loves her. Don tries to give her an honest answer: " 'I know I want to be married to you. I am satisfied to go to work every morning, because I know that I am supporting you and that you are there for me. I would never want to leave you, and I would never want you to leave me. Is that what you mean by love?' This answer leaves her unsatisfied. 'But why can't you say you *love* me?' " Yet, as Driscoll points out, Don did in fact say he loved her, but in his own words rather than in her words.

Paula did not see this, says Driscoll, because "she thinks of love as a feeling" and "he thinks of it as a commitment to being with a woman and working to provide for her."[4] This is one reason, he believes, that many men are reluctant to say "I love you," at least with the frequency women do. Repeating this phrase daily or on demand from a woman, says Driscoll, "sounds stupid to them. After it has been said once, these gents argue, there's no reason to repeat it over and over like a trained seal yapping on cue from a handler."[5]

Here is another husband, participating with his wife in a study of love. He says:

What does she want? Proof? She's got it, hasn't she? Would I be knocking myself out to get things for her—like to keep up this house—if I didn't love her? Why does a man do things like that if not because he loves his wife and kids? I swear, I can't figure what she wants.

But his wife says:

It is not enough that he supports us and takes care of us. I appreciate that, but I want him to share things with me. I need for him to tell me his feelings.[6]

What men *do,* every day of their lives, simply doesn't feel like love to this wife, to Driscoll's client Paula, and to Nobody's Valentine, who knows but discounts the fact that her husband is "hard-working and decent."

The resulting misunderstandings between couples occur daily in countless households. In one study, seven couples recorded their activities and marital satisfaction for several days.[7] Every day, they noted down how often the spouse did a helpful chore, like cooking a good meal or repairing a faucet; how often the spouse expressed affection; and how satisfied they were feeling with the marriage. The wives thought their marital relations were best on days when their husbands had verbally expressed affection to them, regardless of what the husbands *did.* But the husbands' degree of satisfaction depended on their wives' deeds, not on their affectionate words!

The researchers then directed the husbands to step up the frequency of expressions of love toward their wives, and asked the wives to keep track of any such demonstrations they noticed. After a while, they called up the husbands whose wives said there had been no change, and asked them why they had not complied with instructions. One husband replied huffily that he certainly had complied . . . by washing his wife's car. The husband thought that was a perfectly good way to express his love for her, but she, of course, hadn't a clue.

The doing-versus-talking distinction in the emotional styles of males and females begins in childhood, when boys tend to develop what psychologists call "side-by-side" relationships, in which intimacy means sharing the same activity—sports, games, watching a movie or sports event together, bantering and joking. Girls tend to prefer "face-to-face" relationships, in which intimacy means revealing ideas and emotions in a heart-to-heart exchange. As adults, women may have a tough time understanding that for many men a "shared intimate activity" can be something as banal as watching TV or being in the same room together doing different things. Words are irrelevant, even superfluous. As a woman I interviewed said:

> My husband and I have a custom of reading the papers and having coffee together every morning. He loves to listen to music in the background, so the radio is usually on. I don't like the music especially—I'd rather have quiet—but I know how much he does. One morning, though, the radio was annoying me, so I got up to read the paper in the other room. My husband protested immediately—"Where are you going?" I said I was leaving so he could enjoy his concert. "Never mind the music," he said, rather crossly, "come back here and I'll turn it off." His tone made me feel cranky, until I realized what he was really saying—he'd rather share the morning with me than with the radio.

This woman is fortunate that she got his message. Being together comfortably is the soul of intimacy to him.

For most women, in contrast, intimacy rests on talk—both "deep talk" about significant feelings and worries and "small talk" about daily events. Without it, many women feel like unwatered plants; they wither. So do their relationships. A common refrain in the explanations divorced women give for the failure of their marriages is "lack of communication." A bad marriage, they say, is by definition one in which there is "no talking."[8]

Moreover, women demand a particular kind of talk. When men talk to each other or to women, they tend to discuss relatively impersonal matters, such as cars, sports, work, and politics. When they reveal anything about themselves, it tends to be their strengths and achievements. Women like to talk about personal matters, such as their feelings and relationships; they are willing, often eager, to reveal weaknesses and fears. When a woman is worried, the first thing she does is call a friend to discuss it. When a man is worried, the first thing he does is distract himself by watching TV, playing racquetball, or drinking with his buddies.

In short, some of the basic functions of talk are different for men and women. For many men, the purpose of talking about feelings and problems is to solve them; for many women, the purpose of talking is to talk—simply to share the feeling. When women report the benefits of intimate conversation, they list relief from stress, feeling better, and self-improvement. The benefits that men report are more constructive, such as getting advice or help in solving problems. Thus, when a woman describes her worries, fears, or anger about a problem, she is often seeking confirmation of her *feeling;* the man interprets her talk as a request for *help.*[9]

In her book *You Just Don't Understand,* Deborah Tannen describes the story of a woman, Eve, who had had a lump removed from her breast. Eve tells her sister, a woman friend, and her husband, Mark, how upsetting it was to undergo the operation, and how unhappy she is with the stitches and the changed contour of her breast. The sister says, "I know. When I had my operation I felt the same way." The friend says, "I know. It's like your body has been violated." But Mark says, "You can have plastic surgery to cover up the scar and restore the shape of your breast." Mark's comment makes Eve feel hurt and angry; she thinks it means he is disgusted with how she looks. But of course he thinks *she* is disgusted with the way she looks and he wants to be helpful. "Eve wanted the gift of understanding," Tannen observes, "but Mark gave her the gift of advice. He was taking the role of problem solver, whereas she simply wanted confirmation for her feelings."[10]

Men and women speak different languages of love, but in psychotherapy, research, and popular lore, the female language has become the dominant one. Women appear to be better than men at intimacy because intimacy is defined as what women do: talk, express feelings, and disclose personal concerns. Intimacy is rarely defined as sharing activities, being helpful, doing useful work, or enjoying companionable silence. Because of this bias, men rarely get credit for the kinds of loving actions that are more typical of them.

"Part of the reason that men seem so much less loving than women," argues Francesca Cancian, a sociologist and author of *Love in America,* "is that men's behavior is measured with a feminine ruler."[11] Many social scientists, she shows, use what she calls "a feminized definition of love" in their research: For instance, they label practical activities and helping the spouse as "instrumental behavior" and expressing feelings as "affectionate behavior." This distinction, she observes, thereby denies the affectionate aspect of practical help.

Yet most men are more likely than women to agree with statements like "When she needs help I help her" and "She would rather spend her time with me than with anyone else" as evidence of the love in their relationships. Many men define "commitment" not as constant reassurances of love, but as the daily work they do to support their families. "Many working-class women agree with men that a man's job is something he does out of love for his family," Cancian observes. "But middle-class women and social scientists rarely recognize men's practical help as a form of love."[12]

To observe this bias in action, consider the following test of "intimacy maturity" in marriage. A team of psychologists evaluates couples according to five components of intimacy: orientation to the other person and to the relationship; caring and concern; sexuality; commitment; and communication. On each dimension, a person is scored as being at one of three levels of maturity: from egocentric and self-serving at the low end to most mature at the high end. "Most mature" reflects "an ability to integrate conflicting needs, cope with frustrations, and value the partner for his or her unique qualities."[13]

Although the five elements of intimacy are different, all of them, including sexuality, are evaluated primarily according to the couples' *feelings* and how well the couples express themselves. People who describe their sex lives only in terms of frequency or variety are being "self-focused," and get a low score. Couples get a high score on sexuality for, among other things, "*talking freely* about the sexual relationship with the partner" and placing "a high value *on the expression of tenderness.*"

The communication component of intimacy, according to the researchers, involves "self-disclosure, initiating, listening, and responding." Egocentric communicators "usually focus exclusively on concrete issues and matters external to the relationship"—who will get the car repaired, what's for dinner, and when the plumber will get here. They place a low value on communicating and usually have "very poor communication skills." (The traditional, hard-working husband married to Nobody's Valentine would get a low score.) People at the most mature level, say the researchers, *"express a very high value on communicating in their relationships. . . .* There is usually evidence of a commitment to *making time to talk,* despite busy schedules and other obstacles, as well as an ability to resolve conflicts meaningfully" (my emphasis).[14] Sounds like a marriage of psychologists to me.

I do not disagree entirely with the researchers' measurement of intimacy; as a woman, I find it perfectly normal. But I wish to highlight the bias inherent in it—to see what it leaves out. The psychologists' equation of "most mature" with "most verbally expressive" represents a validation of the female standard of intimacy and almost entirely excludes the male standard. Their definition of maturity rests entirely on psychological qualities rather than on *behavior.* What about all the men and women who reliably support their families, who put the wishes of other family members ahead of their own preferences, or who act in a moral and considerate way when conflicts arise? Such individuals are surely being mature and loving, even if they are not articulate or do not value "communication."

Moreover, the researchers did not ask the husbands and wives how *they* defined intimacy; they imposed their own complex definition on the couples, just as Masters and Johnson imposed their notion of the normal sexual response cycle on their volunteers. As one result, they failed to sympathize with the fact that sexuality is part of the masculine language of love. They dismiss "frequency and variety" as criteria for sexual intimacy, yet many men express their deepest affections this way.

For instance, Cancian describes an interview with a twenty-nine-year-old carpenter who said that after sex he feels especially close to his wife, that he feels then that they are truly a family: "I don't talk to her very often, I guess, but somehow I feel we have really communicated after we have made love."[15] Many women, of course, want to feel that they have "really communicated"—that is to say, communicated in words—*before* making love. If the tables were turned, Cancian suggests, and sexual behavior were regarded as an expression, indeed a definition, of love the way talking about feelings currently is, it would appear that men want love more than women do.

When men do speak for themselves, their styles of intimacy are as effective as women's in producing feelings of emotional closeness and meaningful connection. Psychologist Scott Swain conducted a study in which he defined intimacy as any action in a friendship "that connotes a positive and mutual sense of meaning and importance to the participants." The participants, not the observers, got to define what intimacy meant to them, and "any action" would do. One young man said that his most intimate experiences with other men consisted of "a lot of outdoor-type things—fishing, hunting, Tom-Sawyer-type things." [16]

Swain's interviews reveal how different male intimacy is from the female standard. Men use the degree of comfort and relaxation they feel with other men as an index of closeness, says Swain. One interviewee explained that he was "more relaxed around guys. You don't have to watch what you say. . . . I wouldn't be careful I shouldn't say something like this, or I shouldn't do this. That's because with the guys, they're just like you." [17] When asked to recall a "meaningful" time with men friends, another young man said:

> The fun things come to mind. We rented a VCR and some movies and watched those, and just all the laughing together comes to mind as most memorable. As to the most meaningful, those also come pretty close to being the most meaningful, because there was just total relaxation, there. That I felt no need to worry. There's no need to worry about anyone making conversation. The conversation will come. And we can laugh at each other, and you can laugh at yourself, which is handy. [18]

When they were asked to describe the "most meaningful occasion spent with a same-sex friend," the men mentioned twenty-six events, of which twenty were spent in "an activity other than talking"—fishing, playing guitars, diving, drinking, weightlifting, winning a court case, being with a close friend whose sister had died. "Can't think of just one thing that stood out in my mind," one man said. "It was more like a push-pull type thing. Like I'd pull him through things and he'd pull me through things." [19]

Several men said that intimacy with women friends is "just talking"; the talk that women like is, to them, "the lighter side of things." For many men, actions speak louder than words and carry greater value for the friendship, as they do in love relationships. They do not need to say to each other, "I like you"; being invited to a game or another activity *means* "I like you." (Many parents try to teach their daughters this fact about boys, explaining that if a boy puts a frog in a girl's lunchbox, it means he likes her. Girls find this hard to believe.) Men convey affection to one another, adds Swain, with "physical gestures, laughing at jokes, doing one another favors, keeping in touch, 'doing stuff,' teasing, and just being around friends."[20]

Of all these expressions of affection and closeness, perhaps the one that women tend to understand least is men's language of teasing and "joking around." Here, for example, is an exchange between a worried mother and Dr. Joyce Brothers:

Dear Dr. Brothers: Our 14-year-old son loves to tease his young sister. While he has a lively sense of humor, she often doesn't appreciate it, and this becomes the cause of some really unpleasant quarrels. Is there anything we can do about this?

Joyce Brothers, being a woman and a psychologist, uses a female yardstick to measure this boy's behavior:

Teasing often is not simple harmless fun. It can be a way of masking hostility, a kind of hit-and-run attack. . . . Ask your son how he'd like it if he were constantly the butt of jokes or if these same tricks were played on him. . . . Discourage the "teasing" and try to get your son to explore what's behind it.[21]

Notice that the direction of the intervention here is to change the boy's way into the girl's way. Joyce Brothers does not advise the parents, "Discourage your daughter's humorlessness and try to get her to explore the reasons she takes her brother's teasing so seriously." The son *does* know what it's like to be the butt of jokes, because that is how boys and men express many of their feelings to one another. Girls and women keep looking for the meaning "behind" the jokes, a doomed enterprise that makes women seem, to men, overly literal and humorless. To many women, like Joyce Brothers, it is obvious that the boy's teasing is hostile and demeaning. To many men, it is just as obvious that the boy's teasing is his way of being affectionate while also being appropriately masculine.

Men use jokes, teasing, and "horsing around" as ways of creating bonds of camaraderie and in-group knowledge. Jokes communicate affection (and other feelings) indirectly, so no one can accuse the speaker of being wimpy or soft; they protect the speaker from the risk of rejection (or counterattack) that a straightforward remark might evoke. One of my husband's golfing friends, on hearing that my husband's son would be playing with them that day, said, "That's good; I hope he's a better player than you are." It's the kind of teasing remark that few women would say to a female friend—it would be regarded as a hurtful putdown—but my husband laughed and knew it to mean "I enjoy golfing with you and like you very much, even if you do beat me more often than I like."

Among men friends, Swain concludes, joking "camouflages the hidden agenda of closeness." Most men recognize the hidden agenda, but many women do not. In Swain's study, for example, one man had learned to waterski from his best friend. He had trouble getting the knack of it, but by joking the friend removed competitive pressure and worries about failure:

> We were just able to make jokes about it, and we laughed at each other all day. And it finally worked out. I mean it was great for me to be that frustrated and that up-tight about it and know the only thing he was going to do was laugh at me.[22]

Of course, men also use jokes to create distance and to express anger or contempt; women who encroach on traditionally male territory do not mistake the hostility behind the sexist put-downs that they are expected to tolerate with "good humor." But the ambiguity in much of male teasing is the reason that jokes are such a good disguise for love and attachment: The speaker can always claim the listener didn't understand his intention. Most males become fluent in joke-speak and its many meanings by adolescence. They know that "What a jerk!," coming from a friend when they fall off a bicycle, conveys amused affection, but the same remark from a passing stranger is an act of hostility.

Just as many people often overlook or misinterpret men's expressions of love, they often overlook or misinterpret men's expressions of distress when they lose love. The pressures that bar men from the direct revelation of their feelings are especially powerful when the feelings imply vulnerability or weakness, as do the emotions of grief, sadness, fear, loneliness, or anxiety. One unhappy consequence of male emotional silence is the mistaken impression that most men lack these feelings and are harder-hearted than women. By not understanding men's expressions of grief, many psychologists and lay people infer that there is something wrong with men because they seem not to feel anything after divorce, loss, or the death of a loved one.

This mistake figures prominently in the diagnosis of depression in men. Women are more likely than men to talk about feeling depressed (in both mild and extreme cases), to seek help for depression, and to be diagnosed as being clinically depressed. Much of the difference in depression rates has to do with the greater likelihood that women will experience abuse, discrimination, and dead-end work.[23] But some of the difference in rates is more apparent than real: Many men fail to be recognized or diagnosed as depressed because, as with love, *what women do when they are depressed constitutes the norm on which the criteria for depression are based.* In clinical research and psychotherapy, most of the measurements of depression and distress are measured on typically female reactions such as crying, staying in bed, talking about one's unhappiness and misery, and developing eating disorders. Because many men do not express grief this way, it is easy to infer that men suffer less than women when relationships are in trouble, or even that men are incapable of love.

Catherine Riessman is one researcher who came to question the female norm for depression after she had interviewed a large number of wives and husbands about their divorces. The men and women spoke at length about their pain, anguish, and loneliness, but in entirely different ways. The men were suffering as much as the women, Riessman learned, but they didn't *say* so. They did not report the usual symptoms of depression, because these are not, she explains, the "culturally approved idioms for men."[24] Thus, in response to straightforward questions, most of the men said they felt sad "some or a little of the time" and that they felt depressed or lonely "none of the time."

Instead, Riessman found, the men expressed grief in ways that are stereotypically masculine, that they have a vocabulary for, that they can reveal without conflict or shame—"frantic work," heavy drinking, driving crazily, singing sentimental songs. Many of the men had low scores on standard depression scales, yet their lives were in shambles. They described a potpourri of symptoms: trouble concentrating at work; difficulties on the job; extreme restlessness and hyperactivity; and numerous physical ailments and stress symptoms. One man confessed that for four months after his separation he "threw up every morning"—but no, no, he wasn't actually "depressed." Another expressed no feelings of sadness, helplessness, or vulnerability, but in the six months since his divorce he had racked up a long list of criminal charges.

All of these signs of distress have one thing in common, says Riessman: "the distancing of the self from feelings of sadness."[25] A few men, asserting that they felt no pain whatsoever, even had scores of *zero* on the depression scale. "I can't put it into words," many men said of their emotions, while describing lives of desperation and chaos. One man, Rick, tried to explain his feelings this way:

> I was running sort of like wide open, 90 miles an hour down a dead-end street, as the song goes . . . yeah I started drinking much more just because it was something to do. . . . And uh I was monumentally unhappy, I did *not* want her to leave, which I discovered after she left, you know. But there's lots of songs about that too you know so [laughs] what can you do.[26]

Rick goes on to describe the sad songs—"maudlin sorts of things in a country vein"—that he wrote after his separation. But you won't find "writing maudlin sorts of songs" or "running sort of like wide open" on any set of criteria for depression.

Rick's narrative of the aftermath of his divorce, Riessman shows, is very different from what most women would say. It contains many metaphors of pressure: "something's got to give," "running wide open," "driving faster," "just pushing it"—images, she observes, that are "in sharp contrast to the overt images of emptiness, loss, and vulnerability and behaviors like crying that are more consistent with depression in women's talk."[27] Rick constantly apologizes for not having the right word, for not being able to explain himself exactly; he borrows images and feelings from songs.

Even Rick's way of speaking differs from a woman's: "He rushes through his account of his emotions," Riessman explains, "not dwelling on the topic as the women tend to do in their accounts. The language also suggests a fear of loss of control—he is on the edge of disorganization, and whatever restraints that usually contain his strong feelings are breaking down. Whether the issue is overwhelming anger or the sorrow of loss, the prevailing image is of running from it." If he gets too close to identifying an emotion, he runs: "Rick states a feeling, backs off from it, restates it, and backs off again, in repeated cycles," says Riessman.[28]

This typical male pattern of coping with loss—run from it, separate yourself from it, escape from it in activity or drugs—is already apparent in childhood and adolescence, once you know where to look. In a study of the emotional experiences of several hundred schoolchildren, Janice Stapley and Jeannette Haviland concluded, as Riessman had, that depression scales are biased "toward measuring deviation from normal female emotional experience" and do not contain questions that would be "sensitive to male emotional experience."[29] For boys, depression presents itself in such deviations from the male norm as being unable to relax with friends and not being interested in sports or "riding around"! Boys were more likely than girls to deny ever having emotional reactions and to avoid telling others how they were feeling. For instance, when asked to *recall* whether they felt sad, disgusted, guilty, or afraid in the last month, most of the boys said no, they hadn't. But when they kept a daily record of their feelings, they reported having them all.

Men's unwillingness and inability to articulate their griefs may take two extreme forms. When driven to despair, some men can find no middle course between violence and withdrawal. Read any newspaper story of a man who has run amok and killed his family, and what will it invariably say in the fourth paragraph? "John Jones's wife, Mary, had just filed for divorce" or "Friends said that Smith had been despondent ever since his wife left him." Look at this list of the factors that most strongly predict the likelihood of a man killing his wife: the use of drugs or alcohol; strong cultural pressures to save face; previous threats of suicide or vengeance; *recent deep depression; recent failed love relationship;* and *recently separated from family unit.*[30] Almost all of these factors are related to loss of a loved one, since depression often follows separation and many men act out that depression by abusing drugs and alcohol.

The other extreme response takes the form of a total emotional shutdown. Psychotherapist Ronald Taffel believes that many severely depressed men retreat behind a façade of stony silence in their families, but that neither they nor their families recognize the symptoms. Taffel writes of his own father:

> In the middle of the night I would find him there. Alone at the kitchen table, he sat bent over a book or the daily newspaper. "What's the matter, Daddy?" I would ask, already knowing what the answer would be. "Oh, it's nothing, Ronnie. I just have something on my mind, so I couldn't sleep." He'd look up at me, the glasses magnifying some expression in his eyes I wasn't able to name. "Don't worry," he would say. "Go back to bed and I'll see you in the morning." The next morning there would be a noticeable pall over the house.[31]

Taffel has studied 125 men, almost none of whom said they were depressed. "Only 14 percent would have received a formal diagnosis of depression," he observes. "But the partners of 62 percent of them described mood difficulties in the men serious enough to color the atmosphere of the entire household. There is a gloomy undertow in these homes, just below the surface of everyday life. Whether the men passively disappear into the woodwork or shake the foundations of the house with their agitation, they share one characteristic— they cannot regulate their own moods . . . and they depend on their partners and children to do so for them."[32]

And so it is that many women and men end up misreading one another's messages of love, affection, and despair. The feminization of love has its counterpart in the masculinization of silence: To the extent that women are encouraged to talk about their emotions, men are in general expected to remain controlled and silent about theirs. Many men are caught in a conflict between the demands for silence that the world makes of them and the demands for talk the woman makes on them. The world usually wins, which is why Nobody's Valentine doesn't get her card.

■ Economics and emotions

Men's and women's styles of expressing love and other emotions did not develop because women are naturally "emotional" and men are naturally "rational"—or, as some women now interpret this old accusation, because women are naturally "open" and men are naturally "up tight." There are no differences between men and women in the emotions they feel or in how intensely they feel them. The differences in expression we see today emerged because women are expected, allowed, and required to reveal certain emotions, and men are expected and required to deny or suppress them. These rules of emotion are not arbitrary; they fit our social arrangements. It wasn't always so.

In the musical *Fiddler on the Roof,* Tevye, coping with the oddity of having daughters who wish to marry for love, asks his wife: "Do you love me?" Golde thinks about all the things she has done for him over their many years together—she's borne their children, shared his bed, cooked and cleaned and scrimped and saved—and concludes that yes, she must love him after all, whatever that means.

The song is charming because the thought of this peasant couple of the nineteenth century discussing their feelings for one another is so clearly an anachronism. We realize as we listen to them that they belong to another era—imagine, a *husband* asking his *wife* if she loves him! That realization itself reminds us how recent, how contemporary, how culture-bound is the modern woman's language of love and her desire for "intimacy." Intimacy? With Tevye, who is trying to eke out a living while most of the world, including his horse, is against him?

In this respect the story of *Fiddler on the Roof* is a dead-accurate reflection of the transformation of love that occurred in America, beginning in the nineteenth century. Francesca Cancian has shown that as the nation shifted from an agrarian to an industrial economy, the relationship between home and work shifted profoundly as well.[33] In the agrarian era, both sexes were responsible for family life, which in turn was indistinguishable from everyone's work life. The family was, in historian John Demos's words, "a little commonwealth," and both spouses participated in economic production and the education and welfare of household members. In the early centuries of America, women had a major role in the family's economic production—weaving, sewing, cooking, planting, tending animals and gardens—and men worked in or near their homes; men were home for meals and other family activities. There was no sharp distinction between home and work, or between public and private arenas of life.

Correspondingly, there was no sharp distinction between the sexes in matters of love. Benjamin Wadsworth, writing in 1712, was typical of the times in his advice to couples that "the duty of love is mutual, it should be performed by each of them." As historian Mary Ryan has observed, "When early Americans spoke of love they were not withdrawing into a female byway of human experience."[34] Nor was parenthood a "female byway" of experience. John Demos, drawing on letters, journals, and other routine glimpses of everyday early life in America, describes "a picture, above all, of active, encompassing fatherhood, woven into the whole fabric of domestic and productive life."[35]

As the industrial revolution gathered steam, however, the workplace became increasingly separated from home and family. By the 1840s, Cancian writes, the split between the "warm, personal, private sphere" and the "cold public sphere" was well under way. The split was physical as well as psychological. Even people's homes changed from the traditional city style of the row house, where people worked downstairs and lived upstairs, to the private home with large lawns and fences, an increasingly far distance from work. Men left their homes to *go* to work, and women had less economic work to do in their homes. The feminine sphere of love and the family was split off from the masculine sphere of self-assertion and work.

"As the daily activities of men and women grew further apart, a new world view emerged," says Cancian. "It exaggerated the differences between 'the home' and 'the world' and polarized the ideal personalities of women and men."[36] People began to attribute to inherent male and female characteristics what were actually requirements of their increasingly separate domains. Thus, women were expected to provide warmth, nurturance, and care, and forgo achievement; men were expected to provide money and success, and forgo close attachments. The masculine ideal, tailored to fit the emerging economy, was to be an independent, self-made, financially successful man. Masculinity now required self-control: no gaudy displays of emotion; no weakness; no excessive self-indulgence in feelings. Femininity required, and soon came to embody, the opposite.

This bit of background is useful for understanding the origins of women's and men's styles of love and other forms of emotional expression. Their conflict over intimacy today stems from this historical split in family and work roles: The female domain of emotional expression is part of women's general responsibility to keep their relationships humming along and deal with any problems that occur. Marriage is the wife's territory, her domain of expertise. It is her *job* to know how everyone is feeling in order to head off problems at the pass. Naturally, she is motivated to talk; she needs to know if anything in the relationship needs fixing, because she will be blamed if she doesn't fix it.

In contrast, the powerful social norms for masculinity specify that men are not supposed to reveal their feelings directly, because to do so would be a sign of weakness, lack of self-control, and other feminine vices. As a result, boys and men develop protective and indirect ways of communicating their emotions, particularly in the two domains of greatest risk to them: their affections and their griefs. To avoid the cultural denigration of emotional weakness, many men will go to great lengths. "Often," says Ron Taffel, "a man's own suffering so threatens his idealized masculine self-identity that he cannot even admit to any pain."[37]

If a man cries in public, therefore, it is serious news. Senator Edmund Muskie wept at the savage treatment of his wife during his 1972 campaign for the Presidency, and was out of politics. When George Bush revealed that he wept over the decision to start the Gulf

War, he was considered humane in some quarters and wimpy in others—but it was still news. When a Honda executive, testifying on safety problems in a line of his company's cars, cried on the witness stand, his tears made the headlines: "Honda Executive Sobs in Testifying on Safety Problems of Vehicles."

> The senior managing director of the Honda Motor Co. began sobbing on the witness stand Wednesday when an attorney gave him a computer readout containing 789 names of victims— about half of them children—who have died in accidents involving all-terrain vehicles like those built by his company.
>
>   Superior Court Judge Ben Hamrick immediately called a recess to allow Tetsuo Chino time to compose himself. "I apologize for getting emotional," Chino told the jury. . . . "As a father of a child, I get emotional."[38]

Well, I would hope so. But what do we usually see when we watch the parade of men (and some women) standing trial for illegal Iran-Contra deals, the Savings and Loan scandal, insider trading schemes, and product liability suits? Almost to a man, they suppress all signs of guilt, shame, empathy, remorse, and fear. They are all so strong, so manly, so patriotic, so—if we truly evaluated them on a female standard—pathologically inhibited.

The pressures on men to be stoic become even more apparent when we observe men in the primary domain in which they are allowed, in fact encouraged, to "be emotional"—as participants and spectators in sports. "In sports many of the usual prohibitions on males are lifted," observes psychotherapist Bernie Zilbergeld. "A man can be as emotional and expressive about his favorite team and players as he wants. He can cheer them on with unabashed enthusiasm and what might even pass for love. He can be ecstatic and jump up and down when they win and he can feel despair and weep when they lose. Playfulness and creativity are allowed. . . . There's even a lot of physical contact: back- and butt-slapping, shoulder and arm touching, and hugging. Sports is one of the few places where men can safely become boys again, where they can drop the façade of Mr.-Up-Tight-And-In-Control and just play. . . . Is it any wonder they love it so?"[39]

So it is not that men are unfeeling; rather that many are trapped in the belief that feeling is feminine. The social pressure on men to be emotionally masculine (the cultural norm), combined with pressure from their wives to be emotionally feminine (the female norm), puts men in a double bind. If a man learns to become more intimate by his wife's definition, more willing to express his fears and griefs, he is also becoming more girlish, more babyish—and both of them will hate that. Men are right to be suspicious of women who say they want expressive men. According to the findings of numerous research studies and the observations of many clinicians, men who deviate from the masculine norm by disclosing their emotions and private fears are typically regarded by both sexes as being "too feminine" and "poorly adjusted."[40]

"Even if the therapist recognizes that the 'difficult' man is really depressed and unhappy, neither partner may want to hear it," says Taffel.[41] "Most men recoil at the suggestion that they are sick, or in pain, or even that something is bothering them. A woman, even if she has initiated treatment, may be threatened by the diagnosis as well, despairing about depending on a mate with so vague and obscurely 'unmasculine' a flaw."

Thus, the role requirements for emotion catch women in a double bind too. Family therapist Olga Silverstein finds that many of her clients say they want their men to be more "intimate," but then they fear that their lovers will become "sissies" and weaklings. "Women don't want to be dominated and bullied," Silverstein says, "but neither do they want men to be babies. They want him to be a 'man.' Then, when he's a man, they don't like it, because that means he's too controlling and they're afraid of him. They all want heroes, but they want warm, tender, loving heroes. . . . Oh! What a fantasy that is!"[42]

To maintain the fantasy, many women resort to the Mind-Reading Delusion. They expect their husbands to be able to read their minds —to know instinctively what they are feeling, what they want for their birthdays, what words they want to hear. The Mind-Reading Delusion allows women to complain about male inexpressiveness without actually having to teach men what it is they want them to do. "Women want men to be strong; we don't want to teach them anything," says Silverstein. "Because once we're teaching a man, he's in an inferior position. We're just as acculturated as he is—he's got to be bigger than life."

So we are left with a paradox: Both sexes actively play their gender roles to perfection, and then lament their consequences and fight over them. It's a truism among family therapists that couples are first attracted to each other because they fit the stereotypes so well. She likes him because he is strong, silent, manly, assertive, and competent; he likes her because she is nurturant, affectionate, talkative, and open. And what do they most bitterly complain about after the first flush of love? Exactly the qualities they were attracted to. She laments that he doesn't talk to her about his problems or discuss everyday events the way her girlfriends do; he complains that she nags him all the time to talk. Neither of them has changed, of course. A man who is emotionally inexpressive may be regarded as calm or cold, steady or aloof. A woman who is emotionally expressive may be regarded as warm or hysterical, responsive or irrational. The only thing that's different is the eye of the beholder.

Many couples do not see what is wrong with saying, in effect, "Okay, the wife can be the person who worries about the kids and cries when she's unhappy, and the husband can be the person who fixes the lights and lets everybody cry on his shoulder." But disillusionment and misunderstanding are the inevitable consequences of this division of labor. Each style has its benefits, but also serious disadvantages.[43]

For instance, unquestionably women gain much from their practice in talking about feelings. It's fun. They get support from others. They are able to reveal their deepest insecurities and fears, and feel validated and understood. They form close bonds with their friends, because sharing emotions is a gift of trust. They can speak the dominant language of psychotherapy.

But women's expressive style carries a price tag. It leads many women to rehearse their problems and constantly brood about them, rather than learning to distract themselves or take action to solve them. Some women come to believe that talking *is* doing something about the problem, and that talking is enough. Endless rumination —the habit of looking inward, dissecting feelings and experiences— can keep people from taking the action they need to extricate themselves from their difficulties and their depressions.[44] Many men are amazed at women's ability to "wallow" in their problems and emotions, instead of doing the manly thing—finding solutions or laughing them off. They have a point. When women repeatedly discuss their fears and worries, they often feel better in the short run, but also can make themselves more fearful and anxious in the long run. Men, by suppressing their fears and forcing themselves to act, or by not taking their fears seriously, may conquer their anxiety or at least learn to live with it.

For a couple, the risk of talking too much about feelings is that the relationship may come to live only in talk; it rests entirely in the way it is spoken of, how it is analyzed. This hothouse effect creates a pseudo-intimacy. It allows people to overlook what they *do* to and for each other, instead equating love with the self-righteousness of their intentions and the "honesty" of their emotions. As two sex therapists caution:

> Communication is certainly a desirable aim, but when it is made an end in itself it creates a hypochondriacal attitude toward the relationship and breeds precisely the illness it fears. Talking about problems is a way of evoking an apparent intimacy that the partners would otherwise be incapable of establishing. The relationship becomes its own topic, and idle talk stands proxy for the relationship itself; one feels what one says one feels.[45]

As we have seen, of course, there are comparable hazards for men in their don't-talk-just-do-it strategy. Too many men, as they move from childhood to adulthood, become inarticulate about their feelings. "Men, just like women, deserve understanding and support," Bernie Zilbergeld observes. "Unfortunately, they often don't get it because they have a hard time making a case for themselves, for expressing what's going on with them and how they feel about it. If I ask a man in therapy how he feels, his eyes glaze over. Or he makes an assertion: 'I feel my wife should be more assertive.' "[46]

This inability to identify feelings becomes especially troubling when a serious problem occurs that requires discussion and evaluation—a problem that cannot be solved with jokes, distractions, and avoidance. Under extreme stress, couples who rely only on sex-stereotyped ways of coping resort to extreme responses: endless tears for her, total silence for him. This pattern is frequently seen in couples suffering over the death of a child. The wife is angry that her husband "doesn't feel anything"; the husband is angry that "she won't let go of her grief and get on with it." In truth, each is grieving in his or her own way, and each must learn from the other. The man who tries to suppress his feelings entirely, and the woman who indulges her feelings indiscriminately, will both fail to get beyond them.

Why is the view that women are better at love so persistent, even though it means that many women will be unhappy with "inexpressive" husbands and many men will be unhappy that their best efforts at love go unrecognized? Why is women's verbal expression of grief acknowledged as real depression, but men's silent anguish or destructive behaviors regarded as the absence of feeling? Why is it that women and men continue to collude in the allocation of love in particular, and emotion in general, to women's expertise?

The answer is not that society values women's ways of loving and really thinks they are better than men's. The female standard of emotional expression is a norm, all right, but only for women. It does not encompass men in the way that male norms in physiology, law, medicine, and history are said to encompass women. If the female standard were truly the human ideal, men who adhered to it would be admired, and more men would aspire to achieve it. Instead, most men who weep, speak their feelings, and reveal fears and passions are denigrated as being too weak, shrill, feminine, and emotional. The male norm of emotional suppression continues to be held up as the public ideal of adult behavior. Men's ways may not get them much credit in the home, but that is because they are valued —indeed, they are a required component of masculinity and a general standard of mental health—in the public domain.

The feminization of love persists for the same reason that the search for sex differences in the brain persists: because it so beautifully justifies the doctrine of separate spheres—the belief that women's role is taking care of people and men's role is taking care of the world. By not recognizing what men do as love, and by sentimentalizing women's way of loving that is based on words and feelings, we support not only an emotional division of labor but a social and political one.

"In the 19th century, it was men who had to change more than women in response to social and economic changes, moving from agrarian to industrial occupations," says psychologist Rachel Hare-Mustin. "In this century, women's lives are changing faster than men's, with women expected to meet the competing demands of the workplace and the family."[47] Men, she adds, had women to help them ease the transition from family to work. Women today have little help in this combination, with the result that many of them, as sociologist Arlie Hochschild has described, work a "second shift" in addition to their paid jobs: fulltime work in the home.[48]

By fostering the belief that women are naturally better than men at love, nurturance, caring for children, and managing the family, the feminization of love legitimizes women's double burden and excuses men from participating more fully in the emotional life of the family. Women, like men, *behave* lovingly by caring for others and by doing nurturant (unpaid) work for their families. But the emphasis on the expressive, verbal side of love diminishes the importance of these loving actions. It sentimentalizes love into a mystical emotion, ignoring the material and practical basis of attachment, sexuality, nurturance, and mutual assistance. The work of caring for others is devalued or taken for granted.

Beliefs about women's superiority in love deflect our attention from the more threatening matters of inequality and powerlessness. In many families, the feminization of love is the ideology; the masculinization of power is the practice.

■ *The sounds of silence*

My father is the quietest man I know, contemplative as a monk, affable, a good listener. I've never heard him shout in anger, and we've seldom spoken of intimate matters. Silence is an integral element of our relationship.[49]

—Richard Laliberte, "A Silent Bond"

Silence is power. The person who is silent may neither wish to be powerful nor feel powerful, but silence is power nonetheless. The silent partner feels no obligation to speak, no duty to change; he is mysterious, his wishes and feelings unknown. His silence causes those around him either to walk on tiptoe, to avoid the moods they imagine he feels, or to pursue him for connection, communication, and affection. The silent man has a resource that others want: information about what he is thinking, what he desires, how he is reacting, whether he approves of them.

Richard Laliberte pursued his father for many years, hoping for a word of encouragement, personal revelation, support, and love. He describes how he labored for a year on a gift for his dad—a portfolio of his father's life work—and all his father managed to say was "I like it." The son writes:

> I'm left with a familiar feeling of disappointment at his not saying more, but it's tempered by my now realizing he doesn't need to say more. I've learned to read his emotions from signals other than direct expression. I've developed an appreciation of how the deepest truths, if spoken at all, come softly murmured.

Laliberte's pursuit of his father had a happy ending: not because the father changed, but because the son did. The son decided to accept his father for the quiet man he is, realizing that his father will never confer lavish praise or words of love on him but that his father's love is nonetheless deep and abiding.

Do you think that Laliberte's decision is a sign of rationalization or of wisdom? Certainly he is right to understand that saccharine assertions of love are not necessarily good and that silence itself is not necessarily bad; it depends on what the silence means. Companionable silence differs from sulky silence. The temperamental silence of the shy person differs from the sullen silence of the hostile or depressed person, as Ron Taffel well knows. Recall that his father's silence, a mask of depression, left "a noticeable pall over the house." But the silence of both fathers had this in common: It controlled everyone else's behavior.

The silent man does not always retreat in order to maintain power in some authoritarian sense. On the contrary, many silent men retreat because they feel themselves to be powerless: powerless at work, powerless in the wife's territory at home. They are silent because they feel silenced, inarticulate compared to their wives.

Unpracticed in their wives' form of talk, they feel threatened when their wives demand the intimacy of conversation. "Talking about the relationship as she wants to do," says Francesca Cancian, "will feel to him like taking a test that she has made up and he will fail."[50] So he reacts by withdrawing or with passive aggression.

Whatever the reason for silence, the typical response of other people to it is pursuit, and the eventual result is the familiar pursue-withdraw family pattern. Typically, wives (and children) pursue for more closeness; husbands withdraw to preserve distance. Wives pursue for talk; husbands retreat for silence. Each, of course, thinks the other started it: He says he withdraws to get away from her nagging, and she says she pursues because he is always so withdrawn.

When this pattern is a result of traditional differences in love styles, the familiar advice that is given to women—back off, stop chasing, accept him for what he is, and let him move a little in your direction—usually works. In the case of my friend Roberta and her husband Henry, for instance, Roberta first tried teaching her husband how to talk to her, but his best efforts came out as vaguely insulting ("I like the sound of you chattering away in my ear," he said gamely). Eventually, she says, she simply stopped trying to turn him into one of her girlfriends, and recognized that everything about his *behavior* toward her was loving and attentive: the cups of coffee that materialized at her elbow, just when she wanted them; the arrival of a book she idly said she would like to read; the dinners out on tired nights. "I would rather have a loving, quiet man," she decided, "than a sweet-talking egotist."

More often, however, the pursue-withdraw pattern is not a dance of gender, but of power. "Male silence reflects male power," says psychologist Andrew Christensen, who has been studying couples in conflict. "The one who has more power doesn't need to speak; the one who is one-down needs to demand or persuade to get information. When the situation is reversed—when the man has less power in some aspect of the marriage—he will become the demanding one. This reversal is commonly seen with sex, one area in which women generally have the power to say no; now the man pursues and demands, and she withdraws."[51] In such cases of a power imbalance, advice to the woman to "back off" serves to let the man set the standard of behavior they will both follow: his. It gets the woman to stop pressing for change and allows the man to define how much "intimacy" he is prepared to give, how much work he will do in the household, and how much he will acquiesce to the woman's requests.

In one of Arlie Hochschild's case studies, a couple she calls Nancy and Evan had fallen into a pattern of bickering and quarreling.[52] Nancy continually pursued Evan to do more housework and care of their four-year-old, Joey, but Evan didn't see why he should change his life just because Nancy wanted a demanding career as a social worker. Nancy was feeling guilty that she was exhausted all the time and had lost interest in having sex with her husband, and he was angry at her frequent "nagging."

This ongoing quarrel was resolved, Hochschild reports, in the following "compromise." The couple decided to divide all of the household responsibilities in half: upstairs and downstairs. "Upstairs," which would be Nancy's responsibility, included preparing meals, shopping, cleaning, doing laundry, and child care. "Downstairs," which would be Evan's responsibility, included the garage, his basement workshop, and the dog. And one more thing: in order to maintain this "equitable" division of labor, Nancy would cut back her career work to half-time.

Nancy and Evan justified this new arrangement by perceiving their conflict not as one of power or inequality, but one of personalities. They decided that since Evan was "lazy," whereas Nancy was "compulsive," and since men and women are "naturally" different when it comes to household matters, it made sense to divide things this way. If Evan were to have changed for the sake of the marriage, they both would have regarded him as making a "sacrifice." Neither of them thought Nancy was making a sacrifice, however. She did what women are supposed to do.

Although it takes two to play the pursue-withdraw game, most people, including family therapists, have tended to focus on the problem of the pursuer—who, being the subordinate member of the family, is usually the woman. The woman's "emotionality," her "demands and nagging," are usually construed as the problem, not the man's silence, aloofness, or lack of participation. Much of the emphasis on intimacy and talk obscures the underlying dynamics of who is doing what in the family. By emphasizing women's emotionality rather than men's silence, we overlook, among other things, what women might be feeling emotional *about*.

Thus, many women end up in a no-win situation. Because women have primary responsibility for the success of the marriage, the care and feeding of their husbands, and the raising of children, they are also considered responsible for any problems that might occur. Because women are supposed to be the love experts, they also catch the blame when they don't love correctly: if they love "too much" or not enough, if they are too needy or not needy enough, if they are too cold or too involved. In their roles as wives and mothers, they are responsible for handling the emotions and distress of all family members; but, as females, they are also the repository of "emotions," irrational creatures who cannot cope and need help. When families seek therapy as a unit, therefore, it is typically the mother who becomes the focus of intervention, even if the family's problem originates with the behavior of the husband or children.

For example, in a study of children of men who had been prisoners of war, the researchers wanted to know if the children were suffering because of their fathers' experiences.[53] The answer was yes, they were. The fathers were feeling depressed and agitated, but, dutifully adhering to male rules, they had cut themselves off emotionally from their families. As a result, the children did have a high incidence of emotional problems. Yet the researchers concluded that these problems were the *mothers'* fault. The reason: The men's troubles disturbed their wives, which in turn affected their ability to be good mothers, which in turn was disturbing the children.

This is not an isolated example. Psychologist Paula Caplan and her associates analyzed 125 articles in professional journals, and found that "mother blaming" is a widespread assumption in clinical psychology and family therapy. Mothers are held responsible for almost any disorder that their offspring might develop, including bedwetting, schizophrenia, aggression, learning problems, and homicidal transsexualism. The concepts of competent motherhood and incompetent fatherhood are almost nowhere to be seen in the clinical literature.[54]

Caplan also found that clinicians use a double standard in evaluating mothers and fathers. A mother is typically described in emotional terms: She is cold and rejecting, but the same behavior is considered normal for a father who is "just that way." A mother who is *not* cold and rejecting, of course, is likely to be labeled hysterical, irrational, or overprotective. Fathers are typically described in terms of the *work they do,* but mothers in terms of the *emotion they display* or fail to display. In one article the authors, describing the parents of a patient, reported that "the father is a bricklayer and the mother is nervous." (Once you are aware of this habit, you will see it everywhere. In a review I read of a biography of Edward R. Murrow, the reviewer noted that Murrow's mother was an "overprotective, hard-driving moralist," whereas his father was a "hardworking subsistence farmer.")

Mother-blaming is truly insidious. I read in the paper a wife's complaint: She is always being blamed for her husband's overweight. She feeds him low-calorie foods, she explains, but he pigs out on sweets at work and during midnight binges. "Short of handcuffing myself to his arms so I can police him around the clock, there is no way I can monitor everything that goes into my husband's mouth," she says. Well, exactly. But does she conclude that her husband is responsible for his own eating habits, and that if people want to be rude about his weight, they can be rude to him directly? Not at all. She says:

> He was his mother's son and allowed to eat junk a lot longer than he has been my husband. If you want to criticize someone for permitting him to pig out on junk food, bring it up the next time you see *her.*[55]

Of course, some mothers *are* dreadful and behave badly. Some mothers *do* deserve blame and responsibility for the awful things they do. (The alternative to mother-blaming, after all, is not sentimental mother-worshipping, the equally erroneous view that mothers are always, instinctively, "naturally" right.) The point is that a child can be having difficulties for many reasons. As Caplan observes, "We need to consider the child's temperament—perhaps this child would give any parent trouble. We need to look at the father's behavior. We need to look at the child's friends, classmates, and other outside influences. Most people don't do this. If there's a problem, someone is to blame, and it's almost always the mother."[56]

The reason for mother-blaming is not entirely malevolent. From the therapist's standpoint, it is easier to tell one partner to shut up than to get the other partner to speak up; it is easier to modify the woman's pursuit than to modify the man's withdrawal (he might withdraw right out of therapy if you press him too hard). How, after all, do you modify silence? Besides, both the therapist and the woman are used to talking about feelings, and the woman will be used to seeking advice on how to fix things. Even if it is his silence that has driven her crazy, it seems easier to focus on her "craziness" than on his provocation.

This focus on the woman's emotions as the source of family troubles, however, overlooks both the power and function of the man's silences and his unspoken authority to make the major decisions. To see this process in action and its implications for family change, I want to describe in some detail a case study of a family that was treated by therapist Deborah Luepnitz.[57]

The McGinn family sought help for their fifteen-year-old son, Kip, who had become depressed and suicidal. Kip had been hospitalized with an asthma attack—he had not been taking his medication —and the mother, Margo, had come to the hospital on her own to demand to see a therapist and learn about his treatment. She herself had been hospitalized for depression many years before, and she wanted to protect her son from a similar horrible experience. The admitting physician sent a note to Luepnitz, describing the details of the case, and included this observation: "Mother is overinvolved— talks for patient. Father is sales manager in a department store."

Margo McGinn began the first therapy session by saying that she blamed herself for having picked on her son to be more responsible and to do more work around the house. She had stopped reminding him about his medication, since he resented it, and she felt guilty about that too. She thought she was the cause of his problems and was alarmed to find him in a psychiatric hospital. The father, Gus, said of his wife that she "does act a bit hasty or irrational, but she means well." He admitted that he didn't spend much time with his son and really didn't know him very well; in therapy sessions, he often turned to his wife for details about his son's medical history or problems. Gus had no idea why Kip had stopped taking his medication, adding that Kip was "a bit of a mystery."

What was the matter with this "hasty, irrational" mother and "hardworking" father? Traditional therapists, Luepnitz observed, would diagnose the family dynamics as being something like this: The son's problem was "immaturity" or "stubbornness." The mother's problem was that she had become "overinvolved" with Kip because of his medical problem, and this was rewarding his childishness; her coalition with Kip was aberrant and pathological. The father didn't really have a problem, except that he didn't get to spend as much time with his son as he would have liked. As for solutions, the traditional therapist would probably use the father as a buffer between mother and child, advising him to help keep the mother off the son's back and let the boy grow up. The father, although less involved with his family than the mother, would thereby be elevated in status as the savior in this crisis. He would be treated as the ultimate authority.

But Luepnitz perceived this family in quite a different way, without regarding the father's "stoic, rational" behavior as the norm and the ideal. In her view, Kip's problem was his illness and his depression—depression, notice, not immaturity. Margo's coalition with Kip was not aberrant or pathological, but a normal response to the father's emotional and physical absenteeism. The problem was not only Margo's overinvolvement with Kip, but Gus's underinvolvement; he had left all of Kip's caretaking to his wife. The problem was not only Margo's guilt, but Gus's lack of guilt for not being more involved with his son and his failure to try to understand the boy. (Kip was "a bit of a mystery" to him.) The problem was not that Margo was too emotional, but that Gus delegated all emotions to her and ran away from her feelings and his own. The problem was not that Margo had too much power in ruling the family roost, but that she had no real power, no acknowledgment or validation of the work she did.

Luepnitz saw that Margo was caught in a tangle of conflicting instructions about how she was supposed to care for Kip. Ever since Kip's birth, a procession of experts had told Margo that she would have to protect him. "We were told he was special," she said. "He is allergic to literally hundreds of things. When he was little, the doctors said his room should be kept free of dust. How do you keep a child's room free of dust? And you have to cook him all kinds of special foods." The "you" in those sentences, of course, was herself. Margo had spent thousands of hours with allergists, nutritionists, guidance counselors, and teachers; endless hours keeping her son's room free of dust, cooking special meals for him, and attending to his health. Gus rarely did any of this, because, as his wife explained, "He was working." Then, having done all of these things for Kip, Margo was told by another set of experts that she was "overprotective." Yet when she dutifully followed their instruction and stopped "nagging" her son to take his medication, the result was that Kip stopped taking it—and nearly died.

Instead of regarding Margo as an overprotective, meddling, infantilizing mother, Luepnitz saw her as a woman struggling to do the right thing. "I think you did a heroic job in the face of all that advice," she told Margo. "Some people would have thrown in the towel." Margo smiled "like a person who had never heard a compliment," Luepnitz reported. "I told her so." At this point, Gus leaped in to say: "To me, compliments are unnecessary. A person knows if they're doing a good job or not." Margo was silent for a moment, and then turned to Kip and asked if he had taken his medicine that day.

This vignette gave the therapist a key to the family problem: Margo had been doing extraordinary work on behalf of her family, caring for two other children as well, without getting support or so much as a "thank you" for a job well done. Instead of expressing anger at her husband directly for his insensitive remark, instead of finding a way to get acknowledgment from him directly, Margo McGinn did what many wives who feel unvalued do: She turned to her son. What seemed like nagging to the son and father ("Did you take your medicine today?") was her way of restoring self-esteem: "I may get nothing from Gus, but at least I can feel good about being a caring mother; *somebody* needs me."

In treating this family, Luepnitz did not ask the husband to fly in with a solution from his habitual roost on the periphery of the family. Instead, she realized that all members of this family needed to redistribute their emotions and their responsibilities. Luepnitz described her goal in reflecting on Gus's comment that his wife is so "irrational":

> To my ear, it carried not only his personal frustration with his wife but also a long cultural history of bifurcating the rational and the irrational, uncritically valuing the former and devaluing the latter. . . . The therapist must then work toward a more

equitable distribution of the family's affect—that is, the therapist helps the "rational" family members claim their own emotions.

Luepnitz began by raising the emotional issue of Margo's own hospitalization so many years ago. This event had become a big family secret and everyone conspired to keep the lid on it. In doing so, they were obeying the male norm of silence and Gus's authority to enforce it. Gus's rule was to "forgive and forget," avoid emotional revelations, and prevent the family from becoming "upset."

[Therapist:] Gus, are you afraid that something bad could come as a result of discussing the past?
[Gus:] It will take her all week to get back. She'll be hysterical, and the kids have to go to school all upset.

Notice that Gus cast the problem in terms of the emotions that his wife and children will suffer; not his own feelings, which he was trying to suppress.

In spite of the risk of being "hysterical" for a week, Margo, with all family members present, decided to tell her story. She had had two children close together, including Kip, who was sick as an infant, and she was "worn out." Her husband asked their parish priest for permission to use birth control, but the priest emphatically refused. Margo understood that her husband was devout, she said, but she was "crushed" that he put the Church before her mental and physical health and wishes. She soon became pregnant again. She said: "I felt like a nonperson. I don't know how else to say it":

A person with no rights. Like something you wind up and it cleans up everyone's mess and cooks and has babies and gets up at dawn and does it over again. Now I feel like shit saying this. You know I love them, but I really couldn't manage. And one day, when Cindy was two, I just stopped coping. Gus found me crying and I couldn't stop.

Margo McGinn was sent to a mental hospital, where she was treated with electroshock, "terrible drugs," and "cloth restraints." She was horribly alone. Her parents never called or came to see her, and Gus, having been told by doctors that his visits would only make her "more agitated," never visited her at all. When she came home, they never spoke a word about her experience.

Margo's account left the family in tears; even Gus had tears in his eyes. The oldest son challenged Gus's decision to send her to the hospital, but Gus said only that people's thinking about mental illness was different in those days and the decision had been difficult for him. He said nothing further about his own feelings until Margo observed:

> It's funny to talk about it this way because it makes you feel less guilty. Like my family had a part, and the Church had a part, and the doctors, and it wasn't all my fault.

Now her husband asked a question he had been trying to avoid for years: "You forgot me. Don't you blame me for it?" And she replied: "I did, because you were like a patsy for those priests. But when it was all over, it was like you really changed and became really sweet again. . . ."

Eventually, after several more sessions, Gus came forward with his own feelings. Luepnitz asked Gus how his father's death had been for him, and his first inclination was to give the manly reply: It hadn't hit him very hard. Margo interrupted to say she thought it *had* hit him hard, because he had been "down" during the following year and had had a bad year at work. (A man may be "down" or "blue," but never "depressed.") Luepnitz reported:

> He denied ever feeling suicidal, and said that when he felt "down" he worked longer, or occasionally talked to his cousin who was a priest. Sounding a little irritated, he said, "Believe me, there's not a lot of time to be depressed when you have a demanding job and three kids, one with a lot of health problems" . . . making a link between Kip's poor health and his avoidance of his own emotions.

Luepnitz, ever the keen therapist, said: "You sound a little angry. Are you?" To which Gus replied: "Again, we're going on and on about something that happened ten years ago."

[Therapist:] Gus, if your dad were here, what would you want to tell him?

[Gus, after a pause:] If I could tell him something? I would want him to see how great the kids have turned out. Despite our problems. They're bright. They're all good kids. I love 'em.

Gus started to cry then, full crying. After a long silence Luepnitz asked whether he would want to be different from his father in any way, and Gus said: "Yeah, I don't want to keel over when I'm sixty. I want to take time to smell the roses. I want to be with my family more."

The McGinn family consists of unique individuals caught in a common pattern: the traditional father's emotional absenteeism from the family; his silences; the entire family's denigration of the woman's caretaking contributions; the focus on the woman's emotions rather than the men's (Gus *and* Kip); the allocation to the woman of the responsibility for how everyone turns out; and the immediate blame she gets if anyone has a problem. This arrangement, argues Luepnitz, is fostered by a society that " 'milks' mothers for their labor, devalues their 'relational' skills, blames them for whatever goes awry in the family, and makes it financially dangerous for them to leave it." In turn, she adds, fathers, "feeling excluded, sense defeat and bury themselves deeper into work, affairs, or the bar."[58]

New approaches in family therapy begin from the premise that all members of a family are caught in a web of society's making, and that you cannot understand the behavior of any individual without examining the filaments of that web. The example of the McGinns beautifully illustrates the benefits for all concerned of getting unstuck. All members of the McGinn family learned something, and all of them changed. The emotional balance became more equitable, and so did the balance of power and responsibility.

Gus stopped putting down Margo as "irrational," and reclaimed his own emotions of depression, loss, and anxiety. He was able, Luepnitz reported, "to face the fact that he had wounded Margo deeply, and also the fact that he himself had been wounded." He could compliment his family. He started doing more housework—as Margo exclaimed, "And cleaning! Believe me, it was worth every moment and every penny of this therapy just to get to the point we're at with housework!" Gus decided that a career switch out of his detested job was unrealistic, but that he could take college courses at night in subjects that interested him.

Margo, Luepnitz reported, lost the lifelong burden of shame and guilt she had been carrying. "She was no longer the 'loony' being protected by four conflict-avoiding family members," said Luepnitz. "She was not the family's servant, but a person with interests, who had a sense of deserving pleasure and who earned a living wage. She no longer felt that her ability to show anger and other emotions was irrational or bad, but that it was a strength, important and real."

And Kip, no longer a pawn between his parents, no longer needing to use his own symptoms to solve theirs, no longer feeling hopeless that illness would destroy his life, began to grow up.

■ Love story

As a child, I was nuts about cowboys, guns, and Palomino ponies, and so when I first saw the musical *Annie Get Your Gun* I was in heaven. Annie Oakley was a woman who could ride, wear cowgirl outfits, and shoot. She became my hero at once. She sang "Anything you can do, I can do better," and she outshot her rival, Frank Butler. I loved Annie Oakley so much that I entirely blocked out the end of the musical, when she realizes that "You can't get a man with a gun." Annie deliberately blows her next competition with Butler, who of course then realizes he loves her after all. I couldn't understand why a woman would give up being the world's best sharpshooter (even for Frank Butler, who was definitely terrific), or why Frank Butler would love Annie only if she gave up sharpshooting.

I wish I had known then what I know now: In the real-life story of Annie Oakley and Frank Butler, she never had to make that choice. Annie did get her man with a gun. In 1875, as a teenager, she defeated Frank Butler in an arranged competition. "It was her first big match—my first defeat," wrote Butler. "The next day I came back to see the little girl who had beaten me, and it was not long until we were married."[59] For the next fifty years they worked and traveled together in Europe and America, Annie as featured sharpshooter in the Buffalo Bill Wild West show and Frank as her manager. They remained devoted, and Frank continued to express his affections for Annie in published love poems and interviews with the press. They died, within eighteen days of one another, in 1926.

"Why was the true love story of Annie Oakley and Frank Butler discarded as the basis for the musical?" asks writer Bonnie Kreps.[60] Because, she argues, the real story was not romantic enough—which is to say, it did not fit our myths of love. The strong silent hero does not rescue the poor weak lamb. The woman does not have to trade love for competence; she's allowed to have both. The man does not have to squeeze himself into some frozen mold of masculinity, competing with the woman over who does what better. Instead, he speaks, in a human voice, of his love and admiration for the "little girl who had beaten me." The true love story would never sell.

The feminization of love in America, the glorification of women's ways of loving, is not about the love between autonomous individuals. It celebrates a romantic, emotional love that promotes the myth of basic, essential differences between women and men. It supports the opposition of women's love and men's work. In so doing, it derails women from thinking about their own talents and aspirations, rewarding instead a narrowed focus on finding and keeping Mr. Right.[61]

The stereotype of woman-as-love-expert blurs the similarity between the sexes in their human needs for love, intimacy, and attachment, *and* for autonomy and self-development.[62] It allows men's needs for attachment to remain covert and repressed, while women's needs become overt and exaggerated. It encourages women to overfocus on relationships and men to underfocus on them. As Francesca Cancian says, "When women are unhappy, they usually think they need more love; but the objective evidence suggests that they need more independence."[63] When men are unhappy, they usually think they need more success; but the objective evidence suggests that they need more time, as Gus learned, "to smell the flowers."

Women who live only for love will inevitably love too much. The need will become bottomless and unfillable, like the equally unquenchable thirst among some who live only for work, for more and more wealth. The trouble with romantic love, says Bonnie Kreps, is that it blinds women to the less charming realities of life with the

Prince. Many women become what she calls a Reverse Sleeping Beauty: They kiss the Prince and promptly fall asleep. This is why so many of love's experts become, too easily, love's victims.

To move toward an alternative vision of human love, women and men would have to budge from their current certainty that their sex is the only one that knows how to love.

We would stop blaming women for everything that happens in the family and make men as accountable as women for the quality of family life. We would recognize that men's silences and absences have as deep and powerful an effect on the people around them as do the words and interventions of women.

We would value, as a society, the loving work that women and men do for one another. We would value, along with the ability to express feelings, productive work in the home and the physical care of others. We would acknowledge the ways men love, instead of assuming that they are hopeless incompetents in the domains of feeling and the family.

We would break the polarity between the "male" model of stoicism and the "female" emotions it defends against. There is a place for stoicism. No one wants a firefighter to burst into tears at the sight of a fire, and in a crisis everyone should know how to behave without collapsing into puddles of anxiety. But there is also a place for feeling; empathy, remorse, regret, worry, sadness, and compassion are our links to other people and to the human condition, as that Honda executive well knew.

None of this means, in my opinion, that women should try turning their husbands into their girlfriends, or that men should try to make their wives into one of the boys. Such efforts are bound to backfire, even when both participants know the other person's love language. One friend of mine told her lover, "Herb, I don't want you to do the male thing just now. I don't need advice. I've had a bad day, and I just want you to hold me and console me." He looked absolutely perplexed. "What good will that do?" he said.

Nor am I recommending some vague androgynous ideal, in which women have to give up their love of intimate chat and men have to give up teasing and kidding around. Instead, I am arguing for flexibility, the ability to speak both languages when required. I admit that narrow rules for a division of emotional labor are easier to follow. I think it will be as uncomfortable, even frightening, for women to modify their fondness for talk and risk independent action, when this is called for, as for men to modify their silences and risk vulnerability. It's much easier for women to focus on changing men, even if the results are few and puny, than to develop their own programs of self-development. It's much easier for men to withdraw into silence than to try to articulate the fears and losses that jeopardize masculine identity.

But perhaps we can begin by accepting the fact that neither sex has all the answers. Couples can regard each other as a source of charming anecdotes, a repository of a different kind of expertise, and a resource in emergencies. They can exchange help, knowledge, talents, stories, and experiences. An abiding intimacy, in contrast to the fleeting intimacy of momentary emotions, does not require that partners be the same. It requires a reciprocity of affection, power, and respect for differences—the basis of a love between equals, the love between Annie Oakley and Frank Butler.

8

Speaking of Gender

The darkened eye restored

. . . 'tis woman's strongest vindication for speaking that the world needs to hear her voice. . . . The world has had to limp along with the wobbling gait and the one-sided hesitancy of a man with one eye. Suddenly the bandage is removed from the other eye and the whole body is filled with light. It sees a circle where before it saw a segment. The darkened eye restored, every member rejoices with it.[1]

—Anna Julia Cooper, 1892

If women are not deficient men, or better than men, or different from men, or the same as men, what are they? For that matter, if men are not deficient women, or better than women, or different from women, or the same as women, what are *they*? How can we think of gender, speak of gender, without imposing a flat uniformity on the diversity of experience and without transforming differences into deficiencies?

One problem is that many people persist in believing that men and women differ in important qualities, in spite of innumerable studies that have failed to pin these qualities down and keep them there. For instance, we've seen that former (average) differences in intellectual skills, such as mathematical, verbal, and spatial abilities, have gradually vanished or are too trivial to matter. Other differences have faded quickly with changing times, as was the fate of "finger dexterity" (when males got hold of computers) and "fear of success" (when females got hold of law schools). But people *love* sex differences, and not just the familiar anatomical ones. They love to notice and identify ways in which the sexes seem to differ psychologically, and then to complain or laugh about what "women" are or what "men" do.

It is time to break away from the old, literal emphasis on counting differences, because most of those differences, as two psychologists once observed with a tinge of exasperation, are a matter of "now you see them, now you don't."[2] What does that fact alone tell us about efforts to compare the sexes? How serious should we be about the phenomena that are here today and gone tomorrow, like "fear of success" or "the Cinderella complex"?

As I was working on this book a friend asked me where I fell on the maximalist/minimalist debate in the study of women. As we've seen, maximalists (including cultural feminists) take the view that there are major, fundamental differences between the sexes; minimalists, whom we might call material feminists, believe that there are no significant differences other than those temporarily imposed by society. My first inclination was to treat my friend's question jokingly—"On some issues I'm a maximum minimalist, on others I'm a minimum maximalist"—but as I thought about it, I decided that the question itself is the problem.

The reason is that all polarities of thinking, like all dichotomies of groups, are by nature artificial, misleading, and oversimplified. In this book, I've tried to show that on some issues the differences between women and men *are* trivial. On matters of intellectual ability, brain function, competence, morality, empathy, hostility, greed, the need for intimacy and attachment, love and grief, and the capacity for sexual pleasure—on these I am a minimalist. But on some issues I am a maximalist. It is absurd to speak of "sex differences" in rape rates, for instance, as if men are merely somewhat more likely than women to rape; the rate for women is virtually zero. It is absurd to speak of sex differences in the experience of pregnancy, or even in the different consequences that parenthood has in men's and women's lives; parenthood transforms most women's lives in a way that it does not transform most men's.

It is time to ask again the old unfashionable questions: Who benefits from the official theories and private stories we tell about presumed sex differences? Who pays? What are the consequences? Who gets the jobs and promotions? Who ends up doing the housework? If a woman wishes to believe that her problem is PMS or codependency rather than an abusive or simply unresponsive husband, how does she benefit? How does she lose? If a man wishes to believe that a woman is naturally better at relationships, emotions, and caretaking, how does he benefit? How does he lose? If society promotes the view that women are less reliable than men because of their hormones and their pregnancies, what are the consequences for equity at work, in the law, in politics?

This way of thinking gets us out of the "who's better" approach that, as far as I'm concerned, goes merely in circles. Too often, questions are framed this way: "Is the pattern of traditional male development (going straight up the ladder, marching through life in ten-year stages) better or worse than the pattern of female development (following a path with twists, interruptions, and unpredictable transitions)?" Such questions are unanswerable, because "better" or "worse" depends on what a person values, chooses, and wants out of life, and what rewards or disadvantages follow from those choices.

Instead, we might examine some results of the *belief* that women's life paths do not fit them for an academic or corporate career the way men's development does. One consequence is that women were once excluded from universities and still are excluded from advancement at the highest corporate levels; another is that men who focus wholly on career are excluded from the pleasures and crises of daily family life. We might ask how it came to be that only one professional path is acceptable, and who decides which one is correct. We might observe that the very question of whether women's life paths are worse or better than men's deflects us from the fact that men are setting the standard of normalcy.

I believe that we can think about the influence of gender without resorting to false polarities. There are alternatives to the familiar goal of counting trivial differences in personality traits, skills, and mental abilities, while recognizing the profound differences that continue to divide men and women in their daily lives. The first approach looks outward, to a renewed emphasis on the external factors and contexts that perpetuate or reduce differences. The second looks inward, focusing on the ways that women and men perceive, interpret, and respond to events that befall them—the stories they tell about their lives.

■ *The power of context . . . and the context of power*

Have you ever watched a roomful of four-year-olds at play? If so, you have probably been struck by how different the boys and girls are. Many of the boys will be shouting and racing around, leaping head-first off tables, punching and pummeling one another. The girls will seem far more mild-mannered, playing peacefully and patiently, giggling and whispering to one another. Some will be clinging to the teacher, eager to please, afraid to get too far from her.

Observations like these have persuaded many people that basic personality differences between the sexes must be ingrained, since they appear at so early an age. Psychologists have churned out theories of why boys are so much higher in activity level and are more independent than girls, and why girls are more passive and dependent than boys. Recently, however, developmental psychologist Eleanor Maccoby took another look at these classic studies of children and came up with some startling new interpretations of them.

Starting in early childhood, boys and girls do develop different styles of play and influence, as any parent knows. But Maccoby found that children do not differ in "passivity" or "activity" in some consistent, trait-like way; *their behavior depends on the gender of the child they are playing with.* Among children as young as three, for example, girls are seldom passive with each other; however, when paired with boys, girls typically stand on the sidelines and let the boys monopolize the toys. This gender segregation, Maccoby says, is *"essentially unrelated to the individual attributes of the children who make up all-girl or all-boy groups"* (my emphasis).[3] Instead, it is related to the fact that between the ages of 3½ and 5½, boys stop responding to girls' requests, suggestions, and other attempts to influence them. When a boy and girl compete for a shared toy, the boy dominates—unless there is an adult in the room. Girls in mixed classrooms stay nearer to the teacher, it turns out, not because they are more dependent as a personality trait, but because they want a chance at the toys! Girls play just as independently as boys when they are in all-girl groups, when they will actually sit *farther* from the teacher than boys in all-male groups do.

By elementary school, the interaction and influence styles of boys and girls have diverged significantly. Girls tend to form intimate "chumships" with one or two other girls; boys form group friendships organized around games and other activities. Boys in all-boy groups are more likely than girls to interrupt one another; use commands, threats, or boasts; refuse to comply with another child's wishes; heckle a speaker; call another child names; top someone else's story; and tell jokes. Girls in all-girl groups are more likely than boys to agree with another speaker verbally; to pause to give another girl a chance to speak; to acknowledge what a previous speaker said. Among boys, Maccoby concluded, "Speech serves largely egoistic functions and is used to establish and protect an individual's turf. Among girls, conversation is a more socially binding process."[4]

Of course, to many people the more interesting question is *why* boys stop responding to girls, and why these same-sex patterns develop at all. It may be that children are mimicking the adult patterns of male dominance that they observe. It may result from an average difference in a biological disposition for rough-and-tumble play; in all primate species, young males are more likely than females to go in for physical roughhousing. I think both factors are undoubtedly involved. But my point here is that, for whatever reason, one result of this early divergence between males and females is that a culture gap develops between them, and our society, which rewards and fosters this gap, assures that it becomes increasingly wide by the time children reach adulthood.

The result of this process is that gender, like culture, organizes for its members different influence strategies, ways of communicating, nonverbal languages, and ways of perceiving the world. Just as when in Rome most people do as Romans do, the behavior of women and men depends as much on the gender they are interacting with than on anything intrinsic about the gender they are. For example, my friend Elliot Aronson, who is a social psychologist, has noticed that when he watches football or violent movies with other men he reacts differently than he does when he is watching something violent with his wife. "I can tolerate violence, in sports or films, much more than my wife can," he says. "So when we saw *Raging Bull*, I knew as I watched that she found many of the violent scenes offensive. That awareness colored my own reactions. By the time we left the theater we each had accommodated to the other: I disliked the movie more than I might have if I'd seen it with my male buddies, and she disliked it less."

This kind of silent accommodation goes on all the time, in a process that Candace West and Don Zimmerman call "doing gender."[5] We "do" gender unconsciously, adjusting our behavior and our perceptions depending on the gender of the person we are working, playing, or chatting with. What research like Maccoby's shows is that men and women do not have a set of fixed masculine or feminine traits; the qualities and behaviors expected of women and men vary, depending on the situation the person is in. A token woman in a group of men will feel highly aware of her femaleness, and so will the group.[6] Almost everything she does will be attributed to her gender, which is why she is likely to be accused of being too feminine (thus not "one of the boys") or too masculine ("trying to be something she's not")—but what's really at issue is her visible difference from the majority. A token man in a group of women will have the comparable experience.

I observed this phenomenon not long ago at a conference of women psychoanalysts, who had gathered to discuss "barriers to female achievement." Being psychoanalysts, they were naturally inclined to emphasize the unconscious barriers in the psyche. I, in contrast, spoke of the barriers in women's work environments: the difficulty of being the token, the systematic obstacles to advancement, the way that dead-end jobs themselves create dead-end dreams. (As the token social psychologist, I felt uncomfortable speaking in these terms, but proceeded anyway.) When I finished, the lone male psychoanalyst in the audience rose to comment. "As I was listening to you, I disagreed with what you were saying," he said. "But then, when I got up to speak, I felt uncomfortable, my heart began to pound, and I realized it was because I am the only man in this room." The audience laughed sympathetically, but a woman on the panel next to me said, "Just like a man—the only guy in the room and he still has to be the first person to speak." She was, of course, further supporting my argument. She was attending to the fact of his being a man, and attributing his behavior to it.

The prevalent inclination to regard masculinity and femininity as permanent personality traits has overshadowed the importance of the context in which men and women live. In their everyday lives, men *and* women often behave in "feminine" ways (for example, when they are playing with their children or providing a supportive shoulder for a friend to cry on) and sometimes men *and* women behave in "masculine" ways (for example, when they are competing for a promotion). But by regarding masculinity and femininity as polar opposites, with one side usually better than the other, we forget that, in practice, most of us "do" both.

My women friends, for instance, are always amazed at how macho their otherwise affectionate and doting husbands become when they go off with the guys. "It's a transformation," one friend says, "that I attribute to high concentrations of testosterone in one room." She's right about the apparent transformation—most men like to "do" masculinity, with its rules of stoicism, playfulness, and competition, when they are with other males. But my friend is a lot more "girlish" (or whatever the female equivalent of macho is) over lunch with her women friends than she is in planning sessions at her mostly-male advertising agency. She loves to "do" femininity with other women.

This flexibility has proven to be a good thing. People who are rigidly masculine or feminine across all situations are less healthy, mentally and physically, than people who can adopt the best qualities associated with both extremes. Under some conditions the qualities we label feminine are good for both sexes, and under some conditions the qualities we label masculine are good for both sexes. In the family, for example, the positive qualities of traditional femininity—compassion, nurturance, warmth, and so on—are associated with marital satisfaction *in both sexes.*[7] Naturally; everyone wants a spouse who is affectionate and caring. And at work, the positive qualities of masculinity—assertiveness, competence, self-confidence—are associated with job satisfaction and self-esteem *in both sexes.* Naturally; everyone wants a co-worker who is capable.

Conversely, the extremes of femininity and masculinity can be unhealthy—literally. Psychologist Vicki Helgeson, who conducted an in-depth study of men and women who had had heart attacks, found that for men, negative characteristics associated with masculinity (such as arrogance, hostility, cynicism, and anger) were related to having had more severe attacks, whereas the men who were more empathic and nurturing were more likely to have had less severe heart attacks and better relationships. Yet for women, too much femininity produced a poorer prognosis; the sickest women were those who had become overinvolved with others to the exclusion of caring for themselves.[8]

Most men and women, however, are flexible about masculinity and femininity not only across situations, but over the course of their lives. It's always amused me to think of how many theories are based on studies of college students, who do not even represent all young people their age, let alone older people. Our ideas about sex differences in moral reasoning, sexual attitudes and motives, and the need for love, among other topics, have been limited by this narrow evidence. Similarly, psychoanalytic thinking has emphasized the powerful and presumably lasting effects on masculinity and femininity of unconscious perceptions of events that occur during the first five years, or the first three years, or, increasingly, the first few months.

Theories based on studies of people at one phase of their lives, like those based on unconscious infantile dynamics, overlook the ways in which people's experiences and attitudes cause them to change. Psychologist Lawrence D. Cohn analyzed 65 studies, involving more than 9,000 people, to determine the extent of sex differences in personality throughout adolescence and adulthood. He found that sex differences in ego development and personality traits were greatest among junior- and senior-high-school students, largely because girls mature earlier than boys. But these differences, he found, "declined significantly among college-age adults, *and disappeared entirely among older men and women*" (my emphasis).[9] Both sexes go through phases of egocentrism and conformity at somewhat different ages, but differences between them eventually disappear; in adulthood, men and women do not differ in "maturity of thought" and complexity of reasoning. Similarly, in moral reasoning (the centerpiece of cultural feminism) as in other dimensions of personality development, both sexes ultimately converge.

Across the many fields of psychology, context repeatedly overwhelms personality in the search for meaningful differences between men and women.[10] Context, however, refers to far more than a person's immediate situation. It includes everything in the environment of a person's life: work, family, class, culture, race, obligations, the immediate situation and its requirements, the likelihood of experiencing violence and discrimination, access to health care and education, legal status, and so on. These factors not only affect sex differences, of course; they are responsible for differences and conflicts *within* each gender. The arguments within feminism, for example, of whether black women "should" be identifying with white women or with black men are as unresolvable as debates over whether women are "like" men or different. On some issues, such as rape or fetal protection laws, gender is the unifying principle. On others, such as health delivery to the poor, class is the unifying principle. And on others, such as differing educational opportunities for blacks and whites, race is the unifying principle.[11]

These matters of context aren't very sexy, I realize. When I drew up a table to summarize what research currently shows about differences between men and women (see next page), I noticed an interesting pattern. Almost all of the public conversation and debate about differences falls in the left-hand column, home of all the hot and timely topics such as male-female differences in the brain, moral reasoning, pacifism, empathy, and the need or capacity for attachment and love. Yet, in fact, that column is precisely where the differences *aren't*. The differences of magnitude turn up in the right-hand column, home of the mundane yet persistent inequities in income, power, family obligations, housework, medical and legal treatment, and so on. As the sociologist Cynthia Epstein has observed, we focus on the "deceptive distinctions" between men and women and thereby ignore the important ones.[12]

By seeing the behavior of women and men in context, as flexible capabilities rather than solely as steadfast qualities of the person, we move away from the unfathomable question of what women or men are "really, essentially" like. By seeing the worlds of men and women as cultures that can be as different as Norwegian and Brazilian, we can identify the elements of those worlds that perpetuate or eliminate differences. These cultures, however, are not merely different and equal; they are vastly unequal in power, resources, and status.

Do Men and Women Differ?

Where the differences aren't	*Where the differences are*
Attachment, connection	Care-taking
Cognitive abilities	Communication
Verbal, mathematical,[a]	▪ interaction styles
reasoning, rote memory,	▪ uses of talk
vocabulary, reading,[b] etc.	▪ power differences
Dependency	Emotions
Emotions	▪ Contexts that produce them
▪ Likelihood of feeling them	▪ Forms of expression
Empathy	▪ "Feminization of love"
Moods and "moodiness"	▪ "Feminization of distress"
Moral reasoning	Employment, work opportunities
Need for achievement	Health and medicine
Need for love and attachment	▪ medication and treatment
Need for power	▪ longevity differences
Nurturance[c]	Income
Pacifism, belligerence	Life-span development
(e.g., depersonalizing enemies)	▪ effects of children
Sexual capacity, desire, interest	▪ work and family sequence
Verbal aggressiveness, hostility	Life narratives
	Power and status at work, in relationships, in society
	Reproductive experiences
	Reproductive technology and its social/legal consequences
	"Second shift": housework, child care, family obligations
	Sexual experiences and concerns
	Violence, public and intimate
	Weight and body image

[a] Males excel at highest levels of math performance; in general population, females have slight advantage.
[b] Males are more susceptible to some verbal problems. However, many alleged sex differences seem to be an artifact of referral bias: More boys are *reported* for help than girls, but there are no sex differences in the *actual* prevalence of dyslexia and other reading disabilities (see Shaywitz et al., 1990).
[c] As a capacity; in practice, women do more of the actual care and feeding of children, parents, relatives, friends.

As a result, it is easy to mistake a power difference for a cultural one, as many of us do in the case of language.

Deborah Tannen's deservedly popular book, *You Just Don't Understand,* advances the two-cultures theory of miscommunication: the idea that men and women have trouble understanding one another because they come from two different worlds.[13] Tannen's book is chock full of charming, "Eureka!"-style stories of recognition. For example, she contrasts men's comfort with public speaking—on radio call-in shows, at meetings, in groups of friends—with women's preference for private speaking, the domain of intimate conversation. Tannen describes this difference as that between *report-talk* and *rapport-talk.* Men, she says, use conversation "to preserve independence and negotiate and maintain status in a hierarchical social order"; women use conversation as "a way of establishing connections and negotiating relationships."[14] (This difference, as we saw, begins in childhood.)

At the same time that Tannen's book was rising on the best-seller lists, another book on language appeared that made much less of a splash. The reason, I think, is apparent in the title. It is called *Talking Power: The politics of language.* The author, linguist Robin Lakoff, agrees that there are many differences in the nature, function, and style of male and female talk. Where she disagrees is in the origins of those differences; they aren't just quaint and amusing habits designed by the god (or goddess) in charge of Exasperating the Sexes. They aren't even just a matter of socialization and learning. They aren't even entrenched conversational styles.

"Men's language is the language of the powerful," argues Lakoff. "It is meant to be direct, clear, succinct, as would be expected of those who need not fear giving offense. . . . It is the language of people who are in charge of making observable changes in the real world. Women's language developed as a way of surviving and even flourishing without control over economic, physical, or social reality. Then it is necessary to listen more than speak, agree more than confront, be delicate, be indirect, say dangerous things in such a way that their impact will be felt after the speaker is out of range of the hearer's retaliation."[15]

What would happen to your language if you played a subordinate role in society? You would learn to persuade and influence, rather than assert and demand. You would become skilled at anticipating what others wanted or needed (hence "women's intuition"). You would learn how to placate the powerful and soothe ruffled feelings. You would cultivate communication, cooperation, attention to news and feelings about others (what men call gossip). In short, you would develop a "woman's language." But the characteristics of such a language develop primarily from a power imbalance, not from an inherent deficiency or superiority in communication skills, emotion, or nurturance. They develop whenever there is a status inequity, as can be seen in the languages of working-class Cockneys conversing with employers, blacks conversing with whites, or prisoners conversing with guards.

This power imbalance is the reason that women, far more than men, are able to do what linguists call "code-switching." That is, women learn to speak the standard Male Dialect as well as their own nonstandard Female, whereas men are less able to switch from their speech to female speech. As Lakoff observes:

> Women in business or professional settings often sound indistinguishable from their male counterparts. Speakers of nondominant forms must be bilingual in this way, at least passively, to survive; speakers of the dominant form need not be. (So women don't generally complain that men's communication is impossible to understand, but the battlecry 'What do women want?' has echoed in one form or another down the centuries.)[16]

Tannen's book is appealing because it describes how women and men differ in their use of language, and it characterizes many familiar misunderstandings. Yet I had the same reaction after reading it that I had after reading Carol Gilligan's descriptions of male and female moral reasoning, or Nancy Chodorow's descriptions of male and female attachment styles. After feeling a flash of recognition, along with gratitude that the authors show that women's ways are as good as men's and maybe better, I came away with the sense that men and women are monumentally but intrinsically different. What Tannen's approach overlooks is that people's ways of speaking, just as Eleanor Maccoby observed with children, often *depend more on the gender of the person they are speaking with than on their own intrinsic "conversational style."* Psychologist Linda Carli demonstrated this by observing pairs of individuals—male-male, male-female, and female-female—discussing a topic on which they disagreed.[17] Women spoke more tentatively than men did, she found, only when they were speaking to men! With men, they offered more disclaimers ("I'm no expert," "I may be wrong," "I suppose," "I mean," "I'm not sure"). They used more hedges and moderating terms, like the use of *like* ("drinking and driving is, like, dangerous"). And they used more tag questions that solicit agreement ("It's unfair to prevent eighteen-year-olds from drinking when they can be drafted and killed in war, isn't it?").

Carli even discovered why many women use such hesitations and tags when they speak with men: It works. "Women who spoke tentatively were more influential with men and less influential with women," she reports.[18] Tag questions and hesitations annoyed other women, but they seemed to reassure the men. Even though the men regarded an assertive woman as being more knowledgeable and competent than a woman who said the same thing but with hesitations, they were more *influenced* by a woman who spoke tentatively. They liked her more and found her more trustworthy. When a woman uses tentative language with a man, Carli concludes, she may be communicating that she has no wish to enhance her own status or challenge his. This makes him more inclined to listen.

Indeed, whenever social scientists have looked beneath (or around) many of the apparent linguistic differences between women and men, they often find that qualities thought to be typical of women are, instead, artifacts of a power imbalance. (We saw in Chapter 2, for example, that "women's intuition" is really subordinate's intuition, regardless of the sex of the subordinate.) Both men and women who hold positions of authority display the nonverbal signs of authority, such as looking at you while they speak instead of shyly turning away. And women *and* men who are in the one-down position in a relationship, such as being witnesses in a courtroom, reveal the hesitations and uncertainties of so-called "women's speech" (pauses, hedges, "sort of's," and the like).[19]

"Women's language" often seems illogical to men, full of chatter about unimportant things. But because men have written the rules of language, says Lakoff, "women become by default the quintessential *they*. Women are the other, the outsider: unintelligible and therefore not needing to be heard."[20] The fact that women are the outsiders, not that they have some universal conversational style, is what creates differences between the sexes.

Lakoff offers the example of the Malagasy tribe, a closed, remote society of Madagascar. Because almost nothing happens to the Malagasy, news of any kind becomes a valued commodity, and the ability to hoard information is a sign of power. Powerful individuals therefore speak in a way that seems deliberately misleading and annoying to Westerners. "But this strategy is typical only of male Malagasy speakers," Lakoff notes. "Women do just the reverse: speak directly and to the point. . . . As a result, women are considered poor communicators: they just don't know how to behave in a conversation, don't know how to transmit information properly, and are therefore illogical."[21]

No one decides that a certain form of language is logical, notices that women happen to speak differently, and then rationally concludes that women are illogical. On the contrary, the dominant group first notices the ways in which subordinates differ from themselves; they then assume that these differences occur because the subordinates are illogical; they then conclude that there is something about the subordinates' brains, bodies, or abilities that makes them think and speak illogically. This is illogical reasoning.

As long as women are The Other, anything they do will be wrong. If they try to speak Male-Speak, as Geraldine Ferraro did when she ran for Vice President, they may be regarded as tough and unladylike. If they speak Female-Speak, in the manner of Vanna White, their language may be seen as incompetent and inconsequential. Some women respond to this dilemma by valuing "women's speech" for its subtleties and attention to feelings, its polite unwillingness to interrupt the (dominant) speaker, and its modest hesitations. I think this response is fine, as long as it doesn't deflect everyone from the long-range goal of reducing that power imbalance, improving communication, and making sure that women are *heard* in the public domain. Achieving this goal will require a critical density of women in the public sphere and in positions of authority, so that how any one woman speaks will not be the focus of everyone's attention. Lakoff herself is optimistic:

> As long as there is a power imbalance, women will be in a double bind communicatively: any way they communicate that differs from the way men do will be stigmatized as different and therefore worse; any attempt they make to approximate the ways of men will be stigmatized as unfeminine, indicative of bad character, and uppity. . . . But as long as we remain aware and committed, things are likely to continue to get better. We just have to keep the faith.[22]

■ *The power of story: Gender as narrative*

The communications researcher George Gerbner once defined the human being as "the only species that tells stories—and lives by the stories we tell." This idea—that narratives that describe our lives are the key metaphor in understanding human behavior—is sweeping psychology and many other fields.[23] Our plans, memories, love affairs, hatreds, ambitions, and dreams are guided by plot outlines. "Understanding one's past, interpreting one's actions, evaluating future possibilities—each is filtered through these stories," says psychologist Mary Gergen. "Events 'make sense' as they are placed in the correct story form."[24]

Thus we say, "I am this way because, as a small child, I fell into a vat of cherry juice, and then my parents . . ." We say, "Let me tell you the story of how we fell in love." We say, "When you hear what happened, you'll understand why I was entitled to take such gruesome revenge." We say, "I can't be a neurosurgeon, because, when I was sixteen . . . and then . . ." As psychologist George Howard puts it, life is the story we live by, pathology is a story gone mad, and psychotherapy is an exercise in "story repair."[25] Stories need not be *fictions,* in the child's meaning of "tell me a story." They are narratives that provide a unifying theme to organize the events of our lives. They attempt to be true, but they are rarely the whole truth and nothing but the truth.

It is here, in the stories that men and women tell about their lives, that we find the greatest divergence between them.[26] In the classic myth of the hero, the man ventures forth from everyday life to conquer supernatural forces in the name of his quest. He returns, victorious, and is richly rewarded. "Where is the woman in this story?" asks Mary Gergen. "She is only to be found as a snare, an obstacle, a magic power, or a prize."[27] Anthropologist Marvin Harris has noted that "When the King told his knights, 'If you slay the dragon, I'll give you one of my daughters,' no one doubted that the daughters would go when given."[28] What effect does this story, endlessly repeated in its ancient and contemporary forms, have on women's identities and dreams?

And the classic woman's story, whether in ancient fairy tales like "Cinderella" and "Sleeping Beauty" or their modern equivalents in romance novels and films like *Pretty Woman,* is a narrative of passivity, chance, and fate. Horrible things, all of them beyond her control, happen to the beautiful heroine who awaits rescue by her Prince. Until he saves her, she is doomed to a life of sweeping, cleaning, struggling, prostitution, or corporate executivehood. If she isn't beautiful, pliant, and willing to give it all up for love, she doesn't get rescued. What effect does this story, endlessly repeated throughout our culture, have on women's identities and dreams?

I want to emphasize again that there is nothing essential to men's and women's natures that causes the difference in their stories. We've seen how, as women became the love experts in this century, their love stories changed. We've seen how stories of the body, of sexuality, of the brain have changed, along with the times. In the space of only a few years, social movements and economic upheavals can alter the stories that people are able to envision for themselves. And in our private lives, we frequently change explanatory themes as a result of love, tragedy, everyday experience, political conversion, or psychotherapy.

Moreover, it is not that all men tell one kind of story, and all women tell another; that men are always ruthless knights and women are willing pawns; that men value only success and women value only people. As I have been arguing, the virtues and vices of human character are distributed across the sexes, arrogance and compassion included. Men and women differ, however, in the kinds of stories they tell, which reflect the different lives they lead. And, even more interestingly, they differ in what they feel obliged to include or leave out of their narratives, which reflects the roles they play and the faces they present to the world. We saw that men and women, in talking about their divorces, speak of their break-ups and their grief differently. They both feel pain, yet they publicly tell different stories.

Would a celebrity football player, age twenty-four, reveal his abiding and faithful love for his wife? Would a famous congresswoman reveal how she ruthlessly abandoned her husband when he was ill and savagely destroyed the careers of her opponents? Almost never. Gergen, who has been studying modern autobiographies of famous people, finds common metaphors in men's stories that are rarely found in women's. The stories of powerful white men typically fit the traditional male narrative: These authors became heroes, pursue their quest, overcome crises, and ultimately win victory. Women and children may come along for the ride, but (if they figure in the story at all) they must not interrupt it; even if they have the impertinence to get sick and die, the male narrators barely notice.

Thus, Lee Iacocca's best-selling autobiography describes his rise to the top of an automotive career, but he says little about his wife. Mary, a diabetic, had two heart attacks, each one following a crisis in Iacocca's career at Ford or Chrysler. He writes: "Above all, a person with diabetes has to avoid stress. Unfortunately, with the path I had chosen to follow, this was virtually impossible." Too bad for Mary. Gergen comments:

> Obviously his description of his wife's death was not intended to expose his cruelty. It is, I think, a conventional narrative report—appropriate to his gender. The book (and his life) are dedicated to his career. It appears that Iacocca would have found it unimaginable that he should have ended his career in order to reduce his wife's ill-health. As a Manstory, the passage is not condemning; however, read in reverse, as a wife's description of the death of her husband or child, it would appear callous, to say the least.

Likewise, Chuck Yeager reveals in his autobiography—his shining tale of having the Right Stuff to be a pilot—that his wife, who had

had four children in quick succession, became gravely ill during her last pregnancy. "Whenever Glennis needed me over the years, I was usually off in the wild blue yonder," Yeager wrote. Would a woman write that sentence about her husband? Would she be so cavalier— to use an appropriately sex-specific word—about her husband's needs?

And Richard Feynman, the humorous, brilliant, Nobel Prize– winning physicist, was married to a woman who was ill with tuberculosis for seven years. Feynman, hard at work on the atomic bomb, borrowed a car to get to her bedside on the day she was dying. This is what he had to say:

> When I got back (yet another tire went flat on the way), they asked me what happened. "She's dead. And how's the program going?" They caught on right away that I didn't want to talk about it.

Was the tire really more memorable to Feynman than his wife's death? Unlikely. The point is *the narrative of the story*: deaths, even of loved ones, are not to interfere in the Quest, the Task, the Goal.

Many men write of their Quest in a tone of hostility, aggression, and domination: the triumph of conquering impossible odds, defeating the other guy, or beating "nature's incalculable odds" (this last from John Paul Getty on the exhilaration of drilling his first oil well). Men's stories, says Gergen, "celebrate the song of the self"; men are even willing to play the "bastard." In letters, journals, and autobiographies, many eminent male writers and less-eminent celebrities sing of the self as John Cheever, in his published Journals, did in this entry:

> I wake. My older son has returned safely from school. The trees are full of birds. I mount my wife, eat my eggs, walk my dogs. It is the day before Easter.[29]

My son, *my* wife, *my* eggs, *my* dogs, *my* sexual pleasure! Not a paragraph, I think, that could have been written by most female diarists. (Well . . . Katharine Hepburn did call her autobiography *Me*, refrained from revealing her emotions about private matters such as her brother's death, and unflinchingly described her independent professional accomplishments—and for this "male" narrative she was castigated by *The New York Times Book Review*.)

Pick up a typical celebrity autobiography by a male athlete, and chances are that you will learn about his sexual exploits, put-downs of women, childish tantrums, and drunken braggadocio. Writer Merrill Markoe, who read a few of these literary efforts, decided that "The parading of infantile character flaws as though they were badges of honor and distinction is a male trait. . . . The combination of arrogance without shame and insensitivity without humility or hindsight is the sole domain of attractive successful white men." [30]

Eminent women who write their autobiographies almost never tell the same narrative plot. Women enjoy their successes, press to win, and work hard to succeed; they may be as motivated, as self-absorbed, and as pushy as men, but they do not talk about these matters the same way. Beverly Sills, a star at the New York City Opera, gave up her singing career for two years to accompany her husband to Cleveland, where he worked. She writes: "My only alternative was to ask Peter to scuttle the goal he'd been working toward for almost twenty-five years. If I did that, I didn't deserve to be his wife." Gergen's analysis of women's stories—Nien Cheng, who wrote of her survival during years of imprisonment in China, Martina Navratilova on her tennis career, Sills, and others—shows that while men tell of sacrificing their lives to their careers, women tell the same story in reverse.

In the writings of accomplished women, Gergen finds, we hear about the audience response, affection for the opponent, and continuity with goals other than professional achievement, rather than seeing such goals in opposition to achievement. "I've never been able to treat my opponent as the enemy," writes Navratilova (but do we doubt what a fierce competitor she is?). "One of the things I always loved best about being an opera singer was the chance to make new friends every time I went into a new production," writes Sills (but do we doubt what a highly motivated and ambitious singer she was?). Merrill Markoe, wanting to be fair to those arrogant male celebrity athletes, read the comparable "trashy" autobiographies of female celebrities such as Joan Collins, Shelley Winters, and Tina Turner. The women wrote mainly about failed marriages and relationships, embarrassing personal foibles, and family tragedies (but do we really believe they are all soft-hearted sweeties?).

The autobiographies of famous people tell explicit stories; contemporary magazines often tell implicit ones. Popular magazines, for instance, reveal an interesting difference in one way that men and women may think about their lives. As you can see in the table opposite, most of the magazines directed to women include a horoscope, a mystic, or a numerologist; not one man's magazine does. Even newer magazines for older women, such as *Lear's* and *Mirabella*, have them. Why? The surface answer is that horoscopes are cheap to produce, advertisers compete to position their ads next to them, and readers like them.

I am not suggesting that women are more superstitious or gullible than men—or, in the cultural-feminist reinterpretation of this difference, more open-minded and spiritual! Actually, studies of the general population find that women are only slightly more likely than men to believe in astrology (some of the most popular astrology columns are written by men), and that even this difference shrinks when education is factored in.[31] But if we examine one meaning of horoscopes in women's magazines, I believe we find a subtle measure of a difference in women's and men's feelings of control over their lives, in their perception of opportunities and destinies.

It is no coincidence that the magazines called *Fame, Success, Money,* and *Fortune* (which both sexes read) do not have horoscopes, because astrology contradicts the capitalist message that anyone can become anything with enough hard work. Likewise it is significant that magazines about careers, families, and motherhood—*Working Woman, New York Woman, Family Circle, Good Housekeeping*—do not have horoscopes. Mothers and employed women, apparently, know that their fate has little to do with the stars and everything to do with time management. But the magazines for women about relationships, beauty, youth, and the pursuit of perfection—goals which women feel increasingly to be out of their control, increasingly a source of anxiety—tell women they can have it all, at least if their stars and cosmetics are in place.

What follows from the way people tell their stories, and how they interpret their challenges and destinies? What images inspire them

Presence or Absence of Horoscopes in Leading Magazines

Women's magazines		Men's magazines	
Cosmopolitan	yes	Esquire[d]	no
Elle	yes[a]	Fame	no
Glamour	yes	Field & Stream	no
Harper's Bazaar	yes	Forbes	no
In Fashion	yes	Fortune	no
Lear's	yes	GQ	no
Mademoiselle	yes	Golf	no
Marie Claire	yes	M (The Civilized Man)	no
Mirabella	yes[b]	MGF (Men's Guide to Fashion)	no
Moxie	yes[c]	Manhattan, Inc.	no
New Woman	yes	Men's Fitness	no
Sassy	yes	Money	no
Self	yes	Penthouse	no
Seventeen	yes	Playboy	no
Taxi	yes	Popular Mechanics	no
Vogue	yes	Soldier of Fortune	no
Woman	yes	Sports Afield	no
Family Circle	no	Sports Illustrated	no
Good Housekeeping	no	Success	no
Ladies' Home Journal	no	Tennis	no
McCall's	no		
New York Woman	no		
Redbook	no		
Working Woman	no		

NOTE: General-interest magazines directed at both sexes (*Atlantic, Harper's, People, Time,* etc.) have been omitted. Most of these do not have horoscopes, with the notable exception of *TV Guide.*

[a] Has a horoscope *and* a numerology column.
[b] Has a "Mystic of the month" column.
[c] Had a column by a self-proclaimed "psychic" answering reader's queries.
[d] The British edition of *Esquire* began a "Horoscope for Men" in 1991.

and which ones restrict them? We develop and shape our identities in the narratives we tell about our lives, and we are as influenced by the stories we feel do *not* apply to us as by those that do. Two of our most popular cultural stories illustrate their power over our individual and collective imaginations: the struggle of the artist and the valor of the soldier, both of which rest on male narratives.

The writer Ursula Le Guin has skillfully dissected the male story of the artist, a narrative specifying that the artist must sacrifice himself to his art. (This idea is a justification for the "artist as bastard" subplot.) Given such a narrative, Le Guin observes, it follows that any attempt to combine art with housework and family is "impossible, unnatural."[32] How, then, have women writers told their stories? Often in terms of how to escape their families, how to find rooms of their own. The "heroic" female writers had books instead of babies, because otherwise, the story went, both the art and the children would suffer. Yet, as Le Guin points out, the "you-can't-write-if-you-procreate myth" applies to women only. Male writers may have children, as long as someone else is attending to them and they don't interrupt the basic plot of Heroic Male Writer on his Anguished Quest. Narratives about great artists, Le Guin shows, have lacked the possible vision that having a family, or merely having the experience of being female, might *enhance* writing:

It seems to me a pity that so many women, including myself, have accepted this denial of their own experience and narrowed their perception to fit it, writing as if their sexuality were limited to copulation, as if they know nothing about pregnancy, birth, nursing, mothering, puberty, menstruation, menopause, except what men are willing to hear, nothing except what men are willing to hear about housework, childwork, lifework, war, peace, living and dying as experienced in the female body and mind and imagination.[33]

Le Guin hastens to add she doesn't want to reverse the myth, arguing that you *have* to have children to be a great writer. She does not hold with the sentimental belief that motherhood puts a woman artist "in immediate and inescapable contact with the sources of life, death, beauty, growth, corruption. . . ." The point is that our vision of the artist has been based on, and limited by, a male narrative, and this story leaves out much that is important to men as well as to women.

Cultural narratives and metaphors are so powerful that when they are violated by actual human beings, many people feel momentarily dizzy. War is a male story par excellence; in the Persian Gulf War, which reflected a "man-to-man" battle between George Bush and Saddam Hussein, we were inundated with images of brave male soldiers "rescuing" an "innocent" nation that had been "raped" by evil villains. What, then, of the 30,000 women (about six percent of the total troops) who served in this war, in every way but combat? How can women do any rescuing of a damsel nation in distress?

The media solution was to emphasize repeatedly, in articles and images, all the mothers who were tearfully leaving small children at home. *People* magazine did a cover story on "Mom Goes to War." Writer Nell Bernstein, who looked, observed that "it was nearly impossible to find an article that mentioned women soldiers without also mentioning the children they left behind."[34] What the articles did not say, however, was that the majority of women in the military are not mothers, and that a higher percentage of male soldiers have children than female soldiers do. These facts do not fit the traditional story we tell, that war is male, fought by men *for* women. "When women start muscling in on the action," says Bernstein, "the ancient paradigms of war and peace are threatened." Indeed; perhaps it's time for new ones.

And so each sex deviates from its proper story at some peril. "Both seemed imprisoned by their stories," says Gergen; "both bound to separate pieces of the world, which if somehow put together, would create new possibilities—ones in which each could share the other's dreams."

We can be imprisoned by stories; or we can be liberated by them. This has been, in a way, a book about the stories that women and men tell about themselves and one another, and about the scientific stories that society favors. Interest in power and circumstance as the guiding story of human behavior has faded in favor of the individual, internal stories of biology and psychodynamic processes.[35] Of course we are influenced by biology, personality, and unconscious motives. Yet when we choose to emphasize these pieces of the human story over all others, the consequences can be significant. And the consequences differ for men and women, as we can see in the following two examples:

▪ *The story of depression.* Last year, a popular television show presented a report on postpartum depression.[36] Postpartum depression is nearly as popular a topic these days as PMS, and for many of the same reasons; hormones explain so *many* problems that women have.[37]

In this case, the interviewer spoke with a woman who revealed how unhappy and teary she had been after the birth of each of her three children. She worried that she wasn't a contented mother "like other women." In fact, she confessed, at the point of her deepest depression she had fantasized about throwing her baby down an escalator in a shopping mall. Her husband was worried. His wife wasn't the "cute, fun girl" she once was. Fortunately, this woman learned that her problem was easily resolved: She was suffering from postpartum depression, a condition easily treated with antidepressants. Cut to shots of happy wife, happy husband, playing with happy children.

Now, perhaps this woman does have an extreme chemical imbalance that is best treated with antidepressants. I am not unilaterally opposed to the use of medication, and if it helps her, all the better. Let us simply consider the possibility that there is more to this story than a tale of hormones gone awry. Not once during this show, for example, did it occur to the murmuring sympathetic interviewer, or to the woman herself, that this young mother's unhappiness might be due to having *three babies in four years and a Navy spouse who was out of town much of the time.* Three babies in diapers, with no help from another adult? Who *wouldn't* feel exhausted and weepy? What woman could be a "cute, fun girl" under such conditions?

Moreover, not once during this show did the interviewer or a psychologist point out that feelings of incompetence are perfectly normal for mothers to have (especially in a society that doesn't much value what mothers do), and so are fantasies of throwing the baby over a banister (it doesn't mean you will actually do it). No one told this woman that depression can result from sheer fatigue and the daily relentlessness of caring for three babies. No one suggested that perhaps she would benefit by getting together with other mothers of small children; finding ways to organize and share child care; and insisting that her husband do his share around the house. No one interviewed the authors of a recent study, who found that the predictors of postpartum depression were in fact *pre*partum depression, "inadequate social support, reduced closeness to husband, and poor self-esteem." [37]

In this context, consider the 1990 report of a comprehensive three-year study of depression, conducted under the auspices of the American Psychological Association. This study made news, but rarely with the excitement of front-page headlines. The *Los Angeles Times* relegated it to a short item on page 25, with the boring headline "Study Analyzes Women's High Depression Risk." That hardly sounds newsworthy, until we begin reading:

> Women are twice as likely as men to suffer from major depression, for reasons more often cultural than biological, according to the results of a three-year study released Wednesday.
>
> Poverty, unhappy marriage, reproductive stress and sexual and physical abuse are stronger factors than biological conditions in accounting for the difference in depression rates between men and women, the American Psychological Assn. researchers reported . . .
>
> "The task force found that women truly are more depressed than men, primarily due to their experience of being female in our contemporary culture," [Ellen McGrath, chair of the research group] said. [38]

The APA study contradicted the widespread belief that the origins of clinical depression are primarily biochemical, and therefore that any difference between men and women in the prevalence of depression must likewise be due to biochemical differences between them. The APA study spoke in a currently unfashionable language, locating the origins of human misery in human experience. And so it was relegated to page 25 of my daily newspaper.

▪ *The story of success.* Popular explanations of why more women have not reached the highest pinnacles of power have tended to blame women, in one way or another, for a failure of motivation or a personal inability to combine family and career. Certainly, in many professional situations, women are more likely than men to blame themselves for not succeeding, to lose self-confidence, and to lower their ambitions.

However, in a review of the research on gender and power in organizations, Belle Rose Ragins and Eric Sundstrom found that these psychological symptoms proved to be *results* of powerlessness, not causes. Men tend to develop more power as they progress through their careers, whereas most women do not. The reason, Ragins and Sundstrom learned, was "a consistent difference favoring men" in men's and women's access to power and having the resources to make use of it. "The processes involved in the development of power differ for men and women," they concluded, and "the path to power for women resembles an obstacle course."[39] Powerlessness, in short, perpetuates powerlessness.

What are the results of the popularity of the story of hormones over life experiences, of intrapsychic fears of success over objective obstacles to success? They translate into how we treat our children and the expectations we have for ourselves; they affect our deepest emotions and visions of ourselves; they determine how we respond to adversity and the normal problems of adult life. We must be careful about the explanations and narratives we choose to account for our lives because, as we will see next, we live by the stories we tell.

■ *Choosing a story: Victims, survivors, and the problem of blame*

Context and story offer interesting new ways of thinking about the lives of women and men, but neither of these approaches, in my mind, is sufficient on its own. Exclusively environmental views hold that we are wholly created by the system we live in and the events that happen to us. Exclusively cognitive views, such as those held by many psychotherapists today, hold that there is nothing good or bad, but thinking makes it so: that we are wholly created by our stories, by the ways we perceive and explain the events that happen to us.

I'm unsatisfied with both extremes. To overemphasize the power of context is to ignore the power that people have to transcend tragedy, envision new possibilities, and create meanings in their experiences. To overemphasize the power of the mind to do these things, however, is to ignore the very real conditions of people's lives. Context and story affect each other.

The example I've chosen to illustrate this point is the problem of recovery from sexual abuse. This subject is delicate and difficult to write about without giving offense, for it lies on the misty intersection of political analysis and psychological trauma. Yet I believe it illustrates the mismeasure of woman that I have been describing throughout this book: the pathologizing of female experience and of women themselves; what happens when we overlook the important inequalities between women and men, in this case their differences in power and sexual privilege; and the consequences of transforming a societal problem into a purely personal and psychological one.

In the late 1970s and early 1980s, feminists began writing about an issue that was, at first, too shocking for many to accept: the sexual molestation of children. Louise Armstrong, in *Kiss Daddy Goodnight*, revealed her own horrifying experience of incest and placed it in the perspective of a national problem. Community studies found that the frequency of sexual abuse of children was much higher than had been assumed, that most of the victims were female, and that most of the perpetrators were not crazy strangers but familiar relatives and neighbors.[40] To the feminist writers, these facts were evidence that incest and other forms of child abuse were not the aberrations of a few sick men but the results of a system that endows men with the sense of entitlement to control and abuse women and children.

Now, all of us may choose among an array of explanations for the reality of sexual abuse. Who is primarily at fault—the father who molests, the mother who defends him, or the community and legal system that fails to rescue abused children? What are the reasons it happens—that society is patriarchal and sexist, that the perpetrator is mentally ill, that the mother should have been having sex more often with the father or he would never have felt the "need" to turn to his daughter? And what are the consequences of abuse—does it affect everything that later happens to the child, or is it part of many other formative experiences?

In the last decade, ever so quietly, the "story" of the problem of abuse, solutions for treatment, and targets of blame have been changing. For example, the pseudonymous Jan Grey, who founded the SARA society ("Sexual Assault Recovery Anonymous"), has written an autobiography of her recovery from abuse. The promotional flyer for the book identifies the main characters in Jan's story thus:

- The victim, Jan, sexually abused by her stepfather.
- Jan's mother, the *real* abuser, the bad mom, "who enmeshed Jan in a codependent relationship. At times, she emotionally and physically abused Jan; at times she vied with Jan for Bob's affection." (The mother isn't even named, although all other characters in the story are.)
- Bob, the stepfather, who had been "sexually abused by his mother" (*another* bad mother!) and was simply playing his part in the "intergenerational chain of abuse."
- Kevin, Jan's son, "who provided the motivation for the escape from a dysfunctional lifestyle."
- Ian, "the last man in her life, who refused to play codependent and assisted Jan on the road to recovery."

Who is mostly to blame in this narrative? The mothers, Jan's and Bob's. Who are, the rescuers? The Innocent Son and the Good Boyfriend, her savior.

Jan Grey's story is typical of a significant shift in public and professional attitudes toward the problem of incest. A decade ago, when incest was first in the news, public horror and outrage focused on the perpetrator—the father or other adult relative. Louise Armstrong, in *Kiss Daddy Goodnight: Ten years later,* describes what happened next: "The onslaught of experts. The 'disease' model. The proud cry that incest was to be 'de-criminalized.' And with all that, the ever-important building block: the 'profile' of the 'incest mother' ":

From the outset, all the heavy artillery was aimed at this mother. The entire construction of the "family disease" model depended on her existence. . . . She provided the entire rationale for the "illness model," for the de-criminalization of paternal child molestation.

Without this abstract "her," we would have been forced to confront the political/power abuse as we had posed it.[41]

Armstrong is angry at the way that public analysis of sexual abuse has shifted focus from the perpetrator, the man, to the "enabler," the woman. "The mother can't win," she observes. "She's wrong no matter what happens. If she leaves, she didn't support her husband and work it through to keep the family intact. If she stays, somehow she's condoning it."[42]

This change in narrative was, in turn, part of the larger cultural shift away from collective political action to an individualizing mental-health movement. Each battered or raped woman, each molested or raped child, was regarded as an instance of rare and bizarre family pathology. Sociologist Nancy Matthews, who traced the evolution of the anti-rape movement in Los Angeles, has documented the ways in which the "feminist political agenda of relating violence against women to women's oppression was marginalized, ridiculed, and suppressed." One way that funding agencies accomplished this was by redefining rape as an individual problem rather than, as Matthews says, "a personal experience with political implications."[43]

Historian Lloyd deMause, who analyzed the content of themes in political speeches and the media in the 1980s, argues that the public focus on individual horror stories of abusers and survivors deflects attention from the real story: how the massive cutbacks in funding for children's programs, child-abuse programs, prenatal care, unemployment programs, and "dozens of other government activities directly affecting the welfare and lives of children" led to the maltreatment, neglect, abuse, or deaths of thousands of children.[44] Nancy Scheper-Hughes, in her book *Child Survival,* put it more strongly: *"the time of greatest public outcry against child abuse is also the time of the widespread, official planning of sacrifice of children in public policy"* (emphasis in original).[45]

And so the political, economic, and social context of abuse is increasingly out of sync with the narratives that are told about it, with profound consequences for individual well-being and for social policy. To illustrate some of them, let's examine the assumptions and functions of many of the sexual-survivor groups that have sprung up across the United States and Canada.

Most of the women who find their way into these groups are troubled and unhappy, and they report a long litany of reasons that are familiar in contemporary culture: Depression. Conflict with their children and partners, and feeling unvalued by both. Children in trouble. Unhappiness with weight and looks. Alcohol abuse. Feeling helpless to improve their lives. Feeling sexually vulnerable and powerless. Having been in a series of bad relationships.

Indeed, these problems are often the results of childhood sexual abuse, but many of them are also the sadly familiar laments of women who were not abused as children. The prevalence of these problems in women's lives, combined with the reality of widespread sexual abuse, pose a complex question for individual sufferers and for society: How does a woman come to focus exclusively on *past* sexual abuse as the major reason for her unhappiness, when many other *current* factors are often involved as well?

In studying this question, Dara Culhane, a medical anthropologist, has read many of the personal testimonials of survivors of abuse, attended numerous survivor-group meetings, and interviewed many professionals and paraprofessionals in the field. In addition, she has been conducting an ethnographic field study of fifty women, ranging in age from the late twenties to the early forties (the age range typical of women in "adult survivor" groups). The women in her study are single, divorced, and married, lesbian and heterosexual, working class and middle class.[46]

Culhane learned that women find their way into survivor groups for a range of reasons and by a variety of routes—they read a book, talk to a friend, are seeing a therapist, call a crisis hotline. The most common precipitating events are the death of a parent (usually the one who committed the abuse), the birth of a child, the woman's child reaching the age she was when she was abused, and, particularly for single, middle-class women, career stagnation or ambivalence about work. At this point the woman feels she is unable to chisel away at her mountain of difficulties, and phones a private psychotherapist or support service for help. She might say, "I'm having all these problems and I was abused" or "I don't remember having been abused but I have all the symptoms of it."

Once in therapy, a survivor group, or a self-help group, the woman is encouraged to talk freely about her experience of having been abused as a child. The therapist or group then concentrates on helping the woman reallocate responsibility for the abuse, assuring her that she was not an evil or seductive child, that the abuse was not her fault, that the adult was to blame. The next step in the process is to make links with the woman's current problems. "In most of the popular counseling and survivor groups," says Culhane, "progress in therapy is *defined* as the recognition of those links. You are 'more healed' when you come to understand that most of your problems result from your having been a victim of sexual abuse."

In this section I want to consider two case studies that illustrate different routes to this "healing" realization and how it serves to help women cope with their complex problems. One illustrates the path of a woman who always knew she had been abused, and who thought about it more or less intensely at different times in her life but never connected it with her ongoing difficulties. The other illustrates a more recent phenomenon: women who never actually remember having been abused, but who use their current problems to *infer* that they were. I begin with a woman whom Culhane interviewed (naturally, her name and certain identifying details have been changed).

■

Emma, now age thirty-eight, is a working-class woman from the midwest. Her mother, who had Emma at fifteen, was an alcoholic, and her father had disappeared, so Emma was raised by her grandparents. Between the ages of eight and twelve, Emma was sexually molested by her grandfather. She told no one about it, but ran away from home at twelve. She was caught and sent to a foster home, where she lived until age fourteen. She ran away again; drifted around the city; had a child at sixteen; was abandoned by her boyfriend; had another child at eighteen with another man; left him; got married and lived with her husband for seven years; then left him for the man she has now been with for eight years. Emma has struggled to keep her two children with her all this time. She is on welfare and has no marketable skills.

When Emma was thirty-three, one of her woman friends invited her to spend a weekend at her cabin in the country. Emma arranged care for her kids, and told the man she was living with that she would be away for a few days. He became angry and threatened to leave her if she went. Emma was frightened, thought he wouldn't be there when she got back, but she left for the weekend anyway. She is proud of this first small effort to do what she wanted and still talks frequently about how exhilarating it was to stand up to him.

When Emma returned, she and her partner began to have serious problems. She started making more demands on him, which made him angry. Sexually, they fell into a vicious circle: She was turned off to him because he admitted to having numerous affairs with other women; he said he was having affairs because she had lost sexual interest. Emma was also having problems with her teenage daughters, who were, she said, "getting wild and running around."

One day Emma told her social worker that she was feeling depressed and unable to cope. The social worker referred Emma to a mental-health clinic, where she was diagnosed as being depressed and given antidepressants. At some point Emma told her counselor that her grandfather had molested her as a child, and the counselor immediately referred her to a survivor's group.

The group experience was a shock and a relief for Emma. She hadn't known that other women were sexually mistreated; she had never talked about it. At first, she felt awkward in the group, aware of the class differences between her and the other women, most of whom were professionals. "But the more we talked the more I realized we had in common and the less those differences mattered," Emma said.

Today, Emma has been in therapy for five years. She is still on antidepressants, still going to the mental health clinic, and still going to meetings of the survivor group. What became of the problems that sent her to therapy in the first place—depression, being unskilled and on welfare, conflicts with her daughters, her constant battles with her partner about sex, and his infidelities?

When Culhane asked Emma how things were going now, Emma said, "I'm much stronger in myself, I really like this group, my relationship with my women friends in this group is really good. We talk about our problems all the time. I'm not as much of a doormat as I used to be; I stand up for myself more." What about the daughters? "Well, they've calmed down, we are doing better, and *they understand now that the reason I've done some of the things I've done is that I was abused.* They know now that it's not their fault that I was mean or short-tempered; they know where my problems came from: having been molested by my grandfather."

And, reflecting on her relationship with her partner, Emma said, "It's better. He understands now that when I say no, I'm not rejecting him, so he's not hurt by that any more. And I say no when I want to say no, and he understands." At which point she burst into tears and added, "I'm sure he's still fooling around all the time. But I understand that he does it because he's a sex addict." Culhane said, softly, "But it still hurts." And Emma, weeping, replied, "Yes, but I understand."

■

Emma's sexual abuse by a grandfather who betrayed her trust was one of many difficult experiences in her life—moving around from place to place as a child, her mother's inability to care for her, her father's abandonment of her, living with terrible foster parents, having two children as a teenager, having problems with unreliable men, being unemployed and unskilled. Yet Emma has come to believe that the root cause of her life's difficulties was the specific past trauma. Everything else pales in comparison to its importance to her.

Indeed, Emma's realization of how much she had in common with the middle-class professional women in her group is part of the creation of a new identity based on victimization. The common bond is the shared victim experience. It's not that this identity is bad or wrong; it can be very helpful in recovering from sexual abuse. But it is not the only one possible, especially if a woman is also being victimized because of her race or class. What Emma's story leaves out is the way that her current realities—the context of her life— are affecting her.

"Emma is a woman with very little power to begin with, very few resources to begin with, who is trying her best to get through a life that is crisis after crisis after crisis, all of which she is somehow held responsible for," Culhane observes. "The message she keeps hearing from the culture at large is that her kids are 'running wild' because she's a bad mother, that her partner is unfaithful because she's not living up to her sexual obligations. The sexual-abuse explanation allocates responsibility for these problems in something outside herself and her supposed moral failings. Her kids are running around because she abused them, and she abused them because she was abused by her grandfather. Likewise her sexual problems with her partner have nothing to do with her partner's behavior, but with the fact that she was abused as a child. And where's the partner? Doing what he's always done. The two of them now understand that she was sick and he is sick, but nothing changes."

For women like Emma, the survivors' group is a life raft. It saves them from drowning. It gives them friends who understand, who offer the consolation of shared experience. It gives them a clear explanation in the past for their present unhappiness. It alleviates the terrible feeling of guilt they carry for not being perfect lovers and mothers, and for not being able to transform their men into perfect partners. Indeed, the women whom Culhane interviewed said that as a result of their support groups they feel "stronger in themselves"—better able to assert themselves and make choices among available options.

Yet almost all of them also described lives that had remained essentially the same, their available options being limited or even reduced by virtue of their being female, poor, and working class. Culhane heard a few success stories of women who went back to school, moved ahead in their professions, or stopped fighting with their children. "But most of them had the resources to make these changes anyway," she says, "or they had problems that would have gone away in time. Even difficult teenagers grow up."

Culhane once asked a prominent social worker if she thought there were class differences in the consequences for women who have been abused. The woman said: "Oh yes. Middle-class survivors tend to become very successful; they overachieve, do well in school, become leading members of their professions; whereas poorer women who are survivors tend to get involved in drug and alcohol abuse." But, of course, middle-class women generally have the opportunities to do well in school and poor women do not. "Her answer crystallized just what is wrong with the tendency to attribute everything that happens to a woman to childhood abuse," says Culhane. "It's as though the poor woman is sitting there and saying, 'Shall I go and get my Master's Degree or shall I go to the local bar? Oh, I guess I'll go to the bar.' And the middle-class woman has the same set of choices: 'Shall I go to the bar, or shall I go and get my law degree? I'll flip a coin; oh, it tells me to get a law degree.' "

Without intending to take away anything from the help that survivor groups offer women like Emma, therefore, we can also observe the limitations of a story that has an exclusive focus on past reasons for current problems. It overlooks the current realities that entrap survivors, and, by assuming that all survivors share economic opportunities as well as psychological suffering, it blurs the different prospects that people have to recover from trauma and to make abiding changes in their lives.

The sexual-abuse-victim story crystallizes many of society's anxieties, in these insecure times, about the vulnerability of children, the changing roles of women, and the norms of sexuality. It draws like a magnet those who feel vulnerable and victimized, and who wish to share in society's sympathy. For these reasons, it has a powerful emotional appeal to all manner of people who were by no means abused in the way that Emma was.

For some women, the sexual-victim identity is appealing because it is a lightning rod for the inchoate feelings of victimization they have as a result of their status in society at large. It provides a clearer focus than such vague enemies as "the system," sexism, deadening work, welfare, or boredom. For them, "sexual abuse" is a metaphor for all that is wrong in women's lives. For them, the mechanism of "repression" is a convenient way to participate in this metaphor. It allows them to partake of the culture of recovery and to assuage their emotional needs. These motives are apparent in the many women and men who are "recalling" abuse that they believe happened in previous lives or in their cribs. At one conference I heard a man tearfully reveal that he had been "abused" at the age of eighteen months . . . by his mother, who, he revealed, fondled his penis while giving him a bath. A woman next to me whispered, "Are my twin boys going to sue me in twenty years for having destroyed their psyches by bathing them as babies?"

In some of the published accounts of stories of recovery, the search for the "offender" expands to include most of the men in authority the narrator has known.[47] Almost always, the men who allegedly have molested the narrator are the symbols of patriarchy: the father, the father's wealthy friends, the judge, the magistrate, the doctor, the psychiatrist, the company president, the priest. "These accounts may or may not be literally true," says Culhane, "but obviously the woman feels 'molested' by the powers that be. These men are key to the woman's unhappiness: their betrayal, their lack of honoring their obligations to her, are the cause of her misery, depression, shame. The men who are identified as the molesters tend to be representative figures—father, church, law, industry, psychiatry. Which is not to say they literally did it; but symbolically they did do it."

The power of these symbolic abusers—and the power of the narrative of the Victim Who Survives—are reasons that many women, and increasingly men, are attracted to the victim identity, which is rapidly expanding its boundaries. Incest in childhood *is* abuse, because it is committed by a trusted relative, and *is* extremely detrimental to a child's emerging sense of self, autonomy, and agency.[48] But is it as traumatic to be flashed by an exhibitionist, fondled briefly in the subway, or kissed against one's will at the end of a date? Increasingly, the answer is yes: If you feel abused, you were abused. "As you move into the self-help and popular-psychology sector," says Culhane, "the definition of 'sexual abuse' expands like a hot air balloon. One woman got flashed by an exhibitionist on the subway, another woman was molested by her father and her three brothers for six years, and 'their pain is the same.' And their current life problems—whatever they might be—are said to result automatically from these experiences. That is why I found that trying to define 'sexual abuse' was like trying to nail Jell-O to the wall."

Likewise, almost any symptom can serve as an indicator of abuse. The consequences of abuse are said today to include everything from brief mood swings and unlucky love affairs to drug addiction, weight problems, and severe clinical depression. In their book for women survivors of child sexual abuse, Ellen Bass and Laura Davis offer a list of the effects of abuse that a woman might recognize in herself, which include the following:

(1) Do you feel that you're bad, dirty, or ashamed?
(2) Do you feel powerless, like a victim?
(3) Do you feel there's something wrong with you deep down inside? That if people really knew you, they would leave?
(4) Do you feel unable to protect yourself in dangerous situations?
(5) Do you have a sense of your own interests, talents, or goals?
(6) Do you have trouble feeling motivated?
(7) Do you feel you have to be perfect?[49]

This symptom checklist, of course, is similar to the self-diagnosis of codependency or being an Adult Child of Alcoholics: It is general enough to include everybody and is particularly descriptive of many women. (How many women today feel able to protect themselves in dangerous situations?) Women who were severely abused as children *are* more likely than others to be depressed and to have low self-esteem as adults. But there is no good evidence from longitudinal studies showing that abuse invariably causes the entire litany of women's life problems.

Moreover, *it does not follow that all women who are depressed, sexually conflicted, or have low self-esteem were invariably abused as children*. Yet many of them are being encouraged to root around in their memories for evidence that they were. One result is the rise of therapist-induced "memories," in which the therapist, convinced that the symptoms are a sign of abuse, and the client, eager to find an explanation of her many anxieties, come to identify sexual abuse as *the* reason for everything that causes the client's misery. Psychologist Nicholas Spanos and his colleagues have been studying the mechanism of "therapist-induced memories," of everything from sexual abuse to past lives.[50] There is a sensitive line between the therapist's normal probing for evidence of certain psychological problems and literally *creating* them by the force of suggestion. Some therapists so zealously believe in the widespread prevalence of certain problems—such as incest, multiple personality disorder, or, in some circles, Satanic possession—that, sometimes consciously but more often unconsciously, they induce the client to "remember" events that never actually happened. These *pseudomemories* feel real to the individual, but in fact they are responses to the demands of the situation in which they are generated, as Spanos demonstrated in his laboratory. The mechanism of agreement with the therapist's beliefs and implicit suggestions explains how people in psychoanalysis have "Freudian" dreams, people in primal scream therapy "remember" being born, people in fetal therapy "remember" their lives in the womb, and people in past-lives therapy "remember" being Julius Caesar (or whoever).

This phenomenon does not mean, of course, that there is no such thing as multiple personality disorder, repressed memories of traumatic events, or childhood sexual abuse. It does mean that we should be cautious about accepting uncritically every case of "me too!" that makes the news, and ask why these stories are now so appealing to so many.

An example of this process may be seen in Betsy Petersen's book *Dancing with Daddy,* an account of incest in an upper-middle-class family.[51]

∎

Betsy Petersen thought she had had a happy childhood. Her father, an eminent and admired physician, died when she was 37. Seven years later, she entered therapy to learn how to get along better with her two young sons, who were unruly and disobedient. She was angry with them all the time, and couldn't control their quarrels and tantrums. She felt that she was an inadequate mother and wife.

A year after her therapy began, her mother called to say she had found a box of letters that her father had left expressly for Betsy, and she would put it in the mail. Petersen thought the box would contain evidence of an affair she suspected her father of having, but while awaiting it, she became unexpectedly anxious. What would her father have left her? Suddenly the source of her fear appeared to her: *"I'm afraid my father did something to me."* Petersen began to cry. What could he have done? She did not remember incest, but she cudgeled her memory and family documents for evidence ("perhaps it had happened—if it had happened—in the apartment in San Francisco, when my father came back from the war"). Although no evidence turned up, Petersen became suspicious that she could not remember what happened in the seven more months that the family lived in that apartment. She feared that the incest began at that time, when she was three years old.

In therapy, Petersen revealed that she didn't know whether her "memory" of incest was real or imagined. The therapist replied that Petersen's account felt surreal because when incest occurs, everyone pretends that it isn't going on. The therapist added that there was a good chance the incest actually happened. It would explain, she said, Petersen's difficulties with her children, her ambivalent relationship with her father, the nightmares she had been having, and her sexual insecurities—the problems that had brought her to therapy or subsequently come up there.

The box of letters arrived and proved to be a letdown. There was no confirmation of incest, but there was evidence of her father's extramarital affair (which her mother knew about). For six months Petersen had no nightmares and stopped reading books about incest. Then the bad dreams returned. Because she still had no memory of "what my father had done to me," she tried to reconstruct it from the memories of him she did have and from her feelings of discomfort about sex. To aid the process of self-discovery, she wrote a story about the experience of being molested in her crib at the age of three, and the story evoked powerful feelings.

Petersen then began to have fragmentary memories and images of molestation. Although she cannot remember to this day how often the incest took place (after every parental quarrel, when her father would take out his anger on her? Once a month? Twice a week?), the fact that her father molested her was, she felt, unmistakable. She learned in therapy that her body was revealing what her mind had suppressed: Her occasional back pain was evidence that her heavy father once lay on top of her when she was small and defenseless. "I can't remember [my father lying on top of me]," she writes, "—but my body remembers."

In the next phase of recovery, Petersen began to talk about her realization that her father had abused her. "As I told more people," she writes, "telling became a reliable way I could make myself feel better." She joined a survivors group, where she learned how much she had in common with other incest victims. She told her husband, who was supportive and sympathetic, reassuring her how much he loved her, even when she felt dirty and sexually insecure. She told a woman friend, who said that Betsy was lovable and "really special." Then she told her children, explaining that *she was not really angry at them but at her parents.* "We wanted to help them understand," she writes, "that my distress had nothing to do with them."

Petersen at last became angry, at big things and small ones: at her mother, for failing to protect her. At her father, for not being the Daddy every girl wants and deserves. At her mother, for being annoyed once when Betsy got into mischief and interrupted her rest. At her parents, for "only" giving her swimming lessons, trampoline lessons, horseback-riding lessons, and tennis lessons, but not ballet lessons. "The only thing I wanted, they would not give me," she laments. "I had nothing of my own; my father made sure of that."

■

True to the formula of the sexual-survivor ideology, Betsy Petersen's process of self-discovery increasingly linked all of her adult difficulties to her incestuous experiences with her father. The incest explained her current nightmares and sleep irregularities, eating disorders, compulsive cleanliness, shame about sexuality, anxieties, obsessive drive for self-improvement, colon problems, back pain, insecurity about money, difficulties in wishing for something for herself, the obnoxious behavior of her sons and her impatience with them, why she could not say no to them, and even why she cooked a hot breakfast for her dogs every morning. It explained, as if no other woman had this problem, her vulnerability to fad diets (she would be perfect and have perfect children if only she could stick to the perfect healthy diet). It explained, as if no other new mother had this problem, her awkwardness with her firstborn son (he cried when she tried to nurse him). It explained why her babies didn't sleep throughout the night and why she kept going to them: "It's clear to me now that they awoke at night because they weren't getting what they needed from me during the day." It explained, as if no other adult in modern times had this problem, the malaise of alienation: "Sometimes it feels like the world is tilting and I'm sliding off, sliding off the planet into outer space: dark and cold, nothing to hold on to, nobody to hold on to me." It explained, as if no one else is numb to the world's ills, her apathy toward social problems, prejudice, war, and the Holocaust.

For Betsy Petersen, all current events are processed through the lens of incest. "Before I knew my father had molested me," she writes, "the feelings cycled endlessly and attached themselves to the world outside my skin: If only my children weren't so demanding, I could think, I wouldn't feel so crazy." This is hardly a rare lament among mothers! But Petersen's solution is not to make the boys less demanding but herself less "crazy" about their demands. One day her son, whining to be taken out for some corn dogs, screamed: "You said you'd get me some meat, you stupid asshole!"—and threw his shoe against the wall. Petersen writes: "And suddenly I was *so mad*. My stomach hurt." She was not, of course, angry about her son's behavior. She was angry "about all the times I wanted to say no to my father but was too afraid of his anger."

Similarly, Petersen is appalled by the greedy desires of many American middle-class children, including her own: "Their wanting overwhelms me: Buy me this, give me that, I want, I want, I want, and I have to give them what they want and I can't take care of myself until everyone else has gotten everything he wants . . ." Does she see in their materialism, perhaps, a commentary on living in a culture of ads and acquisitions? Does she see in her inability to "take care of myself" the woman's role requirement of putting children and husbands first? No: She cannot say no to them because her father had lived in fear that his hard-earned wealth would be taken away from him: "And I had to pay for that."

After reading Petersen's book, I find I am doubtful about whether her father molested her or not (although readers are told that such doubts may be evidence that they themselves were victimized—or are perpetrators). But let us assume that some form of incest occurred and that it affected Petersen adversely in various ways. Is it therefore appropriate to attribute everything that troubles her—from cooking breakfast for her dogs to feelings of alienation—to that abuse? Nowhere in her book do we learn anything about her husband and his role in the family (where was he when she was taking all the responsibility for their uncontrollable sons?); about her own work as a writer; about the community they live in. "Can't we condemn the sexual exploitation of children," asks Culhane, "without reducing all of life's complex problems to reflex-like responses to such abuse? Must we always seek one-dimensional solutions to multidimensional problems?" [52]

Betsy Petersen seems to have completely shut out "the world out-side my skin," and that is the problem. Of course it is important for women to talk about feelings of victimization, guilt, and powerless-ness; to speak up when they feel they have been abused; and to identify the links along the continuum of abuse, from daily harass-ments to rape. The question is, what story emerges from the per-sonal revelations of the survivor movement, with what results for society? The feminist rallying cry of the 1970s, "the personal is political," meant that personal experience can be used to illuminate the darker corners of society's closets. Today that slogan has been reversed: The political is personal, and only personal.

Indeed, the original feminist analysis of the sexual abuse of chil-dren—that it is not merely a problem of a few disturbed individuals —has been co-opted, diluted, and defused. The effort to achieve social change has been co-opted into a focus on psychological solace. The reality of the victimization of children is diluted by a chorus of insecure adults clamoring that they are victims too. The horror of a child being treated for gonorrhea of the throat is defused by the claims of some adults that they had venereal disease as a child too, in a previous life.

Louise Armstrong, reflecting on how public conversation about the problem of incest has changed since her book first appeared, muses:

Where is everybody? I sometimes ask, meaning the survivors. The voices of no-nonsense, unsentimental, unromantic reason.

Oh (the answer comes back), they're in therapy.

Nothing wrong with that. We all need help and support. But here's a tricky feature. Where you have systematic power abuse, the exclusive reliance on individualized solutions defuses the possibility of a strong collective voice, and of action for change. Exclusively personal solutions do nothing to defy the ongoing tacit permission for abuse.[53]

I do not in any way mean to disparage survivor groups that help abused women to feel better and stronger about themselves. I have only admiration for the women who are able to overcome the effects of their victimization and get on with their lives. My worry about the popularity of support groups is that too many women in them, longing for community and conversation, come to incorporate the language of victimhood and survival into the *sole organizing narrative* of their identity. It becomes their major story, a story whose moral rarely goes further than "Join a group (or write a book) and talk about the problem."

Such stories soothe women temporarily while allowing the perpetrators to go free. Indeed, they allow the whole system to go free: a system that rests on the neglect of children, the blame of mothers, and the entitlements of men who commit the abuse. That's why society likes these stories so much. Nothing changes.

■ *Bridges*

> Both men and women, in the short term, have something to gain from things not changing, in not redressing the balance of power, or changing the rules of the game. But for both sexes, in the long run, clinging to old habits is dangerous and, in this world, deadly.[54]
>
> —Robin Lakoff

> The darkened eye restored, every member rejoices with it.[55]
>
> —Anna Julia Cooper

The debates about sex differences—and about who is differing from whom, and why—are not academic. Our society is presently in the midst of an intellectual revolution that may prove to be as significant as what Copernicus, Darwin, and Freud wrought in their fields. The earth is not the centerpiece of the solar system, human beings are not the centerpiece of creation, the ego is not the centerpiece of the mind, and man is not the centerpiece of experience and knowledge—neither the generic man nor the individual man.[56]

This effort at expanding our vision seems the essence of sweet reason to me, but, as Bertrand Russell once said, all social movements go too far. This one will too. For some, the goal of dethroning the universal male means setting up a universal female in his place. It means that everything men do, have done, have written or composed, have thought or written, have invented or created, is worth-less or hopelessly biased. Some academic conventions reverberate with the acronym DWEM, which stands for all the people whose hopelessly-biased work is now supposed to be expunged from the curriculum: dead white European males. Oh, dear; I'm rather fond of Beethoven, Socrates, Shakespeare, Aristotle, Renoir, Cervantes, Galileo, Oscar Wilde, George Bernard Shaw. . . .

In contrast to the contemporary impulse to pit the contributions of one group against those of another—male versus female, East versus West, black versus white—I wish to argue here on behalf of Anna Julia Cooper's vision one hundred years ago: a vision of the whole, rather than of segments. I believe it is possible to eradicate (or at least minimize) the assumption of "normal" men and "differ-ent" women. But we will not accomplish this in the movement to-ward particularization, in which each gender, race, or ethnicity seeks only its own validation, celebrates only itself, and rewrites its history and character in false phrases of its own superiority.

We need some new stories, and we need to be critical of many of the existing ones. For ourselves as individuals, one way we can evaluate our stories is not by whether they are "true" or "false"—most of the time, in trying to find the reasons for the complicated things we do, we can never know. But we can try to examine what the story leaves out, for all stories leave out something. Genetic stories tend to omit experience; psychoanalytic stories tend to over-look the environment; my own favorite social-psychological stories tend to ignore biology; childhood-blame stories leave out current events. We do best, I believe, by adding explanations to our quiver of life stories rather than limiting ourselves to only one.

Further, rather than trying to find the "right" story or the "offi-cial" story, we can direct our attention to the origins, contexts, and consequences of stories. What are the supports for narratives that rely heavily on a vocabulary of disease, deficiency, victimhood, and astrological destiny rather than a vocabulary of power, context, and current relationships? As I've tried to show, society has a consider-able investment in promoting the former set of stories as explana-tions for why women are the way they are, and why they differ from men.

For example, over the years we have heard a lot about the problems of those poor Superwomen, the jugglers who strive to balance work and family. The attention goes to the woman who is doing the juggling. We hear how stressed she is, how impossible her task is, how likely she is to fail, how work is killing her (or making her sick), how much better off she will be if she quits knocking her head against a wall and goes home to raise her children.

In fact, the preponderance of the evidence utterly contradicts these popular impressions.[57] Women who juggle are better off in many ways than those who don't (though they *are* more tired!). The story of "superwomen," however, draws the heat away from anyone or any institution that might be able to make it easier on the woman who has a family and a job. It draws attention away from husbands and employers, the division of family obligations, and the structure of corporations. It places the burden of adjustment on the woman, thereby eliminating the need to make adjustments elsewhere.

In the last chapter we saw how one quarreling couple, Evan and Nancy, came up with a compromise story, a rearrangement of their family obligations based on their new narrative of Nancy's "compulsiveness" and Evan's "laziness." To sociologist Arlie Hochschild, who interviewed them, one consequence of this story was quite simply the survival of the marriage. Nancy and Evan's story allows them to maintain their belief that they have an equal marriage, even as she gives up half of her career time and even though her "half" of the housework is all of it, minus walking the dog. According to Hochschild, many women would rather have a stable marriage than risk the pursuit of an equitable one, and Nancy and Evan's resolution allows them to do it.

Nancy and Evan may live happily ever after. But their story is being multiplied thousands of times across the country, at which point it becomes a social problem, not just an individual one. A recent Roper survey found that, next to money, the issue of "how much my mate helps around the house" is the "single biggest source of resentment" in many women's lives.[58] The story that couples tell about their marriages may serve either to paper over that resentment or to move them toward a resolution that works.

Likewise, a story fails when it is sustained at great personal or social cost: when it has unforeseen long-term consequences, when the individual pays the price of living a lie, when a hidden toll is being taken, when it narrows vision instead of expanding it, or when it systematically leads to the exclusion or maltreatment of large segments of the population.

This is one reason that I am so concerned about the current fashion for cultural feminism, the appealing theories that women have a natural ability to be connected, attached, loving, and peaceful, that they speak in a different voice, have different ways of knowing, or different moral values. Of course, many of the women who promote these ideas do so with the intention of raising women's self-esteem and promoting their welfare in society. Nevertheless, the philosophy of cultural feminism has functioned to keep women focused on their allegedly stable and innate personality qualities, instead of on what it would take to have a society based on the qualities we value in both sexes.

Further, quite apart from their lack of research validation, these ideas get men off the hook in family arrangements, ignore men's affections and attachments, and underwrite the ideology that women are best suited to certain kinds of jobs. At their worst, they distract us from the hard work we have to do, women and men together, to humanize jobs, foster children's welfare, save the environment, and combat corporate mindlessness.

Stories have consequences, but stories change, and how and why they do is the heart of the human enterprise. Our narratives can reclaim the psychological qualities historically associated with female deficiency, but within a framework of synthesis rather than opposition. Dependency, typically viewed as feminine and a sign of childish regression, is a basic human need. Women do not need to stop being conciliatory in order to be leaders, or to stop caring for others in order to be autonomous. Connection and autonomy are both necessary in human life. The goal for both sexes should be to add qualities and skills, not lose old ones.

We can tell more flexible stories, ones that recognize that our qualities, skills, and actions change over the life span. People develop, learn, have adventures and new experiences; and as they do, their notions of masculinity and femininity change too. The rules of gender are not frozen at one moment in time, whether the psychologically fashionable time is thought to be infancy, childhood, or adolescence.

We can become aware of the hidden agendas not only in old-fashioned stories but also in modern ones. It is easy to discern the political purpose of the diagnosis of drapetomania, that nineteenth-century "disease" that afflicted slaves with an uncontrollable urge to escape from slavery. Yet it is equally important to identify the uses of diagnoses such as PMS and Self-defeating Personality Disorder today. It is easy to see the bias in labeling as "sick" those women, years ago, who refused to play their traditional roles and wanted instead to be lawyers, scientists, and artists. It is equally important to recognize the bias in labeling as "sick" (e.g., "addicted") those women today who play the traditional role of caretaker too well.

We can realize that our favorite life stories may not apply to everyone in the same ways. We have learned that the male model of adult development does not apply to all women, the medical model of sexuality does not apply to all women or men, the female model of emotional expressivity does not apply to all men. Likewise, there is no one right way to have (or combine) a marriage, a baby, or career; no one right way to be straight or gay; no one right way to be a parent. There is, in sum, no one right way to be, no single story that fits all.

Finally, we can resist the temptation to see the world in opposites. Western ways of thinking emphasize dualisms and opposites, and pose many questions of human life in fruitless either-or terms. Are we rational or emotional creatures? Will we win or lose? Is this decision good or bad? Are we uniquely human or basically mammalian? Are we shaped by nature or nurture, mind or environment? Are we masculine or feminine? As long as the question is framed this way—"What can we do about *them*, the other, the opposite?"—it can never be answered, no matter which sex is being regarded as "them." The question, rather, should be this: What shall we do about *us*, so that our relationships, our work, our children, and our planet will flourish?

# *Notes*

In addition to references to the bibliography, the Notes contain full citations for magazine and newspaper articles, interviews, unpublished academic articles, and miscellaneous other sources.

EPIGRAPH

1. De Beauvoir quoted in Schwartzer, 1984, p. 103.

INTRODUCTION: THE UNIVERSAL MALE

1. Minnich, 1990. See also Miller, Taylor, and Buck, 1991.
2. The assistant professor of English is Valerie Babb. The story was reported in *The New York Times,* March 4, 1991, p. B4.
3. Quoted in Anderson and Zinsser, 1988, Volume 1, p. xviii.
4. Waring, 1989. See also Gayle Kirshenbaum, "Why Aren't Human Rights Women's Rights?" *Ms.,* July/August 1991, pp. 12–14.
5. Minnich, 1990, p. 39. Minnich observes that many students "do not see the men represented and discussed in their courses *as men* but, rather, as philosophers, writers, painters, significant historical figures, important composers. But they do see the women *as women* because they have learned from the use of prefixes in course titles and the omissions in their courses that women are oddities in the dominant tradition, that women are always a kind of human, a kind of writer or whatever, and never the thing-itself" (p. 79).
6. Ibid., p. 79.
7. Schafran quoted in *Ms.,* January/February 1989, p. 137.
8. American Psychological Association, brief for *amicus curiae* in support

of respondent Ann B. Hopkins. Washington, D.C.: American Psychological Association, 1988.

9. Gould, 1981, p. 74.

CHAPTER 1: MEASURING UP

1. Donovan and Sanford, 1986, p. 33.
2. Sample findings on women's "problems": Self-esteem, Donovan and Sanford, 1986; on value of work, Major, 1987; hurt rather than angry, Mary K. Biaggio, "Sex Differences in Anger: Are they real?", paper presented at the annual meeting of the American Psychological Association, Atlanta, 1988; separate sense of self, Aries and Olver, 1985.
3. Cheryl B. Olson, "The Influence of Context on Gender Differences in Performance Attributions: Further evidence of a 'feminine modesty' effect." Paper presented at the annual meeting of the Western Psychological Association, San Francisco, 1988.
4. Silverstein, Peterson, and Purdue, 1986; Silverstein et al., 1988, 1990.
5. Garner et al., 1980.
6. Adam Drewnowski and Doris K. Yee, "Adolescent Dieting: Fear of fatness and the role of puberty." Paper presented at the annual meeting of the American Psychological Association, Atlanta, 1988. See also Striegel-Moore, Silberstein, and Rodin, 1986.
7. Joan S. Girgus, Susan Nolen-Hoeksema, and Martin E. P. Seligman, "Why Do Sex Differences in Depression Emerge During Adolescence?" Paper presented at the annual meeting of the American Psychological Association, New Orleans, 1989; Attie and Brooks-Gunn, 1987.
8. Silverstein, personal interview with author, quoted in Carol Tavris, "Is Thin Still In?" Woman's Day, March 3, 1987, p. 35.
9. Susan Wooley and O. Wayne Wooley, "Thinness Mania," American Health, October 1986, pp. 68–74. Quote, p. 72.
10. For statistics on the prevalence and risks of breast implants, see Wolfe, 1991. See also Doug Podolsky, "Breast Implants: What price vanity?" American Health, March 1991, pp. 70–75. In 1991 the head of the Food and Drug Administration, Dr. David Kessler, observing that too many women were being lulled into believing that breast implants were risk-free, urged physicians to inform potential clients of the risk involved. (The New York Times, August 1, 1991.)
11. Betty Goodwin, "Soft Sell: Leading ladies throw moviegoers a curve," Los Angeles Times, February 1, 1991, p. E3. This article also contains the quotes by Gale Hayman and Margaret Sharley, deputy general manager of Lancôme. See also Amy Louise Kazmin, "The Voluptuous

Woman Makes a Comeback," *Los Angeles Times*, February 22, 1991, pp. E1 and E7, for interviews with designers.

12. Paddy Calistro, "For Good Measure," *Los Angeles Times Magazine*, April 8, 1990, p. 32.

13. Source: National Osteoporosis Foundation, Washington, D.C.

14. See Bennett and Gurin, 1982.

15. Ernsberger and Nelson, 1988.

16. Attie and Brooks-Gunn, 1987; Striegel-Moore, Silberstein, and Rodin, 1986.

17. Wooley, personal interview with author, quoted in Carol Tavris, "Is Thin Still In?" *Woman's Day*, March 3, 1987, p. 114.

18. Quoted in Kazmin, p. E7. (See Note 11.)

19. Gilligan, 1982, p. 6.

20. Ibid., pp. 12–13. See also Gilligan, Ward, and Taylor, 1988; Josselson, 1987.

21. Offer and Sabshin, 1984.

22. Apter, 1990, pp. 2–3.

23. Ibid., p. 71.

24. Baruch, Barnett, and Rivers, 1982.

25. See, for example, Mary Crawford, "The Discourse of Humor: Two levels," paper presented at the annual meeting of the American Psychological Association, Boston, 1990; see also Crawford and Gressley, 1991, and Wade, 1986.

26. Robert Sapolsky, "The Case of the Falling Nightwatchmen," *Discover*, July 1987, pp. 42–45.

27. Ibid., p. 44. The data that Sapolsky reanalyzed come from Benbow and Stanley, 1980.

28. T. Lang, *The Difference Between a Man and a Woman* (New York: The John Day Co., 1971), pp. 203–204.

29. Le Bon quoted in Gould, 1981, pp. 104–105.

30. Sperry, 1982.

31. Quoted in Gina Kolata, "Math Genius May Have Hormonal Basis," *Science*, 222 (December 23, 1983), p. 1312.

32. Ibid., p. 1312.

33. Transcript from radio show "Focus on the Family: 'Dr. James Dobson interviews Dr. Donald Joy—The innate differences between males and females.' " 1984, 1986, CS-099, pp. 4, 78.

34. Gary Smalley and John Trent, *The Language of Love* (Pomona, CA: Focus on the Family Publishing, 1988). Quote, pp. 35–36.

35. See Bleier, 1988; Fausto-Sterling, 1985; Harrington, 1987; Hubbard, 1990. For an excellent history of psychological revisionism in the study of the brain, see Shields, 1975.

36. *Newsweek*, "Guns and Dolls," May 28, 1990, p. 59.

37. Smalley and Trent, p. 36. (See Note 34.)
38. Levy, 1983.
39. The discussion and critique of Geschwind and Behan, 1982, is from Bleier, 1988.
40. Ruth Bleier, "Sex Differences Research in the Neurosciences." Paper presented at the annual meeting of the American Association for the Advancement of Science, Chicago, 1987.
41. The study of the corpus callosum is from de Lacoste-Utamsing and Holloway, 1982.
42. Hyde and Linn, 1986, 1988. Males are more likely to have speech problems, such as stuttering, and to be referred for treatment for dyslexia—though not more likely to actually be dyslexic (see Shaywitz et al., 1990). See also Feingold (1988), who found that gender differences in SAT scores have "declined precipitously" in the last forty years. In 1950, school-age boys and girls differed markedly in verbal ability (girls excelled), abstract reasoning (boys excelled), and "clerical ability" (girls excelled). By 1980, boys had completely caught up with girls in verbal ability. Girls had completely caught up in verbal and abstract reasoning and numerical ability, and halved the difference in mechanical reasoning and space relations. The only exception to the rule of "vanishing gender differences," Feingold found, was the gender gap at the highest levels of math performance.
43. Hyde, Fennema, and Lamon, 1990.
44. Caplan, MacPherson, and Tobin, 1985. Researcher quoted on p. 786.
45. Robert Crooks and Karla Baur, *Our Sexuality,* 4th edition (Redwood City, CA: Benjamin Cummings, 1990), p. 64. To see how easy it is to slip from describing gender "differences" to speaking of one gender's "superiority," regard this statement by the authors: "Because the right hemisphere is the primary repository of spatial abilities, it is not surprising that male rats, with *quantitatively superior right hemispheres,* perform better than do their female counterparts on maze-learning tasks that require skill with spatial relationships. . . ." (My emphasis.)
46. Kinsbourne, 1980, p. 242.
47. Fairweather quoted in Bleier, 1988, p. 154.
48. Fishman, 1983; Lakoff, 1990; McConnell-Ginet, 1983, 1984; Tannen, 1990 (esp. pp. 75–76).
49. McGlone, 1980, p. 226.
50. Bleier, 1987, pp. 11–12. (See Note 40.)
51. Frances K. Conley, "Why I'm Leaving Stanford: I Wanted My Dignity Back," *Los Angeles Times,* June 9, 1991, pp. M1, M6.

CHAPTER 2: BEAUTIFUL SOULS AND DIFFERENT VOICES

1. Richard Restak, "Rx for Medical Profession: Women," *San Francisco Chronicle (This World)*, May 18, 1986, p. 17.
2. Quoted in Mednick, 1989, p. 1122.
3. Lindsy Van Gelder, "It's Not Nice to Mess with Mother Nature," *Ms.*, January/February 1989, pp. 60–63. Quote, p. 61.
4. Ynestra King, quoted by Van Gelder, p. 61. On ecofeminism, see also Kirkpatrick Sale, "Ecofeminism—A New Perspective," *The Nation*, September 26, 1987, pp. 302–305.
5. For an excellent article on the rise of cultural feminism, see Alice Echols, 1984. Adrienne Rich, Susan Griffin, and Mary Daly are among the best-known proponents of this view. The argument that women have developed special "ways of knowing" has also been very popular; see Belenky et al., 1986.
6. West, 1988, p. 18.
7. Menstruation ritual described in Christ, 1979, p. 282.
8. Standing, 1980, p. 138.
9. Pain researcher Ronald Melzack, interviewed by Claire Warga for "Pain's Gatekeeper," *Psychology Today*, August 1987, pp. 51–56. Melzack observed that "Some women feel intense guilt, anger, and failure when they anticipate a 'natural, painless birth' and are then confronted with such severe pain or complications that they require an epidural block or a cesarean section."
10. Hallie Iglehart, *Womanspirit: A guide to women's wisdom* (San Francisco: Harper & Row, 1983).
11. Quotes from Caldicott and the member of the international peace conference, in Zur, 1989, p. 315.
12. Risman, 1987.
13. Kaye and Applegate, 1990.
14. Chodorow, 1978, p. 167.
15. Eisenberg and Lennon, 1983, p. 126.
16. Snodgrass, 1985.
17. Kohn, 1990, p. 82.
18. On "kin work," see Di Leonardo, 1987; interaction work, Fishman, 1983; emotion work, Hochschild, 1983; on the "second shift" of housework, Hochschild, 1989.
19. Gelles and Straus, 1988; Tavris, 1982/1989.
20. Tavris and Wade, 1984.
21. Elshtain, 1987, pp. 192–193.
22. Ibid., p. 197.
23. Ibid., p. 178 (Nadya Popova); p. 176 (Marisa Masu).
24. Ibid., p. 190. In 1990, Saudi women tried getting out of their houses

and into men's cars by appealing to the fact that they would need to be able to drive in case of war. Saudi men were not fooled and continue to forbid women to drive.

25. Ibid., p. 157. According to Paul Boyers, Elshtain reports, letters to newspapers at the time of the bombings—from both sexes—frequently expressed regret "that atomic bombs had not been used to destroy all human life in Japan."

26. See Helen Zia, "Women in Hate Groups," *Ms.,* March/April 1991, pp. 20–27.

27. Cited in Ruth Rosen, "The Anti-war Gender Gap is Back," Op-ed column, *Los Angeles Times,* November 26, 1990.

28. Zur, 1989; the study of the analysis of the polls is in Zur and Morrison, 1989.

29. On the history of matriarchal theories, see Tavris and Wade, 1984.

30. Quote appears in Sarah Pomeroy's review of Gerda Lerner's *The Creation of Patriarchy,* "When No One Wore the Pants," *The New York Times Book Review,* April 20, 1986, p. 12.

31. Stone, 1979, pp. 120–121, 130.

32. Eisler, 1987.

33. Pomeroy, 1975, p. 14.

34. Anderson and Zinsser, 1988, Vol. I, p. 5.

35. Stone, 1979, p. 122.

36. See Anderson and Zinsser, 1988, Vol. I, p. 8; also Pomeroy, 1975.

37. Iglehart, p. 17. (See Note 10.)

38. Pomeroy, 1975, p. 8.

39. Ibid., p. 15.

40. Elizabeth Fox-Genovese, review of Riane Eisler's *The Chalice and the Blade,* "Androcrats go home!," *The New York Times Book Review,* October 4, 1987, p. 32.

41. Iglehart, p. 11. (See Note 10.)

42. The example of Sweden, and many other points, are contained in *The Seville Statement on Violence,* a report prepared by twenty scientists from twelve nations, who met in Seville to draft a research position against the popular notion of the inevitability of war. "Humanity can be freed from the bondage of biological pessimism," they concluded. "The same species who invented war is capable of inventing peace." The Seville Statement has been published in many places, including Kohn, 1990, pp. 269–272; and in Jo Groebel and Robert Hinde (Eds.), *Aggression and War: Their Biological and Social Bases* (Cambridge, England: Cambridge University Press, 1989).

43. Pomeroy, 1975, p. 15.

44. These conditions are analyzed in more detail in Tavris and Wade, 1984.

45. Elshtain, 1987, pp. 181–182. Elshtain cites Evan Connell's book on Custer's last stand, *Son of the Morning Star* (San Francisco: North Point Press, 1984) as an example of a historical account that "neither deifies nor demonizes" Custer, the Indians, or anyone else in that terrible story.
46. Quoted in Anderson and Zinsser, 1988, Vol. II, p. 430.
47. Fox-Genovese. (See Note 40.)
48. Jean Baker Miller, *Toward a New Psychology of Women* (Boston: Beacon Press, 1976), p. 27.
49. Mary Lou Randour, *Women's Psyche, Women's Spirit* (New York: Columbia University Press, 1987), p. 11.
50. Gilligan, 1982, p. 100.
51. Quoted in Barbara Dolan and Melissa Ludtke, "Coming From a Different Place," *Time*, Special issue on "Women: The road ahead," Fall 1990, pp. 64–66. Quote on p. 66.
52. Gilligan, 1982, p. 8.
53. Chodorow, 1978, p. 169.
54. Lerner, 1989, p. 280.
55. West, 1988, p. 20.
56. Greeno and Maccoby, 1986, p. 315.
57. Mednick, 1989, pp. 1119, 1120.
58. Gilligan, 1982, p. 71.
59. See Crosby, 1991.
60. Quotations from Jeffrey (the first quote) and Karen (the second): Gilligan, 1982, pp. 32–33.
61. Quotations from Jake (the first quote) and Amy (the second): Ibid., p. 37.
62. See, for example, Cohn, 1991; Colby and Damon, 1987; Friedman, Robinson, and Friedman, 1987; Lifton, 1985; Mednick, 1989; Thoma, 1986.
63. Thoma, 1986, p. 176.
64. Colby and Damon, 1987, p. 327.
65. Cochran and Peplau, 1985, p. 483.
66. Benton et al., 1983.
67. Helgeson and Sharpsteen, 1987.
68. Gilligan, 1982, p. 41.
69. Colby and Damon, 1987, p. 327.
70. Kanter, 1977, p. 161.
71. Major, 1987; Major, McFarlin, and Gagnon, 1984.
72. Hare-Mustin and Marecek, 1986.
73. Lerner, 1989, p. 281.
74. Goodrich et al., 1988, p. 20. See also Siegel, 1988.
75. See, for example, Rojcewicz, 1971, who examined the relationships

among suicide, war, and homicide. The suicide rate declines during wartime, reflecting the social conditions of wartime rather than the presence of actual fighting. The decreased suicide rate during wartime is linked to greater social integration, increased patriotism, and greater sense of purpose resulting from a state of war.

76. This study is described in an unpublished doctoral dissertation by W. S. Barnes. I found it cited in Deaux and Major, 1990, p. 89.
77. Denmark et al., 1988.
78. Elshtain, 1987, p. 258.
79. Hare-Mustin, 1987; see also Lott, 1990.

CHAPTER 3: THE 70-KILOGRAM MAN AND THE PREGNANT PERSON

1. The story of Myra and Jim is from Mason, 1988, pp. 32–34.
2. Quoted in "News: Body/Mind," *Self,* February 1990, p. 64.
3. *The New York Times,* May 10, 1988, p. 27.
4. Quoted in Laqueur, 1987, p. 2.
5. Giacomini, Rozée-Koker, and Pepitone-Arreola-Rockwell, 1986. Quote, p. 418.
6. See Laqueur, 1987, 1990.
7. Schiebinger, 1987.
8. Perri Klass and Lila Wallis, "Macho Medicine," *Lear's,* October 1989, pp. 65, 67.
9. Margrit Eichler, Anna Lisa Reisman, and Elaine Borins, "Gender Bias in Medical Research." Unpublished manuscript, Ontario Institute for Studies in Education, Toronto, Ontario, Canada.
10. The diabetes article is Patricia Schreiner-Engel et al., "The Differential Impact of Diabetes Type on Female Sexuality," *Journal of Psychosomatic Research,* 31 (1987), pp. 23–33. The article on hormones and "human" mood in twelve males is B. C. McAdoo et al., "A Study of the Effects of Gonadotropin-releasing Hormone on Human Mood and Behavior," *Psychosomatic Medicine,* 40 (1978), pp. 199–209.
11. Klass and Wallis, p. 65. (See Note 8.)
12. See, for example, Jones and Jones, 1976; Jeavons [Wilkinson] and Zeiner, 1984.
13. See Keh-Ming Lin et al., "Ethnicity and psychopharmacology," *Culture, Medicine, & Psychiatry,* 10 (1986), pp. 151–165. Chaisson also interviewed in the *LA Times,* September 25, 1989, p. A1.
14. See Hamilton and Parry, 1983; McGrath et al., 1990; Margaret Jensvold, "Gender Issues in Pharmacological Treatment of Depression," paper prepared for the National Task Force on Women and Depression, American Psychological Association, 1989.
15. The text is *Psychopharmacology* (New York: Raven Press, 1987).
16. McGrath et al., 1990.

17. Interview with author, February 21, 1988.
18. Lee Goldman et al., "Costs and Effectiveness of Routine Therapy and Long-term Beta-adrenergic-antagonists After Acute Myocardial Infarction," *New England Journal of Medicine, 319* (1988), 152–156.
19. Palumbo, 1989. The cholesterol debate deserves a lengthy discussion on its own. But for a review of the research and issues—including the ages at which high cholesterol is riskiest for men—I recommend Thomas J. Moore's provocative book, *Heart Failure* (New York: Random House, 1989).
20. This is from the Framingham Heart Study 30-year follow-up. Washington, D.C.: National Institutes of Health, April 1987. See also Wolfe, 1991.
21. Wolfe, 1991, p. 214.
22. *Los Angeles Times,* October 5, 1989, pp. A1, A39.
23. Latman, 1983; Ostensen, Aune, and Husby, 1983.
24. Interview with author.
25. Polefrone and Manuck, 1987.
26. Perri Klass, "Bearing a Child in Medical School," *The New York Times Magazine,* November 11, 1984, pp. 120–125.
27. Tobin et al., 1987; Khan et al., 1990.
28. Rosenberg, Palmer, and Shapiro, 1990. The researchers also found, by the way, no reduced risk of heart attack in women who smoke low-nicotine cigarettes. "The estimated risks did not vary according to the nicotine or carbon monoxide yield of the cigarette," they concluded. (See Palmer, Rosenberg, and Shapiro, " 'Low Yield' Cigarettes and the Risk of Nonfatal Myocardial Infarction in Women," *New England Journal of Medicine,* June 15, 1989.)
29. Quoted in Eisenstein, 1988, p. 218.
30. West, 1988, pp. 58–59.
31. Ibid., p. 60.
32. Littleton, 1987, p. 1282.
33. Quoted in Littleton, 1987, p. 1292.
34. Littleton, 1987, p. 1292.
35. Ibid., p. 1302.
36. Judicial Council of California, "Achieving Equal Justice for Women and Men in the Courts: The draft report of the Judicial Council Advisory Committee on gender bias in the courts." The report, which was released in March 1990, is available from the Judicial Council of California, San Francisco. So far twelve states have issued reports on gender bias in the legal system, and another dozen or so have studies in progress.
37. Robert Satter, *Doing Justice: A trial judge at work* (New York: American Lawyer Books/Simon & Schuster, 1990).
38. Mason, 1988, p. 53.

39. Ibid., p. 56.
40. Sheila James Kuehl, "Understanding the Battered Reality," op-ed article, *Los Angeles Times,* January 7, 1990.
41. Ibid.
42. West, 1988, p. 59.
43. Quoted in Russell, 1982, p. 92.
44. West, 1988, p. 66.
45. *Los Angeles Times,* "Sexual Harassment Standards Rejected," January 24, 1991.
46. This story was reported in the *Los Angeles Times,* May 10, 1989, and produced a storm of protest from both sexes!
47. Huling quoted in Sam Roberts, "No Easy Task: Balancing Scales of Justice for Battered Women in Prison," *The New York Times,* March 4, 1991. See also Miles Corwin, "Waiting in Isolation," *Los Angeles Times,* January 15, 1991.
48. The story of this Massachusetts woman and of James Lutgen were reported by Ellen Goodman in her column; *Los Angeles Times,* May 23, 1989.
49. California Judicial Council: quote from Kathleen West, tab 7 ("Achieving Equal Justice in Criminal and Juvenile Law"), p. 81. (See Note 36.)
50. Ibid., quote from anonymous attorney also testifying, p. 82.
51. See Caplan, 1989, and Chesler, 1986. For a moving, personal account of how women are treated in family court, see Viva, "Women and Children . . . Last," *New York Woman,* November 1989, pp. 111–115. The author writes: "Having been through the system myself, I can confirm that this treatment would make any normal person crazy. The procedure, it seems, is to drive the mother crazy, then label her crazy, then say she's too crazy to be trusted with her child."
52. Chamallas with Kerber, 1990, p. 818.
53. Kaminer, 1990, p. 24.
54. Quoted in Eisenstein, 1988, p. 105.
55. Rothman, 1989, p. 248.
56. Littleton, 1987, p. 1306.
57. Caroline Whitbeck originated the "flowerpot theory of pregnancy"— the view that men have the seeds and women provide the pot for them to grow in. Quoted in Rothman, 1989, p. 248.
58. Ibid., p. 21. On this issue, see also Corea, 1985.
59. Ibid., p. 42.
60. Ibid., p. 107.
61. Littleton, 1987, p. 1304.
62. Dworkin, 1977, p. 227.
63. Littleton, 1987, p. 1337.

64. Mason, 1988, p. 45.
65. Ibid., p. 25.
66. Ibid., pp. 41–42.
67. MacKinnon, 1990, pp. 220–221.
68. Littleton, 1987, p. 1326.
69. Interview with author.
70. Ibid.
71. Littleton, 1987, p. 1297.
72. Ibid., p. 1313.

CHAPTER 4: MISDIAGNOSING THE BODY

1. Lionel Tiger, "Male Dominance? Yes, Alas. A Sexist Plot? No," *The New York Times Magazine,* October 25, 1970, pp. 35–37ff.
2. *Los Angeles Times,* May 10, 1990. This is the same judge, A. Andrew Hauk, whom we met in Chapter 3 giving a woman a reduced sentence for the crime of robbery.
3. Woman interviewed by Emily Martin, 1987, p. 132.
4. Judy Lever and Michael G. Brush, *Pre-menstrual Tension* (New York: Bantam, 1981).
5. For example, see "A Nightly Checklist for PMS," *American Health,* December 1989, p. 58.
6. The debate on nature and prevalence of "PMS" symptoms is in Fisher, 1987, pp. 1–2.
7. Cited in Peele, 1989, p. 141, and in Golub, 1988.
8. From an (undated) publicity letter to health professionals written by Joseph T. Martorano, M.D., Director of the "P.M.S. Medical Group: A Center for the Treatment of Premenstrual Syndrome" in New York. The letter announces that "PMS MEDICAL GROUP has been effectively treating thousands of women." That's a lot of sick women.
9. News item on Vitamin E, "The Oil of Relief," *American Health,* April 1988; on caffeine, "A Cuppa Trouble?", October 1989.
10. Jeffrey Bland, "Break the Cycle of Monthly Discomfort," *Delicious!,* March 1988, pp. 10–12.
11. "Relief for PMS Symptoms," *Cooking Light,* March/April 1988, p. 19.
12. Frank, 1931, p. 1054. On the concern of employers, p. 1053.
13. Martin, 1987, p. 118.
14. G. H. Seward's 1944 paper, "Psychological Effects of the Menstrual Cycle on Women Workers," quoted in Martin, 1987, p. 120.
15. Actually, Greene and Dalton introduced the term "premenstrual syndrome" in 1953, as an improvement over Frank's "premenstrual tension"; they wanted, they said, "to prevent missing the diagnosis when tension was absent or overshadowed by a more serious complaint."

While acknowledging that "PMS covers a wide spectrum from normality to gross abnormality," Dalton nevertheless argues that "PMS does exist and has only one definition: it is a syndrome needing treatment." (Dalton, 1987, p. 135.)

16. Martin, 1987, p. 120. See also Laws, 1983, who argues that the emphasis on PMS was a direct response to the challenges of feminism; and Anne Fausto-Sterling (1985), among the first to sound the alarm against the growing PMS bandwagon.

17. Mary Brown Parlee, "The Science and Politics of PMS Research." Invited address presented at the annual meeting of the Association for Women in Psychology, Newport, R.I., 1989. See also Parlee, 1987.

18. Parlee, 1989. (See Note 17.)

19. See for example DeJong et al., 1985; Hammarback and Backstrom, 1989.

20. American Psychiatric Association, 1987, p. 369.

21. There is considerable confusion, among researchers and clinicians, as to whether PMS and LLPDD are the same or even related phenomena. Some researchers consider LLPDD to be a subset of the more severe symptoms of PMS; others think that PMS simply refers to normal menstrual changes, whereas LLPDD is a distinct disorder; others think the two labels refer to the same phenomenon. In practice, however, most of the studies attempting to confirm LLPDD as a diagnostic category use the same measures as studies of PMS do; and they lack criteria for degree of symptom severity, let alone criteria of "interference with work or relationships."

22. Parlee, 1989. (See Note 17.) The original paper she is referring to is Parlee, 1973.

23. Ibid.

24. Quoted in Lynn Payer, "Hell Week," *Ms.,* March 1989, pp. 28–31. Quote on p. 28.

25. Gise, 1988, p. xi (preface).

26. Parlee, 1989. (See Note 17.) See also Freeman et al., 1990.

27. Freeman et al., 1990, p. 349. Katharina Dalton, however, who at age seventy-five still operates a private practice in London as of this writing (1991), continues to prescribe progesterone; Suzie Mackenzie, "A Woman's Problems," *The Guardian,* May 8, 1991.

28. Halbreich and Endicott, 1983; Gallant and Hamilton, 1988; Hamilton et al., 1984; Koeske, 1987. For a critical analysis of PMS, see also Fausto-Sterling, 1985. For a dissenting opinion, that retrospective questionnaire methods are not unduly problematic, see Richardson, 1990.

29. Koeske, 1987, p. 141.

30. Parlee, 1982.

31. AuBuchon and Calhoun, 1985.
32. McFarlane, Martin, and Williams, 1988.
33. AuBuchon and Calhoun, 1985; Gallant and Hamilton, 1988.
34. McFarlane, Martin, and Williams, 1988, pp. 216, 217.
35. Houser, 1979.
36. See Birke and Best, 1980.
37. Golub, 1988, p. 17.
38. Dalton, 1987. On the opposite argument, that stress and emotional events cause menstruation and may seem to coincide with the premenstrual phase, see Koeske, 1987.
39. Dabbs and Morris, 1990, p. 210.
40. Daniel Goleman, "Aggression in Men: Hormone Levels Are a Key," *The New York Times,* July 17, 1990, pp. B1, B8.
41. The Massip case was reported in the *Los Angeles Times,* December 24, 1988; information on Ronnie Shelton is from William Wilbanks, professor of criminal justice at Florida International University. To date, no man has successfully used a hormone excuse for diminished responsibility, although some have tried. On PMS as a legal defense, see Nelkin and Tancredi, 1989. In England, charges against two women were reduced from murder to manslaughter because they used a PMS defense, and PMS was used successfully in Canada to mitigate a sentence. France recognizes PMS as a legal insanity defense. It seems only a matter of time before American courts will do so as well. See also Elizabeth Holtzman, "Premenstrual Syndrome as a Legal Defense," in Gise, 1988; Peele, 1989.
42. Harriet Lerner, "PMS," in *New Directions for Women, 13* (July/August 1984), p. 4.
43. The WHO study consisted of 500 women from each of ten different nations. See Ericksen, 1987.
44. Koeske, 1987.
45. On the psychological interpretation of physical symptoms of all kinds, see Pennebaker, 1982.
46. Gelles and Straus, 1988.
47. This study and others on the same point—the myth that "alcohol and drugs are the real causes of violence in the home"—are described in Gelles and Straus, 1988, pp. 44–48.
48. Discussed in Martin, 1987, p. 125.
49. Linda Roach Monroe, "Menopause: Baby Boomers' Next Step," *Los Angeles Times,* December 5, 1989, pp. E1–3.
50. McKinlay, McKinlay, and Brambilla, 1987.
51. See Martin, 1987; Laqueur, 1987, 1990.
52. Quoted in Laqueur, 1987, p. 31.
53. Ibid., p. 32.

54. Martin, 1987, general description of menstruation, p. 45; "cata-strophic disintegration," p. 48.
55. Ibid., p. 50.
56. Ibid.
57. Ibid., p. 48.
58. Ibid., p. 43.
59. Quoted in Martin, 1987, p. 52.
60. Miller, 1946, p. 808.
61. Quoted in Lynn Payer, "Unnecessary Evil," *Savvy*, April 1988, pp. 96–98. Quote on p. 96. See also Payer, 1987.
62. See Payer, 1987; Wolfe, 1991.
63. Payer, 1988, p. 97. (See Note 61.)
64. Ibid. See also Wolfe, 1991.
65. The National Women's Health Network publishes frequent newsletters on all issues pertaining to women's health, including evaluations of the studies on hormone replacement therapies. See their newsletter, *The Network News*, March/April 1990 and July/August 1990. The Network is located at 1325 G Street, N.W., Washington, D.C. 20005.
66. Stampfer et al., 1991. See also the commentary on This Study, in the same issue of *The New England Journal of Medicine*, by Goldman and Tosteson, 1991.
67. Quoted in Andrea Boroff Eagan, "The Estrogen Fix," *Ms.*, April 1989, pp. 38–43. Quote on p. 43.
68. Metzger and Hammond, 1988, p. 493.
69. See Wolfe, 1991, for a consumer review of the studies; see also Barrett-Connor, 1989; Steinberg et al., 1991; and van Leeuwen and Rookus, 1989.
70. National Osteoporosis Foundation, Washington, D.C.; Dr. Charles Chesnut, Osteoporosis Research Center, University of Washington. See also Goldman and Tosteson, 1991.

CHAPTER 5: MISDIAGNOSING THE MIND

1. Checklist adapted from "No Life to Live," by Melinda Blau, *American Health*, May 1990, pp. 57–61.
2. Silvia S. Canetto, "Suicide Attempts and Substance Abuse: Similarities and Differences." Paper presented at the annual meeting of the American Psychological Association, New Orleans, 1990. This paper is also in press in the *Journal of Psychology*, 1992.
3. Caplan, 1987; see also Blackman, 1989.
4. Landrine, 1988, p. 39. The source of these two "disorders" is K. M. Stampp, *The Peculiar Institution: Slavery in the Antebellum South* (New York: Knopf, 1956). See also Dumont, 1987.

5. *Diagnostic and Statistical Manual of Mental Disorders*, American Psychiatric Association, 1987. (Hereafter DSM-III-R.) On its worldwide success and number of language translations, p. xviii. On the warning about its relevance to legal judgments, p. xxix. On the yearly revenue, Caplan, 1991.

6. Judith Herman, "Self-defeating Personality Disorder [and] Sadistic Personality Disorder: A conceptual critique and review of recent research." Unpublished paper, Department of Psychiatry, Cambridge Hospital, Cambridge, MA, 1990. Herman observes that no one has been much interested in studying "Sadistic Personality Disorder" or diagnosing patients as having it, supporting the impression of many that it was, as she says, a "paper concept created to neutralize criticisms of gender bias."

7. For a history of the Work Group's revision and criticism of the proposed diagnosis of Self-defeating Personality Disorder, see Caplan, 1987 and 1991; Rosewater, 1987; Laura S. Brown, "Diagnosis and the Zeitgeist: The politics of masochism in the DSM-III-R," paper presented at the annual meeting of the American Psychological Association, Washington, D.C., 1986; Lenore E. Walker, "Diagnosis and Politics: Abuse disorders," same convention; and Sarah Boxer, "The Parable of the Cheek-Turners and the Cheek-Smiters," *Discover*, August 1987, pp. 80–83.

8. DSM-III-R, p. 371.

9. Ibid., p. xxi.

10. Ibid., p. xxii.

11. This comment comes from an anonymous reviewer of Paula J. Caplan and Maureen Gans's paper, "Is There Empirical Justification for the Category of 'Self-Defeating Personality Disorder'?", that the authors had submitted to the *Journal of Personality Disorders*. This article was published in the February 1992 issue of *Feminism and Psychology*. See Caplan's 1987 paperback edition of *The Myth of Women's Masochism* ("Afterword: A warning") for a published description of this history.

12. Dumont, 1987, p. 11.

13. On the reliability of personality disorders in the DSM: Dumont, 1987; Kutchins and Kirk, 1986; Matarazzo, 1990; Zimmerman, 1988; and the preface to the DSM-III-R itself.

14. Dumont, 1987, p. 11.

15. Ibid., p. 10.

16. Landrine, 1989. The extracted descriptions of various personality disorders are from this article.

17. Ibid., p. 332.

18. The three psychologists are Sprock, Blashfield, and Smith, 1990. In the published version, this is what Sprock et al. had to say: "Whether

this weighting [of diagnostic criteria by gender] is inappropriate and reflects gender bias is an issue that was not addressed in this study. Further research is needed to examine the influence of sex roles and gender bias on the diagnosis of personality disorders" (p. 590).

19. DSM-III-R, p. 426.
20. On the reasons for the "self-defeating" behavior of normal people, see Baumeister and Scher, 1988; Rebecca Curtis, "Choosing to Suffer and Conditions Leading to Self-Defeating Behaviors," paper presented at the annual meeting of the American Psychological Association, New York City, 1987. On the masochism experiment, see Stone and Hokanson, 1969.
21. Robertson and Fitzgerald, 1990. In this study, forty-seven therapists were randomly assigned to view one of two versions of a videotaped simulation of a depressed male client. The tapes were identical except for the client's occupational and family roles, which were portrayed as either traditional or nontraditional. Later, the therapists evaluated the client on various dimensions, assigned a diagnosis, and outlined their proposed treatment. Nontraditional men were judged as being more disturbed than traditional men were, and were treated more harshly.
22. C. Brownsmith and D. Pearlmutter, "Position Paper on DSM-III-R." Women's Study Group, American Orthopsychiatric Association, New York, 1986.
23. Paula J. Caplan and Margrit Eichler, "Draft Proposal of a Category Proposed for Inclusion in the American Psychiatric Association Diagnostic and Statistical Manual of Mental Disorders-IV: Delusional Dominating Personality Disorder." For the published paper on "DDPD," see Pantony and Caplan, 1991.
24. Pantony and Caplan, 1991. Quote, pp. 129–130.
25. Ibid., p. 122.
26. Letter from Allen Frances and Harold Alan Pincus to the DSM-IV Work Group on Personality Disorders, September 19, 1988, p. 1. This memo and subsequent correspondence published in Caplan, 1991.
27. Thomas A. Widiger and Allen J. Frances, "Diagnosis of Self-defeating Personality Disorder." Paper presented at the annual meeting of the American Psychological Association, Atlanta, 1988. Quote, p. 28.
28. Letter from Gunderson to Paula Caplan, October 16, 1989. Published in Caplan, 1991.
29. Letter from Gunderson to Caplan, November 14, 1989. Published in Caplan, 1991.
30. Quoted in Wendy Kaminer, "Chances Are You're Codependent Too," *The New York Times Book Review*, February 11, 1990, pp. 1, 26–27. Schaef describes codependency as a "progressive, fatal disease," in *Escape from Intimacy*. See also review by Jennifer King, "Close Encounters," in *New Age Journal*, July/August 1989, pp. 59–61.

31. Blau, p. 61. (See Note 1.)
32. The booklet is cited in Alison Humes, "The Culting of Codependence," 7 *Days*, November 1, 1989.
33. Ibid., p. 26.
34. Interview with author.
35. David Schreiber, "Why Women Should Be Cautious about CD [chemical dependency] Treatment," *AuContraire*, June 1982. See also his article "Hysterectomies, Mastectomies and Co-dependencies," in *Viewpoints: The quarterly publication of the Minnesota Chemical Health Association*, Winter 1984.
36. Gierymski and Williams, 1986.
37. Edwards, Harvey, and Whitehead, 1973, p. 130.
38. Gomberg, 1989, pp. 118, 119.
39. Letters to *American Health* magazine, October 1990, p. 6.
40. Kaminer, p. 27. (See Note 30.)
41. Laura Brown, "What's Addiction Got To Do With It: A feminist critique of codependence." *Psychology of Women Newsletter* of Division 35, American Psychological Association, Winter 1990, p. 4.
42. Katz and Liu, 1991, pp. 98–99.
43. Ellen Herman, "The Twelve-Step Programs: Cure or cover?" Article reprinted in the *Utne Reader*, November/December 1988, pp. 52–63. Quote on p. 61. See also the rest of the full section of that issue, "Are You Addicted to Addiction? A skeptical look at AA and other 12-step programs."
44. Interview with author, quoted in Carol Tavris, "Do Codependency Theories Explain Women's Unhappiness—or Exploit Their Insecurities?" *Vogue*, December 1989, pp. 220–226.
45. Strube, 1988, p. 240.
46. Interview with author, quoted in Tavris. (See Note 44.)
47. Beth Ann Krier, "Everyday Addicts," *Los Angeles Times*, July 29, 1990, p. E10.
48. Harriet G. Lerner, "Women Who Read Too Much: Reflections on the advice-giving industry," *Women's Review of Books*, April 1990, pp. 15–16. Quote, p. 16.
49. Interview with author, quoted in Tavris. (See Note 44.)
50. For example, psychiatrist Timmin Cermak, interviewed in Blau, p. 61. (See Note 1.)
51. Bepko and Krestan, *Too Good for Her Own Good* (New York: Harper & Row, 1990), p. ix.
52. Some psychologists already are. See Philipson, 1985.
53. Canetto, 1990 and in press. (See Note 2.)
54. Dumont, 1987, p. 12.
55. Peele and Brodsky, 1991.
56. Katz and Liu, 1991, p. 17.

CHAPTER 6: BEDTIME STORIES

1. Fritz Kant, *Frigidity: Dynamics and treatment* (Springfield, IL: Charles C. Thomas, 1969), p. 29. (Typographical error in original.)
2. Symons, 1979, p. v.
3. Echols, 1984, p. 59.
4. Sam Kash Kachigan, *The Sexual Matrix* (New York: Radius Press, 1990), p. 162.
5. Ibid., p. 161.
6. Charles Darwin, *The Descent of Man and Selection in Relation to Sex* (New York: Appleton & Co., 1871).
7. Hrdy, 1988, p. 120.
8. Ibid., p. 121.
9. Angus John Bateman, "Intra-sexual Selection in Drosophila," *Heredity*, 2 (1948), pp. 349–368. Quote, p. 365.
10. For a basic text on sociobiology, see E. O. Wilson, *On Human Nature* (Cambridge, MA: Harvard University Press, 1978); also Symons, 1979.
11. Hubbard, 1990, p. 110. See also Haraway, 1988.
12. Hrdy, 1988, p. 122.
13. Ibid., p. 126.
14. See, for example, Goodall, 1986, and De Waal, 1989.
15. Hrdy, 1988, p. 129.
16. On primate fathers, see Taub, 1984; Tavris and Wade, 1984. The observer in the infant study was Patricia Wright, cited in Hrdy, 1988.
17. Altmann, 1980.
18. Hrdy, 1988, p. 141.
19. Ibid., p. 137. See also Haraway, 1988.
20. Ibid., p. 139.
21. Kinsey et al., 1953, p. 641.
22. Ibid., p. 102.
23. Masters and Johnson, 1970, p. 297.
24. Kaplan, 1974, p. 45.
25. Irvine, 1990, p. 10.
26. Ibid., pp. 51–52.
27. Tiefer, "Gender and Meaning in DSM-III (& III-R) Sexual Dysfunctions." Paper presented at the annual meeting of the American Psychological Association, Boston, 1990a.
28. Irvine, 1990, p. 197.
29. Quoted in Irvine, 1990, pp. 197–198.
30. Ibid., p. 86.
31. Robinson, 1976. See also Leonore Tiefer, "Historical, scientific, clinical and feminist criticisms of 'the human sexual response cycle' model." Unpublished paper, Montefiore Medical Center, 1991.

32. Comments by Carole Wade, here and following, from interview with author.

33. Mary Harrington Hall, "A Conversation with Masters & Johnson," *Psychology Today,* July 1969, pp. 50–58. "Physiologically, they're identical," p. 52; "textbook concept," p. 54.

34. Irvine, 1990, p. 226.

35. American Psychiatric Association, 1987, [hereafter DSM-III-R], p. 290. The version of "the" sexual response cycle enshrined in the current DSM is *appetitive* (fantasies about and desire to have sexual activity); *excitement* (a subjective sense of pleasure and accompanying physiological changes); *orgasm;* and *resolution* (muscular relaxation).

36. Tiefer's critique of the DSM, here and following pages: 1990a, "Gender and Meaning." (See Note 27.)

37. DSM-III-R, 1987, p. 292.

38. Ibid., p. 294.

39. Ibid.

40. Quoted in Irvine, 1990, p. 137.

41. Leonore Tiefer, "Sexual Biology and the Symbolism of the Natural." Paper presented at the International Academy of Sex Research, Sigtuna, Sweden, 1990b. See also Tiefer, 1986.

42. Tiefer, 1990a, "Gender and Meaning." (See Note 27.)

43. Davidson, Darling, and Conway-Welch, 1989.

44. Ladas, Whipple, and Perry, 1982, p. 87. The authors of *The G Spot* made many such assertions with no scientific evidence to back up their claims. They explained why with this disclaimer: "We do not expect," they wrote, "anyone to accept what we are saying unconditionally. We also hope that it will be subjected to scientific rigorous scrutiny" (p. xvi). This was odd; most scientists are in the habit of gathering evidence before writing a book. But by writing first and then hoping for the evidence, the authors were able to bypass the usual procedures of scholarly publication—detailed reporting and peer review of methods, statistics, and results.

45. For example, see Freese and Levitt, 1984: Data from ninety-two women "provided no evidence of a general relationship between strength of voluntary pelvic muscle contractions and orgasmic function." Similarly, see Trudel and Saint-Laurent, 1983.

46. Grafenberg, 1950, p. 145.

47. The three articles in the February 1981 issue of the *Journal of Sex Research* were Edwin Belzer, "Orgasmic Expulsions of Women: A review and heuristic inquiry"; Perry and Whipple, "Pelvic Muscle Strength of Female Ejaculators: Evidence in support of a new theory of orgasm"; and Frank Addiego, E. Belzer, J. Comolli, W. Moger, J. Perry, and B. Whipple, "Female Ejaculation: A case study."

48. Goldberg et al., 1983, p. 29.

49. Ibid., p. 36.
50. Crenshaw's "research" was first reported in an "exclusive interview" in that scholarly sex publication *Forum* (July 1983, pp. 5–10). Desmond Heath, "An Investigation into the Origins of a Copious Vaginal Discharge During Intercourse," *Journal of Sex Research, 20* (1984), pp. 194–215. (This article was mostly a case study of one woman.) Perry's disclaimer was cited in the September 1982 issue of *Forum*.
51. Zaviačič et al., 1988a.
52. Heli Alzate, Letter to the Editor ("A clarification to Perry"), *Journal of Sex & Marital Therapy, 11* (1985), pp. 67–68. Quote on p. 68.
53. Zaviačič et al., 1988b. Spot found in all women, p. 313; "urge for micturition" in all subjects, p. 313.
54. Ibid., p. 315. (Typographical error in original.)
55. Heli Alzate and Maria Ladi Londoño, "Vaginal Erotic Sensitivity," *Journal of Sex & Marital Therapy, 10* (1984), pp. 49–56.
56. Zwi Hoch, Letter to the Editor ("The G Spot"), *Journal of Sex & Marital Therapy, 9* (1983), p. 166.
57. Winton, 1989.
58. Quoted in Irvine, 1990, pp. 63–64.
59. For a discussion of this issue, see Tiefer, 1986, 1988.
60. On sexual dysfunction in "normal" couples, see Frank, Anderson, and Rubinstein, 1978.
61. See, for example, Hite, 1976.
62. See Lerner, 1989, Chapter 2, "Parental Mislabeling of Female Genitals."
63. Bland, 1984, p. 9.
64. Faulkner, 1980, p. 162.

CHAPTER 7: LOVE'S EXPERTS, LOVE'S VICTIMS

1. On the inexpressive male, see Balswick and Peek, 1976; Mirra Komarovsky wrote of men's "trained incapacity to share" in *Blue-collar Marriage* (New York: Vintage, 1964).
2. "Dear Abby," *Los Angeles Times*, March 14, 1990, p. E3.
3. This statistic is from Harper's Index, *Harper's* magazine, February 1991, p. 19. The Index cited Hallmark Cards.
4. Driscoll, 1991, p. 61.
5. Ibid., p. 62.
6. This couple is quoted in Cancian, 1987, p. 76.
7. Wills, Weiss, and Patterson, 1974.
8. Riessman, 1990, p. 97.
9. On the different functions of talk: See Lakoff, 1990; Maltz and Borker, 1982; McConnell-Ginet, 1983; Tannen, 1990.

10. Tannen, 1990, pp. 49–50.
11. Cancian, 1987, p. 74. Joseph Pleck, 1981, also argues that men enjoy and need their family relationships more than they get credit for.
12. Ibid., p. 76.
13. White et al., 1986, p. 155.
14. Ibid., p. 156.
15. Quoted in Cancian, 1987, p. 77.
16. Swain, 1989, p. 72. "Tom-Sawyer-type things," p. 74.
17. Ibid., p. 75.
18. Ibid.
19. Ibid., p. 77.
20. Ibid., p. 80.
21. *Los Angeles Times,* January 28, 1991, p. C3.
22. Swain, 1989, p. 82.
23. For a review of the research on women and depression, see McGrath et al., 1990.
24. Riessman, 1990, pp. 156–157.
25. Ibid., p. 153.
26. Ibid., p. 144.
27. Ibid., p. 145.
28. Ibid.
29. Stapley and Haviland, 1989, p. 307.
30. This list of predictors is from police psychologist Theodore Blau, who was interviewed by Robert Trotter for "Psychologist With a Badge," *Psychology Today,* November 1987, p. 26.
31. Ronald Taffel, "The Politics of Mood," *The Family Therapy Networker,* September/October 1990, pp. 49–53, 72. Quote, p. 49.
32. Ibid., p. 51.
33. Cancian, 1987.
34. Wadsworth and Ryan cited in Cancian, 1987, pp. 15–16.
35. Demos, 1986, p. 47.
36. Cancian, 1987, p. 19.
37. Taffel, p. 53. (See Note 31.)
38. *Los Angeles Times,* October 15, 1987, p. A1.
39. Zilbergeld, 1992; see also Stephanie Shields, *Gender and the Social Meaning of Emotion.* Book manuscript in preparation, University of California at Davis.
40. See, for example, Peplau and Gordon, 1985; Robertson and Fitzgerald, 1990; Shields, 1987.
41. Taffel, p. 52. (See Note 31.)
42. Comments by Silverstein, here and following, from staff interview with Olga Silverstein, "On the Couch," *Vogue,* February 1989, pp. 387, 456–457.

43. In a review of numerous studies of men's and women's expressive styles, Wendy Wood and her associates found that neither sex has an advantage "in the adaptiveness and desirability of their different styles of emotional life." See Wood, Rhodes, and Whelan, 1989.

44. On the relationship between self-focused rumination and depression, see Nolen-Hoeksema, 1990.

45. Arentewicz and Schmidt, 1983, p. 6.

46. Interview with author.

47. Hare-Mustin, 1991.

48. Hochschild, 1989.

49. Richard Laliberte, "A Silent Bond," *The New York Times Magazine*, April 29, 1990, pp. 26, 28.

50. Cancian, 1987, p. 93. Scott Swain agrees. "The deficit model of male expressiveness does not recognize men's active style of intimacy," he argues, which in turn "may alienate and threaten men who then assume that intimacy is a challenge they will fail." Swain, 1989, p. 85.

51. Interview with author. See also Christensen and Heavey, 1990, who assessed thirty-one couples in two conflict situations: one in which the husband wanted a change in the wife, and one in which the wife wanted a change in the husband. The demand/withdraw pattern depends on the situation, not gender: When the wife wanted a change in the husband, he was likely to withdraw; but when the husband wanted a change in the wife, *she* was just as likely to withdraw.

52. Hochschild, 1989. This couple is also analyzed thoughtfully by Hare-Mustin, 1991.

53. Study cited and discussed in Caplan, 1989, p. 53.

54. Ibid., p. 46.

55. Ann Landers's column, *Los Angeles Times,* September 30, 1990, p. E11.

56. Interview with author. See also Caplan, 1989.

57. The McGinn case study is from Luepnitz, 1988, pp. 230–279. Specific citations are as follows: her compliment to Margo and the exchange with Gus, p. 242; her thoughts on the rational/irrational bifurcation, p. 236; Gus's worry that "she'll be hysterical," p. 250; Margo's account of her hospitalization, pp. 250–251; Margo's exchange with Gus about who was to blame, p. 253; Luepnitz's exchange with Gus about his emotions after his father's death, pp. 259–260; Gus, "I want to be with my family more," p. 260.

58. Luepnitz, 1988, p. 273; Gus's benefit of therapy, p. 274; Gus doing more housework, p. 271; Margo "was no longer the 'loony,' " p. 275. For a similar nonblaming approach to family therapy, see Goodrich et al., 1988; Lerner, 1989.

59. Butler's memoirs cited in Kreps, 1990, p. 78.

60. Ibid., p. 79.
61. See Holland and Eisenhart, 1991, who studied college women at two southern schools over a period of several (recent) years. They found that peer pressure and patriarchal culture are sharply curtailing the aspirations and expectations of young women today: Many are entering college with high hopes and ambitions, and leaving with the single goal of catching the right husband.
62. Studies of love, intimacy, grief, and attachment find no sex differences of any significance. Men and women are equally likely, for example, to have "secure" attachments or those marked by anxiety, ambivalence, and avoidance; see Shaver, Hazan, and Bradshaw, 1988. Paul Wright (1988) warns of the hazards of falsely dividing men and women into two exaggerated extremes, since the same kinds of experiences and exchanges take place to some degree in all close friendships.
63. Cancian, 1987, p. 81.

CHAPTER 8: SPEAKING OF GENDER

1. Anna Julia Cooper, *A Voice From the South*. Quoted in Minnich, 1990, p. vii.
2. Deaux and Major, 1987, p. 369.
3. Maccoby, 1988, p. 755.
4. Maccoby, 1990, p. 516. Here, she is referring to the work of Maltz and Borker, 1982, among others.
5. West and Zimmerman, 1987.
6. On tokens, see Kanter, 1977; Nieva and Gutek, 1981; Tavris and Wade, 1984.
7. Antill, 1983.
8. Helgeson, 1990.
9. Cohn, 1991, p. 252. His conclusion on the "single path to maturity," p. 263.
10. On context, see Deaux and Major, 1987, 1990; Eagly, 1987; Jacklin, 1989.
11. For instructors and other individuals who are interested in issues of class and race in the field of gender studies, see Phyllis Bronstein and Kathryn Quina (Eds.), *Teaching a Psychology of People* (Washington, D.C.: American Psychological Association, 1988).
12. Epstein, 1988.
13. Tannen, 1990. Maltz and Borker, 1982, also propose a "two cultures" view of sex differences in communication patterns.
14. Tannen, 1990, p. 77.
15. Lakoff, 1990, p. 205.
16. Ibid., p. 202.

17. Carli, 1990.
18. Ibid., p. 941.
19. See Snodgrass, 1985, on "women's intuition"; O'Barr, 1983, and Erickson et al., 1978, on the courtroom research; Dovidio et al., 1988, on visual displays and power. See also McConnell-Ginet, 1983.
20. Lakoff, 1990, p. 199.
21. Ibid., p. 203.
22. Ibid., p. 214.
23. On narratives in psychology, see Howard, 1991; Mair, 1988; Sarbin, 1986.
24. Mary Gergen, 1992.
25. Howard, 1991, p. 194.
26. See Heilbrun, 1989, and Le Guin, 1989, on writing women's lives; on differences in the way men and women who have the same occupation perceive their work, see Weingarten and Douvan, 1985. Cultures too differ in the form a story might take, which is the source of much misunderstanding and conflict. For instance, when Anglo women talk about the reasons for the breakup of their marriages, they tell a linear story of events through time: "He did this, then I did that, and finally he did this intolerable last straw." But Puerto Rican women tend to describe their breakups in terms of significant episodes, in no particular historical order. Each story symbolizes to the speaker what her marital problems were, but whereas an Anglo interviewer can "hear" and understand the first woman, she remains "out of sync" with the second. Many people are "out of sync" with what other cultures, races, and genders are trying to say to them. See Riessman, 1987.
27. Gergen, 1992. All subsequent excerpts from her research on autobiographies are from this source.
28. Carol Tavris, "Male supremacy is on the way out. It was just a phase in the evolution of culture" (Interview with Marvin Harris), *Psychology Today,* January 1975, pp. 61–69. Quote, p. 66.
29. Excerpt reprinted in *The New Yorker,* January 28, 1991, p. 29.
30. Merrill Markoe, "Write Like a Man," *New York Woman,* April 1990, pp. 58ff.
31. See George H. Gallup, Jr., and Frank Newport, "Belief in Paranormal Phenomena Among Adult Americans" (Special Report/Gallup Poll), *Skeptical Inquirer, 15* (Winter 1991), pp. 137–146.
32. Le Guin, 1989, p. 222.
33. Ibid., p. 228.
34. Nell Bernstein, "Babes in Arms," *Image,* March 24, 1991, pp. 7–9.
35. For an analysis of this point, see Kahn and Yoder, 1989, and Mednick, 1989.

36. The show was *20/20*, August 2, 1991.
37. Mimia C. Logsdon, John C. Birkimer, and Angela B. McBride, "A Further Look at Predictors of Postpartum Depression." Paper presented at the annual meeting of the American Psychological Association, San Francisco, 1991. The evidence regarding postpartum depression is actually quite similar to that regarding PMS. That is, hormonal changes following childbirth are normal; most of the women who suffer extreme clinical depression, however, tend to have had a lifetime history of depressive episodes or other problems.
38. *Los Angeles Times*, December 6, 1990, p. A25. For the actual study on depression, see McGrath et al., 1990.
39. Ragins and Sundstrom, 1989, p. 51.
40. See, for example, Armstrong, 1978/1987; Koss, 1990; Russell, 1982; Walker, 1989; Wyatt and Powell, 1988. The theory that women are *defined* by their sexual victimization is most forcefully argued by MacKinnon, 1987.
41. Armstrong, 1978/1987, pp. 265–266.
42. Ibid., p. 290.
43. Nancy Matthews, "Stopping Rape or Managing Its Consequences? State intervention and feminist resistance in the Los Angeles anti-rape movement, 1972–1987." Doctoral dissertation, University of California at Los Angeles, 1989. "Feminist political agenda," p. 263; "a personal experience," p. 323. See also Matthews, in press.
44. deMause, 1984, p. 79.
45. Scheper-Hughes and Stein, 1987, p. 342.
46. Culhane's findings and the story of Emma come from my interview with her. This work is further described in her unpublished paper, "Critical Frameworks from Contemporary Anthropology and the Case of Adult Survivors of Sexual Abuse," Simon Fraser University, 1991.
47. For example, see Elly Danica, *Don't: A woman's word* (Charlottetown, Prince Edward Island: Gynergy Books, 1988).
48. On the psychological consequences of severe abuse, see Wyatt and Powell, 1988.
49. Ellen Bass and Laura Davis, *The Courage to Heal: A guide for women survivors of child sexual abuse* (New York: Harper & Row, 1988), p. 35.
50. See Spanos et al., 1991.
51. Betsy Petersen, *Dancing With Daddy* (New York: Bantam, 1991). Quotes are as follows: "Perhaps it had happened . . . in San Francisco," p. 64; "I can't remember—but my body remembers," p. 159; "Telling . . . make myself feel better," p. 83; "We wanted to help them understand," p. 88; "The only thing I wanted," p. 158; "It's clear to me now that they awoke at night," p. 5; "Sometimes it feels like the world is tilting," p. 23; "Before I knew my father had molested me," p. 79;

story of conflict with son, being really angry at father, p. 92; "Their wanting overwhelms me," p. 117; "And I had to pay for that," p. 119.

52. Dara Culhane, "Sins of the Father," review of Petersen's book in *The New York Times Book Review*, August 4, 1991.

53. Armstrong, 1978/1987, p. 286.

54. Lakoff, 1990, p. 199.

55. See Note 1.

56. See, for example: Crawford and Marecek, 1989; K. Gergen, 1985; M. Gergen, 1988; Hare-Mustin and Marecek, 1990; Minnich, 1990; Tiefer, 1988.

57. See Crosby, 1991, for an excellent review of the research evidence on the benefits to women (physically and mentally) who combine paid work and family.

58. Roper Organization survey of 3,000 women, released September 1990. Quoted in Bettijane Levine, "Heavy-duty Anger," *Los Angeles Times,* September 23, 1990, pp. E1, E8–9.

Bibliography

Altmann, Jeanne (1980). *Baboon mothers and infants*. Cambridge, MA: Harvard University Press.

American Psychiatric Association (1987). *Diagnostic and statistical manual of mental disorders, Third Edition—Revised*. Washington, D.C.: American Psychiatric Association.

Anderson, Bonnie S., & Zinsser, Judith P. (1988). *A history of their own: Women in Europe from prehistory to the present, Vols. I and II*. New York: Harper & Row.

Antill, John K. (1983). Sex role complementarity versus similarity in married couples. *Journal of Personality & Social Psychology, 45*, 145–155.

Apter, Terri (1990). *Altered loves: Mothers and daughters during adolescence*. New York: St. Martin's Press.

Arentewicz, Gerd, & Schmidt, Gunter (1983). *The treatment of sexual disorders: Concepts and techniques of couple therapy*. New York: Basic Books.

Aries, Elizabeth J., & Olver, Rose R. (1985). Sex differences in the development of a separate sense of self during infancy: Directions for future research. *Psychology of Women Quarterly, 9*, 515–532.

Armstrong, Louise (1978, 1987). *Kiss daddy goodnight: Ten years later*. New York: Pocket Books.

Attie, Ilana, & Brooks-Gunn, Jeanne (1987). Weight concerns as chronic stressors in women. In R. C. Barnett, L. Biener, & G. K. Baruch (Eds.), *Gender and stress*. New York: The Free Press.

AuBuchon, P. G., & Calhoun, K. S. (1985). Menstrual cycle symptomatology: The role of social expectancy and experimental demand characteristics. *Psychosomatic Medicine, 47*, 35–45.

Balswick, Jack O., & Peek, Charles W. (1976). The inexpressive male: A tragedy of American society. In D. S. David & R. Brannon (Eds.), *The forty-nine percent majority: The male sex role*. Reading, MA: Addison-Wesley.

Barrett-Connor, Elizabeth L. (1989). The risks and benefits of long-term estrogen replacement therapy. *Public Health Reports, 104* (supplement), 62–65.

Baruch, Grace K.; Barnett, Rosalind C.; & Rivers, Caryl (1982). *Lifeprints: New patterns of love and work for today's women.* New York: McGraw-Hill.

Baumeister, Roy F., & Scher, Steven J. (1988). Self-defeating behavior patterns among normal individuals: Review and analysis of common self-destructive tendencies. *Psychological Bulletin, 104,* 3–22.

Belenky, Mary F.; Clinchy, Blythe M.; Goldberger, Nancy R.; & Tarule, Jill M. (1986). *Women's ways of knowing: The development of self, voice, and mind.* New York: Basic Books.

Benbow, Camilla P., & Stanley, Julian (1980). Sex differences in mathematical ability: Fact or artifact? *Science, 210,* 1262–1264.

———— (1983). Sex differences in mathematical reasoning ability: More facts. *Science, 222,* 1029–1031.

Bennett, William, & Gurin, Joel (1982). *The dieter's dilemma: Eating less and weighing more.* New York: Basic Books.

Benton, Cynthia; Hernandez, Anthony; Schmidt, Adeny; Schmitz, Mary; Stone, Anne; & Weiner, Bernard (1983). Is hostility linked with affiliation among males and with achievement among females? A critique of Pollak and Gilligan. *Journal of Personality and Social Psychology, 45,* 1167–1171.

Birke, Lynda, & Best, Sandy (1980). The tyrannical womb: Menstruation and menopause. In The Brighton Women and Science Group (Eds.), *Alice through the microscope: The power of science over women's lives.* London: Virago.

Blackman, Julie (1989). *Intimate violence.* New York: Columbia University Press.

Bland, Lucy (1984). Purity, motherhood, pleasure or threat? Definitions of female sexuality 1900–1970s. In S. Cartledge & J. Ryan (Eds.), *Sex & love: New thoughts on old contradictions.* New York: Salem House (Harper Collins).

Bleier, Ruth (1988). Sex differences research: Science or belief? In R. Bleier (Ed.), *Feminist approaches to science.* New York: Pergamon.

Cancian, Francesca M. (1987). *Love in America: Gender and self-development.* Cambridge, England: Cambridge University Press.

Canetto, Silvia S. (in press). Suicide attempts and substance abuse: Similarities and differences. *Journal of Psychology.*

Caplan, Paula J. (1987). *The myth of women's masochism.* New York: Signet.

———— (1989). *Don't blame mother: Mending the mother-daughter relationship.* New York: Harper & Row.

———— (1991). How *do* they decide who is normal? The bizarre, but true, tale of the *DSM* process. *Canadian Psychology, 32,* 162–170.

Caplan, Paula J.; MacPherson, Gael M.; & Tobin, Patricia (1985). Do sex-related differences in spatial abilities exist? *American Psychologist, 40,* 786–799.

Carli, Linda L. (1990). Gender, language, and influence. *Journal of Personality and Social Psychology, 59,* 941–951.

Chamallas, Martha, with Kerber, L. K. (1990). Women, mothers, and the law of fright: A history. *Michigan Law Review, 88,* 814–864.

Chesler, Phyllis (1986). *Mothers on trial: The battle for children and custody.* New York: McGraw-Hill.

Chodorow, Nancy (1978). *The reproduction of mothering.* Berkeley, CA: University of California Press.

Christ, Carol (1979). Why women need the goddess. In C. Christ & J. Plaskow (Eds.), *Womanspirit rising: A feminist reader in religion.* San Francisco: Harper & Row.

Christensen, Andrew, & Heavey, Christopher L. (1990). Gender and social structure in the demand/withdraw pattern of marital conflict. *Journal of Personality and Social Psychology, 59,* 73–81.

Cochran, Susan D., & Peplau, L. Anne (1985). Value orientations in heterosexual relationships. *Psychology of Women Quarterly, 9,* 477–488.

Cohn, Lawrence D. (1991). Sex differences in the course of personality development: A meta-analysis. *Psychological Bulletin, 109,* 252–266.

Colby, Anne, & Damon, William (1987). Listening to a different voice: A review of Gilligan's *In a different voice.* In M. R. Walsh (Ed.), *The psychology of women: Ongoing debates.* New Haven, CT: Yale University Press.

Corea, Genoveffa (1985). *The mother machine.* New York: Harper & Row.

Crawford, Mary, & Gressley, Diane (1991). Creativity, caring, and context: Women's and men's accounts of humor preferences and practices. *Psychology of Women Quarterly, 15,* 217–231.

Crawford, Mary, & Marecek, Jeanne (1989). Psychology reconstructs the female: 1968–1988. *Psychology of Women Quarterly, 13,* 147–165.

Crosby, Faye J. (1991). *Juggling.* New York: The Free Press.

Dabbs, James M., Jr., & Morris, Robin (1990). Testosterone, social class, and antisocial behavior in a sample of 4,462 men. *Psychological Science, 1,* 209–211.

Dalton, Katharina (1987). What is this PMS? In M. R. Walsh (Ed.), *The psychology of women: Ongoing debates.* New Haven, CT: Yale University Press.

Davidson, J. Kenneth; Darling, Carol A.; & Conway-Welch, Colleen

(1989). The role of the Grafenberg Spot and female ejaculation in the female orgasmic response: An empirical analysis. *Journal of Sex & Marital Therapy, 15,* 102–120.

Deaux, Kay & Major, Brenda (1987). Putting gender into context: An interactive model of gender-related behavior. *Psychological Review, 94,* 369–389.

Deaux, Kay, & Major, Brenda (1990). A social-psychological model of gender. In D. L. Rhode (Ed.), *Theoretical perspectives on sexual difference.* New Haven, CT: Yale University Press.

DeJong, R.; Rubinow, D. R.; Roy-Byrne, P.; Hoban, M. C.; Grover, G. N.; & Post, R. M. (1985). Premenstrual mood disorder and psychiatric illness. *American Journal of Psychiatry, 142,* 1359–1361.

de Lacoste-Utamsing, Christine, & Holloway, Ralph L. (1982). Sexual dimorphism in the human corpus callosum. *Science, 216,* 1431–1432.

deMause, Lloyd (1984). *Reagan's America.* New York: Creative Roots, Inc.

Demos, John (1986). *Past, present, and personal: The family and the life course in American history.* New York: Oxford University Press.

Denmark, Florence; Russo, Nancy F.; Frieze, Irene H.; & Sechzer, Jeri A. (1988). Guidelines for avoiding sexism in psychological research. *American Psychologist, 43,* 582–585.

De Waal, Frans (1989). *Peacemaking among primates.* Cambridge, MA: Harvard University Press.

di Leonardo, Micaela (1987). The female world of cards and holidays: Women, families, and the work of kinship. *Signs, 12,* 1–20.

Donovan, Mary Ellen, & Sanford, Linda T. (1986). The elements of self-esteem. In C. Tavris (Ed.), *EveryWoman's emotional well-being.* New York: Prentice-Hall.

Dovidio, John F.; Ellyson, Steve L.; Keating, Caroline F.; Heltman, Karen; & Brown, Clifford E. (1988). The relationship of social power to visual displays of dominance between men and women. *Journal of Personality and Social Psychology, 54,* 233–242.

Driscoll, Richard (1991). *The binds that tie.* Lexington, MA: Lexington Books.

Dumont, Matthew P. (1987, December). A diagnostic parable (first edition —unrevised) [Review of *DSM-III-R.*] *Readings: A Journal of Reviews and Commentary in Mental Health,* pp. 9–12.

Dworkin, Ronald (1977). *Taking rights seriously.* Cambridge, MA: Harvard University Press.

Eagly, Alice H. (1987). *Sex differences in social behavior: A social-role interpretation.* Hillsdale, NJ: Erlbaum.

Echols, Alice (1984). The taming of the id: Feminist sexual politics: 1968–1983. In C. S. Vance (Ed.), *Pleasure and danger: Exploring female sexuality.* Boston: Routledge and Kegan Paul.

Edwards, Patricia; Harvey, Cheryl; & Whitehead, Paul C. (1973). Wives of alcoholics: A critical review and analysis. *Quarterly Journal of Studies on Alcohol, 34,* 112–132.

Eisenberg, Nancy, & Lennon, Randy (1983). Sex differences in empathy and related capacities. *Psychological Bulletin, 94,* 100–131.

Eisenstein, Zillah R. (1988). *The female body and the law.* Berkeley, CA: University of California Press.

Eisler, Riane (1987). *The chalice and the blade.* San Francisco: Harper & Row.

Elshtain, Jean B. (1987). *Women and war.* New York: Basic Books.

Epstein, Cynthia F. (1988). *Deceptive distinctions: Sex, gender, and the social order.* New Haven, CT: Yale University Press

Ericksen, Karen P. (1987). Menstrual symptoms and menstrual beliefs: National and cross-national patterns. In B. E. Ginsburg & B. F. Carter (Eds.), *Premenstrual syndrome.* New York: Plenum.

Erickson, Bonnie; Lind, E. Allan; Johnson, Bruce C.; & O'Barr, William M. (1978). Speech style and impression formation in a court setting: The effects of "powerful" and "powerless" speech. *Journal of Experimental Social Psychology, 14,* 266–279.

Ernsberger, P., & Nelson, D. O. (1988). Refeeding hypertension in dietary obesity. *American Journal of Physiology, 154,* R47–55.

Faulkner, Wendy (1980). The obsessive orgasm: Science, sex and female sexuality. In The Brighton Women and Science Group (Eds.), *Alice through the microscope: The power of science over women's lives.* London: Virago.

Fausto-Sterling, Anne (1985). *Myths of gender: Biological theories about women and men.* New York: Basic Books.

Feingold, Alan (1988). Cognitive gender differences are disappearing. *American Psychologist, 43,* 95–103.

Fisher, Hyman W. (Ed.) (1987). *The premenstrual syndrome.* London: Royal Society of Medicine Services.

Fishman, Pamela M. (1983). Interaction: The work women do. In B. Thorne, C. Kramarae, & N. Henley (Eds.), *Language, gender and society.* Rowley, MA: Newbury House.

Frank, E.; Anderson, C.; & Rubinstein, D. (1978). Frequency of sexual dysfunction in "normal" couples. *New England Journal of Medicine, 299,* 111–115.

Frank, Robert T. (1931). The hormonal causes of premenstrual tension. *Archives of Neurology and Psychiatry, 26,* 1053–1057.

Freeman, Ellen; Rickels, Karl; Sondheimer, S. J.; & Polansky, M. (1990, July 18). Ineffectiveness of progesterone suppository treatment for premenstrual syndrome. *Journal of the American Medical Association, 264,* 349–353.

Freese, Margaret P., & Levitt, Eugene E. (1984). Relationships among intravaginal pressure, orgasmic function, parity factors, and urinary leakage. *Archives of Sexual Behavior, 13,* 261–268.

Friedman, William J.; Robinson, Amy B.; & Friedman, Britt L. (1987). Sex differences in moral judgments? *Psychology of Women Quarterly, 11,* 37–46.

Gallant, Sheryle J., & Hamilton, Jean (1988). On a premenstrual psychiatric diagnosis: What's in a name? *Professional Psychology: Research and Practice, 19,* 271–278.

Garner, David; Garfinkel, Paul; Schwartz, Donald; & Thompson, Michael (1980). Cultural expectations of thinness in women. *Psychological Reports, 47,* 483–491.

Gelles, Richard J., & Straus, Murray A. (1988). *Intimate violence: The causes and consequences of abuse in the American family.* New York: Touchstone.

Gergen, Kenneth J. (1985). The social constructionist movement in modern psychology. *American Psychologist, 40,* 266–275.

Gergen, Mary M. (Ed.) (1988). *Feminist thought and the structure of knowledge.* New York: New York University Press.

Gergen, Mary M. (1992). Life stories: Pieces of a dream. In G. Rosenwald & R. Ochberg (Eds.), *Storied lives.* New Haven, CT: Yale University Press.

Geschwind, Norman, & Behan, Peter (1982). Left-handedness: Association with immune disease, migraine, and developmental learning disorder. *Proceedings of the National Academy of Sciences, 79,* 5097–5100.

Giacomini, M.; Rozée-Koker, P.; & Pepitone-Arreola-Rockwell, F. (1986). Gender bias in human anatomy textbook illustrations. *Psychology of Women Quarterly, 10,* 413–420.

Gierymski, Tadeusz, & Williams, Terence (1986, Jan–Mar.). Codependency. *Journal of Psychoactive Drugs, 18,* 7–13.

Gilligan, Carol (1982). *In a different voice.* Cambridge, MA: Harvard University Press.

Gilligan, Carol; Ward, Janie V.; & Taylor, Jill M. (Eds.) (1988). *Mapping the moral domain: A contribution of women's thinking to psychological theory and education.* Cambridge, MA: Harvard University Press.

Gise, Leslie H. (Ed.) (1988). *The premenstrual syndromes.* New York: Churchill Livingstone.

Goldberg, Daniel C.; Whipple, Beverly; Fishkin, Ralph E.; Waxman, Howard; Fink, Paul J.; & Weisberg, Martin (1983). The Grafenberg spot and female ejaculation: A review of initial hypotheses. *Journal of Sex & Marital Therapy, 9,* 27–37.

Goldman, Lee, & Tosteson, Anna N. A. (1991, September 12). Uncertainty about postmenopausal estrogen: Time for action, not debate [Editorial]. *The New England Journal of Medicine, 325,* 800–802.

Golub, Sharon (1988). A developmental perspective. In L. H. Gise (Ed.), *The premenstrual syndromes*. New York: Churchill Livingstone.

Gomberg, Edith S. L. (1989). On terms used and abused: The concept of "codependency." *Drugs and Society: Current issues in alcohol/drug studies, 3,* 113–132.

Goodall, Jane (1986). *The chimpanzees of Gombe: Patterns of behavior*. Cambridge, MA: Harvard University Press.

Goodrich, Thelma J.; Rampage, Cheryl; Ellman, Barbara; & Halstead, Kris (1988). *Feminist family therapy: A casebook*. New York: W. W. Norton & Co.

Goodwin, Jean; Cheeves, Katherine; & Connell, Virginia (1988). Defining a syndrome of severe symptoms in survivors of severe incestuous abuse. *Dissociation, 1,* 11–16.

Gordon, Suzanne (1991). *Prisoners of men's dreams: Striking out for a new feminine future*. Boston: Little, Brown.

Gould, Stephen J. (1981). *The mismeasure of man*. New York: W. W. Norton & Co.

Grafenberg, Ernest (1950). The role of urethra in female orgasm. *The International Journal of Sexology, 3,* 145–148.

Greene, Raymond, & Dalton, Katharina (1953). The premenstrual syndrome. *British Medical Journal, 1,* 1007–1014.

Greeno, Catherine G., & Maccoby, Eleanor E. (1986). How different is the "different voice"? *Signs, 11,* 310–316.

Halbreich, U., & Endicott, J. (1983). Retrospective report of premenstrual changes: Factors affecting confirmation of daily ratings. *Psychopharmacology Bulletin, 18,* 109–112.

Hamilton, Jean A., & Parry, Barbara L. (1983). Sex-related differences in clinical drug response: Implications for women's health. *Journal of the American Medical Women's Association, 38,* 126–132.

Hamilton, Jean A.; Parry, Barbara L.; Blumenthal, S.; Alagna, S.; & Herz, E. (1984). Premenstrual mood changes: A guide to evaluation and treatment. *Psychiatric Annals, 14,* 426–435.

Hammarback, S., & Backstrom, T. (1989). A demographic study in subgroups of women seeking help for premenstrual syndrome. *Acta Obstetrics & Gynecology Scandinavia, 68,* 247–253.

Haraway, Donna (1988). Primatology is politics by other means. In R. Bleier (Ed.), *Feminist approaches to science*. New York: Pergamon.

Hare-Mustin, Rachel T. (1987). The problem of gender in family therapy theory. *Family Process, 26,* 15–27.

——— (1991). Sex, lies, and headaches: The problem is power. In T. J. Goodrich (Ed.), *Women and power: Perspectives for therapy*. New York: W. W. Norton & Co.

Hare-Mustin, Rachel T., & Marecek, Jeanne (1986). Autonomy and gender: Some questions for therapists. *Psychotherapy, 23,* 205–212.

———— (1990). Gender and the meaning of difference: Postmodernism and psychology. In R. T. Hare-Mustin & J. Marecek (Eds.), *Making a difference: Psychology and the construction of gender*. New Haven, CT: Yale University Press.

Harrington, Anne (1987). *Medicine, mind, and the double brain: A study in 19th-century thought*. Princeton, NJ: Princeton University Press.

Heilbrun, Carolyn G. (1989). *Writing a woman's life*. New York: Ballantine.

Helgeson, Vicki S. (1990). The role of masculinity in a prognostic predictor of heart attack severity. *Sex Roles, 22,* 755–774.

Helgeson, Vicki S., & Sharpsteen, Don J. (1987). Perceptions of danger in achievement and affiliation situations. *Journal of Personality and Social Psychology, 53,* 727–733.

Hewlett, Sylvia A. (1991). *When the bough breaks: The cost of neglecting our children*. New York: Basic Books.

Hite, Shere (1976). *The Hite report*. New York: Macmillan.

Hochschild, Arlie R. (1983). *The managed heart*. Berkeley, CA: University of California Press.

———— (1989). *The second shift: Working parents and the revolution at home*. New York: Viking.

Holland, Dorothy C., & Eisenhart, Margaret A. (1991). *Educated in romance: Women, achievement, and college culture*. Chicago: University of Chicago Press.

Houser, Betsy B. (1979). An investigation of the correlation between hormonal levels in males and mood, behavior, and physical discomfort. *Hormones and Behavior, 12,* 185–197.

Howard, George S. (1991). Culture tales: A narrative approach to thinking, cross-cultural psychology, and psychotherapy. *American Psychologist, 46,* 187–197.

Hrdy, Sarah B. (1988). Empathy, polyandry, and the myth of the coy female. In R. Bleier (Ed.), *Feminist approaches to science*. New York: Pergamon.

Hubbard, Ruth (1990). *The politics of women's biology*. New Brunswick, NJ: Rutgers University Press.

Hyde, Janet S.; Fennema, Elizabeth; & Lamon, Susan J. (1990). Gender differences in mathematics performance: A meta-analysis. *Psychological Bulletin, 107,* 139–155.

Hyde, Janet S., & Linn, Marcia C. (Eds.) (1986). *The psychology of gender: Advances through meta-analysis*. Baltimore, MD: Johns Hopkins University Press.

———— (1988). Gender differences in verbal ability: A meta-analysis. *Psychological Bulletin, 104,* 53–69.

Irvine, Janice M. (1990). *Disorders of desire: Sex and gender in modern American sexology*. Philadelphia: Temple University Press.

Jacklin, Carol N. (1989). Female and male: Issues of gender. *American Psychologist, 44,* 127–133.

Jeavons [Wilkinson], Candace M., & Zeiner, Arthur R. (1984). Effects of elevated female sex steroids on ethanol and acetaldehyde metabolism in humans. *Alcoholism: Clinical and Experimental Research, 8,* 352–358.

Jones, B. M., & Jones, M. K. (1976). Women and alcohol: Intoxication, metabolism, and the menstrual cycle. In M. Greenblatt & M. A. Shuckit (Eds.), *Alcoholism problems in women and children.* New York: Grune & Stratton.

Josselson, Ruthellen (1987). *Finding herself: Pathways to identity development in women.* New York: Jossey-Bass.

Kahn, Arnold S., & Yoder, Janice D. (1989). The psychology of women and conservatism: Rediscovering social change. *Psychology of Women Quarterly, 13,* 417–432.

Kaminer, Wendy (1990). *A fearful freedom: Women's flight from equality.* Reading, MA: Addison-Wesley.

Kanter, Rosabeth M. (1977). *Men and women of the corporation.* New York: Basic Books.

Kaplan, Helen S. (1974). *The new sex therapy.* New York: Brunner/Mazel.

Katz, Stan J., & Liu, Aimee (1991). *The codependency conspiracy.* New York: Warner.

Kaye, Lenard W., & Applegate, Jeffrey S. (1990). Men as elder caregivers: A response to changing families. *American Journal of Orthopsychiatry, 60,* 86–95.

Khan, Steven S.; Nessim, Sharon; Gray, Richard; Czer, Lawrence S.; Chaux, Aurelio; & Matloff, Jack (1990). Increased mortality of women in coronary artery bypass surgery: Evidence for referral bias. *Annals of Internal Medicine, 112,* 561–567.

Kiesler, Sara; Sproull, Lee S.; & Eccles, Jacquelynne S. (1985). Pool halls, chips, and war games: Women in the culture of computing. *Psychology of Women Quarterly, 9,* 451–462.

Kinsbourne, Marcel (1980). If sex differences in brain lateralization exist, they have yet to be discovered. *The Behavioral and Brain Sciences, 3,* 241–242.

Kinsey, Alfred; Pomeroy, Wardell; Martin, Clyde E.; & Gebhard, Paul H. (1953). *Sexual behavior in the human female.* Philadelphia: W. B. Saunders Co.

Koeske, Randi D. (1987). Premenstrual emotionality: Is biology destiny? In M. R. Walsh (Ed.), *The psychology of women: Ongoing debates.* New Haven, CT: Yale University Press.

Kohn, Alfie (1990). *The brighter side of human nature: Altruism and empathy in everyday life.* New York: Basic Books.

Koss, Mary P. (1990). The women's mental health research agenda: Violence against women. *American Psychologist, 45,* 374–380.

Kreps, Bonnie (1990). *Subversive thoughts, authentic passions.* San Francisco: Harper & Row.

Kutchins, Herb, & Kirk, Stuart A. (1986, Winter). The reliability of DSM-III: A critical review. *Social Work Research and Abstracts, 22,* 3–12.

Lakoff, Robin T. (1990). *Talking power: The politics of language.* New York: Basic Books.

Landrine, Hope (1988). Revising the framework of abnormal psychology. In P. Bronstein & K. Quina (Eds.), *Teaching a psychology of people.* Washington, D.C.: American Psychological Association.

——— (1989). The politics of personality. *Psychology of Women Quarterly, 13,* 325–340.

Laqueur, Thomas (1987). Orgasm, generation, and the politics of reproductive biology. In C. Gallagher & T. Laqueur (Eds.), *The making of the modern body.* Berkeley, CA: University of California Press.

——— (1990). *Making sex: Body and gender from the Greeks to Freud.* Cambridge, MA: Harvard University Press.

Latman, N. S. (1983). Relation of menstrual cycle phase to symptoms of rheumatoid arthritis. *American Journal of Medicine, 74,* 957–960.

Laws, Sophie (1983). The sexual politics of pre-menstrual tension. *Women's Studies International Forum, 6,* 19–31.

Le Guin, Ursula K. (1989). *Dancing at the edge of the world.* New York: Harper & Row.

Lerner, Harriet G. (1989). *Women in therapy.* New York: Harper & Row.

Levy, Jerre (1983). Language, cognition, and the right hemisphere: A response to Gazzaniga. *American Psychologist, 38,* 538–541.

Lifton, Peter D. (1985). Individual differences in moral development: The relation of sex, gender, and personality to morality. In A. J. Stewart & M. B. Lykes (Eds.), *Gender and personality.* Durham, NC: Duke University Press.

Littleton, Christine A. (1987). Reconstructing sexual equality. *California Law Review, 75,* 1279–1337.

Lott, Bernice (1990). Dual natures or learned behavior: The challenge to feminist psychology. In R. T. Hare-Mustin & J. Marecek (Eds.), *Making a difference: Psychology and the construction of gender.* New Haven, CT: Yale University Press.

Luepnitz, Deborah A. (1988). *The family interpreted: Feminist theory in clinical practice.* New York: Basic Books.

Maccoby, Eleanor E. (1988). Gender as a social category. *Developmental Psychology, 24,* 755–765.

——— (1990). Gender and relationships: A developmental account. *American Psychologist, 45,* 513–520.

MacKinnon, Catharine A. (1987). Feminism, Marxism, method, and the state: Toward feminist jurisprudence. In S. Harding (Ed.), *Feminism and methodology*. Bloomington, IN: Indiana University Press.

——— (1990). Legal perspectives on sexual difference. In D. L. Rhode (Ed.), *Theoretical perspectives on sexual difference*. New Haven, CT: Yale University Press.

Mair, Miller (1988). Psychology as storytelling. *International Journal of Personal Construct Psychology, 1,* 125–137.

Major, Brenda (1987). Gender, justice, and the psychology of entitlement. In P. Shaver & C. Hendrick (Eds.), *Sex and Gender: 7.* Newbury Park, CA: Sage.

Major, Brenda; McFarlin, Dean B.; & Gagnon, Diana (1984). Overworked and underpaid: On the nature of gender differences in personal entitlement. *Journal of Personality and Social Psychology, 47,* 1399–1412.

Maltz, Daniel N., & Borker, Ruth A. (1982). A cultural approach to male-female miscommunication. In J. J. Gumperz (Ed.), *Language and social identity*. Cambridge, England: Cambridge University Press.

Martin, Emily (1987). *The woman in the body: A cultural analysis of reproduction*. Boston: Beacon.

Mason, Mary Ann (1988). *The equality trap*. New York: Touchstone.

Masters, William, & Johnson, Virginia (1966). *Human sexual response*. New York: Bantam.

——— (1970). *Human sexual inadequacy*. New York: Bantam.

Matarazzo, Joseph D. (1990). Psychological assessment versus psychological testing. *American Psychologist, 45,* 999–1017.

Matthews, Nancy A. (in press). *Managing rape: The feminist anti-rape movement and the state*. London: Routledge.

McConnell-Ginet, Sally (1983). Intonation in a man's world. In B. Thorne, C. Kramarae, & N. Henley (Eds.), *Language, gender and society*. Rowley, MA: Newbury House.

——— (1984). The origins of sexist language in discourse. In S. J. White & V. Teller (Eds.), *Discourses in reading and linguistics (Annals of the New York Academy of Sciences, vol. 433)*. New York: New York Academy of Sciences.

McFarlane, Jessica; Martin, Carol L.; & Williams, Tannis M. (1988). Mood fluctuations: Women versus men and menstrual versus other cycles. *Psychology of Women Quarterly, 12,* 201–223.

McGlone, Jeannette (1980). Sex differences in human brain asymmetry: A critical survey. *The Behavioral and Brain Sciences, 3,* 215–263.

McGrath, Ellen; Keita, Gwendolyn P.; Strickland, Bonnie; & Russo, Nancy F. (Eds.) (1990). *Women and depression: Risk factors and treatment issues*. Washington, D.C.: American Psychological Association.

McKinlay, John B.; McKinlay, Sonja M.; & Brambilla, Donald (1987). The relative contributions of endocrine changes and social circumstances to depression in mid-aged women. *Journal of Health and Social Behavior,* 28, 345–363.

Mednick, Martha T. (1989). On the politics of psychological constructs: Stop the bandwagon, I want to get off. *American Psychologist, 44,* 1118–1123.

Metzger, D. A., & Hammond, C. B. (1988). Are estrogens indicated for the treatment of postmenopausal women? *Drug Intelligence and Clinical Pharmacy, 22,* 493–496.

Miller, Dale T.; Taylor, Brian; & Buck, Michelle L. (1991). Gender gaps: Who needs to be explained? *Journal of Personality and Social Psychology, 61,* 5–12.

Miller, Norman F. (1946). Hysterectomy: Therapeutic necessity or surgical racket? *American Journal of Obstetrics and Gynecology, 51,* 804–810.

Minnich, Elizabeth K. (1990). *Transforming knowledge.* Philadelphia: Temple University Press.

Nelkin, Dorothy, & Tancredi, Laurence (1989). *Dangerous diagnostics: The social power of biological information.* New York: Basic Books.

Nieva, Veronica F., & Gutek, Barbara A. (1981). *Women and Work.* New York: Praeger.

Nolen-Hoeksema, Susan (1990). *Sex differences in depression.* Stanford, CA: Stanford University Press.

O'Barr, William M. (1983). The study of language in institutional contexts. 2nd International Conference on Social Psychology and Language (Bristol, England). *Journal of Language & Social Psychology, 2,* 241–251.

Offer, Daniel, & Sabshin, Melvin (1984). Adolescence: Empirical perspectives. In D. Offer & M. Sabshin (Eds.), *Normality and the life cycle.* New York: Basic Books.

Ostensen, M.; Aune, B.; & Husby, G. (1983). Effect of pregnancy and hormonal changes on the activity of rheumatoid arthritis. *Scandinavian Journal of Rheumatology, 12,* 69–72.

Palumbo, Pasquale J. (1989, July 7). Cholesterol lowering for all: A closer look. *Journal of the American Medical Association, 262,* 91–92.

Pantony, Kaye-Lee, & Caplan, Paula J. (1991). Delusional dominating personality disorder: A modest proposal for identifying some consequences of rigid masculine socialization. *Canadian Psychology, 32,* 120–133.

Parlee, Mary B. (1973). The premenstrual syndrome. *Psychological Bulletin, 80,* 454–465.

——— (1982). Changes in moods and activation levels during the menstrual cycle in experimentally naive subjects. *Psychology of Women Quarterly, 7,* 119–131.

——— (1987). Media treatment of premenstrual syndrome. In B. E. Ginsburg & B. F. Carter (Eds.), *Premenstrual syndrome.* New York: Plenum.

Payer, Lynn (1987). *How to avoid a hysterectomy.* New York: Pantheon.

Peele, Stanton (1989). *Diseasing of America: Addiction treatment out of control.* Lexington, MA: Lexington Books.

Peele, Stanton, & Brodsky, Archie, with Arnold, Mary (1991). *The truth about addiction and recovery: The life-process program for outgrowing destructive habits.* New York: Simon & Schuster.

Pennebaker, James W. (1982). *The psychology of physical symptoms.* New York: Springer-Verlag.

Peplau, Letitia Anne, & Gordon, Steven (1985). Women and men in love: Sex differences in close relationships. In V. O'Leary, R. Unger, & B. Wallston (Eds.), *Women, gender and social psychology.* Hillsdale, NJ: Erlbaum.

Philipson, Ilene (1985). Gender and narcissism. *Psychology of Women Quarterly, 9,* 213–228.

Pleck, Joseph (1981). *The myth of masculinity.* Cambridge, MA: MIT Press.

Polefrone, Joanna M., & Manuck, Stephen B. (1987). Gender differences in cardiovascular and neuroendocrine response to stressors. In R. C. Barnett, L. Biener, & G. K. Baruch (Eds.), *Gender and stress.* New York: The Free Press.

Pomeroy, Sarah B. (1975). *Goddesses, whores, wives, and slaves: Women in classical antiquity.* New York: Schocken.

Ragins, Belle Rose, & Sundstrom, Eric (1989). Gender and power in organizations: A longitudinal perspective. *Psychological Bulletin, 105,* 51–88.

Richardson, John T. E. (1990). Questionnaire studies of paramenstrual symptoms. *Psychology of Women Quarterly, 14,* 15–42.

Riessman, Catherine K. (1987). When gender is not enough: Women interviewing women. *Gender and Society, 1,* 172–207.

——— (1990). *Divorce talk: Women and men make sense of personal relationships.* New Brunswick, NJ: Rutgers University Press.

Risman, Barbara J. (1987). Intimate relationships from a microstructural perspective: Men who mother. *Gender and Society, 1,* 6–32.

Robertson, John, & Fitzgerald, Louise F. (1990). The (mis)treatment of men: Effects of client gender role and life-style on diagnosis and attribution of pathology. *Journal of Counseling Psychology, 37,* 3–9.

Robinson, Paul (1976). *The modernization of sex.* New York: Harper & Row.

Rojcewicz, Stephen J. (1971). War and suicide. *Life-Threatening Behavior, 1,* 46–54.

Rosenberg, L.; Palmer, J. R.; & Shapiro, S. (1990, January 25). Decline in the risk of myocardial infarction among women who stop smoking. *New England Journal of Medicine, 322,* 213–217.

Rosewater, Lynne B. (1987). A critical analysis of the proposed self-defeating personality disorder. *Journal of Personality Disorders, 1,* 190–195.

Rothman, Barbara K. (1989). *Recreating motherhood: Ideology and technology in a patriarchal society.* New York: W. W. Norton & Co.

Russell, Diana E. H. (1982). *Rape in marriage.* New York: Macmillan.

Sarbin, Theodore R. (1986). The narrative as a root metaphor for psychology. In T. R. Sarbin (Ed.), *Narrative psychology: The storied nature of human conduct.* New York: Praeger.

Scheper-Hughes, Nancy, & Stein, Howard F. (1987). Child abuse and the unconscious in American popular culture. In N. Scheper-Hughes (Ed.), *Child survival.* Holland: Kluwer Academic/Reidel.

Schiebinger, Linda (1987). Skeletons in the closet: The first illustrations of the female skeleton in eighteenth-century anatomy. In C. Gallagher & T. Laqueur (Eds.), *The making of the modern body.* Berkeley, CA: University of California Press.

Schwartzer, Alice (1984). *After "The second sex": Conversations with Simone de Beauvoir.* New York: Pantheon.

Shaver, Phillip; Hazan, Cindy; & Bradshaw, Donna (1988). Love as attachment: The integration of three behavioral systems. In R. J. Sternberg & M. L. Barnes (Eds.), *The psychology of love.* New Haven, CT: Yale University Press.

Shaywitz, S. E.; Shaywitz, B. A.; Fletcher, J. M.; & Escobar, M. D. (1990, Aug. 22–29). Prevalence of reading disability in boys and girls. Results of the Connecticut Longitudinal Study. *Journal of the American Medical Association, 264,* 998–1002.

Shields, Stephanie A. (1975). Functionalism, Darwinism, and the psychology of women: A study in social myth. *American Psychologist, 30,* 739–754.

————— (1987). Women, men, and the dilemma of emotion. In P. Shaver & C. Hendrick (Eds.), *Sex and gender: 7.* Newbury Park, CA: Sage.

Siegel, Rachel J. (1988). Women's "dependency" in a male-centered value system: Gender-based values regarding dependency and independence. *Women & Therapy, 7,* 113–123.

Silverstein, Brett; Carpman, Shari; Perlick, Deborah; & Perdue, Lauren (1990). Nontraditional sex role aspirations, gender identity conflict and disordered eating among college women. *Sex Roles, 23,* 687–695.

Silverstein, Brett; Perdue, Lauren; Peterson, Barbara; Vogel, Linda; & Fantini, Deborah A. (1986). Possible causes of the thin standard of bodily attractiveness for women. *International Journal of Eating Disorders, 5,* 135–144.

Silverstein, Brett; Perdue, Lauren; Wolf, Cordulla; & Pizzolo, Cecilia (1988). Bingeing, purging, and estimates of parental attitudes regarding female achievement. *Sex Roles, 19,* 723–733.

Silverstein, Brett; Peterson, Barbara; & Perdue, Lauren (1986). Some correlates of the thin standard of bodily attractiveness in women. *International Journal of Eating Disorders, 5,* 145–155.

Snodgrass, Sara E. (1985). Women's intuition: The effect of subordinate role on interpersonal sensitivity. *Journal of Personality and Social Psychology, 49,* 146–155.

Spanos, Nicholas P.; Menary, Evelyn; Gabora, Natalie J.; DuBreuil, Susan C.; & Dewhirst, Bridget (1991). Secondary identity enactments during hypnotic past-life regression: A sociocognitive perspective. *Journal of Personality and Social Psychology, 61,* 308–320.

Sperry, Roger W. (1982). Some effects of disconnecting the cerebral hemispheres. *Science, 217,* 1223–1226.

Sprock, June; Blashfield, Roger K.; & Smith, Brenda (1990). Gender weighting of DSM-III-R personality disorder criteria. *American Journal of Psychiatry, 147,* 586–590.

Stacey, Judith (1990). *Brave new families.* New York: Basic Books.

Stampfer, Meier J.; Colditz, G. A.; Willett, W. C.; et al. (1991, September 12). Postmenopausal estrogen therapy and cardiovascular disease—ten-year follow-up from the Nurses' Health Study. *New England Journal of Medicine, 325,* 756–762.

Standing, Hilary (1980). "Sickness is a woman's business?": Reflections on the attribution of illness. In The Brighton Women and Science Group (Eds.), *Alice through the microscope: The power of science over women's lives.* London: Virago.

Stapley, Janice C., & Haviland, Jeannette M. (1989). Beyond depression: Gender differences in normal adolescents' emotional experiences. *Sex Roles, 20,* 295–308.

Steinberg, K. K.; Thacker, S. B.; Smith, S. J.; et al. (1991, April 17). A meta-analysis of the effect of estrogen replacement therapy on the risk of breast cancer. *Journal of the American Medical Association, 265,* 1985–1990.

Stone, Lewis, & Hokanson, Jack E. (1969). Arousal reduction via self-punitive behavior. *Journal of Personality and Social Psychology, 12,* 72–79.

Stone, Merlin (1979). When God was a woman. In C. Christ & J. Plaskow (Eds.), *Womanspirit rising: A feminist reader in religion.* San Francisco: Harper & Row.

Striegel-Moore, Ruth H.; Silberstein, Lisa R.; & Rodin, Judith (1986). Toward an understanding of risk factors for bulimia. *American Psychologist, 41,* 246–263.

Strube, Michael J (1988). The decision to leave an abusive relationship: Empirical evidence and theoretical issues. *Psychological Bulletin, 104,* 236–250.

Swain, Scott (1989). Covert intimacy: Closeness in men's friendships. In B. J. Risman & P. Schwartz (Eds.), *Gender in intimate relationships.* Belmont, CA: Wadsworth.

Symons, Donald (1979). *The evolution of human sexuality.* New York: Oxford University Press.

Tannen, Deborah (1990). *You just don't understand.* New York: William Morrow.

Taub, David M. (1984). *Primate paternalism*. New York: Van Nostrand Reinhold.

Tavris, Carol (1982, 1989). *Anger: The misunderstood emotion* (2nd ed.). New York: Simon & Schuster/Touchstone.

Tavris, Carol, & Wade, Carole (1984). *The longest war: Sex differences in perspective* (2nd ed.). San Diego: Harcourt Brace Jovanovich.

Thoma, Stephen J. (1986). Estimating gender differences in the comprehension and preference of moral issues. *Developmental Review, 6*, 165–180.

Tiefer, Leonore (1986). In pursuit of the perfect penis: The medicalization of male sexuality. *American Behavioral Scientist, 29*, 579–599.

——— (1988). A feminist perspective on sexology and sexuality. In M. M. Gergen (Ed.), *Feminist thought and the structure of knowledge*. New York: New York University Press.

Tobin, J. N.; Wassertheil-Smoller, S.; Wexler, J. P.; Steingart, R. M.; Budner, N.; Lense, L.; & Wachspress, J. (1987). Sex bias in considering coronary bypass surgery. *Annals of Internal Medicine, 107*, 19–25.

Trudel, Giles, & Saint-Laurent, Suzanne (1983). A comparison between the effects of Kegel's exercises and a combination of sexual awareness relaxation and breathing on situational orgasmic dysfunction in women. *Journal of Sex & Marital Therapy, 9*, 204–209.

van Leeuwen, F. E., & Rookus, M. A. (1989). The role of exogenous hormones in the epidemiology of breast, ovarian and endometrial cancer. *European Journal of Cancer and Clinical Oncology, 25*, 1961–1972.

Wade, Carole (1986). Humor. In C. Tavris (Ed.), *EveryWoman's emotional well-being*. New York: Prentice-Hall.

Walker, Lenore E. (1989). Psychology and violence against women. *American Psychologist, 44*, 695–702.

Waring, Marilyn (1989). *If women counted: A new feminist economics*. San Francisco: Harper & Row.

Weingarten, Helen R., & Douvan, Elizabeth (1985, October). Male and female visions of mediation. *Negotiation Journal* (no volume), 349–358.

West, Candace, & Zimmerman, Don H. (1987). Doing gender. *Gender & Society, 1*, 125–151.

West, Robin (1988). Jurisprudence and gender. *The University of Chicago Law Review, 55*, 1–72.

White, Kathleen M.; Speisman, Joseph C.; Jackson, Doris; Bartis, Scott; & Costos, Daryl (1986). Intimacy maturity and its correlates in young married couples. *Journal of Personality and Social Psychology, 50*, 152–162.

Williams, Walter L. (1987). *The spirit and the flesh: Sexual diversity in American Indian Culture*. Boston: Beacon.

Wills, Thomas A.; Weiss, Robert L.; & Patterson, Gerald R. (1974). A behavioral analysis of the determinants of marital satisfaction. *Journal of Consulting and Clinical Psychology, 42,* 802–811.

Winton, Mark A. (1989). Editorial: The social construction of the G-spot and female ejaculation. *Journal of Sex Education & Therapy, 15,* 151–162.

Wolfe, Sidney M., & the Public Citizen Health Research Group (1991). *Women's health alert.* Reading, MA: Addison-Wesley.

Wood, Wendy; Rhodes, Nancy; & Whelan, Melanie (1989). Sex differences in positive well-being: A consideration of emotional style and marital status. *Psychological Bulletin, 106,* 249–264.

Wright, Paul H. (1988). Interpreting research on gender differences in friendship: A case for moderation and a plea for caution. *Journal of Social and Personal Relationships, 5,* 367–373.

Wyatt, Gail E., & Powell, Gloria J. (1988). Identifying the lasting effects of child sexual abuse: An overview. In G. E. Wyatt & G. J. Powell (Eds.), *Lasting effects of child sexual abuse.* Newbury Park, CA: Sage.

Zaviačič, Milan, et al. (1988a). Concentrations of fructose in female ejaculate and urine: A comparative biochemical study. *The Journal of Sex Research, 24,* 319–325.

——— (1988b). Female urethral expulsions evoked by local digital stimulation of the G-Spot: Differences in response patterns. *The Journal of Sex Research, 24,* 311–318.

Zilbergeld, Bernie (1992). *The new male sexuality.* New York: Bantam.

Zimmerman, Mark (1988). Why are we rushing to publish DSM-IV? *Archives of General Psychiatry, 45,* 1135–1138.

Zur, Ofer (1989). War myths: Exploration of the dominant collective beliefs about warfare. *Journal of Humanistic Psychology, 29,* 297–327.

Zur, Ofer, & Morrison, Andrea (1989). Gender and war: Reexamining attitudes. *American Journal of Orthopsychiatry, 59,* 528–533.

■ *Acknowledgments*

I have been writing this book, in one way or another, for 20 years. In these two extraordinary decades it seems as though every assumption about the "nature" of women and men has been scrutinized and dissected, and I feel fortunate to be able to draw on the research and writing of the many women and men who have transformed our ways of thinking about gender. I am grateful to the many feminists who spurred a movement that is enriching and provoking, and that learns from its digressions and blind alleys as it seeks a thoroughfare to the future.

Two friends in particular, Carole Wade and Leonore Tiefer, came into my life 20 years ago and have been inspiring me ever since. Carole and I have written several books together, and my good fortune in finding such a happy and harmonious collaboration, to say nothing of finding such a happy and harmonious friendship, continues to delight me. Far more tangibly, the results of Carole's sharp questions, sharp ideas, and sharp editorial pencil are apparent everywhere in these pages. I am also immeasurably grateful to Leonore Tiefer for our abiding friendship; for the countless conversations we have had over the years about gender, science, and social change; for so generously allowing me to quote from her unpublished papers; and for the fun we had writing up the true story of the G-Spot. Everyone should have friends like Tiefer and Wade to goad us out of complacent thinking and move our ideas and commitments forward.

My special thanks to the following friends and colleagues who so conscientiously read all or parts of the manuscript and offered excellent, thoughtful suggestions for improvement: Anne Peplau, Paula Caplan, Faye Crosby, Harriet Goldhor Lerner, Vicki Michel, and Mary Brown Parlee.

I am also indebted to the following people for providing me with research papers, articles in press, unpublished manuscripts, and other helpful materials: Martin Bobgan, Elaine Borins, Silvia Canetto, Paula Caplan, Faye Crosby, Cynthia Fuchs Epstein, Mary Gergen, Tadeusz Gierymski, Edith Gomberg, Rachel Hare-Mustin, Nancy Henley, Judith Herman, Carol Jacklin, Harriet Goldhor Lerner, Eleanor Maccoby, Jeanne Marecek, Nancy Matthews, Vicki Michel, Mary Brown Parlee, David Schreiber, Patricia Schreiner-Engel, Stephanie Shields, Brett Silverstein, Leonore Tiefer, Candace Wilkinson, and Bernie Zilbergeld. Judge David Rothman was kind enough to make available to me the Judicial Council of California's report on gender bias in the courts.

My warm thanks to Dara Culhane for the research results and interview time she so generously shared with me while in the middle of writing her doctoral dissertation; and for her careful reading and editing of the section on the sexual survivor movement in Chapter 8. Thanks also to Jacqueline Goodchilds, Estelle Ramey, and Brett Silverstein for their excellent and informative interviews. Susan Campbell was an invaluable help in providing research assistance, ideas, and case studies.

I would also like to thank the American Psychological Association for inviting me to give the master lecture on gender at their 1990 convention and for permission to draw material from that lecture in this book; and to *Vogue* and *Woman's Day* magazines, for assignments on many aspects of the mismeasure of woman, some of which I have drawn on here.

I know many writers who lament their associations with editors who don't edit and agents who don't even read their work; but I am blessed by not knowing what they are talking about. Therefore I am aware of how much I owe to Frederic Hills, my fine and meticulous editor at Simon & Schuster, for his critical eye, superb editorial contribution to the manuscript, and enthusiasm. Robert Lescher, my knight in agent's clothing, offered unwavering support for this work from the beginning and excellent editorial help as well. And I would like to thank Burton Beals, Daphne Bien, and the rest of the editorial team at Simon & Schuster for their part in the production of this book.

I am grateful beyond measure for my mother, Dorothy Tavris, a feminist ahead of her time, for her example of commitment and courage, and for being a mother whom I cannot blame for anything; and for the legacy of my father, Sam Tavris, a feminist ahead of his time, for all the books about great women and great DWEMs that he gave me in my childhood, and for being a father who treated me as his son and daughter.

Finally, I thank my husband, Ronan O'Casey, my Case study on all manner of things, and my stepson Matthew for many of the anecdotes that infuse this book—and for the optimism they inspire in me that the battle of the sexes will one day find a lasting truce.

—Carol Tavris

Index